ENVIRONMENTAL LIABILITY AND THE INTERPLAY BETWEEN EU LAW AND INTERNATIONAL LAW

The role of law in responding to global environmental problems and the interplay between different levels of regulation and governance is becoming increasingly relevant in the field of liability and reparation for environmental damage. This book examines the relationship and reciprocal influences between the EU and the international legal order in a multilevel and comparative perspective, in relation to the ongoing efforts to elaborate effective regimes of liability and reparation for environmental damage. It offers a comparative analysis of legal developments in the field of environmental liability within the EU and at the international law level and addresses questions concerning the impact of such interaction on the development, implementation and enforcement of appropriate responses to environmental damage within the respective legal orders and on a global level.

Given the book's focus and the transnational legal dimension of the issues covered, this volume will be of great interest to legal academics and researchers working in the environmental law field from an EU law and international law perspective, as well as more generally to scholars interested in the study of the relationship between EU and international law. Outside academia, the book will also be of great interest to practitioners wishing to get insights into the application of the law of environmental liability in the EU and at the international law level.

Dr Emanuela Orlando is Lecturer in Environmental Law at the School of Law, Politics and Sociology of the University of Sussex.

Routledge Research in International Environmental Law

Enforcement of International Environmental Law
Challenges and Responses at the International Level
Martin Hedemann-Robinson

Marine Pollution, Shipping Waste and International Law
Gabriela Argüello

Compensation for Environmental Damage Under International Law
Jason Rudall

International Environmental Law Compliance in Context
Mechanisms and Case Studies
Belen Olmos Giupponi

Sustainable Fisheries Management and International Law
Marine Fisheries in Bangladesh and the Bay of Bengal
Abdullah Al Arif]

Marine Conservation and International Law
Legal Instruments for Biodiversity Beyond National Jurisdiction
Sarah Louise Lothian

Nature Law and Policy in Europe
Edited by Andrew L.R. Jackson

Environmental Liability and the Interplay between EU Law and International Law
Dr Emanuela Orlando

www.routledge.com/Routledge-Research-in-International-Environmental-Law/book-series/INTENVLAW

Environmental Liability and the Interplay between EU Law and International Law

Emanuela Orlando

Routledge
Taylor & Francis Group
LONDON AND NEW YORK

First published 2024

by Routledge
4 Park Square, Milton Park, Abingdon, Oxon OX14 4RN

and by Routledge
605 Third Avenue, New York, NY 10158

Routledge is an imprint of the Taylor & Francis Group, an informa business

British Library Cataloguing-in-Publication Data
A catalogue record for this book is available from the British Library

ISBN: 978-1-138-93666-9 (hbk)
ISBN: 978-1-032-53874-7 (pbk)
ISBN: 978-1-315-67670-8 (ebk)

DOI: 10.4324/9781315676708

Typeset in Times New Roman
by Apex CoVantage, LLC

To my family

Contents

Preface

This book is a largely revisited, expanded and updated version of my PhD thesis, which I successfully defended at the European University Institute (EUI), in Florence, several years ago. Since then, the legal landscape in the field of liability and reparation for environmental harm has spread and diversified further, through various developments and ramifications, providing even more ground to explore and reflect upon. At the same time, scholarly debates on the role of law in responding to environmental problems have been increasingly animated by the need to understand the legal effects of globalisation and how to manage the interactions and the relationship between different systems of norms and different levels of regulation and governance. In capturing these developments and dynamics, this book sought to go beyond the initial scope of the PhD thesis and has thus expanded the aims and objectives of the original doctoral study to encompass more recent developments in the field of environmental liability and the analysis of the interconnections, synergies and interactions between EU and international law in this context.

Acknowledgements

Given the long gestation process of this book, I met several people who helped me, in different ways, to develop and refine my thinking about the topic, and whom I wish to thank. First and foremost, I would like to thank two distinguished academics who represent my two role models. In particular, I would like to express my sincere and everlasting gratitude to my PhD supervisor, Professor Francesco Francioni, not only for the outstanding supervision during the entire PhD, but also, and especially, for the constant support and unfaltering encouragement throughout my studies, and even after. I also owe a special and most heart-felt thanks to Professor Ludwig Kramer, who served as an external jury member of my PhD thesis, and with whom I then had the privilege, the pleasure and the honour to collaborate academically.

I would also like to thank Professor Bruno de Witte for his valuable comments and suggestions on my PhD thesis; Professor Massimiliano Montini who involved me in interesting research and consultancy projects that enabled me to gain significant and helpful practical experience on the functioning of EU environmental law and governance; Professor Ana Vrdoljak, for her wonderful encouragement and optimism; Professor Elisa Morgera, for the inspiring discussions on global environmental law; and Professor Joanne Scott, with whom I had the pleasure to discuss my research on the interaction between EU law and international law during my visiting Fellowship at the EUI in 2017.

While completing this book I was also fortunate enough to benefit from the incredibly supportive, friendly and intellectually enriching environment of Sussex Law School. I would like to thank in particular my colleagues, Professor Jo Bridgeman and Professor Donald McGillivray, for their support and positive encouragement while writing this book, and Professor Christian Henderson for having read an earlier draft of this manuscript. I would also like to thank Professor Susan Millns, former head of Sussex Law School, for giving me the time and space to do the research necessary to complete an earlier draft of this book. All errors remain of course mine.

Many sincere thanks also go to the production team at Routledge. I am hugely grateful especially to Siobhán Poole, the Commissioning Editor, who oversaw the slow development of this book since the very beginning and who has been extremely supportive, and patient, throughout the entire process.

Finally, my most heart-felt acknowledgments go to my family: to Giovanni and to my parents, for their love, understanding, and never-ending trust and encouragement in each step of my personal and professional life; and to my son Giorgio, the joy of my life, for brightening up my days and for constantly reminding me that writing a book is not the most important thing in one's person life . . .

Emanuela Orlando

Firenze, Brighton—28 December 2022

Abbreviations

ARISWA	Articles on the International Responsibility of the States for Wrongful Acts
ATCA	Alien Tort Claim Act
CBD	Convention on Biological Diversity
CERCLA	Comprehensive Environmental Response, Compensation and Liability Act
CITES	Convention on International Trade of Endangered Species
CJEU	Court of Justice of the European Union
CLC	Convention on Civil Liability for oil pollution damage
EEZ	Exclusive economic zone
ELD	Environmental Liability Directive
EU	European Union
GMO	Genetically modified organism
IAEA	International Atomic Energy Agency
ICJ	International Court of Justice
ILC	International Law Commission
ITLOS	International Tribunal for the Law of the Sea
LMO	Living modified organism
MEAs	Multilateral environmental agreements
NGO	Non-governmental organisation
OECD	Organisation for Economic Co-operation and Development
OPA	Oil Pollution Act
TEU	Treaty on European Union
TFEU	Treaty on the Functioning of the European Union
UNCC	United Nations Compensation Commission
UNCLOS	United Nations Convention on the Law of the Sea
UNECE	United Nations Economic Commission for Europe
UNEP	United Nations Environment Programme
UNGA	United Nations General Assembly
WTO	World Trade Organization

Introduction—relevance of the topic and scope of the analysis

1. Background: the problem

In the era of economic globalisation and growing technological development, the need for a comprehensive and effective set of rules on liability and reparation for environmental harm remains a pressing contemporary issue. Despite some tragic accidents in the past—such as the disasters of Chernobyl and Bhopal and the explosion of the Sandoz chemical factory in Switzerland—which raised attention on the environmental liability topic and prompted important regulatory initiatives at the domestic, regional (European) and international levels, the reality demonstrates that significant environmental harm still occurs, notwithstanding the existence of sophisticated frameworks on safety and prevention, and often without reliable mechanisms in place for remediation or compensation. Indeed, some ten years after the severe pollution of the Rhine caused by the Sandoz chemical blast, a new and serious ecological disaster took place on another important waterway, the Danube. The Baia Mare disaster occurred in January 2000.[1] The accident was provoked by the sudden rupture of the dam of the wastewater reservoir used in the process of extraction of non-ferrous metals by the Aurul mining company. The range and gravity of the harm was so widespread that it has been defined as the worst ecological catastrophe to hit Central-Eastern Europe since Chernobyl. A similar scenario occurred in 2015 in Brazil where the collapse of a huge tailing dam caused the discharge of 32m to 40m cubic meters of mining waste across the countryside, destroying villages and killing fish and aquatic life.[2] The accident is considered Brazil's worst environmental disaster.[3] Other episodes of grave environmental damage have occurred elsewhere including, in the United States, the ecological disaster caused by the Exxon Valdez oil spill off the coast of Alaska in 1989 followed, ten years later, by an even greater oil spill caused by the explosion and subsequent sinking of the Deepwater Horizon oil rig in the Gulf of Mexico. In both cases, the consequences for the environment, the population and the economies of the regions have been devastating. A year after the Gulf of Mexico's spill, the nuclear reactor meltdown at the Fukushima Daiichi nuclear power station in Japan resulted in the largest accidental release of radioactive materials into the ocean.[4]

These are just a few out of an extensive and growing list of environmental accidents which illustrate in dramatic fashion the significant environmental hazards

DOI: 10.4324/9781315676708-1

associated with the operation of industrial and technological activities considered essential to our economic development. These examples also highlight the persistent gaps and limitations of existing legal frameworks. Except for a few cases where the legal and institutional response to the accident enabled the payment of appropriate compensation and the imposition of adequate civil and criminal sanctions to the polluters,[5] in most cases victims face numerous hurdles in the pursuit of legal redress. On the one hand, the available regulatory and administrative frameworks are often not designed to specifically address situations of such magnitude and complexity. On the other hand, traditional liability rules borrowed from the private law context of neighbourhood relationships fall short in providing appropriate remedies to the victims of massive instances of pollution, let alone in ensuring proper restoration of the environment. Originally conceived to operate in a relatively straightforward context characterised by the bilateral relationship between the victim and their tortfeasor and by the existence of a clear and identifiable prejudice, classic mechanisms of tort liability are often ill equipped to address more widespread and diffuse forms of environmental damage.[6] Further difficulties are related to the uncertainties over causation or to the deficiencies in scientific knowledge concerning the possible harmful effects of a given substance or activity, especially when compounded by the long latency period between the harmful emission and the manifestation of the damage. When translated in legal terms, the specific features that characterise many instances of environmental harm become a series of legal hurdles that plaintiffs must face when claiming compensation in courts.[7] Ecological harm is also often left uncovered by existing frameworks, which normally address traditional forms of property damage or economic losses.

Over time, legal systems have progressively adjusted to cope with the peculiarities of environmental pollution and to facilitate the pursuit of redress by those harmed by hazardous substances or activities. Both statutory reforms and judicial interpretation contributed to the elaboration of rules aimed at introducing greater flexibility in the causality nexus, for example through presumptions of causality or reversal of the burden of proof. Judicial practice in the field of toxic torts and product liability offers interesting examples in this sense, with potential for cross-fertilisation in the field of environmental pollution. A common process of objectivisation of liability has also taken place across different jurisdictions, whereby fault was progressively replaced by strict standards of liability for certain categories of hazardous and ultra-hazardous activities.[8] Furthermore, specific liability regimes, other than classic civil liability rules, were developed to specifically address damage to the environment and to natural resources.

Albeit significant, these reforms have however only partially contributed to ensure the full realisation of environmental justice for victims and for the environment. Despite the emergence of certain converging trends, there still exist disparities among different jurisdictions in the regulation of liability, the available remedies and the legal responses to environmental harms. Moreover, besides the inherent limitations of classic tort liability principles to deal with complex instances of environmental pollution, the prospects to obtain redress through civil justice are often undermined by jurisdictional, procedural and economic obstacles, which form additional barriers to an effective access to justice. These problems are magnified in a transnational context and in the case of transboundary pollution affecting two or more jurisdictions. In these cases, the international relevance of the damage, the differences in the liability standards and remedies available across the affected countries, and the lack of coordinated procedural frameworks to claim and enforce liability across different legal systems pose additional difficulties for claimants seeking redress. Particularly problematic are the cases of environmental harms, often accompanied by the breach of human rights standards, caused by the activities of transnational corporations. Here, the peculiarities and complexities of corporate structures, the involvement of different jurisdictions and legal systems, and the lack of harmonised and coordinated legal frameworks addressing liability and environmental remedies *de facto* allow the responsible companies to escape their liability. While several cases of environmental disasters in the Global South have prompted sensational transnational tort litigation against parent companies in Europe and in the United States, these cases led to limited success for the victims and for the environment.[9] Corporate law concepts, such as the principle of corporate separate personality, and the absence of binding standards of due diligence have in the past acted as shield for companies whose activities cause environmental damage.

Given the difficulties in achieving justice through the judicial system, settlements are in many cases reached out of court. Even in these situations, though, the compensation agreed and paid by the operator (if they pay at all) is usually much less than the actual amount of the damage caused, and that paid to the victims comes to significantly less than their original claim.[10] The case of Bhopal is perhaps the most tragically representative example of the failure of the legal and institutional system to provide justice for the victims and to establish the accountability of the responsible companies, as more than 38 years after the disaster victims are still waiting for appropriate compensation.[11] But other cases display similar scenarios. While compensation proceedings for victims of the Baia Mare cyanide spill were ongoing, the Aurul mining company was declared insolvent. The accident, and the consequent transboundary damage, provoked international tensions between Hungary and Romania, with discussion on the latter's international responsibility. Yet, reports and findings after the event indicate that 'the locals affected by the accident were never compensated, neither by the Australian company that went bankrupt nor by the Romanian authorities that tried to deny the true scale of the disaster'.[12] Similarly, victims affected by the collapse of the tailing dam operated by Samarco mining company in Brazil had to face complex jurisdictional and legal battles in their pursuit for compensation.[13] When compared with the landmark settlement achieved in the Gulf of Mexico oil spill and the firm response of the US government to that disaster, these cases highlight once more the injustice, inequalities and discrepancies faced by victims of environmental harms in different parts of the world. In the absence of a uniform set of rules and principles on environmental liability and on the responsibilities of companies, redress for victims and the environment remains contingent and unpredictable.

A further aspect that emerges from the past experience is that many of these types of accidents could have been avoided through the use of appropriate preventive measures or simply more care. While the nuclear disaster at Fukushima was connected to natural forces (i.e. a violent earthquake and a subsequent tsunami), the tragedies of Chernobyl, Bhopal, Baia Mare and surely BP were the result of human errors and of the failure to take the necessary preventive and precautionary measures.

2. The concept, role and function of liability in the environmental context

It cannot be denied that the presence of effective rules on environmental liability is a crucial element of environmental protection strategies. Yet, liability rules are only one important component of a complex puzzle. In a legal framework aimed at protecting the environment, liability rules must go hand in hand with appropriate and comprehensive strategies for harm prevention and the management of risks. There is a close and multifaceted relationship between the concepts of liability and prevention in the environmental field. On the one hand, liability rules usually step in when preventive approaches have failed. On the other hand, liability is conceptually associated to the idea of prevention, based on the understanding, particularly popular among legal scholars with a law and economic background,[14] that liability rules may provide incentives to potential polluters to take appropriate care and invest in more environmentally friendly technologies.[15] The debate in this context revolved especially around the question of the most appropriate form and standards of liability—i.e. whether strict liability or fault-based—that could be used to reach this preventive effect.[16] This emphasis on the deterrent and preventive function of liability is often juxtaposed to other conceptual approaches that focus instead more on compensation and corrective justice, and which present environmental liability as an instrument primarily aimed at providing redress to the victims of environmental pollution and/or to rectify a wrongdoing. In this justice-focused perspective to liability, scholars have also placed attention to the distributive justice dimension of liability rules and their role in enabling a fair apportionment of the burdens and benefits of risky activities.[17]

Of course, these considerations offer a rather oversimplified account of the subtleties of the extensive legal scholarship discussing the concepts and functions of liability rules. In fact, discussions about the functions of liability often intersect with a further distinction that can be drawn between, on the one hand, the instrumentalist and functionalist conceptions of liability (particularly popular among law and economics scholars) and, on the other hand, a principled approach which connects liability to fundamental principles of justice.[18] Scholars adhering to the latter approach tend to view liability rules as being essentially ‘a set of ethical principles about individual behaviours toward others’,[19] or equally ‘a set of rules and principles of personal responsibility the main function of which is to justify the imposition of obligations to repair harm’.[20] These justice-based conceptions of liability tend to approach the subject from a more ‘internal’ perspective, which is primarily centred on the interests of those individually affected by the application of liability rules (i.e. victims and the injurer)[21] and on their correlative rights and obligations.[22] By contrast the normative/instrumentalist approaches to liability appear more oriented towards the 'external' and societal dimension of liability rules and are more concerned about using liability to promote the pursuit of socially desirable goals,[23] whether these be accident prevention through deterrence, or more generally the creation of incentives to minimise the social costs of accidents.[24] Somewhat in the middle between these two approaches, but mostly within the justice-based theorisations of tort law, are those understandings of tort liability which emphasise the distributive justice function of liability rules, and which therefore correlate justice with fairness. By contrast to ideas based on corrective justice, the accent here is not so much placed on the rectification of wrongdoing (corrective justice), but on the distributive effects of liability, whereby '[w]hen courts make rules about the circumstances in which tort liability to repair harm will arise . . . they contribute to the establishment of a pattern of distribution of that resource and burden within society'.[25]

Far from being a purely theoretical speculation, the different approaches to the functions and role of tort law bear an influence in the determination of the most appropriate standard of liability. Scholars adopting a corrective justice approach to liability tend to prefer fault over strict liability, as being more in line with the idea of personal responsibility and the rectification of wrong as the main functions of tort law.[26] Conversely, strict liability becomes the preferable standard when the imposition of liability rules is associated to considerations of fairness and justice and the aim of ensuring a fair distribution of the burden and benefits of mutually beneficial but harmful activities.[27] The assumption from this perspective is that those who choose to create and impose risks on other individuals or on society, while also profiting from the operation of certain activities, will have to bear the relevant costs. This understanding of liability which emphasises its distributive justice rationale has been particularly influential in determining a preference for a strict standard of liability in statutory legislation and international regulatory frameworks addressing damage caused by hazardous but economically beneficial activities.[28] Finally, scholars taking a law and economics approach see the preference for negligence (fault-based) or strict liability as ultimately depending on which of the two standards, in a specific situation, would be best apt to provide incentives to risk creator to take optimal care to avoid damage.[29]

While these theoretical discussions on the role and functions of liability featured mostly among private law scholars concerned about the application of tort law more in general, they have a particular relevance in the environmental field, as they contributed to inform the structures and underlying rationales of liability regimes for environmental damage caused by hazardous activities. Indeed, while the immediate objective of environmental liability regimes is providing compensation of victims of pollution and reparation for the damaged natural resources, it is not infrequent that prevention features as an additional justification for the adoption of rules on environmental liability. EU Directive 35/2004 on the prevention and remedying of environmental damage ('the Environmental Liability Directive') is very explicit in this sense.[30]

The recognition of a preventive function to liability in the environmental field is also in part related to the regulatory and administrative nature of most environmental law. Environmental legislation and regulation can be closely intertwined with liability.[31] Environmental laws that establish permitted levels of emissions or discharges into the environment, standards of environmental quality or the conservation status for certain natural resources can positively contribute to inform definitions of environmental damage, for example by concurring to define 'the point at which pollution becomes a damage'; they can also inform the assessment of the reasonableness of an activity in private nuisance, or even the standard of care in negligence action and personal injury cases.[32] In these contexts, liability rules may positively complement existing mechanisms to incentivise compliance and enhance the enforcement of administrative environmental laws.[33] This is especially so where breaches of regulatory standards are taken into account in the determination of fault in liability.[34] In public international law, the notion of a wrongful act (i.e. violation of an international environmental law obligation binding upon the State) is a constitutive element for the operation of the rules on State responsibility, which represent one of the main mechanisms for the enforcement of international law. However, strict liability rules can also exert a complementary and supportive function in the implementation of international environmental agreements.[35] In the EU, the adoption of the Environmental Liability Directive took place at a time where the question of implementation and enforcement of EU environmental law was very high on the EU Commission agenda. The Directive operates a strict standard of liability for most instances of environmental damage falling within its scope of application. On the assumption that liability rules would incentivise operators' compliance with environmental prevention standards, the adoption of an EU-wide environmental liability regime represented, at least in part, an attempt to provide an indirect tool for the enforcement of environmental law.

3. Environmental liability and access to justice

3.1. Access to justice in environmental matters

Academic and policy-making debates around environmental liability have often centred around the structural elements of an environmental liability regime, such as the appropriate standard of responsibility (i.e. whether strict or fault-based) and the scope and definition of compensable damage and the relevant remedies. However, the operation, implementation and ultimately the effectiveness of such framework cannot prescind from the existence of appropriate legal mechanisms enabling an effective access to justice for those affected by environmental pollution.

Back in the 1970s, a few legal scholars, such as Mauro Cappelletti, Bryan Garth and Nicolo Trocker, already drew attention on the importance of access to justice 'as a movement to make particular rights effective', referring in particular to those rights which started to be legally recognised as an expression of the welfare State, such as rights related to environmental protection.[36] Their findings highlighted the relevance of a paramount shift from the individualistic foundations of access to justice in the liberal and laissez-faire State of the late eighteenth and nineteenth century—where 'access to judicial protection meant essentially the aggrieved individual's formal right to litigate or defend a claim'[37] without much speculation on the effective 'ability, *in practice*, of a party to recognize his legal rights and to prosecute or defend them adequately'[38]—to modern conceptions of access to justice as a means to empower citizens to uphold and effectively protect their substantive rights. With the advent of social reforms in the twentieth century, it became clear that the conferral of individual and social rights would be meaningless if these were not accompanied by appropriate legal means for their effective protection and enforcement.[39] In this context, substantive (as opposed to formalistic) conceptualisations of access to justice started to emerge in Europe both as a duty of the State to ensure equal and effective access to judicial protection and as a fundamental human right protected in domestic constitutional law and under the European Convention of Human Rights.

In the specific field of environmental protection, the discussions and legal developments concerning the question of access to justice must be examined in connection with another prominent development which is represented by the progressive recognition, across several domestic systems but also in EU law,[40] of certain legal interests that transcend the classical distinction between public and private and can therefore be more appropriately qualified as 'diffuse'. Thus, the concept of 'diffuse interests' started to animate academic debates and in certain jurisdictions was even formally introduced as a legal category in domestic law[41] to indicate a certain kind of legal interests, such as environment or consumer protection, which are indivisible in nature and attributed 'to an indeterminate number of people'.[42] The formal recognition of diffuse interests in domestic law reflects the need to allow for the protection and enforcement of certain social, economic and cultural rights, which by their very nature cannot be captured within the structures of private law, by empowering the citizens concerned by those rights to stand for their protection. Some scholars also tend to distinguish diffuse interests from collective interests, with the latter being regarded as 'the aligned, identical interests of many people'[43] connected *inter se* by a defined juridical link.[44] In any event, both categories indicate the recognition that there are certain concerns which are situated beyond the purview of private individual rights and beyond the 'public interest' strictly defined. Thus, while the public interest was traditionally conceived as the realm of State regulation, the qualification of environmental protection as a diffuse interest has entailed a redefinition of the public sphere as to also include that 'societal space' situated between the State and the individual and comprising the diffuse and collective interests of the citizens.[45] Diffuse interests represent, therefore, a sort of meta- or 'trans-individual'[46] category, the legal protection of which transcends orthodox distinctions between public and private law and requires instead the coordinated application of different legal tools and the concerted involvement of different societal actors in the protection of a common good. In the environmental field, it reflects the acknowledgement of the environment as a 'common heritage, a public good belonging equally to all citizens'.[47] With respect to access to justice, the understanding of the environment as a common good has an important implication as it requires, at a minimum, that the representation of environmental interests in court does not remain the exclusive prerogative of public authorities, but it becomes open also to citizens and those concerned about environmental protection. Access to justice in environmental matters becomes therefore an instrument for environmental democracy.[48] If properly implemented, it would enable individual citizens and other concerned parties to have a say in matters affecting their living conditions and to challenge the decisions of public authorities that affect the environment.[49]

While the idea of diffuse interests, as a distinct legal category, does not yet find a specific equivalent in international law, there are some parallel developments denoting a movement in a similar direction. It can be argued that the emergence of the notion of common concern of humankind reveals an analogous shift from a territorially based approach to the protection of the environment and of natural resources, defined through the lenses of State sovereignty, to the acknowledgment that there are 'global ecological concerns arising beyond the national jurisdiction of States and/or within the jurisdiction of individual States'.[50] While formally this concept has been usually referred to climate change and biodiversity protection, there are suggestions to consider the 'global environment' and the protection of the earth's biosphere as a common concern of humanity.[51]

3.2. Access to justice and environmental liability

But how do the earlier outlined conceptual developments play out in terms of framing access to justice approaches in the field of environmental liability? One way to answer this question is to reflect on the concept of environmental damage in the light of the earlier outlined recognition of environmental protection as a common good, and to distinguish, on the one hand, the harm suffered by private individuals and communities whose property, health and means of livelihood are affected by environmental pollution and, on the other hand, harm to the environment and to natural resources *per se* considered. Classic principles of tort law or civil liability are usually available to individuals who suffer damage to their land, personal injury or, in some cases, economic losses as a consequence of environmental pollution, meaning that those environmental tort victims can bring an action in court against the polluter to claim compensation—provided of course that they can fulfil other requirements of a tort action, such as proof of causation and, where necessary, proof of the defendant fault or breach of duty of care. However, the definition of right-holder in tort law is notoriously very narrow, focused on individual rights. In some instances, such as in the English tort of private nuisance, it is restrictively interpreted as requiring the possession by the claimant of an ownership entitlement on the land, or the demonstration of having a sufficient interest in the land, thereby excluding other potential claimants who, despite not being owners or suffering a personal injury that they could claim under negligence, may still be indirectly affected.[52] Thus, if we consider the judicial standing component of the principle of access to justice, the representation of environmental interests in court is the aspect where the classic tort law paradigm is mostly challenged. Traditional approaches to *locus standi* in the private law of tort liability appear inadequate to encompass the 'ecological' dimension of environmental damage, such as damage to an ecosystem, to a protected species or to a river and the impairment of a habitat, *per se* considered, unless this damage translate into the impairment of a legally protected individual right. They appear equally inadequate to address the non-economic type of damages suffered by the human communities or indigenous people living in the proximity to the impaired natural resources and bearing special cultural and historical connections with those resources and with the surrounding environment.[53] There is, in this respect, a close connection between the substance and the procedure, in that by curtailing the rights to judicially represent the collective interests in the environment, procedural rules regarding standing result eventually in the recognition of a narrow and one-sided notion of environmental damage.

In response to those shortcomings, some jurisdictions started to endorse legislative and jurisprudential developments that went in the direction of expanding the range of subjects entitled to bring an action in court to claim reparation for environmental damage. In France, already in 1995, the law conferred to environmental protection associations the possibility to bring a civil action before a criminal court in case of environmental damage resulting from a violation of environmental provisions.[54] Under this law, legal standing for environmental associations is based on the recognition of an injury ('préjudice') that directly or indirectly harms the collective interests that the association has, according to its statute, the objective to protect.[55] More recently, a number of court decisions in France have opened the way to a more liberal interpretation of those provisions, enabling claims for reparation of environmental damage filed by environmental protection associations or by other entities representing the environment, not only in criminal courts as a 'civil party petition', but also in civil courts and even in the absence of a demonstrated violations of environmental standards.[56] Of particular relevance is the decision rendered by the French Criminal Court of Cassation in relation to the catastrophic pollution of the Brittany coast, in northern France, as a result of the *Erika* oil tanker's shipwreck.[57] In that decision, the court accepted claims for environmental damage compensation filed by environmental protection associations on the basis not only of the material or moral damage to the collective interests which the associations had the statutory purpose to protect, but also for the harm suffered by the environment as such, and which directly or indirectly harmed those same interests that it was the associations' statutory task to safeguard. Compared to earlier decisions recognising environmental damage solely through the lenses of the material and moral injury suffered by NGOs in connection with their statutory environmental protection objectives, this case signals a further step forward towards the recognition of ecological damage—as damage suffered by the environment *per se*—as an autonomous head of damage.[58]

From a comparative law perspective, this is not an isolated phenomenon, and examples of legislative provisions opening the door to environmental organisations and public interest groups seeking to claim compensation under civil liability for environmental damage can be found also in other jurisdictions.[59] In fact, almost at the same time when the Loi Barnier was adopted in France, in the Netherlands an article of the Dutch Civil Code was amended to recognise the capacity of associations to bring an action to protect the collective interests that itself promotes. This provision was used by Dutch courts to grant environmental NGOs the right to ask for an injunction under tort law in case of events or activities that violate environmental law and cause environmental impairment,[60] as well as the entitlement to sue for damages albeit limitedly to the clean-up costs and the costs of other preventive and mitigating measures.[61] Even more progressively, certain legal systems, such as Portugal, admit a civil *actio popularis*, which enables public interest organisations, environmental NGOs and even 'every citizen enjoying their civil and political rights, regardless of having or not a direct interest in the matter'[62] to claim compensation for environmental harm directly from the polluter.[63]

An alternative approach to the judicial representation of environmental interests consists instead in conferring standing to the State (i.e. public authorities or authorised representatives) and/or other selected parties as part of a more radical shift from civil liability models towards an administrative type of environmental liability. This is the approach adopted by two US environmental liability statutes, namely the Comprehensive Environmental Response Compensation and Liability Act (CERCLA), and the Oil Pollution Act (OPA), which grant standing to the federal, State or Indian tribal government.[64] Similarly, in Italy, former Article 18 of Law 349/1986[65] (the law on environmental damage that preceded the transposition of the EU Environmental Liability Directive) conferred initially to the State in the person of the Ministry of the Environment or its local subdivisions (municipalities, provinces and regions) the possibility to claim redress for ecological damage when this was caused by an intentional or negligent violation of legal or administrative provisions.[66] However, under this approach, the rights of access to justice for members of the public or for environmental public interest groups and NGOs remain usually rather limited. Under the aforementioned Italian law, environmental associations only had a right to intervene in decisions concerning environmental damage and may act in judicial review against unlawful acts.[67] Similarly, the aforementioned US statutes provide for opportunities for public involvement with the decision regarding damage restoration plans, but they do not have the right to bring a direct action against the polluter or to file claims for compensation for injury to natural resources.[68]

Overall, however, in Europe the norms on standing for environmental organisations, public interest groups and even members of the public have generally been softened following the adoption of the Aarhus Convention, which grants procedural rights to information, participation in decision-making and access to justice in environmental proceedings.[69] The normative influence of this convention has been remarkable, as demonstrated *inter alia* by the recent adoption of a similar regional treaty in Latin America, the Ezcazú Regional Agreement on Access to Information, Public Participation and Justice in Environmental Matters in Latin America and the Caribbean.[70] In practice, the Aarhus Convention is subject to implementation in domestic law. Therefore, the extent to which its Article 9 could be applied to grant the public or even associations a direct action for environmental damage reparation depends ultimately on each State party's national legislation.

While most discussion regarding access to justice in environmental matters tends to concentrate on the question of standing, the formal entitlement to file a claim before a court of law is not the only component of this principle. There are different dimensions and different aspects involved in the notion of access to justice, which emerge both from the law and practice related to the environment and from human rights norms. Article 6 of the European Convention on Human Rights stipulates a right to fair trial, which includes the right to be heard 'within a reasonable time by an independent and impartial tribunal established by law'.[71] This provision clearly puts forward a 'more qualified meaning of access to justice', appealing to the application of substantive standards of fairness and justice in the adjudication proceedings,[72] and which appears of particular relevance to guarantee individual victims of corporate human rights and environmental abuses the access to a judiciary whose decision-making capacity is free from political and other illicit interferences.[73] Moreover, insofar as access to justice includes the right to a remedy, an effective access justice entails the removal of the barriers—actual or potential, procedural and substantive—that may undermine the pursuit of an effective remedy. At the procedural level, the excessive length and delays of the proceedings or, conversely, a too strict time limit to file a claim for compensation under civil liability, may create barriers in the access to remedies. In the environmental field, too strict time limitations to file a claim for reparation may become an obstacle since some type of pollution-related harm to human health or ecosystems often manifest themselves only after a long period of latency. Furthermore, in cases with a transnational element, additional procedural barriers can arise in the form of jurisdictional uncertainties regarding the competent court or the law applicable. Furthermore, when a case involves transboundary victims of environmental harm trying to sue in the foreign court where the polluting company is based, a basic principle of non-discrimination and equal treatment becomes a fundamental component of access to justice, since '[i]f nuisances do not stop at the borders it makes little sense to treat the victims differently depending on where they happen to live'.[74] The need of ensuring a regime of equal right of access and non-discrimination in matters of transfrontier pollution was put forward in a OECD recommendation already in 1977[75] and has since them become a cardinal tenet of the international law related to transboundary impacts.[76] With specific respect to access to environmental justice, the principle of non-discrimination is enshrined in both the Aarhus Convention and the Escazú agreement. Article 3(9) of the Aarhus Convention defines it as the right of the public to

> have access to information, have the possibility to participate in decision-making and have access to justice in environmental matters *without discrimination as to citizenship, nationality or domicile* and, in the case of a legal person, without discrimination as to where it has its registered seat or an effective centre of its activities.

Other barriers that at the substantive level may hamper access to justice and make difficult the pursuit of effective remedies are the actual or perceived costs of litigation, the availability of public funding and access to legal aid, and the availability of legal representation. Article 9(4) of the Aarhus Convention requires that judicial procedures in environmental matters be 'not prohibitively expensive'. This requirement, particularly in combination with EU law, determined some important changes in the law and policy related to the cost of judicial proceedings in some EU Member States and in the UK, pre-Brexit. In transnational civil liability cases, the availability of potentially more favourable rules on legal funding or the existence of contingency fees may be an important factor determining the plaintiffs' choice of jurisdiction, where such choice is possible. It has been argued, for example, that certain jurisdictions such as the UK or the US, where contingency fee arrangements and collective redress mechanisms are available, appear as a more attractive forum for plaintiffs seeking to pursue foreign direct liability claims.[77] In Vedanta, the UK judges in admitting the English court jurisdiction over the claim against the parent company and the overseas located subsidiary for damage caused in Zambia, took access to justice considerations into account, noting in particular that given the scale and complexity of the case and the limited funding and legal resources available to the claimants in Zambia, the latter could not secure the necessary legal representation.[78]

An effective access to justice also depends on the type and effectiveness of the remedies available. In environmental cases, the possibility to obtain an injunction, prohibiting the pursuit of a harmful activity, in addition to or alternatively to compensation may be especially important, as it is the availability of interim relief having a suspensive effect on the pursuit of a potentially harmful activity or development. It is not infrequent that the absence of injunctive relief or a delay in obtaining it, combined with the slow judicial proceedings, means that in practice some cases 'are won in court, but lost on the ground' because a given activity has continued to cause further harm to the environment or to people's health before a court decision.[79] Furthermore, in case of damage to the environment, it is important that the remedies are appropriately tailored to the ecological dimension of the damage and the publicness and collectiveness of the interests involved. The classic tort law or civil liability remedy of providing monetary compensation may in fact be problematic from an environmental perspective, particularly from the point of view of assessing and quantifying the damage. Conversely, an approach to remediation focused on achieving restoration of the impaired natural resources may overcome this difficulty, although restoration orders may need to be accompanied by appropriate indications regarding the restoration standard required or desirable. It is therefore increasingly the case in various jurisdictions that the law imposes specific obligation on the polluter to restore the environment and the impaired habitats to the *quo ante* condition, including in some cases with consideration for the loss or impairment of ecosystem services. These types of remedies may coexist with the classic tort law remedies available under common law or civil liability rules.[80]

4. From theory to practice: current developments in environmental liability

4.1. The global picture

As illustrated in the previous sections, the question of environmental liability, including its societal functions and relationship with environmental protection strategies and with the themes of access to justice and prevention, has received over the years considerable attention in academic circles and at the policy-making level. These debates contributed to inform the adoption of significant reforms in this field of law, both at the domestic level and in EU law. Undoubtedly, the legal and regulatory framework concerning the responses to environmental harms has progressively undergone a profound transformation, in close connection with the recognition of the environment as a fundamental societal interest deserving legal protection. One of the most discernible features characterising legal developments in the field of environmental liability has been the move from the classic and narrow private law conceptualisations of environmental damage under tort law and civil liability, as traditional damage to property, persons or other private law protected interest, to the legal recognition of harm to the environment and to natural resources *per se* considered. The notion of 'ecological damage', or natural resources damage, has not only raised the interest of a growing number of legal scholars seeking to better understand its conceptual and legal implications from a domestic and comparative law perspective,[81] but also triggered important changes in the form and structure of liability regimes, including through the elaboration of apposite remedies for natural resources damage and the reconceptualisation of the classic categories of standing. The first steps in this direction can be found at the domestic level, most notably in the US—where the so-called Superfund[82] and the OPA[83] represented some of the pioneering attempts to shift the paradigm of environmental liability from the classic tort law approaches towards a public law model of liability—and through other, perhaps less known, examples in other legal systems.[84] The normative influence of the two aforementioned US liability statutes progressively extended to other jurisdictions where growing public concerns about the risk of accidents causing severe and often almost irremediable environmental contamination fuelled the adoption of specific environmental liability regimes and the raising of liability and remediation standards.[85] EU Directive 2004/35 on environmental liability, which is the object of extensive discussion in the following chapters of this book, is perhaps the most notable example of the global influence exerted by the US models and provides a remarkable illustration of the transnational borrowing of environmental law across different jurisdictions.[86]

But if, on the one hand, these regulatory initiatives in the field of liability and reparation for environmental damage seem to signal a shift away from the traditional private law-based approaches, regarded as insufficient to capture the intrinsic ecological dimension and the collective value of natural resources; on the other hand, a parallel set of developments are shedding new insights on the continued relevance of tort-based litigation in the environmental field. Interestingly, a number of cases brought before domestic courts in Europe and concerning the civil liability of European-based parent companies for the severe environmental pollution and human rights violations occurring during the operation of their foreign subsidiaries or suppliers operating in third countries reveals how civil liability litigation can still represent a powerful tool for the poor victims of environmental harms in the absence of alternative and more effective remedies available in their own jurisdiction.[87] The relevance of tort-based litigation becomes indeed especially evident in this context as this is an area which has so far been characterised by the conspicuous absence of an appropriate international legal framework establishing binding standards of conduct for multinational corporate actors and other businesses operating transnationally and setting up relevant mechanisms for enforcement of those standards and for seeking redress. In this scenario, recourse to private international litigation seeking to rely on the transnational application of domestic law and standards remains often the most viable alternative for foreign victims seeking justice against human rights and environmental grievances. From a normative perspective, the growing domestic courts' case-law on the alleged liability of the parent companies or of the lead businesses in a supply chain also prompt interesting questions on the potential role of these judicial proceedings in forging transnational standards of corporate accountability. Of special relevance in the context of the efforts to fill the gaps left by the absence of a proper regulatory framework at the international level is the intersection between the growing recourse to transnational tort liability cases before domestic courts and certain domestic legislative initiatives aimed at unilaterally setting appropriate standards of care and appropriate human rights and environment-related responsibilities for enterprises operating in third countries.[88] Progress in this direction is currently being made at the EU level, with the recent Proposal for a Directive on Corporate Sustainability Due Diligence.[89]

A further discernible trend is the use of tort liability not only as a means to seek redress, but also as a positive complement to environmental regulation.[90] There is a stream of cases across different national jurisdictions which highlight how private actions in tort can indeed be usefully employed to contest regulatory decisions (for example administrative decisions authorising a given activity which in turn causes severe property damage or personal discomfort)[91] or correct regulatory failures.[92] By offering the opportunity to raise a different view on the legality of a given activity and to contest the regulator's definition of public interest, private law would enable a decentralised and pluralistic mode of decision-making[93]—that is, one which takes into account the diversity and plurality of interests at stake, and that by giving voice to different societal representation, including minority groups and poor communities, promotes the alignment of regulation with environmental justice.[94]

Finally, tort litigation before domestic courts can also act as a catalyst for further regulatory developments at the national and international levels. The recent rise of climate change litigation, for example, has prompted a number of scholars to explore the role of private litigation as a means to raise public awareness on important environmental issues and to address regulatory inaction.[95] In the multi-level dimension that characterises current environmental governance globally, this remark appears particularly relevant as it suggests that transnational civil liability litigation for environmental damage in domestic court can not only serve a gap-filling role to compensate the lack of comprehensive legal framework on the international level, but can also indirectly promote the 'further development of global environmental liability norms'.[96]

Overall, the aforementioned considerations portray a dynamic and variegated scenario in the field of environmental liability, which is increasingly characterised by the coexistence and intersection of public and private legal frameworks, judicial proceedings and bottom-up approaches from citizens and civil society. These developments also bear witness to the importance of putting in place appropriate responses to environmental harm and developing appropriate remedies for environmental damage, including through environmental liability. The question that still remains is whether, at least in Europe, those developments and initiatives at the national and supranational (i.e. EU) levels are sufficient to compensate the slow progress achieved by international law in this context. It is to this question that the discussion will now turn.

4.2. The elusive response of international law

In international law, the topic of environmental liability has been at the centre of a longstanding academic and policy-making debate. The issue moved officially up on the international environmental agenda in 1972, when Principle 21 of the Stockholm Declaration on the Human Environment included the further development of 'international law regarding liability and compensation for the victims of pollution and other environmental damage' among the future priority areas for international cooperation in the environmental field.[97] The relevance of the topic was then reinstated in Principle 13 of the 1992 Rio Declaration which encouraged States to 'cooperate in an expeditious and more determined manner' in the further development of international law regarding liability and compensation for pollution and other environmental damage and in the elaboration of their domestic legislation in this area. These broadly formulated statements did not offer concrete guidance on the contents or scope of application of any prospective environmental liability regimes. Nonetheless, in the years following the 1972 Stockholm Declaration, these two broad principles provided the conceptual framework for a number of significant law-making efforts, including within the International Law Commission[98] and in the field of treaty-making,[99] that attempted to set up appropriate and comprehensive international regimes of liability and remediation for transboundary environmental harm. Presently, the question of the legal liability of business enterprises is also one of the topics that have been touched during the negotiation for a prospective legally binding treaty on business and human rights.[100]

While these legal developments and initiatives testify to the importance of the topic, it is fair to say that the question of liability and reparation for environmental damage remains one of the yet unresolved issues of international law. On the one hand, progress on the definition of specific international principles on the environmental liability of States for the harmful impacts of activities within their jurisdiction or control have so far found important obstacles in the persistent reluctance of the States to accept legal binding rules in this context, outside the operation of the classic customary law on State responsibility. On the other hand, conventional developments on the liability of private operators are limited by the narrow scope of application of these treaty regimes, which are usually tailored to a specific type of damage or specific sectors of activities, thereby leaving a gap for those cases which do not fall under their framework. Additionally, the lengthy negotiation processes and the difficulties in achieving the necessary number of ratifications for the entry into force of these treaties confirm once again the complexity and political sensitivity of the liability topic. There is at present no general international environmental liability treaty, and the failure of the Council of Europe's Lugano environmental liability convention (so far, the only environmental liability treaty with a broad scope of application) to entry into force raises doubts as to whether this would be feasible in practice. There are several factors that need to be considered and which may weigh against the feasibility or even the appropriateness of adopting a global environmental liability regime. These include the absence of a unanimous definition of environment and of environmental damage; the diversity of hazardous activities, which may make it difficult to subject them to a unified regime; and the existence of divergent views concerning the nature and structure of such liability—whether it shall be strict or fault based, and whether it shall be imposed on private operators or on the States or on both.[101]

Additionally, from a public international law perspective, the difficulties in the development of effective remedies for environmental damage are further exacerbated by the lack of a proper institutional system of global environmental governance and of appropriate mechanisms for the implementation and enforcement of international environmental norms.[102] Unlike other branches of international law, such as trade, human rights and investment law, there is no dedicated agency set up within the United Nations specifically to deal with environmental issues, nor are there effective systems for monitoring compliance and securing the appropriate enforcement of international environmental treaties.[103] State implementation of international environmental obligations is thus usually left to 'soft' forms of monitoring mechanisms or to the spontaneous compliance of States through their domestic laws. These persistent weaknesses in the mechanisms of enforcement and adjudication, often combined with restrictive access to justice provisions before international judicial institutions for individuals and public interest groups, do not only undermine the overall effectiveness of international environmental norms, but they also hamper the establishment of appropriate and effective international remedies for environmental damage and for the victims of transboundary pollution.

5. Scope and aims of this book

5.1. Theoretical background

There are important arguments that, at least in principle, support the longstanding quest of the international community towards the definition of comprehensive and legally binding international norms on environmental liability. First, particularly with respect to transboundary or transnational instances of environmental damage involving two or more different jurisdictions, the harmonisation of international rules on liability contributes to set up a level playing field, with respect to standards of accountability and responsibility, and to ensure equal access to remedies for victims of pollution and other environmental harm. Second, collective action at the international level is better suited to address environmental damage to global commons and areas beyond national jurisdiction, which cannot be appropriately addressed through unilateral initiatives at the domestic level.

That said, the difficulties encountered in the elaboration of effective and workable international environmental liability regimes and the elusiveness of reaching consensus on a core set of legally binding and generally applicable norms on liability for transboundary environmental harm have prompted various questions regarding the role of international law in this context. Commenting on the slow progress of international law on the topic, several legal scholars have raised doubts on the practicality of 'engaging in the laborious task of developing a liability regime',[104] voicing concerns related to both the appropriateness of liability itself as an instrument to address preoccupations related to damage that might be caused to the environment[105] and the viability of classic international law-making mechanisms (such as the development of international treaties, or the customary rules of State responsibility) to pursue these objectives.[106] Others tried, more positively, to put forward proposals to improve the meagre success achieved so far by international civil liability negotiations.[107] Meanwhile, some scholars asserted the importance to take a broader outlook to the examination of the legal responses and instruments available to remediate transboundary environmental pollution, emphasising the phenomenon of 'cluster litigation'[108] and noting that 'transboundary environmental legal disputes are not only remedied through instruments of international law'.[109]

The scenario emerging from these findings suggests that while harmonisation by means of environmental liability treaties or the codification of general principles on the international responsibility for environmental harm remains a desirable and legitimate objective, there are principled and pragmatic arguments pointing to the relevance of taking a broader and global perspective to the topic, through an analytical approach that brings together in an integrated fashion the diverse developments happening at the international, regional and domestic levels. This does not mean to abandon the 'old' international law aspirations of universality[110] or a diminished role for international law in this context. Rather, what is put forward is the need to take a different perspective to the analysis of the role, place and function of international law in the field of environmental liability by examining the developments at the international level in connection with the various processes and initiatives taking place at different normative level and regulatory contexts (i.e. domestic law, EU law, private law and public law as well as the intersection between hard law and soft law). Conceptually, this analytical approach entails shifting the focus from 'international law' (traditionally conceived as the law governing interstate relations) towards the process of 'internationalization of law', conceived as a 'dynamic', an 'ensemble of movements' triggered by the interactions between international laws and domestic laws.[111]

It is submitted that such a global and 'integrated approach'[112] is particularly appropriate to the study of legal developments in the environmental field. It has been noted that although 'international environmental law is commonly seen as a specialized sub-field of the "law of nations"', 'it also differs from other areas of international law due to its more global character'.[113] Reflecting both the intrinsic interdependence of ecological systems and the impact of globalisation on legal processes,[114] the realm of environmental law is nowadays characterised by a plurality, interaction and intersection of different legal orders, practices and normative processes (public and private, state and non-state) which are in some cases blurring the divide between international law and domestic (and, arguably, European) law, as well as between hard law and soft law.[115] Moreover, in the environmental field, the interplay between international, domestic and regional/EU legal developments occurs not only through the necessary reliance on national legislation for the incorporation and implementation of international agreements,[116] or through the interpretation of domestic law in the light of the State's international commitments, but it also happens by means of a subtle process of vertical or 'trans-echelon' borrowing[117] of regulatory models between national and international law. While such growing international linkages are blurring the division between legal orders, they are also gradually 'promoting integration and harmonisation'.[118]

Scholars tend to refer to this phenomenon as 'global (environmental) law', a concept that has been defined as 'law that is international, national and transnational in character all at once', comprising an evolving 'set of legal principles developed by national, international and transnational environmental regulatory systems to protect the environment and manage natural resources'.[119] Whether or not one adheres to the view of global environmental law as a distinct body of law, the concept provides a 'promising' and 'transformative research agenda',[120] as it arguably enables a better understanding of how environmental protection can be promoted and enhanced 'through a plurality of legal mechanisms relying on a plurality of legal orders'.[121] Global environmental law is distinct from, and arguably broader than, 'transnational law',[122] the latter being a concept initially coined to study the relationship between private and public international law and the reliance on private international law to resolve transnational problems and now extending to also encompass the various manifestations of law beyond the State,[123] as well as more recently certain trends characterised by the extraterritorial impact of domestic environmental laws and policies.[124] Although scholars have also pointed out how the two notions of global and transnational law are partly overlapping to the extent that in both cases 'law is being denationalised to varying degrees' through legal ordering happening beyond the State, and beyond the categories of international and national law 'as conventionally construed'.[125]

Both concepts of global environmental law and transnational (environmental) law are particularly relevant in enabling a comprehensive and integrated approach to the study and analysis of environmental liability regimes in a global context. Indeed, it has been argued that 'international environmental law has transformed itself into a new area of law: that of global environmental law and/or transnational environmental law' so that simply 'referring to international environmental law does not accurately reflect the new modes of regulation as well as the emergence of multi-level governance, and the new normative power relationships that now permeate international society'.[126] Global law allows an analytical perspective that by examining the common set of legal principles, tools and concepts emerging in domestic, international and transnational law, and the interconnections and interaction of different regulatory frameworks in addressing common environmental problems, it implicitly acknowledges the international law aspirations of universality and the need to provide common and effective legal responses to global environmental problems. In fact, as Walker noted, while '[g]lobal law . . . may or may not be sourced and institutionalised at the planetary level', it reflects 'a practical endorsement of, or commitment to the universal or otherwise global-in-general warrant of some laws or some dimensions of law'.[127] Along similar lines, some scholars have stressed the forward-looking dimension and aspirational nature of global law. The notion of global law would thus reflect the 'publicness of law' in a global space, and the international community's or humanity's striving for the common good, be that justice, fundamental human rights or the protection of the global environment.[128] Global (environmental law) can therefore offer an appropriate analytical lens to investigate the current and prospective developments in the field of environmental liability, which take place globally through the interaction between different layers of regulation and governance, and through both formal legal frameworks and other, less formal, normative frameworks.

At the same time, there are elements of transnational law that increasingly populate the field of environmental liability. These features can be discerned, notably and in the more traditional meaning of the term,[129] when victims of transboundary environmental pollution pursue compensation by relying on the transnational application of domestic law across different jurisdictions; but also through domestic and EU regulatory endeavours seeking to have extraterritorial reach, as well as through the work of international organisations in the elaboration of soft-law frameworks and guidelines.[130]

5.2. Focus, methodological approach and structure of the book

Against this conceptual and theoretical background, this book proposes to examine the question of environmental liability by focusing the analysis on the relationship and interaction between EU and international law. There are various reasons why a focus on the interplay between EU and international law is particularly interesting in this context. To start with, the EU achieved harmonisation in the field of liability and reparation for environmental damage by means of Directive 35/2004, which lays down a minimum common framework in the field of environmental liability across the EU Member States. In spite of the significant scholarly literature on the Directive and its implementation in the domestic systems of the EU Member States,[131] there is still very little exploration of the potential scope for interplay and synergic application of this EU legal instrument with the various environmental liability regimes on the international level. And yet, cases such as the *Commune de Mesquer*[132]—concerning the overlap between the Civil Liability Convention for oil pollution damage and certain EU law provisions under the Waste Framework Directive—demonstrate that, in the multilevel framework which characterises environmental governance in Europe and internationally, the question of potential conflict between different sets of environmental liabilities and responsibilities bears an increasing practical relevance.

The adoption of the Directive was preceded by EU legislative instruments harmonising in the field of jurisdiction and conflict of law[133] and is currently being paralleled by prospective EU legislation laying down common rules on corporate sustainability due diligence for EU-based companies operating in third countries and establishing liability for violations of their obligations regarding their actual and potential human rights and environmental impacts.[134] Both sets of development are relevant when dealing with the harmful environmental impact of EU-based economic activities across different Member States and in third countries. Moreover, they operate in a field where international law is struggling to reach consensus on the adoption of legally binding frameworks.

It has also been asserted that the EU is a regional model of regulatory integration, which can serve as a source of inspiration for the development of international law rules both regionally and globally.[135] This statement rests principally on the recognition of the dual facets of the European Union legal order. On the one hand, it originates and forms an integral part of the international legal order.[136] The European Union is grounded in an international agreement, the EU Treaty, whose validity and means of influence continue to be governed by traditional rules of international law. On the other hand, notwithstanding its roots in the international legal system, the EU legal order remains innovative in many respects. The Treaty of Rome and subsequent EU treaties laid down the basis for the gradual devolvement of an ever-wider range of Member States' competences to a supranational entity, thereby allowing the EU to regulate on a number of matters normally falling within the States' internal affairs. The EU remains in fact 'an example of a particularly effective international law'[137] and has very often been regarded as a 'laboratory' for the developments and the transformations taking place in the international legal order.[138]

Finally, a focus on the EU and its relationship with the international legal order is particularly appropriate in the light of the EU's increasing role as a global environmental actor[139] and its ambitions to play a leading role in the development of global environmental policies.[140] As noted, '[s]ince its very inception, the European environmental policy has always had an outward, international dimension'.[141] Over the years the EU has used different strategies to exert its normative and regulatory influence on the wider world, from its growing participation in the negotiations and as a contracting party in multilateral environmental agreements[142] to other more indirect and subtle ways of extending its normative and regulatory power extraterritorially,[143] seeking slowly and progressively to contribute to shaping developments at the global level.[144] These EU ambitions are currently explicitly reflected in the Treaty on European Union (TEU), which includes both the contribution to the 'sustainable development of the Earth' and the strict observance and the development of international law among the EU's aims.[145] Moreover, Title V TEU on the general principles of the EU external action explicitly portrays the EU as an actor on the international scene, guided by the twin goals of 'promoting multilateral solutions to common problems' and seeking to advance its principles and values, which also include 'respect of the principles of the United Nations Charter and international law' in the wider world.[146] Article 21(2) TEU contains specific references to EU's international action in the field of environmental protection and sustainable development, including among the objectives and tasks of the EU to 'foster the sustainable economic, social and environmental development of developing countries' and to 'help develop international measures to preserve and improve the quality of the environment and the sustainable management of global natural resources, in order to ensure sustainable development'. These provisions are to be read in the light of Article 11 mandating EU institutions to integrate environmental protection requirements into all EU policies and activities, including the external ones. The global, international outlook that characterises the EU's action in the environmental field and its emphasis in contributing actively to law-making at the international level and globally render the analysis of the relationship between EU and international law particularly appropriate to explore the regulatory and normative potential of a multilevel interplay between different legal orders.

In the light of all the aforementioned, and with a specific focus on the question of environmental liability, this book brings together the analysis of relevant legal developments in the EU and in international law, and then examines the complex interaction between the two legal orders with a view to explore the potential for a mutually supportive and synergic relationship between EU and international law in the definition and implementation of appropriate responses to environmental harms. The book starts from the acknowledgment of the difficulties and scant progress made in the field of environmental liability at the international level. Thus, taking an integrated perspective and drawing on the burgeoning legal scholarship in the field of global environmental law and on the extensive literature on the relationship between EU and international law, it seeks to put forward a constructive reading of the current and ongoing developments in this context and to understand whether, if not through harmonisation, it is nevertheless possible to strengthen the remedies for victims of environmental damage through the interaction and combination of different legal regimes and different legal systems. In this perspective, the book also seeks to explore and better understand the impact of the interplay between EU and international law in terms of advancing, or limiting, the further developments of international norms and mechanisms to respond to environmental damage.

With this overall goal in mind, the book has a two-fold objective, which is reflected in its contents and structure. First, it aims to provide a comprehensive analysis of the current developments in the field of environmental liability taking place at the international law level and within the EU legal system, respectively. This part of the enquiry is carried out by taking a comparative perspective, which seeks to identify similarities, or differences, in the legal responses put in place in EU law and in international law to the problem of liability and environmental damage, as well as to discern patterns of convergence or divergence in the evolution of their respective regulatory frameworks. The analysis applies the comparative method in a vertical,[147] trans-echelon[148] perspective, which brings together the analysis of European and international law developments in the field of environmental liability, with a view to discern patterns of norm diffusion vertically across different regulatory levels.[149] The comparative examination is also combined with a transnational and global law perspective on the law and legal developments.

A transnational law approach allows to include within the scope of the comparative analysis also normative developments beyond the State, and beyond the remits of international and EU law as classically construed.[150] The findings of this comparative analysis are functional to address the first dimension of the enquiry which aims to assess the normative impact of the interplay between EU and international law in forging a common understanding of the question of environmental liability and in shaping global legal principles applicable in the field.[151]

The findings of the comparative examination also inform the second dimension or objective of this enquiry, which seeks to ascertain and to critically assess the contribution of the EU to the development and strengthening of international law in the field of environmental liability. In this respect, the research examines the EU's interplay with international law by focusing on the EU participation in international environmental liability treaties and other ways that it contributes to shape international regimes, and by examining how international environmental norms are applied in the EU legal order and interact with EU law.

Overall, both dimensions of the research seek to contribute to answering a more general and fundamental question, that is whether and to what extent the relationship between international law and EU law, with specific respect to liability, responsibility and redress for environmental damage, can be framed as a relationship of coexistence, of potential conflict or instead of complementarity and reciprocal supportiveness.

This book is structured in three main parts. The first two parts (Part I and Part II) focus on the analysis of the legal frameworks and relevant current developments in the field of environmental liability at the international law level and within the EU, respectively. Together Part I and Part II illustrate the various law-making endeavours, in international law and in EU law, aimed at harmonising the field of environmental liability and the efforts to establish a set of common principles on liability and reparation for environmental harm applicable across various jurisdictions. Building upon this, Part III examines different aspects of the relationship between EU law and international law in the field of environmental liability with a view to explore interactions and potential synergies and complementarities.

Notes

1 United Nations Environment Programme, UNEP/OCHA Assessment Mission, 'Cyanide Spill at Baia Mare Romania' (Report, March 2000); J Braswell, 'Quando Chi Inquina non Paga: la Fuoriuscita di Acqua Contaminata da Cianuro a Baia Mare e l'Irrisolto Problema della Responsabilità Internazionale per Danni Ambientali Trasfrontalieri' (2001) Rivista Giuridica dell'Ambiente 909.

2 D Phillips, 'Samarco Dam Collapse: One Year on from Brazil's Worst Environmental Disaster' *The Guardian* (15 October 2016) <www.theguardian.com/sustainable-business/2016/oct/15/samarco-dam-collapse-brazil-worst-environmental-disaster-bhp-billiton-vale-mining > accessed 20 July 2022.

3 S Eisenhammer, 'Brazil Mine Disaster Could Devastate Ecosystem for Many Years' *Insurance Journal* (November 2015) <www.insurancejournal.com/news/international/2015/11/16/389012.htm> accessed 15 September 2022.

4 K Buesseler, M Dai, M Aoyama, C Benitez-Nelson, S Charmasson, K Higley, V Maderich, P Masqué, PJ Morris, D Oughton, and JN Smith, 'Fukushima Daiichi-derived Radionuclides in the Ocean: Transport, Fate, and Impacts' (2017) 9 Annual Review Marine Science 173.

5 An example is the settlement reached between BP and the US Justice Department, following years of litigation related to the Gulf oil spill, where the company agreed to plead guilty to 14 criminal counts, including violations of relevant environmental statutes, and to pay a $4.5 billion criminal penalty. See DM Uhlmann, 'BP Paid a Steep Price for the Gulf Oil Spill But for the US a Decade Later, It's Business as Usual' *The Conversation* (23 April 2020) <www.theconversation.com/bp-paid-a-steep-price-for-the-gulf-oil-spill-but-for-the-us-a-decade-later-its-business-as-usual-136905> accessed 20 July 2022.

6 RL Rabin, 'Environmental Liability and the Tort System' (1987) 24 Houston Law Review 28, 32. The author speaks in these cases of 'collective harm'.

7 H Bocken, 'Developments with Respect to Compensation for Damage Caused by Pollution' in B Markesinis (ed.), *The Gradual Convergence; Foreign Ideas, Foreign Influences, and English Law on the Eve of the 21st Century* (Clarendon Press 1994) 226; A Kiss, 'Present Limits to the Enforcement of State Responsibility for Environmental Damage' in F. Francioni and T. Scovazzi (eds.), *International Responsibility for Environmental Harm* (Graham and Trotman 1991) 4, comparing the pursuit of compensation for environmental harm to a legal 'steeple-chase' 'where different obstacles must be overcome before arriving to the final result'.

8 G Brüggemeier, 'European Civil Liability Outside Europe. The Example of the Big Three: China, Brazil, Russia' (2011) 2 Journal of European Tort Law 1.

9 The problem related to the transfer of hazardous activities and substances to countries in the Global South is significant and longstanding. See, among others, G Handl and RE Lutz (eds.), *Transferring Hazardous Technologies and Substances: The International Legal Challenge* (Graham and Trotman 1989); MT Kamminga and S Zia-Zarifi (eds.), *Liability of Multinational Corporations under International Law* (Kluwer Law International 2000); more recently, C Glinsky, 'Corporate Social Responsibility and Corporate Liability for Environmental Damage' in B Pozzo and V Jacometti (eds.), *Environmental Loss and Damage in a Comparative Law Perspective* (CUP 2021).

10 Background document to the UNECE workshop 'Transboundary Accidental Water Pollution, Liability and Compensation: Challenges and Opportunities' (21–22 May 2007).

11 U Baxi, 'Human Rights Responsibility of Multinational Corporations, Political Ecology of Injustice: Learning from Bhopal Thirty Plus?' (2016) 1 Business Human Rights Journal 21.

12 Environmental Justice Atlas, 'Baia Mare Gold Exploitation, Romania' <https://ejatlas.org/conflict/baia-mare> accessed 18 October 2022.

13 K Ridley and Z Shabalala, 'BHP Labels $ Billion UK Case Over Brazilian Dam Failure Pointless' *Reuters* (22 July 2020) <www.reuters.com/article/us-bhp-britain-court-dam-idUKKCN24N187> accessed 15 September 2022; P Weston, 'Victims of Brazil's Worst Environmental Disaster to Get Day in UK Courts' *The Guardian* (8 July 2022) <www.theguardian.com/environment/2022/jul/08/uk-court-of-appeal-case-victims-brazil-mariana-dam-collapse-aoe> accessed 15 September 2022.

14 See G Calabresi, 'Some Thoughts on Risk Distribution and the Law of Torts' (1961) Yale Law Journal 499.

15 See generally on this debate from an environmental law and economics perspective, M Faure, 'Economic Aspects of Environmental Liability: An Introduction' (1996) 4 European Review of Private Law 85–110.

16 S Shavell, *The Economic Analysis of Accident Law* (Harvard University Press 1987); M Faure, 'Regulatory Strategies in Environmental Liability' in F Cafaggi and H Muir Watt (eds.), *The Regulatory Function of European Private Law* (Edward Elgar 2009).

17 GC Keating, 'Distributive and Corrective Justice in the Tort Law of Accidents' (2000) 74 Southern California Law Review 193–222; P Cane, 'Distributive Justice and Tort Law' (2001) New Zealand Law Review 401.
18 S Deakin, 'The Evolution of Tort' (1999) 19 Oxford Journal of Legal Studies 537.
19 Ibid. citing P Cane, *The Anatomy of Tort Law* (Hart 1997) 24.
20 Cane 'Distributive Justice' (n 17) 403.
21 Keating (n 17) 196.
22 The idea of 'correlativity' is common among tort law scholars focusing on a justice conception of liability. See Cane 'Distributive Justice' (n 17) 403, who refers to the work of E Weinrib.
23 Keating (n 17) 196.
24 See, e.g., G Calabresi (n 14); M Faure, 'Regulatory Strategies' (n 16) 133.
25 Cane 'Distributive Justice' (n 17) 404, who conceives distributive justice concerns as possibly cohabiting with views of tort law as a system of corrective justice.
26 Keating (n 17) 198. See also discussion on negligence versus strict liability for environmental harm in P Cane, 'Are Environmental Harms Special' (2001) 13 Journal of Environmental Law 3.
27 Keating (n 17) 199–200.
28 J Barboza, *The Environment, Risk and Liability in International Law* (Martinus Nijhoff Publishers 2010); R Lefeber, *Transboundary Environmental Interference and the Origin of State Liability* (Kluwer Law International 1996).
29 M Faure, 'Regulatory Strategies' (n 16) 134–135.
30 OJ L 143, 30.4.2004.
31 M Lee, 'The Intersection Between Environmental Law and Tort Law' in L Paddock, R Glicksman and N Bryner (eds.), *Decision Making in Environmental Law* (Edward Elgar 2016).
32 But the debate on these questions is complex, and the extent to which regulation can influence the application of tort law concepts or even pre-empt common law is far from straightforward. See among others, KS Abraham, 'The Relation between Civil Liability and Environmental Regulation: An Analytical Overview' (2002) 41 Washburn Law Journal 379; M Lee, 'Safety, Regulation and Tort: Fault in Context' (2011) 74 Modern Law Review 555. In England, see cases *Barr v Biffa Waste Services* [2012] EWCA Civ 312 and *Coventry v Lawrence* [2014] UKSC 13.
33 M Wilde, *Civil Liability for Environmental Damage—Comparative Analysis of Law and Policy in Europe and the US* (2nd ed., Kluwer Law International 2013) 158–161; Abraham (n 32); P Cane, 'Using Tort Law to Enforce Environmental Regulations?' (2002) 41 Washburn Law Journal 428, 448 ff.
34 Lee 'Safety Regulation' (n 32).
35 J Brunnée, 'Of Sense and Sensibility: Reflections on International Liability Regimes as Tools for Environmental Protection' (2004) 53 International and Comparative Law Quarterly 351; A Daniel 'Civil Liability Regimes as a Complement to Multilateral Environmental Agreements: Sound International Policy or False Comfort?' (2003) 12 Reciel 225.
36 M Cappelletti, B Garth and N Trocker, 'Access to Justice. Variations and Continuity of a World-Wide Movement' (1982) 46 Rabels Zeitshrift fur auslandisches und internationals Privatrecht 664, 666.
37 M Cappelletti and B Garth, 'Access to Justice: The Newest Wave in the Worldwide Movement to Make Rights Effective' (1978) 27 Buffalo Law Review 181, 183.
38 Ibid.
39 Cappelletti and Garth (n 37).
40 C Godt, 'Enforcement of Environmental Law by Individuals and Interest Groups: Reconceptualizing Standing' (2000) 23 Journal of Consumer Policy 79.

41 See G Alpa, 'Interessi Diffusi: Una Categoria Rivisitata' (2014) 2 Economia e Diritto del Terziario 167; A Aragão, 'Les intérêts diffus, instruments pour la justice et la démocratie environnementale' [Vertig0—La revue électronique en sciences de l'environnement' Hors-série 22, Septembre 2015 <https://journals.openedition.org/vertigo/>]; A Aragão and AC Carvalho, 'Taking Access to Justice Seriously: Diffuse Interests and Actio Popularis. Why Not?' (2017) 2 ELNI Review 42.
42 Godt (n 40) 81.
43 Ibid., and cited literature.
44 Aragão (n 41).
45 Godt (n 40) 86.
46 Aragão (n 41).
47 Aragão and Carvalho (n 41) 44.
48 J Darpö, 'Principle 10 and Access to Justice' in L Kramer and E Orlando (eds.), *Principles of Environmental Law* (IUCN/Edward Elgar 2018).
49 Ibid.
50 P Taylor, 'Common Heritage of Mankind and Common Concern of Humankind' in L Kramer and E Orlando (eds.), *Principles of Environmental Law* (IUCN/Edward Elgar 2018) 315.
51 See in this sense, Article 3 of the IUCN Draft Covenant on Environment and Development (5th ed., 2015); A Kiss, 'The Common Concern of Mankind' (1997) 27 Environmental Policy and Law 244.
52 *Hunter v Canary Wharf* [1997] AC 655. But a more relaxed approach to standing is adopted by English courts with respect to judicial review action.
53 See *Re the Exxon Valdez* (1997) 104 F3d 1196, where the US Court of Appeal (nine circuit) rejected the claim of Alaskan natives seeking compensation for the non-economic damage to their cultural heritage and subsistence way of life caused by the catastrophic oil pollution created by the grounding of the Prince William Sound oil tanker. M Wilde, 'Locus Standi in Environmental Torts and the Potential Influence of Human Rights Jurisprudence' (2003)12 Reciel 3.
54 It must be recalled that in the French legal system, it is possible for individuals to bring a civil liability claims in the framework of criminal proceedings.
55 L n. 95–101, 2nd February 1995, JO 3 February (Loi Barnier). A subsequent law on environmental liability, adopted on 1 August 2008, and translated into Article L. L142–4 of the Environmental Code, extended this possibility to local territorial entities.
56 M Boutonnet, 'La réparation du préjudice causé à l'environnement' (2010) 5 Hokkaido Journal of New Global Law and Policy 67.
57 Cour de Cassation, Arret No 3439, 25 September 2012 (10–82938) <www.legifrance.gouv.fr/juri/id/JURITEXT000026430035/> accessed 20 July 2022.
58 UNECE, Task Force on Access to Justice, Study on the Possibilities for Non-Governmental Organisations Promoting Environmental Protection to Claim Damages in Relation to the Environment in Four Selected Countries: France, Italy, the Netherlands and Portugal (2015) <www.unece.org/fileadmin/DAM/env/pp/a.to.j/AnalyticalStudies/TFAJ_Study_env_damage_final.pdf>; Boutonnet (n--) 97; D Papadopoulou, 'The Role of French Environmental Associations in Civil Liability for Environmental Harm: Courtesy of "Erika" ' (2009) 21 Journal of Environmental Law 87.
59 G Betlem, 'Standing for Ecosystems—Going Dutch' (1995) 54 Cambridge Law Journal 153.
60 Ibid.
61 *District Court Rotterdam* 15 March 1991 15 May 1991, UJ 1992/91, reported in (1992) 23 Netherlands Yearbook of International Law 513 (*Borcea* case); in this decision the Court regarded the existence of a public interest in the protection and conservation of birds as coinciding with the NGO's own individual interest, as emerging from its statute EHP Brans, *Liability for Damage to Public Natural Resources—Standing, Damage and Damage Assessment* (Kluwer Law International 2001) 2–43.

62 Aragão (n 41) 47.
63 E Fasoli, 'The Possibilities for Nongovernmental Organizations Promoting Environmental Protection to Claim Damages in Relation to the Environment in France, Italy, the Netherlands and Portugal' (2017) 26 Reciel 30, 33.
64 Comprehensive Environmental Response, Compensation and Liability Act of 1980 (CERCLA) (42 US Code 9601 et seq.); Oil Pollution Act of 1990 (OPA), 33 USC Chapter 40; see also EHP Brans, *Liability for Damage to Public Natural Resources—Standing, Damage and Damage Assessment* (Kluwer Law International 2001) 65–91.
65 Law 8 July 1986 No 349, GU No 162, 15 July 1986, Suppl. Ord. no 59, 5 ff (Article 18); A Bianchi, 'The Harmonization of Laws on Liability for Environmental Damage in Europe: An Italian Perspective' (1994) 6 Journal of Environmental Law 21.
66 Note that this provision was subsequently amended and in part repealed by Legislative Decree 3 April 2006 No 152 (Italian Environmental Code) which transposed into Italian law the EU Directive on Environmental Liability.
67 Article 18(5) Law 349/1986; for more details on the standing of NGOs in Italian law see S Gobbato, 'Legal Standing of Environmental Associations: The New 'Democratic Approach' of the Italian Supreme Administrative Court' (2007) 19 Journal of Environmental Law 259.
68 Brans (n 64) 91.
69 1998 Aarhus Convention on Access to Information, Public Participation in Decision-Making and Access to Justice in Environmental Matters (adopted 25 June 1998; entered into force 20 October 2001) 2161 UNTS 447.
70 Adopted 4 March 2018, entered into force 22 April 2021.
71 Analogous formulations of this right can be found in other human rights instruments, such as the African Charter on Human and Peoples' Rights (Article 7.1); the American Convention of Human Rights (Article 25); and the Charter of Fundamental Rights of the European Union (Article 47).
72 See discussion in F Francioni, 'The Rights of Access to Justice under Customary International Law' in F Francioni (ed.), *Access to Justice as a Human Right* (OUP 2007) 3–4.
73 See A Marx et al., 'Access to Legal Remedies for Victims of Corporate Human Rights Abuses in Third Countries' (EU Study, February 2019) 17, <www.europarl.europa.eu/RegData/etudes/STUD/2019/603475/EXPO_STU(2019)603475_EN.pdf> accessed 15 July 2022, citing corruption and political interferences or pressures on the judiciary as one of the barriers to access to justice which claimants in many host States may experience when seeking to file lawsuits in their country for corporate environmental harms; also L Enneking, 'Judicial Remedies: The Issue of Applicable Law' in JJ Alvarez Rubio and K Yiannibas (eds.), *Human Rights in Business—Removal of Barriers to Access to Justice in the European Union* (Routledge 2017) 40.
74 A Boyle, 'Human Rights and the Environment: Where Next?' (2012) 23 European Journal of International Law 613, 635.
75 OECD, Recommendation of the Council for the Implementation of a Regime of Equal Right of Access and Non-Discrimination in Relation to Transfrontier Pollution (1977) OECD/LEGAL/0152.
76 See Article 15 of the ILC's Articles on Prevention of Transboundary Harm, UN Doc. A/RES/56/82 (2001); A Boyle and C Redgwell, *Birnie, Boyle and Redgwell's International Law and the Environment* (4th ed., OUP 2021) 324 ff.
77 Enneking (n 73) 67.
78 Vedanta Resources PLC and another (Appellants) v Lungowe and others (Respondents) [2019] UKSC 20, [97].
79 Darpö (n 48) 395.
80 For the US see CERCLA (n 64). From a comparative perspective, see in Mexico, Ley Federal de Responsabilidad Ambiental (Diario Oficial de la Federación, 7 Junio 2013); in China, restoration for environmental damage is also available: see MG Faure and L Jing, 'Compensation for Environmental Damage in China: Theory and Practice' (2014) 31 Pace Environmental Law Review 226.

81 Brans (n 64); P Girod, *La Réparation du Dommage Ecologique* (Librairie Génerale de Droit et de Jurisprudence 1974); B Pozzo, *Danno Ambientale ed Imputazione della Responsabilitá—Esperienze Giuridiche a Confronto* (Giuffré 1996); Societé Francaise pour le Droit de L'Environnement, *Le Dommage Ecologique en Droit Interne, Communautaire et Comparé* (Economica 1992).

82 Comprehensive Environmental Response, Compensation and Liability Act (CERCLA) [also known as 'Superfund'], 42 U.S.C. Chapter 103.

83 Oil Pollution Act of 1990 (OPA), 33 U.S.C. Chapter 40.

84 M Hinteregger (ed.), *Environmental Liability and Ecological Damage in European Law* (CUP 2008).

85 RV Percival, KH Cooper and MM Gravens (eds.), 'CERCLA in a Global Context' (2012) Southern Western Law Review 727, 771 arguing that while 'many countries are moving in the CERCLA's direction', 'no country has adopted an environmental remediation program as comprehensive as CERCLA's'.

86 Percival, Cooper and Gravens (n 85); E Orlando, 'From Domestic to Global? Recent Trends in Environmental Liability from a Multi-Level and Comparative Law Perspective' (2015) 24 Reciel 289.

87 See further in Chapter 5 of this book.

88 See, among others, the French corporate Duty of Vigilance Law of 27 March 2017 (Article L. 225–102–4 of the French Commercial Code); the German Act on Corporate Due Diligence in Supply Chains of 22 July 2021, BGBI I 2021, 2959; the Norwegian Act relating to enterprises' transparency and work on fundamental human rights and decent working conditions, LOV-2021–06–18–99.

89 COM (2002) 71 final.

90 Wilde (n 33) 14; on the application of the common law of tort at the intersection with environmental regulation, B Pontin, *Nuisance Law and Environmental Protection: A Study of Nuisance Injunctions in Practice* (Lawtext 2013).

91 M Lee, 'Tort Law and Regulation: Planning and Nuisance' (2011) Journal of Planning & Environment Law 986.

92 Wilde (n 33) 14: '[e]xisting torts may have a useful role to play in providing redress for private harms stemming from . . . regulatory oversight and, at worst, regulatory failures'.

93 D McGillivray and J Wightman, 'Private Rights, Public Interests and the Environment' in T Hayward and JO' Neill (eds.), *Justice, Property and the Environment—Social and Legal Perspectives* (Ashgate 1997) 154–155.

94 T Yang, 'Environmental Regulation, Tort Law and Environmental Justice: What Could Have Been' (2002) Washburn Law Journal 607.

95 J Lin, 'Climate Change and the Courts' (2012) 31 Legal Studies 1, 35–57. HM Osofsky and J Peel, 'The Role of Litigation in Multilevel Climate Change Governance: Possibilities for a Lower Carbon Future?' (2013) 30 EPLJ 303.

96 RV Percival, 'Liability for Environmental Harm and Emerging Global Environmental Law' (2010) 25 Maryland Journal of International Law 37, at 63.

97 Stockholm Declaration on the Human Environment, found in: Report of the UN Conference on the Human Environment (UN Doc. A/CONF.48/14, 16 June 1972).

98 See further in Chapter 2 of this book.

99 See further in Chapter 3.

100 C Lopez, 'Legal Liability for Business Human Rights Abuses Under the Revised Draft of a Treaty on Business and Human Rights' *Cambridge Core Blog* (11 September 2019) <www.cambridge.org/core/blog/2019/09/11/legal-liability-for-business-human-rights-abuses-under-the-revised-draft-of-a-treaty-on-business-and-human-rights> accessed 27 December 2022.

101 F Orrego Vicuna, 'Current Trends in Responsibility and Liability for Environmental Harm under International Law' in K Koufa (ed.), *Protection of the Environment for the New Millennium—2000 International Law Session* (Sakkoulas Publications 2002).

102 F Francioni and C Bakker, 'The Evolution of the Global Environmental System: Trends and Prospects in the EU and the US' in F Francioni and C Bakker (eds.), *The EU, the US and Global Climate Governance* (Ashgate 2014) 28–29.
103 PM Dupuy and J Viñuales, *International Environmental Law* (Cambridge University Press 2015) 245.
104 Brunnée (n 35).
105 Daniel (n 35) 236–8; Brunnée (n 35).
106 Brunnée (n 35); RV Percival, 'Liability for Environmental Harm and Emerging Global Environmental Law' (2010) 25 Maryland Journal of International Law 37.
107 N Sachs, 'Beyond the Liability Wall: Strengthening Tort Remedies in International Environmental Law' (2008) 55 UCLA Law Review 837.
108 A Nollkaemper, 'Cluster-Litigation in Cases of Transboundary Environmental Harm' in M Faure and S Ying (eds.), *China and International Liability: Legal Remedies for Transboundary Pollution* (Edward Elgar 2008) 11, defining cluster litigation as 'a parallel or serial litigation of overlapping or closely related claims before multiple courts'.
109 M Faure and S Ying (eds.), *China and International Liability: Legal Remedies for Transboundary Pollution* (Edward Elgar 2008) 1.
110 M Delmas-Marty, 'Ordering Pluralism' (2009) *Max Weber Programme Working Paper* 2009/06 <https://cadmus.eui.eu/handle/1814/14274> accessed July 2022.
111 M Delmas-Marty, A Supiot and M. Frieyro, 'L'Internationalisation du droit: degradation ou recomposition?' (2012) 389 Esprit 35.
112 Expression borrowed from M Faure and A Nollkaemper, 'International Liability as an Instrument to Prevent and Compensate for Climate Change' (2007) 26 Stanford Environmental Law Journal 123, 126; and from Faure and Ying (n 109) 1–2.
113 E Cusato and others, 'Symposium Introduction: Critical Perspectives on Global Law and the Environment' (2022) 12 Asian Journal of International Law 1.
114 J Husa, *Law and Globalization* (Edward Elgar 2018).
115 T Yang and RV Percival, 'The Emergence of Global Environmental Law' (2009) 36 Ecology Law Quarterly 615.
116 M Delmas-Marty, 'Governing Globalisation Through Law' (2020) European Journal of Risk Regulation 195, 196.
117 JB Wiener, 'Something Borrowed for Something Blue: Legal Transplants and the Evolution of Global Environmental Law' (2001) 27 Ecological Law Quarterly 1295, 1297.
118 Yang and Percival (n 115) 616.
119 Ibid.
120 In this sense, see E Morgera, 'Global Environmental law and Comparative Legal Methods' (2015) Reciel 254; also, K Kulovesi, M Mehling and E Morgera, 'Global Environmental Law: Context and Theory, Challenge and Promise' (2019) 8 Transnational Environmental Law 405.
121 Morgera, 'Global Environmental Law and Comparative Legal Methods' (n 120) 255.
122 Kulovesi, Mehling and Morgera (n 120) 410.
123 R Cotterel, 'What Is Transnational Law?' (2012) 37 Law & Social Inquiry 500.
124 There is a significantly rich and further expanding literature on the concept and applications of transnational law in the environmental field, see V Heyvaert, 'Transnationalization of Law: Rethinking Law through Transnational Environmental Regulation' (2017) Transnational Environmental Law 205.
125 Kulovesi, Mehling and Morgera (n 120) 410; GC Shaffer, 'Transnational Legal Ordering and State Change' in GC Shaffer (ed.), *Transnational Legal Ordering and State Change* (CUP 2012) 3.
126 F Sindico, S Switzer and Q Tianbao, 'The Transformation of Environmental Law and Governance' in F Sindico, S Switzer and Q Tianbao (eds.), *The Transformation of Environmental Law and Governance; Risk, Innovation and Resilience* (Edward Elgar 2021) 3.
127 N Walker, *Intimations of Global Law* (CUP 2014) 55. See also Kulovesi, Mehling and Morgera (n 120) 410.

128 M Siems, *Comparative Law* (3rd ed., CUP 2022) 354.
129 P Jessup, *Transnational Law* (Yale University Press 1956). The term 'transnational law' is considered to have been first coined by Philip Jessup to include 'all law which regulates actions or events that transcend national frontiers'.
130 On the use of soft law at the EU level, through the European Commission's drafting guidelines on the interpretation of legal concepts and legislation, see M Eliantonio, 'Soft Law in Environmental Matters and the Role of the European Courts: Too Much or Too Little of It?' (2018) 37 Yearbook of European Law 496.
131 Among others, E Brans and G Betlem (eds.), *Environmental Liability in the EU: An Introduction* (Cameron & May 2006); G Winter and others, 'Weighing Up the EC Environmental Liability Directive' (2008) 20 Journal of Environmental Law 163; S Cassotta, *Environmental Damage and Liability Problems in a Multilevel Context: The Case of the Environmental Liability Directive* (Kluwer 2012); L Bergkamp and B Goldsmith (eds.), *The EU Environmental Liability Directive: A Commentary* (Oxford University Press 2013).
132 Case C-188/07 *Commune de Mesquer v Total France SA and Total International Ltd* [2008] ECR I-4501.
133 Regulation (EU) No 1215/2012 on Jurisdiction and the recognition and enforcement of judgments in civil and commercial matters (recast) OJ L 351; Regulation (EC) No 864/2007 on the law applicable to non-contractual obligations (Rome II) OJ L 199.
134 European Commission, Proposal for a Directive on Corporate Sustainability Due Diligence and amending Directive (EU) 2019/1937, COM (2022) 71 final.
135 L Kramer, 'Regional Economic International Organizations: The European Union as an Example' in D Bodansky, J Brunnée and E Hey (eds.), *The Oxford Handbook of International Environmental Law* (OUP 2007).
136 A Pellet, 'Les Fondements Juridiques Internationaux du Droit Communautaire' (1994) V-2 Collected Courses of the Academy of European Law 193.
137 K Ziegler, 'International Law and EU Law: Between Asymmetric Constitutionalisation and Fragmentation' in A Orakhelashvili (ed.), *Research Handbook on the Theory of International Law* (Edward Elgar 2011) 272.
138 M Cremona, 'The Union as a Global Actor: Roles, Models and Identity' (2004) 41 Common Market Law Review 553; L Azoulai, 'The Acquis of the European Union and International Organisations' (2005) European Law Journal 196.
139 J Vogler, 'The European Union as an Actor in International Environmental Politics' (1999) 8 Environmental Politics 24; T Delreux, 'The EU as an Actor in Global Environmental Politics' in A Jordan and C Adelle (eds.), *Environmental Policy in the EU. Actors, Institutions and Processes* (Routledge 2012).
140 RKW Wurzel and J Connelly (eds.), *The European Union as a Leader in International Climate Change Politics* (Routledge 2010).
141 A Cardesa-Salzmann and E Morgera, 'The EU's External Action after Lisbon: Competences, Policy Consistency and Participation in International Environmental Negotiations' in M Peeters and M Eliantonio (eds.), *Research Handbook on EU Environmental Law* (Edward Elgar 2020) 71.
142 F Hoffmeister, 'The Contribution of EU Practice to International Law' in M Cremona (ed.), *Developments in EU External Relations Law* (OUP 2008).
143 J Scott, 'Extraterritoriality and Territorial Extension in EU Law' (2014) 62 American Journal of Comparative law 87; J Scott, 'The Global Reach of EU Law' in M Cremona and J Scott (ed.), *EU Law Beyond EU Borders: The Extraterritorial Reach of EU Law* (Oxford University Press 2019).
144 On the normative actorness of the EU, cf literature including I Manners, 'Normative Power Europe: A Contradiction in Terms?' (2002) 40 Journal of Common Market Studies 235; I Hadjiyanni, 'The European Union as a Global Regulatory Power' (2020) 41 Oxford Journal of Legal Studies 243.
145 Article 3(5) Treaty on European Union (TEU).

146 Article 21(1) TEU.
147 A Momirov and A Naudé Fourie, 'Vertical Comparative Law Methods: Tools for Conceptualising the International Rule of Law' (2009) 3 Erasmus Law Review 291.
148 JB Wiener, 'Something Borrowed for Something Blue: Legal Transplants and the Evolution of Global Environmental Law' (2001) 27 Ecological Law Quarterly 1295, 1307.
149 A Dolidze, 'Bridging Comparative and International Law: Amicus Curiae Participation as a Vertical Legal Transplant' (2015) 26 European Journal of International Law 851.
150 R Michaels, 'Transnationalising Comparative Law' (2016) 23 Maastricht Journal of European and Comparative Law 352.
151 On the relevance of comparative analysis to global environmental law scholarship, see Morgera 'Global Environmental Law' (n 120).

Part 1

Environmental liability in international law

In international law, developments in the field of environmental liability have been characterised by significant 'harmonisation' endeavours aimed at establishing or at least identifying a set of general principles applicable to transboundary and/or transnational environmental damage and capable of guiding the judge in the determination of liability and the corresponding allocation of losses. The most remarkable output of these efforts is represented by the several international conventions that set up uniform rules on liability and compensation for damage arising during the operation of hazardous activities. However, a conspicuous part of these efforts has also been directed at defining the role and responsibilities of States in this context, particularly with a view to identify whether and to what extent States can be regarded as having an international duty to provide reparation for the harmful consequences of activities operating within their jurisdiction or under their control. In this respect, two main normative frameworks can be identified. The first is represented by the customary rules and principles of State responsibility for breaches of international law obligations. These general principles are not specific to the environment, but they rather provide a universal set of rules that are applicable across a variety of international law violations, including breaches of international environmental norms. The second framework consists instead of the various attempts to identify and/or to develop a set of legal principles governing the liability of States for the harmful consequences of lawful but high-risk activities, and applicable independently from the commission of a wrongful act.

Part 1 of this book seeks to offer an in-depth analysis of these different international frameworks of liability and responsibility with a view to identify the different 'layers'[1] of environmental liability that have emerged at the international level. In particular, Chapter 1 examines the application of the customary law of State responsibility to instances of environmental damage. Chapter 2 discusses various attempts and proposals to develop a distinct set of international principles on liability and allocation of loss for damage caused by lawful activities. Finally, Chapter 3 examines the several international conventions establishing the liability of private operators according to domestic rules of civil liability or administrative law. Overall, the analysis in this part will seek to understand whether and to what extent, besides and beyond the sector-specific conventions, international law is evolving towards the affirmation of a number of core principles in this field.

DOI: 10.4324/9781315676708-2

1 The law of State responsibility and its application to environmental damage

1. Introduction

From a customary international law perspective, questions of liability and reparation for environmental damage are regulated primarily through the framework of the law of State responsibility. This legal framework comprises a set of general norms and principles that are applicable to violations of international law obligations binding upon States under a treaty or by customary international law. Initially developed during the first half of the last century to address issues concerning the diplomatic protection of aliens, the law of State responsibility subsequently evolved into a broader and general regime addressing breaches of international obligations, including those related to the protection of the environment. This body of rules is now codified in the Articles on States Responsibility for Internationally Wrongful Acts ('ARISWA') which were adopted by the International Law Commission ('ILC') in 2001[2] and are currently regarded as the most authoritative account of State practice on this topic.

Given its general nature, the law of State responsibility is also applicable to breaches of environmental protection obligations. In practice, however, the concrete operation of this body of rules to claim redress for transboundary environmental damage harm is not always straightforward. Part of the difficulties are related to the very nature of those rules, which became consolidated at the beginning of the last century to address a slightly different set of international concerns and to operate in a different context of international relations.[3] There are several questions regarding how such principles and remedies can be relied upon to respond to current environmental challenges. First, the special features of environmental damage raise themselves specific questions that do not often find an easy answer in those broadly defined principles. Moreover, the very structures of the law of State responsibility and the requirement to ground responsibility, and liability, on the violation by the State of an international obligation appear ill-suited to deal with the reality of the manifold and diverse economic activities causing the majority of environmental harms on the planet. Finally, there are problems related to the unclear formulation of the relevant primary obligations and the uncertain standard of conduct that is expected from States in this context.[4] In the light of this, this chapter seeks to examine the extent to which the law of

DOI: 10.4324/9781315676708-3

State responsibility can effectively accommodate claims for reparation of environmental damage.

2. The responsibility of States for wrongful acts: general principles

The starting point for an analysis of the law of State responsibility are the ILC's ARISWA.[5] According to this framework, the responsibility of States arises from the violation of an international obligation undertaken under a treaty or applicable by customary international law. This concept, which is now considered as reflecting customary international law, is expressed in Article 1, according to which 'every internationally wrongful act of a State entails the international responsibility of that State'. 'Wrongful act' is defined in Article 2 as an action or omission that is attributable to the State under international law and that constitutes a breach of an international obligation of the State established in a treaty or by customary law. Accordingly, a violation of an international law obligation and the link of attribution of that violation to the State form the two constitutive elements of State responsibility.

At a conceptual level, the ARISWA principles operates on the basis of a fundamental distinction between primary and secondary rules. The former are the rules establishing the substantive or procedural obligations of States under international law. State responsibility relates to the secondary rules, which are triggered by a breach of a primary obligation ('wrongful act') and determine the consequences of such breach. In this framework 'liability' forms part of the secondary rules concerning the consequences of State responsibility; the term assumes a specific meaning, defined as the state's 'exposure to legal redress once responsibility and injury arising from a failure to fulfil that legal responsibility have been established'.[6] This notion of State liability is thus fundamentally different from the concept of 'liability' employed in certain international treaties establishing the liability of States for damage caused during the operation of certain ultra-hazardous activities. It is also different from the idea of liability referred to in a parallel ILC work concerning the international liability of the States for damage arising from lawful acts. In those contexts, 'liability' refers to the international duty of a State to repair environmental harm independently from the commission of a wrongful act; it is completely detached from the commission of a wrongful act and arises, instead, directly from the occurrence of a transboundary damage causally linked to a hazardous activity located under the jurisdiction of the (liable) State.[7]

A corollary of these different conceptualisations of State responsibility and international liability is that while the occurrence of a damage is an essential element for the operation of the international liability related to hazardous activities, it is not in itself a precondition for the application of the law of State responsibility, unless so provided by the content of the relevant primary obligation.[8] Accordingly, and unless so required by the relevant international environmental norm, the occurrence of a material damage to the environment is not necessary to trigger the responsibility of the State—although damage does remains relevant in the determination of the modalities and scope of reparation. The law of State responsibility can therefore be relied upon for the enforcement of international obligations independently on the proof of actual or imminent damage.[9] Accordingly, the range of remedies available to the injured State include not only compensation for material damage, but also satisfaction, as well as guarantees of non-repetition.

The following sections explore the application of the law of State responsibility to instances of environmental damage. Given the functional relationship of primary and secondary rules in the operation of State responsibility, the analysis starts by examining the evolving scope and content of one the foundational rules governing the States' conduct in transboundary environmental relations—i.e. the principle of harm prevention.

3. Transboundary harm prevention and State responsibility

3.1. Early developments and evolution of the primary rules

Primary international obligations can either be included in treaties or be of customary nature. Treaties remain today the primary source of international obligations in the environmental field. There is nowadays a huge array of international and multilateral agreements addressing different areas of environmental problems and imposing on States duties of protection, harm prevention and sustainable management with respect to different areas of natural resources. It is accepted that, unless the relevant treaty provides otherwise, breach of these international obligations entails the responsibility of the State and, depending on the circumstances, also a corresponding duty to provide reparation. Thus, Article 235 UNCLOS provides that States shall be liable for failure to fulfil their international obligations concerning the protection and preservation of the marine environment, adding that such liability will be determined 'in accordance with existing rules of international law.' State responsibility may arise also from the violation of environmental obligations contained in bilateral treaties aimed at the protection of shared natural resources.[10]

Outside specific treaties, the responsibility of States may originate from the violation of customary rules of international law. Over the years, a number of important principles related to environmental protection have progressively consolidated into rules of customary law or are in the process of gaining that status.[11] Of particular relevance is the well-established principle of not to cause transboundary harm according to which a State that harbours a potential source of harm in its territory has a duty to control it or to otherwise prevent the occurrence of significant transboundary damage to the territory and the environment of other states.

This principle currently represents the overarching rule of international environmental law. Its origins, however, are relatively old and can be traced back to a series of international judicial decisions enacted in the first half of the twentieth century and based on the application of existing principles of international law related to State sovereignty and territorial integrity to novel juridical problems created by the transboundary impacts and harms caused by hazardous activities. The landmark ruling in this respect was rendered by the arbitral tribunal in the *Trail Smelter* case on the 11 March 1941.[12] The case concerned the emission of toxic fumes from a smelter located in the Canadian town of Trail and causing significant damage to the neighbouring US territory. In its decision, the tribunal enunciated the famous *obiter dictum* whereby 'no State has the right to use or permit the use of its territory in such a manner as to cause injury by fumes in or to the territory of another or the properties or persons therein'.[13] It is noteworthy that, in the dearth of international case-law dealing with air pollution, the tribunal grounded its statement on general principles of international law as well as on principles and decisions of US courts regulating similar issues. A similar conclusion regarding the prohibition of no-harmful uses of the territory was reached, albeit within a different factual context, by the International Court of Justice in the *Corfu Channel* case,[14] and was recalled in subsequent decisions related to the uses of shared natural resources.[15]

The relevance of these early decisions in laying the ground for the subsequent development of primary duties of States in a transboundary context cannot be overestimated.[16] However, they also reflected a narrow vision of environmental problems.[17] Environmental issues were mainly conceived and approached through the rather confined lenses offered by the principle of State sovereignty over its territory. As such, at stake were often questions concerning the balancing of the competing sovereign and territorial rights of States vis-à-vis the transboundary impacts of newly developed industrial activities,[18] with little consideration, if any, for more genuine environmental concerns and impacts on natural resources. These cases also reflected a strict criterion of territoriality whereby a State is internationally responsible for transboundary harm caused by the operation of hazardous activities taking place within its territorial jurisdiction.

3.2. From no-harm to prevention

Since these initial developments, a significant evolution in the scope and contents of States' duties and responsibilities in a transboundary context took place in the wake of the increasing environmental awareness and growing concerns for the deteriorating state of the planet. This change in awareness of environmental problems led to the emergence of specific duties of States related to the environment. It also prompted a reformulation of the no-harm principle in an environmental perspective. Principle 21 of the 1972 Stockholm Declaration provided an important input in this sense. It added a specific environmental dimension to the no-transboundary harm principle, making clear that it is not confined to the territorial rights of the affected State but it also includes its environment and natural resources. It also extended the scope of the no-harm duty to include areas beyond national jurisdiction and the global commons. Furthermore, Principle 21 and its subsequent reformulation in Principle 2 of the 1992 Rio Declaration played a fundamental role in bringing a conceptual shift in focus from the initial 'curative' and *ex post* perspective of the no-transboundary harm principle in the *Trail Smelter* ruling towards an anticipatory approach aimed at the prevention of environmental harm.[19] This 'paradigm shift' was accompanied by a redefinition of the role of States with respect to potential transboundary impacts. While the no-harm duty focused on a negative obligation of harm avoidance, the emphasis on prevention entails a proactive attitude and a positive obligation 'to take adequate measures to control and regulate in advance sources of potential significant transboundary harm'.[20]

This evolution started soon to be reflected in the jurisprudence of international courts and tribunals. In the *Gabcikovo-Nagymaros* decision, the ICJ asserted in clear terms, for the first time in its case-law, the importance of 'vigilance and prevention . . . on account of the often irreversible character of damage to the environment'.[21] In the *Pulp Mills* case, the ICJ recognised the customary legal status of the prevention principle. The duty of prevention, as a positive obligation 'to use all the means at . . . disposal to avoid environmental harm',[22] is also closely linked with an implicit requirement to integrate environmental concerns into the planning and development of hazardous activities. As stated by the arbitral tribunal in the partial award in the *Indus Water Kishenganga* case, 'there is no doubt that States are required under contemporary customary international law to take environmental protection into consideration when planning and developing projects that may cause injury to a bordering State'.[23]

Furthermore, both Principles 21 and 2 of the Stockholm and Rio Declarations, and the jurisprudence related to the no-harm and prevention principles situate them in a sustainable development perspective, which seeks to reconcile the duty of environmental protection with the idea of States sovereignty over their natural resources and their interests in pursuing economic development. The *Pulp Mills* ruling clearly reflects this conceptual framing by indicating that the duty of harm prevention does not embody an absolute prohibition of environmental harm, but rather a best effort obligation to use the necessary and appropriate due diligence to ensure that activities under the state's jurisdiction or control do not cause transboundary harm. As we shall see, this approach has in turn important consequences from the point of view of the scope and contents of State responsibility for transboundary environmental damage.

Finally, closely connected to the substantive obligation of prevention are a series of procedural obligations which provide measurable parameters to assess the minimum standard of conduct of the State with respect to transboundary damage arising from industrial and technical activities.[24] These include the duty to inform, notify and consult potentially affected States of proposed activities entailing a risk of transboundary damage, as well as new duties of environmental impact assessment, which have entered into the picture both as specific requirements under international treaties and as a more general requirement under international law.[25] Accordingly, both substance and procedure concur in articulating the international legal framework applicable to States engaging in development projects or hosting activities capable of causing significant harm to the territory and the environment of other States.

3.3. Due diligence and environmental liability

For a long time, extensive scholarly discussions revolved around the question of the relevant standard of conduct expected from States under the no-harm and prevention obligations. A fundamental point of contention was whether these international obligations could be regarded as embodying an absolute prohibition of transboundary damage so that the mere occurrence of significant transboundary damage to other States' territory could *ipso facto* entail the responsibility, and thus the liability (i.e. duty to repair) of the source State. In reality, although advocated by some scholars, particularly with respect to ultra-hazardous activities, the idea of a State's strict liability in international law for transboundary environmental damage has not found support in States' or judicial practice. The question was eventually settled by the ICJ in the *Pulp Mills* case, where the ICJ referring to the due diligence nature of the no-harm obligation stated, 'the responsibility of a party . . . would be engaged if it was shown that it had failed to act diligently and thus take all appropriate measures to enforce its relevant regulations on a public or private operator under its jurisdiction'. This position was reconfirmed by the ITLOS' Seabed Disputes Chamber in its Advisory Opinion on Responsibilities and Obligations in the Area, which rejected the argument that the sponsoring State was subject to strict liability under Article 139(2) UNCLOS and asserted, 'liability for damage of the sponsoring State arises only from its failure to meet its obligation of due diligence'.[26] Although both judicial pronouncements are related specifically to the interpretation of relevant treaties—respectively, the Statute of the River Uruguay and Article 139(2) of UNCLOS—they nevertheless contributed to clarify the standard of conduct and level of due diligence required of States when permitting the operation within their territory or jurisdiction of hazardous and potentially harmful activities. Accordingly, and unless provided otherwise in a treaty applicable between the parties to the dispute, the mere occurrence of transboundary environmental harm does not give rise to the liability of the source State unless such damage can be causally linked to the violation by the defendant State of its due diligence duties of prevention and avoidance of transboundary harm, or of any other norm of international law. The same position is adopted by the ILC in its Articles on Prevention, where it is stated, 'the obligation of the State of origin to take preventive or minimization measures is one of due diligence' and such duty 'is not intended to guarantee that significant harm be totally prevented, if it is not possible to do so'.[27]

A due diligence standard of prevention is certainly more easily accepted by the State than the idea of strict liability, as demonstrated by the opposition encountered by the ILC with its work on the topic of international liability. Moreover, as noted by the International Law Association (ILA), a '[r]igid application of international rules, mandating results, or imposing liability in the event of breach in any circumstances cuts against the grain of notions of State sovereignty'.[28] The inherently flexible nature of due diligence is also better apt to accommodate and balance environmental concerns with the states' rights to exploit their natural resources and pursue economic development,[29] and is thus regarded as more in line with certain views of sustainable development and with the need to accommodate the different needs of States within a diverse international community.[30] In fact, some legal scholars have advocated for a differentiated scope and strictness of the required duty of care commensurate to the hazardous nature of the activity.[31]

From an environmental perspective, however, a due diligence approach leaves an important gap for the case in which such damage is caused accidentally and despite the adoption by the State, or by private operators, of the necessary and appropriate preventive measures. Furthermore, unless the burden of proof is reversed—a proposition rejected by ICJ in the *Pulp Mills* case—it would be for the victim State to provide evidence that its counterpart failed to perform according to the required standard of conduct. This, in itself, can be problematic. Moreover, the flexible and open-ended nature of due diligence may arguably render the assessment of State compliance with the duty of prevention 'contingent and subjective',[32] with the risk of ultimately further diluting the responsibility of the source State.[33] In this respect, international courts have an important interpretative role in carving the contours of due diligence in a slightly more prescriptive fashion.[34] For example, the ICJ clarified in the *Pulp Mills* case that the 'obligation to act with due diligence . . . entails not only the adoption of appropriate rules and measures, but also a certain level of vigilance in their enforcement and the exercise of administrative control applicable to public and private operators, such as the monitoring of activities undertaken by such operators'. The ITLOS, in its advisory opinion on the *Responsibilities and Obligations of Sponsoring States*,[35] put forward an ever more extensive interpretation of this concept by adding a precautionary approach as 'an integral part of the general obligation of due diligence of sponsoring States'. Similarly, the ILC in its commentary to the Articles on Prevention indicated that, while a duty of due diligence does not guarantee that significant harm will be totally prevented, it nevertheless imposes a requirement on the State of origin 'to exert its best possible efforts to minimize the risk'.[36]

3.4. The 'significant harm' threshold

Under the ARISWA, material damage is not a necessary element for responsibility to arise, unless so provided by the primary obligation.[37] The question is, therefore, whether the occurrence of transboundary damage is a constitutive part of the primary obligation of prevention. The ILC's Article on Prevention and the emphasis on a preventive approach in recent international case-law suggest that the duty of prevention already applies where there is a non-minimal risk of environmental harm. The ILC Prevention's Articles define this risk as including either 'a high the probability of causing significant transboundary harm' or 'a low probability of causing disastrous transboundary harm'.[38] Moreover, the prevailing view seems to be that the preventive and anticipatory perspective extends also to the classic duty of no-harm. According to one scholar, the 'no-harm' principle in the environmental field must now be interpreted in connection with the duty of prevention so that the responsibility of the State would already arise if it can be proved that the State has failed to take the appropriate measures to avoid and prevent such harm.[39]

A certain threshold of significance is also required with respect to actual damage. However, the relevant states' and judicial practice on the threshold of significance has evolved. While the rulings in *Trail Smelter* and *Lac Lanoux* set the threshold at a 'serious' level, more recent formulations adopted a milder approach.[40] The ILC's commentary to its 'Principles on Allocation of Loss in the Case of Transboundary Harm Arising Out of Hazardous Activities' indicate that 'significant' is to be understood as 'something more than detectable', although 'it need not be at the level of "serious" or "substantial"'.[41] Nevertheless, 'the harm must lead to a real detrimental effect on matters such as . . . human health, industry, property, environment or agriculture in other states'.[42] Despite of these indications, the determination of the relevant threshold is not without ambiguity, and although the assessment of 'significance' involves factual and objective criteria, it must eventually be made on a case basis.[43] However, the increasing inclusion of emission standards and guidance for the safe concentration levels in international environmental treaties can arguably help in determining the significance threshold.[44] Moreover, the significance threshold is a common feature of several environmental liability regimes at the regional (i.e. EU) and international levels. Experience gained under these frameworks can therefore contribute insights on the interpretation and application of the concept in interstate relations.

3.5. The link of causality

Article 36(1) of the ILC Draft on State responsibility expressly refers to the requirement of a causal link between the wrongful act and the injury as a necessary element for the duty to provide reparation. In the case of the *Trail Smelter*, the arbitral tribunal undertook a very careful analysis and thoroughly assessed the evidence produced by the parties concerning the adverse impact that the sulphur emissions from the smelter had on the production of crops, and they used such evidence to determine the scope of compensable damage. In practice, outside more straightforward and evident instances of transboundary pollution, the need to prove the causal link and connect to the breach of an international obligation can bring several evidentiary difficulties for the claimant State and represent a further obstacle to the pursuit of a successful liability claim. For example, in its ruling of the *Pulp Mills* case, the ICJ had on several counts dismissed Argentina's claim regarding Uruguay's violation of its substantive obligations of prevention, including for lack of sufficient evidence on the causal link between the alleged environmental damage and the operation of the pulp mills. Moreover, and in contrast to relevant trends at the domestic level, the ICJ rejected Argentina's argument that a reversal of the burden of proof may be appropriate in the case of transboundary environmental harm, thereby leaving it to the claimant State to gather the necessary evidence to support its claim regarding a breach of the prevention obligation and to prove the existence of a causal link between the wrongful act and the harm suffered.[45]

4. From transboundary harm prevention and responsibility to States' environmental liability

4.1. The concept of environmental damage

International law does not offer a universally accepted definition of environmental damage. However, the evolution of primary rules on the protection of the environment leaves no doubt that the concept of transboundary harm evolved from the narrower approach of the early case-law to include damage to the environment and to natural resources.[46] Starting from the ICJ's advisory opinion on the Legality of the Threat or Use of Nuclear Weapons,[47] where the ICJ expressly took cognizance of the growing importance of the environment, the decisions of international courts and tribunals have increasingly referred to ecological concerns and the protection of environmental values, even independently from specific connection with the State's territory or property.

Positive support for the inclusion of damage to natural resources and the environment as such in the scope of reparation is also discernible in the application of the law on State responsibility, as long as such damage is causally linked to the breach of an international obligation. An important precedent is the UN Security Council (UNSC) Resolution No. 687 of 1991 adopted in the aftermath of Iraq's invasion of Kuwait.[48] This is one of the first formal acknowledgments of natural resource damage as compensable type of damage under general international law.[49] The resolution asserted the responsibility of Iraq for its unlawful invasion of Kuwait and its liability for any direct loss and damage 'including environmental damage and the depletion of natural resources'. The subsequent work and decisions of the United Nations Compensation Commission (UNCC)—a quasi-judicial and fact-finding body established by the Security Council to resolve claims, assess damage and award compensation to individuals, corporations and governments for damage, including environmental damage, arising from Iraq's invasion and occupation of Kuwait[50]—contributed to further elaborate this concept in international law and to identify the modalities for the reparation of this kind of damage. Furthermore, arguments regarding damage to the environment have also been raised more frequently in the pleadings of the parties to international disputes, and a more recent ICJ decision confirmed that damage to natural resources may be included in the scope of reparation under the international law of State responsibility.[51]

4.2. Reparation under the law of State responsibility

General international law does not contain remedies appositely tailored for environmental harm,[52] although the customary law principle of 'full reparation', enunciated by the Permanent Court of International Justice (PCIJ) in the *Chorzów Factory* case, is in principle applicable also to instances of environmental damage.[53] According to this principle, 'reparation must, so far as possible, wipe-out all the consequences of the illegal act and re-establish the situation which would, in all probability, have existed if that act had not been committed'.[54] Pursuant to this principle, the ARISWA articulate reparation in the form of restitution, compensation and satisfaction, with the idea that these different forms of reparation are not mutually exclusive but may be used in combination to achieve the overall goal of wiping out all the consequences of the wrongful act.[55]

Restitution essentially corresponds to 'restitution in kind' and consists in 're-establishing the situation which existed before the wrongful act was committed'. In the environmental field it may consist in restoring the environment to the *status quo ante* (i.e. the situation existing before the damage inflicted by the unlawful activities in the affected areas). Depending on the situation and circumstances, it might also include replanting trees that were illegally harvested or cleaning up the area from pollution, as far as this is possible. Given its closer connection to the objective of full reparation, restitution has primacy over the other forms of reparation provided that is not materially impossible or entirely disproportionate.[56]

From a comparative environmental law perspective, the articles' preference for restitution is in line with the most updated trends emerging in domestic law and more recent treaty practice. In this respect, there is a certain analogy between the customary international law principle of full reparation, as mitigated by the requirements of reasonableness and proportionality, and the principles retained in the majority of international liability treaties which require the polluter to sustain reasonable costs to restore environmental damage.[57] In some cases, and certainly in most civil liability treaties, reinstatement costs are included in the scope of compensation to be paid by the polluter, and in that sense there is some overlap between restitution in kind and compensation.

One problem with restitution in the environmental field is that there may be situations in which full environmental restoration is not possible, for example because the damage is irreversible (e.g. the extinction of a species or the irreparable destruction of a habitat) or because the environment cannot be restored to its previous conditions. In the *Costa Rica v Nicaragua Certain Activities Case*, for instance, restitution appeared to be 'materially impossible' since it looked 'extremely difficult that Nicaragua could restore the situation existing prior to its activities in the affected area in respect of air quality, soil erosion, and loss of biodiversity'.[58] In this case, both claimant State (i.e. Costa Rica) and the Court convened that compensation would be the most appropriate form of reparation.

Compensation is envisaged for the cases in which restitution is not possible; it can be used as alternative to restitution, or in combination with it.[59] Compensation encompasses 'any financially assessable damage'—that is, 'damage which is capable of being evaluated in financial terms'—suffered by the State or by its nationals.[60] It may therefore include traditional types of damage to property and other economic damage suffered by State nationals as a consequence of environmental pollution, such as 'compensation for a reduction in the value of polluted property'. With respect to this, causation is a criterion to delimit the scope of compensation, as the latter should only cover damage that is directly caused by the wrongful act, with the exclusion of damage which is too indirect or remote.[61] Pure economic losses[62] which are too loosely connected with the wrongful act are usually excluded. In the *Trail Smelter* case, for example, the tribunal excluded from compensation the damages allegedly suffered by business enterprises for loss of business as a result of the reduced economic status of the residents in the damaged area.[63] Compensation may also include the costs incurred by the State in responding to pollution damage, including for clean-up measures and other 'expenses reasonably incurred in preventing or remedying pollution'.[64] Moreover, in the light of State practice at the domestic level and under most civil liability conventions, it is arguable that compensation may also include the costs of reasonable measures of reinstatement of the environment.

4.3. Valuation and assessment of environmental damage

The idea of calculating compensation on the basis of the reasonable costs of reinstatement of the impaired natural resources represents a pragmatic solution to avoid the problems related to the difficulty to attribute a monetary value to the environment and natural resources considered as such. The problem of valuation remains for the case of irremediable damage, or damage in which restoration is not possible or not possible at reasonable costs. A further question concerns the calculation of 'interim losses', that is losses related to natural resources and resulting from the impairment of the ecological services provided by those resources from the moment in which damage occurred to the complete rehabilitation of the environment.

The ARISWA do not provide specific indication on the methodology to use regarding the valuation and assessment of environmental damage. However, in its commentary to the ARISWA, the ILC acknowledges the shortcomings of limiting compensation to environmental damage which is financially quantifiable, suggesting that the difficulties related to the economic valuation of the environment should not in principle preclude compensation for the loss of environmental values.[65] It notes, in particular, 'damage to such environmental values (biodiversity, amenity, etc.—sometimes referred to as "non-use values") is, as a matter of principle not less real and compensable than damage to property, though it may be difficult to quantify'.[66]

In the absence of more specific guidance in international law, inspiration can be drawn from domestic and regional developments—such as in the US[67] and in the EU[68]—which lay down remedies for damage to natural resources and which can provide guidance on the criteria to use in evaluating and assessing these type of damages in interstate compensation claims. At the international level, the work of the UNCC also provides an important precedent. The UNCC's tasks consisted mostly of ascertaining the validity of the various claims brought against Iraq, assessing damage and awarding compensation to successful claimants. Its Governing Council's Decision 7 specified the heads of damage included in the category of 'environmental damage and depletion of natural resources'.[69]

In the Report and Recommendations presented in 2005,[70] the Panel of Commissioners appointed to adjudicate the environment (Fifth Instalment) claims touched on the questions of irreversible damage and temporary loss of natural resources. The Panel found both types of damage admissible under international law, despite some contrary practice arising under certain international liability conventions that limit compensable damage to the reasonable costs of restoration. Notably, the Panel did not regard the exclusion of compensation for pure environmental damage in some international civil liability conventions as a valid basis to assert that international law, in general, prohibits compensation for this type of damage when it results from an internationally wrongful act.[71] In that sense, the Panel seems to suggest that there is a differentiation in the scope of compensable damage between the case when damage results from an internationally wrongful act and international developments concerning strict liability for damage arising out of hazardous (but lawful) activities.[72]

The Panel also argued that the UNSC Resolution left enough scope for including interim losses in the scope of compensation, provided that it can be demonstrated that the claimed losses and expenses for damage to natural resources had resulted directly from Iraq's invasion and occupation of Iraq.[73] It noted, 'the fact that the effects of the loss of or damage to natural resources might be for a temporary duration should [not] have any relevance to the issue of the compensability of the damage or loss, although it might affect the nature and quantum of compensation that may be appropriate'.[74]

As to the question of valuation and assessment of environmental damage, the Panel made interesting recommendations on the assessment of biodiversity damage not having a specific market value. On this point, in the absence of precedents or guidance in international law, the Panel relied in part on classic international law principles—especially the principles of State responsibility and the landmark rulings such as the *Chorzów Factory* and the *Trail Smelter*; in part it availed itself of the methodologies elaborated and developed in municipal systems,[75] including law and economics methodologies,[76] such as attaching a price value to the use of environmental resources (based for example on travel costs and expenditures made by an individual to visit and enjoy a resource) or contingent valuation techniques that measure the willingness of individuals to pay for environmental goods.[77] The Panel also considered the Habitat Equivalency Analysis (HEA), which consists in evaluating the damage in terms of the cost of environmental projects designed to replace ecosystem services previously provided by the irremediably damaged natural resources.

Overall, the UNCC's work opened the way for the formal recognition of ecological damage within the scope of reparation under international law. More recently, the opportunity came for the ICJ to examine, for the first time, the question of assessment and compensation for natural resources damage in the context of the *Costa Rica v Nicaragua Certain Activities case*.[78] In addressing the question of the compensation owed to Costa Rica, the ICJ affirmed that the inclusion of compensation for damage to the environment as such is consistent with the general principles of international law on State responsibility, including the principle of full reparation.[79] It further specified that such damage may include indemnification for the consequent impairment or loss of the ability of the environment to provide goods and services and payment for the restoration of the damage environment.[80] In determining, for the first time in its case-law, the appropriate methodology for monetary calculation of natural resources damage, the Court mediated between different approaches put forward by the parties[81] and applied an 'overall valuation' methodology, consisting in considering and assessing the ecosystem 'as a whole' and 'adopting an overall assessment of the impairment or loss of the environmental good and services prior to recovery',[82] instead of attributing values to specific categories of environmental goods and services. The ICJ's reasoning, however, does not delve too much in the particulars of the methodology used and does not explain how it reached the *quantum* of compensation. This may make it more difficult for international courts or tribunals to use the decision as an authoritative basis when dealing with similar issues in the future.[83] Nevertheless, the ruling sends an important signal for the recognition of ecological damage in international law. It is also interesting that both disputing parties and the Court referred to domestic law developments and practices and to relevant studies produced by international bodies.[84] This shows that, especially for some areas of environmental law which deal with the very nature and ontological dimension of the environment, there is scope for a positive convergence and complementarity between different sources of law at different levels. Although, at the moment, the problem of quantification of environmental damage in international law is still an area for further research and development.

5. Current challenges of the law of State responsibility in the environmental context

5.1. Non-state actors and State responsibility

Despite being generally applicable to questions of transboundary environmental damage, the classic rules of State responsibility reveal their shortcomings when confronted with the complexities of current environmental problems. Part of these limitations relate to the predominantly state-centric approach that characterises the ARISWA, and that is reflected in the rules governing the attribution of a wrongful conduct to the State. According to the general principles of State responsibility, the only conduct attributable to the State at the international level is that of its organs of government,[85] or of others who have acted under the direction, instigation or control of those organs.[86] Conduct of private actors, albeit linked to the State by nationality, habitual residence or incorporation, or simply by the fact that the act or omission is committed on the state's territory, is not as such directly attributable to the State.[87] The ARISWA only envisage certain circumstances in which acts and omissions by non-state actors can be attributed to the State and can engage the State's international responsibility. This is possible when a State empowers the private actor (for example, a corporation) to exercise elements of public authority (Article 4), and when the private actor acts on the 'instructions of, or under the direction or control of' the State (Article 8). Moreover, ICJ has retained a rather stricter approach to the notion of 'control' under Article 8 of the ARISWA, despite other tribunals have offered slightly different, broader, interpretation of this notion.[88] According to the ICJ, 'persons, groups of persons or entities may, for purposes of international responsibility, be equated with State organs even if that status does not follow from internal law, provided that in fact *[they] act in "complete dependence" on the State*, of which they are ultimately merely the instrument'.[89]

The ARISWA's narrow approach to the question of attribution arguably limits significantly the application of the rules on State responsibility in order to vindicate important values concerning human rights or environmental protection. It is also a further manifestation of the existing mismatch between the positivistic and state-centred stance of this body of international rules and the reality characterised by the rise of non-state actors as increasingly prominent participants in the international legal arena.[90] In particular, the strict interpretation of the notion of control under

Article 8 would not be apt to capture the wide range of situations in which a State may directly or indirectly be linked to violations of basic environmental standards carried out by private actors operating in foreign countries.[91]

It is true that the ARISWA do not exclude the responsibility of a State for the transboundary harm caused by private actors, if it can be demonstrated that the State failed to regulate and control these private activities taking place within its jurisdiction. Responsibility, in this case, would directly arise from the State's breach of its duty of prevention and would require the claimant to prove the source state's breach of its due diligence obligations. It could therefore be argued that the question of State responsibility for transboundary damage caused by the hazardous activities of private companies within the state's territorial jurisdiction can be best addressed at the level of the primary norms, by establishing a stricter standard of care, without the need to adjust the rules governing attribution. And yet, there are a number of situations in which the narrow approach to attribution combined with a strict interpretation of the other circumstances in which international law allows the conducts of private actors to be linked back to the State may leave a gap in the protection afforded to individual victims of human rights violations and to the environment. An example of these gaps is the limitations of the law of State responsibility with respect to environmental harm caused by multinational corporations (MNCs), particularly when they act through their subsidiaries or suppliers in third countries. As MNCs typically spread across different jurisdictions, the question arises as to the extent to which the State's duty of prevention, and thus its responsibility for failure to do so, would encompass the harmful conduct carried out by private actors operating extraterritorially. In these cases, the question is whether and on what basis the harmful conduct taking place extraterritorially by private actors can directly or indirectly engage the responsibility of the home state.[92]

To overcome these limitations, an alternative approach has been proposed which would consist in shifting the focus from the rules on attribution to the interpretation, and (re)conceptualisation, of the primary obligation to prevent activities carried out within the jurisdiction *or control* of the State from causing environmental harm in other states. Accordingly, the main question would be whether this primary duty of environmental harm prevention is to be conceived as anchored to a rigid, and arguably outdated, principle of territoriality according to which the responsibility of a State and thus its duties of supervision and control are confined to conduct taking place on its territory. It is submitted that such a strict application of the territoriality principle would contrast with the conceptual evolution that has occurred in the field of human rights and environment. In the environmental field, Principle 21 of the Stockholm Declaration extends the responsibility of the State to activities carried within its territory or 'under its control'; this wording indicates an openness for an interpretation of the no-harm principle in a way to encompass also activities carried out by the state's nationals outside the territorial jurisdiction. In this perspective, some scholars have advanced a 'functional' interpretation of the scope of application of the primary duty of harm prevention on the basis of the control *de facto* retained by the home State over the exported hazardous technology or activity, even when this activity or technology are operating abroad.[93]

This argument finds its factual basis on the acknowledgment that the home State usually exerts, or is capable of exerting, a certain degree of control on their national corporate actors, even when their activities have impacts outside its territorial jurisdiction.[94] Unlike host states, which in several cases are developing countries with poor means to effectively regulate and control the activities of MNCs and other foreign investors in their territory, the home States of the parent company are usually developed countries with the means and the expertise to regulate and control the planning and execution of activities of the corporate entity located within its territory.[95] Therefore, they are arguably 'in the best position to effectively oversee this centre of control through the exercise of its territorial jurisdiction'.[96] On this basis, it would be possible to envisage a primary due diligence obligation of the home State to supervise the activities of the corporate entity, in particular the parent company located in its territory, which is doing business in third countries through its subsidiaries. Correspondingly, it would also be possible to hold the home State responsible for failure to exercise such due diligence duties, especially when there is sufficient knowledge that such conduct may cause a violation of international environmental standards in third countries and has the legal and technical means to prevent such harm.[97]

This far-reaching reading of the due diligence obligation of the home State finds support on the existence of a home state's prescriptive and adjudicative jurisdiction over the extraterritorial activities of corporate nationals in areas such as competition law, consumer protection, anti-bribery and corruption.[98] It would also find support in recent developments in international human rights law. In particular, there is a relatively well-established jurisprudence of the European Court of Human Rights (ECtHR) envisaging an extraterritorial reach of human rights obligations under the European Human Rights Convention (ECHR) whereby the responsibility of the contracting parties may arise 'because of acts of State authorities, whether performed within or outside national boundaries, *which produce effects outside their own territory*'.[99] Furthermore, a consolidated line of ECtHR's case-law indicates that States Parties to the ECHR have a positive duty to protect human rights also against violations by private parties such as corporations. In the environmental field, a leading case in this sense is *Fadeyeva v Russia*, in which the ECtHR held Russia responsible for having violated Article 8 of the ECHR for failing to regulate the environmental pollution of a private company which affected the quality of life at the applicant's home.[100]

Moreover, this question assumed renewed relevance in light of the Advisory Opinion of the Inter-American Court of Human Rights (IACtHR), which addressed specifically the question of State obligations in relation to the environment arising in the context of the human rights protection afforded by the Inter-American Human Rights Convention.[101] The IACtHR acknowledged that the exercise of State jurisdiction is a necessary precondition in order for a State to be held responsible for any conduct that may be attributed to it and that violates any of the rights under the Convention. However, it puts forward a broad reading of jurisdiction in Article 1(1) of the American Convention, which is not limited to the national territory of a State but contemplates circumstances in which the extraterritorial conduct of a

State constitutes an exercise of its jurisdiction.[102] On this basis, the Court asserts that the State obligation to respect and ensure human rights applies to every person who is within its territory or 'who is in any way subject to its authority, responsibility or control'.[103]

In the light of this, there are appropriate grounds to sustain that the times are ripe for a broader reading of home states' duties and responsibilities and that (home) States obligations to protect human rights and the environment include also a duty to regulate the extraterritorial activities of their corporate nationals or of the latter's foreign subsidiaries. Such an approach would find additional support in the recent initiatives at the level of the UN[104] and regionally, within the EU, aimed at the better defining the duties of States to protect human rights with respect to the activities of their corporate actors operating in third countries.[105] At the moment, these remarks are at the level of the progressive development of international law. They may therefore be regarded as responding to a normative reading of current trends rather than reflecting existing positive law. Nevertheless, it seems that the time has arrived for endorsing a more advanced and innovative stance to the question of State responsibility and to expand its reach to make it more relevant to capture a present and pressing challenge in the field of human rights and environment.

5.2. The **erga omnes** *character of environmental harms*

From an environmental law standpoint, the law of State responsibility must also be assessed against its capacity to accommodate the collective and multilateral dimension that characterises the majority of environmental obligations. In this respect, the question is whether the international norms that emerged at the beginning of the last century in a completely different ideological and political era have evolved and adapted to capture the twenty-first century problems of an increasingly interdependent and globalised international community. Is the law of State responsibility capable of providing remedies for the protection of fundamental interests that transcends the individualistic dimension of bilateral interstate relations and are, instead, of concern of the international community as a whole?

The cases examined in the previous sections, such as the *Trail Smelter* or the more recent Costa Rica versus Nicaragua dispute, demonstrate that the law of State responsibility may theoretically work well in the typical bilateral scenario of transboundary environmental damage between two neighbouring states. Less straightforward, however, is the application of these international principles to address damage to common areas located beyond the national jurisdiction of States or to more widespread and pervasive types of environmental degradation, such as biodiversity depletion, air pollution, marine pollution from land-based sources and, last but not least, climate change.

From the perspective of the primary norms, there is almost no doubt that the duties of harm prevention as reflected in Principle 21 of the Stockholm Declaration also apply to damage caused to the high sea or the Antarctic environment and to certain type of global environmental harms.[106] It has been submitted, for example, that the prevention principle entails the responsibility of a State (presumably any state) towards other States for its contribution to climate change and for the harm resulting from the emission of greenhouse gases in its territory.[107] Arguably, the customary nature of this rule would also imply that this is an obligation applicable to all States, not only those who are parties to relevant treaties, such as the UNFCCC or the Paris Agreement in the field of climate change.

However, if we move from the primary norms to the application of the secondary rules on State responsibility, there are two sets of challenges that need to be addressed. First, there is the question of standing: who is entitled to invoke the responsibility of the State in case of damage to areas outside territorial sovereignty (so-called global commons)? Second, particularly with respect to the scenario of diffuse and global environmental harms, such as air pollution or climate change or even the pervasive pollution of the marine environment from land-based sources located in multiple states, there is the question of identifying the responsible State. Here, besides factual difficulties concerning the identification of the causal link between the activities or the harmful emissions and the resulting pollution damage, there is the complex legal issue concerning the attribution, and distribution, of responsibility.[108] Climate change is the typical problem which is characterised by an indefinite plurality of contributing actors, which include both States and private actors, and of affected States and individuals. It has, in fact, even been objected whether a focus on the responsibility of States is appropriate in the case of climate change damage, given that the majority of the harmful GHGs emissions come from private sources and the activities of individuals.[109]

The ARISWA have tried to respond to these emerging concerns and to capture the changing status of the world's international relations. Thus, while Article 42 overall maintains the centrality of the injured State, it acknowledges in its subparagraph (Article 42(b)) the existence of collective and multilateral obligations that are owed to a group of treaty parties ('*erga omnes partes*') or to the international community as a whole ('*erga omnes*'). This provision envisages therefore that a State may be regarded as 'injured', and hence entitled to invoke the responsibility of another State, also in case of the breach of a multilateral or collective obligation. This possibility, however, remains limited to States that are directly or 'specially affected' by the breach.[110]

Article 48 goes further and entitles any State other than an injured State to make a claim against the breach of an international obligation that is established for the protection of the collective interests of a group of States or that is owed to the international community as a whole. So far, this provision has been regarded as being rather an example of progressive development than of codification of international law.[111] And yet, it represents a welcome attempt to take stock of developments in treaty practice and in international courts' jurisprudence pointing to the evolution of the international legal order 'from bilateralism to community interest'.[112] In the environmental field, developments such as the emergence of the notion of 'common concern of humankind' and more recently the drafting of the Global Pact for the Environment constitute further expressions of the idea that the environment is a global responsibility and that all States and the whole international community need to cooperate for the protection of vital environmental components.[113]

Environmental obligations can fit in each of the two scenarios envisaged in Article 48. International environmental obligations of a regional character (for example those aimed at protecting the environment in a given region) would fit in the notion of collective obligations under 48(1)(a). The ILC commentary indicates that this paragraph also extends to 'agreements established by a group of States in some wider common interest'. An illustration of this is provided by the Antarctic whaling case in which Australia launched in 2010 proceedings against Japan for its alleged violations of obligations assumed under the 1946 International Convention for the Regulation of Whaling and of other international obligations for the preservation of marine mammals and the marine environment.[114] Additionally, the duty to protect the environment may be qualified as an obligation owed to the international community as a whole under 48(b); although in practice the characterisation of *erga omnes* obligations and their legal consequences still remain controversial.

That said, with respect to the remedies that are available, the ARISWA differentiate sharply between the position of directly injured States and that of other states. Article 48(2) provides third States only with a right to seek cessation of the breach and assurances of non-repetition. Therefore, non-injured States cannot benefit from the full range of remedies available and cannot claim reparation or compensation in the case of damage to the global environment beyond any clean-up or reinstatement costs which they may incur.[115] From a political perspective, the opportunity for such differentiation was justified by reasons of pragmatism and by the need that Article 48 could be used to legitimise politically motivated acts or unilateral interventions by a State to enforce international law.[116] Still, from an environmental law perspective, this leaves an important gap in the range of remedies that may be available.

6. State responsibility for environmental harm in the international States practice

When moving from the analysis of the theoretical and legal aspects to the examination of State practice and judicial decisions on the question of liability and reparation for environmental harm, the picture appears rather fragmentary. Inter-states environmental liability claims have, indeed, seldom reached international courts. States usually prefer to address their disputes through informal means, such as negotiations and mediation, rather than more formally by recourse to courts. Hence, apart from a handful set of prominent precedents,[117] international practice in this field was for long time characterised by informal intercourses between States, rather than recourse to formal means of dispute settlement. The reasons behind this situation are manifold. Victim states' reluctance to formally invoke the responsibility of a State is often grounded on a sentiment of silent complicity and tolerance for the potentially harmful consequences of activities considered crucial for the States' own economic progress. A remarkable example of this attitude is the reaction (or lack thereof) of the international community in the aftermath of the Chernobyl's tragic disaster and the absence of any allegation regarding the URSS's responsibility, despite subsequent evidence of the human and managerial errors which were at the origin of the incident. A further reason is that States tend to avoid recourse to adversarial mechanisms that are often considered 'too heavy, unpredictable and of a politically damageable use'.[118] This is particularly the case if the claim is based on the assertion of international responsibility for a wrongful State conduct since 'inevitably such claims carry the implication of a moral reproach'.[119] Moreover, as noted by Dupuy and Viñuales, court litigation is often regarded as a last resort in international law and as an avenue to pursue only where other means of dialogue and exchange, such as mediation and negotiation, have proved unsuccessful.[120] Additionally, in the environmental field, the establishment of non-compliance mechanisms for the enforcement of international treaty provisions is a further illustration of the preference of States for 'soft' approaches to responsibility based on peer-pressure.[121]

That said, over the more recent decades, there have been important developments in interstate environmental litigation, including cases in which questions of environmental harm have been linked to an explicit claim of State responsibility for violation of an international law obligation. One of the earliest disputes with a distinct environmental law dimension was that related to the nuclear testing experiments conducted by France in the Pacific in the period between 1966 and 1972 and resulting in a fallout of radioactive material on Australia's and New Zealand's territory. The two States commenced separate proceedings before the ICJ claiming that France had violated their right of territorial sovereignty, the right to be free from nuclear testing as well as the right of the international community to the preservation of the maritime, aerial and terrestrial environment from artificial radioactive contamination.[122] The ICJ did not eventually rule on this dispute since, further to a number of official statements and assurances by the French government that there would be no further atmospheric nuclear tests, it declared the claim deprived of any object.

More recently, two disputes brought before the ICJ raised expressly the question of international State responsibility and reparation for transboundary environmental damage. The first concern the claim brought by Ecuador in 2008 regarding the alleged 'serious damage to people, to crops, to animals and to the natural environment' caused by the aerial spraying by Colombia of toxic herbicides near its border.[123] The dispute represented at the time one of the rare occasions where a State had recourse to the ICJ in order to expressly seek a declaration of international responsibility for the violation of international law related to the prohibition of transboundary harm and the prevention of environmental damage. In its claim, Ecuador recognised the environmental facet of the international law principles of territorial sovereignty and integrity and emphasised the relevance of the precautionary principle in the assessment of State's compliance with its primary duties of prevention.[124] The case was eventually discontinued due to the disputing States reaching a settlement on the matter. However, it represented an important precedent under at least two respects. First, it demonstrated the growing relevance of environmental concerns to represent integral part of states' international claims. In the dispute, the question of responsibility and reparation for environmental damage was not raised as a merely indirect and ancillary question, but was at the heart of Ecuador's claim. Second, the case may be taken as an indication of a gradual change in the attitude of States with respect to the invocation of other states' responsibility and liability in the environmental context, as well as a potentially greater willingness to refer requests of compensation for environmental damage to a judicial forum.

Indeed, two years later, in 2010 the ICJ was once again sized with a specific question of State responsibility for environmental damage. In the joined cases of *Certain Activities carried out by Nicaragua in the Border Area* (Costa Rica v Nicaragua) and *Construction of a Road in Costa Rica along the San Juan River* (Nicaragua v Costa Rica), the ICJ was asked to consider the claimant States' respective requests for reparation for the alleged significant transboundary damage arising as a consequence of the defendant States' violation of the primary obligation not to cause significant transboundary harm and other substantive and procedural environment related obligations. In its application, Costa Rica mentioned specifically the serious damage inflicted to its protected rainforests and wetlands and the damage intended to the Colorado River, wetlands and protected ecosystems. The Court's decision issued in 2015 affirmed the responsibility of Nicaragua for the breach of Costa Rica's territorial sovereignty and its duty to make reparation for the damage, including environmental damage, caused by its unlawful activities. However, the Court grounded Nicaragua's liability only on the violation of Costa Rica's territorial sovereignty, without consideration for the duty of harm prevention.

The significance of these cases, however, needs to be assessed against the widespread preference of States towards more informal means of addressing environmental controversies. The analysis of relevant State practice shows indeed that questions of reparation for transboundary environmental harm are most frequently resolved via negotiated settlements either at the interstate level between the States involved or between the affected State and the private company responsible for the damage.[125] This attitude is in line with the more general preference of States for less adversarial mechanisms for the resolution of international disputes. In general, extra-judicial settlements, with the direct or indirect involvement of the State, may also have the advantage to overcome the often cumbersome and lengthy process that characterises court litigation not only at the international level but also at the domestic level. They might also be particularly appropriate for the so-called mass tort cases where damage is so widespread and the transnational legal ramifications so complex that domestic court proceedings often prove inadequate.[126] There are in fact several instances in which the victim State pursued compensation directly with the private corporation. Some scholars refer to this trend as a 'privatization' of 'what would be environment-related international State compensation claims'.[127] An example is the settlement negotiated between the Swiss company Sandoz and the affected private and public victims of the pollution disaster caused by a fire that occurred at a Sandoz warehouse near Basel and the subsequent spill of toxic chemicals into the Rhine. The accident was described as one of Western Europe's worst environmental disasters.[128] Interestingly, in this case it was apparent that Switzerland had in various respects fallen short of meeting its international obligations under a number of treaties imposing a primary duty of environmental protection of the Rhine against chemical pollution. And yet, it was noted, 'no trace of Switzerland's responsibility can be found in the communiqués from the conference of the Rhine ministers held after and in connection with the accident'[129] or in the proceedings of the European Community's council meeting shortly after the disaster. Instead of acting against Switzerland and invoking its responsibility under international law, the government of the riparian States had preferred to seek reparation directly from the responsible company.[130]

A similar approach was taken with respect to the Baia Mare mining disaster in Romania, where a significant leakage of cyanide from the Aurul gold mining company—a joint venture of an Australian company and the Romanian government—caused massive pollution of the Tisza and then Danube rivers. Despite the magnitude of the damage and the failure of Romanian authorities to comply with relevant international regulations and standards, including those established under the UN Convention on the Protection and Use of Transboundary Watercourses and International Lakes,[131] there were no formal proceedings brought against Romania at the international level. Hungary and Serbia initially demanded that Romania pay compensation for the transboundary pollution of the Tisza and Danube rivers, invoking its responsibility. However, they eventually decided to direct their claims directly against the private operator of the mine, the Australian company Esmeralda Exploration, and the Romanian company Aurul. A civil compensation case was therefore started by Hungary against Aurul SA in Hungarian courts.[132] Another example is the spill from the Montara oil well in 2009 when 40 million litres of oil and gas leaked from a faulty rig into the Timor Sea, at the southeast of Australia. Indonesia, whose shore were severely affected by the spill, launched a lawsuit against the Australian rig operator and its Thai parent company. The lawsuit was eventually dismissed in 2018, but a parallel lawsuit was launched in the form of a class action by Indonesian seaweed farmers claiming compensation for the severe marine pollution which led to significant impairment of their seaweed industry and consequent loss of their livelihood.[133] In 2021, the federal court ordered the Australian subsidiary of the Thai oil company that owned the oil well to pay compensation amounting to little more than A$ 34,000 in damages for each farmer.[134]

Overall, the examination of international practice seems to suggest that most States implicitly acknowledge that they do have a role to play in relation to situations of significant transboundary environmental damage, even when such damage is the result of activities carried out by private actors operating within their jurisdiction. Yet, they prefer to be involved in question of reparation and redress outside the formality of international judicial procedures and outside the formal connotation of wrongfulness that characterises the State responsibility framework.

7. Concluding remarks and assessment

The ARISWA have provided an important contribution to unifying international law with respect to secondary rules governing the consequences of breaches of primary environmental law obligations. However, there still remain some shortcomings when relying upon this body of rules to claim reparation for environmental harm. From a strictly legal perspective, the requirement of a wrongful act to activate the secondary rules on State responsibility, compounded with the due diligence standard of prevention at the level of the primary norms, make it difficult to capture accidental damage in which there is not an evident breach by the State of its primary duties of environmental harm prevention or of any other international law obligation. Such difficulties are further accentuated by the fluid and open-ended contours of due diligence and by the narrow approach to the question of attribution of private conducts to the State.

The overview of State practice has also illustrated that in case of environmental damage, States tend to avoid recourse to formal international dispute settlement mechanisms before an international court or tribunal, let alone to formally invoke the other state's responsibility and liability. Although recent years have seen an incremental rise in interstate environmental litigation, these are essentially bilateral disputes between two States that concerned relatively straightforward instances of transfrontier pollution or the management of shared natural resources. Moreover, most of these cases concern actual or potential transboundary impacts arising from activities in which there is a direct involvement of the State. By contrast, in the more ordinary cases of environmental damage caused by privately operated activities and technologies, the widespread tendency is to opt for the more informal processes of negotiated settlements, often directly with the private company responsible for the damage.

Finally, when examined from the perspective of the individual victims of the damage, the pursuit of international claims in an interstate context is not the easier option. International litigation proceedings are usually long and cumbersome. With few exceptions, international dispute settlement mechanisms are anchored to the idea of the State as the primary actor in the international legal arena and as the only one to have standing.[135] This means that the decision whether to bring the claim is left entirely to the state's discretion, whereas NGOs or the individuals who suffer *in primis* the consequences of environmental harm have no control over the process and no voice in the proceedings or over any ensuing outcome.[136] In the absence of special treaty arrangements granting individuals access to international tribunals, their relevant rights and interests will be upheld only indirectly usually through the exercise of diplomatic protection by the State of their nationality. Moreover, the State's decision to bring the claim is often motivated by political considerations rather than by genuine environmental concerns.[137]

Further important shortcomings are represented by the voluntary and consensual nature of judicial settlement processes, particularly in the environmental field where there is no compulsory or centralised system of enforcement.[138] In that context, the possibility to have the issue heard by an international court is ultimately dependent on the consent of the defendant state. Moreover, and except from when a broad consent to the ICJ jurisdiction is provided on the basis of the optional clause in Article 36(2) ICJ Statute, the consensual character of international dispute settlement implies that the final outcome of the case depends on the scope of the court's jurisdiction.[139] At present, only a few environmental treaties contain specific provision for the compulsory adjudication of environmental controversies,[140] and they generally limit jurisdiction to disputes concerning the interpretation or application of the treaty in which the dispute settlement clause is found. This means that the relevant court or tribunal 'may not be able to decide all aspects of environmental harm that may have been caused in a particular case'.[141] In the *Pulp Mills* case, for example, the ICJ could not consider a specific claim for damage to air and atmospheric pollution as it was regarded outside its scope of jurisdiction under the relevant treaty.

The shortcomings involved in interstate litigation based on the law of State responsibility to pursue redress for transboundary environmental harm eventually led both scholars and policy-makers to explore possible alternatives. The first alternative is represented by the various scholarly attempts to identify a principle of international State liability for the harmful impacts of hazardous activities which would operate outside, and in parallel, to the framework of State responsibility but which would be detached from the requirement of wrongful act. The second alternative consisted in shifting the focus from the responsibility of States under international law to the civil liability of private operators under domestic law. It is to analysis of these two alternatives that the discussion of the next two chapters will now turn.

Notes

1 The idea of 'layers' of environmental liability in this context has been borrowed from J Brunnée, 'Of Sense and Sensibility: Reflections on International Liability Regimes as Tools for Environmental Protection' (2004) 53 International and Comparative Law Quarterly 351.

2 ILC, 'Draft Articles on Responsibility of States for Internationally Wrongful Acts' in *Yearbook of the International Law Commission,* vol. II (Part Two) (ARISWA 2001).

3 P Okowa, 'Responsibility for Environmental Damage' in M Fitzmaurice, DM Ong and P Merkouris (eds.), *Research Handbook on International Environmental Law* (Edward Elgar 2010).

4 T Scovazzi, 'State Responsibility for Environmental Harm' (2001) 12 Yearbook of International Environmental Law 43, 46.

5 ILC (n 2).

6 LFE Goldie, 'Concepts of Strict and Absolute Liability and the Ranking of Liability in Terms of Relative Exposure to Risk' (1985) 16 Netherlands Yearbook of International Law 175, 180; P Sands et al., *Principles of International Environmental Law* (4th ed., CUP 2018) 738.

7 A Rosas, 'Issues of State Liability for Transboundary Environmental Damage' (1991) 60 Nordic Journal of International Law 29.

8 ILC, 'Draft Articles on Responsibility of States for Internationally Wrongful Acts, with commentaries' (2001) *Report of the International Law Commission*, Supplement No. 10 UN Doc A/56/10, 92 [Commentaries to Draft Articles on State Responsibility].

9 A Boyle and C Redgwell, *Birnie, Boyle and Redgwell's International Law and the Environment* (4rd ed., OUP 2021) 223.

10 E.g. *Case Concerning Pulp Mills on the River Uruguay* (Argentina v Uruguay) (Merits) [2010] ICJ Rep 14.

11 U Beyerlin, 'Different Types of Norms in International Environmental Law: Policies, Principles and Rules' in D Bodansky, J Brunnée and E Hey (eds.), *The Oxford Handbook of International Environmental Law* (OUP 2007); PM Dupuy, G Le Moli and JE Viñuales, 'Customary International Law and the Environment' (2018) C-EENRG

Working Papers 2018–2, <www.ceenrg.landecon.cam.ac.uk/system/files/documents/CEENRG_WP_19_CustomaryInternationalLawandtheEnvironment.pdf> accessed 12 July 2022.

12 *Trail Smelter Arbitration (United States v Canada)* (1938 and 1941) 3 R.I.A.A. 1905.

13 Ibid. 1965.

14 *Corfu Channel Case (United Kingdom v Albania)* (Merits) [1949] ICJ Rep 4.

15 *Lac Lanoux Arbitration* (*France v Spain*) (1957) 12 RIAA 281; *Gut Dam Arbitration (Canada v United States)* (1968) 8 ILM 118.

16 RM Bratspies and RA Miller (eds.), *Transboundary Harm in International Law* (CUP 2009).

17 J Brunnée, 'The Responsibility of States for Environmental Harm in a Multinational Context—Problems and Trends' (1993) 34 Les Cahiers de Droit 827, 831.

18 G Handl, 'National Uses of Transboundary Air Resources: The International Entitlement Issue Reconsidered', (1986) 26 Natural Resources Journal 405.

19 This 'paradigm shift' is very well illustrated in the work of LA Duvic-Paoli, *The Prevention Principle in International Environmental Law* (CUP 2018).

20 G Handl, 'Transboundary Impacts' in *The Oxford Handbook of International Environmental Law* (n 11) 538.

21 *Gabcikovo-Nagymaros Project (Hungary v Slovakia)* (Merits) [1997] ICJ Rep 7, para 140.

22 *Pulp Mills* (n 10) [101].

23 *Gabcikovo-Nagymaros* (n 20) [141]; *Indus Water Kishenganga Arbitration (Pakistan v India)* (Partial award) (PCA 2013) [449].

24 X Hanqin, *Transboundary Damage in International Law* (CUP 2003) 185; I Plakokefalos, 'Prevention Obligations in International Environmental Law' (2012) 23 Yearbook of International Environmental Law 1, 3.

25 *Pulp Mills* (n 10) [105].

26 ITLOS, *Responsibilities and Obligations of States Sponsoring Persons and Entities with Respect to Activities in the Area* (Advisory Opinion) 1 February 2011, ITLOS Reports, p 10 [189].

27 ILC, 'Draft Articles on Prevention of Transboundary Harm from Hazardous Activities, with Commentaries', (2001) UNGA Official Records A/56/10, 154 ('ILC Draft Articles on Prevention').

28 International Law Association (ILA), *Study Group on Due Diligence in International Law* (Second Report), July 2016, <www.ila-hq.org/index.php/study-groups?study-groupsID=63> accessed 1 June 2022.

29 ILC's Draft Articles on Prevention (n 27) 154.

30 ILA (n 27).

31 G Handl, 'International Accountability for Transboundary Environmental Harm Revisited: What Role for "State Liability"?' (2007) 37 Environmental Policy and Law 116.

32 Y Kerbrat, 'Le droit international face au défi de la réparation des dommages à l'environnement. Rapport général sur le thème de la deuxième demi-journée' in *Le Droit International Face au Défi de la Protection de l'Environnement* (SFDI—Pédone 2010) 125.

33 For a similar view see Plakokefalos (n 24) 36.

34 On this, *Pulp Mills* (n 9) [197]; S Maljean-Dubois, 'International Litigation and State Liability for Environmental Damages: Recent Evolutions and Perspectives' in Jiunn-Ron Yeh (ed.), *Climate Change Liability and Beyond* (National Taiwan University Press 2017).

35 (n 26).

36 ILC Draft Articles on Prevention (n 27) 154.

37 ILC, 'Draft Articles on Responsibility of States for Internationally Wrongful Acts, with Commentary' (Articles on State Responsibility) in Report of the International Law Commission on the Work of its 53rd session, UN GAOR, 56th Sess. Supp. No 10, UN Doc A/56/10 (2001), 36. Cfr with Article 139(2) UNCLOS as interpreted by the ITLOS

in its Advisory Opinion (n 26) [176] where the occurrence of damage is instead a precondition for liability.
38 ILC Draft Articles on the Prevention, Article 2.
39 Scovazzi (n 4).
40 In the *Trail Smelter* case, the tribunal held that the injury must have a 'serious consequence' to justify a claim. See S Maljean-Dubois (n 34) 16, citing Y Kebrat.
41 ILC, 'Principles on Allocation of Loss in the Case of Transboundary Harm Arising Out of Hazardous Activities, with Commentaries' (2006) *Yearbook of the International Law Commission*, Vol. II, Part II, 123. Similarly, ILC's Draft Articles on Prevention (n 27) and the 1997 UN Convention on the Law of Non-Navigational Use of International Watercourses.
42 ILC, Principles on Allocation of Loss (n 41), commentary to Principle 2.
43 ILC's Draft Articles on Prevention, 153.
44 Sands and Peel (n 6) 711.
45 CR Payne, 'Pulp Mills on the River Uruguay' (2011) 105 American Journal of International Law 94.
46 A Boyle, 'Reparation for Environmental Damage in International Law: Some Preliminary Problems' in M. Bowman and A Boyle (eds.), *Environmental Damage in International and Comparative Law: Problems of Definition and Valuation* (OUP 2002) 17.
47 *Advisory Opinion on the Legality of the Threat or Use of Nuclear Weapons* [1996] ICJ Rep 2.
48 UNSC Resolution 678, S/RES/678 (1990) November 29.
49 CR Payne, 'Legal Liability for Environmental Damage: The United Nations Compensation Commission and the 1990–1991 Gulf War' in C Bruch, C Muffett and S Nichols (eds.), *Governance, Natural Resources and Post-Conflict Peacebuilding* (Earthscan/Routledge 2016) 723–724.
50 UN Security Council Resolution of 3 April 1991, No 687, Concerning the Restoration of Peace and Security in Iraq and Kuwait, U.N. Doc. S/RES/687 (1991).
51 *Certain Activities Carried out by Nicaragua in the Border Area (Costa Rica v Nicaragua)* (merits) [2015] ICJ Rep 665.
52 Boyle (n 46) 22.
53 Articles on State Responsibility (n 37), 99 and 101.
54 *Chorzów Factory (Germany v Poland)*, PCIJ Series A No 17, 29.
55 Articles on State Responsibility Articles with Commentaries' (n 37) 95.
56 Ibid. 96.
57 See further in Chapter 3 of this book.
58 *Costa Rica v Nicaragua* (n 51), Separate Opinion of Judge Bhandari, para 5.
59 Articles on State Responsibility (n 37) 95.
60 Ibid. 99.
61 Article 31(1) links reparation to the concept of injury: 'The responsible State is under an obligation to make full reparation for the injury *caused* by the internationally wrongful act'. Article 31(2) articulates the degree of proximity required between injury and the internationally wrongful act: 'Injury includes any damage, whether material or moral, *caused* by the internationally wrongful act' [emphasis added].
62 The expression 'pure economic losses' refers to economic damages that are unconnected with personal injury or property damage—for example, the losses suffered by people who are dependent for their economic subsistence on the use of public natural resources.
63 Reported in ILC, Survey of Liability regimes relevant to the topic of international liability for injurious consequences arising out of acts not prohibited by international law, prepared by the Secretariat, Doc A/CN.4/543 (2004).
64 Articles on State Responsibility (n 37), 101.
65 Ibid.
66 Ibid.

67 Comprehensive Environmental Response, Compensation, and Liability Act (CERCLA) 42 U.S.C. § 9601 et seq. (1980); Oil Pollution Act (OPA) 33 U.S.C. § 2701 et seq. (1990).
68 EC/2004/35 Directive on Environmental Liability with regard to the prevention and remedying of environmental damage OJ L 143.
69 Decision taken by the Governing Council of the UNCC during its third session, at the 18th meeting, held on 28 November 1991, as revised at the 24th meeting held on 16 March 1992: Criteria for additional categories of claims. Governing Council Decision 7.S/AC.26/1991/7/Rev 1, 17 March 1992.
70 *Report and Recommendations Made by the Panel of Commissioners Concerning the Fifth Instalment of "F4" Claims*, 30 June 2005, United Nations Security Council, Doc. S/AC. 26/2005/10.
71 UNCC, *Report and Recommendations Made by the Panel of Commissioners Concerning the Fifth Instalment of "F4" Claims*, UN Doc. S/AC.26/2005/10 (2005), para 58 <www.uncc.ch>.
72 Doc. S/AC.26/2005/10 of 30 June 2005, para 58.
73 Ibid. 55.
74 Ibid. 56.
75 UNCC, *Report and Recommendations Made by the Panel of Commissioners Concerning the Fifth Instalment of "F4" Claims*, UN Doc. S/AC.26/2005/10 (2005) [80].
76 PH Sand, 'Compensation for Environmental Damage from the 1991 Gulf War' (2005) 36 Environmental Policy and Law 244, 247.
77 Sand (n 76). See also N Hanley, 'The Economic Value of Environmental Damage' in *Environmental Damage in International and Comparative Law: Problems of Definition and Valuation* (n 46) 27.
78 *Certain Activities Carried Out by Nicaragua in the Border Area (Costa Rica v Nicaragua) Compensation*, Judgment [2018] ICJ Reports 15.
79 Ibid. [41].
80 Ibid. [42].
81 Ibid. [47–49].
82 Ibid. [78].
83 J Rudall, 'Certain Activities Carried Out by Nicaragua in the Border Area (Costa Rica v Nicaragua)' (2018) 112 American Journal of International Law 288, 292.
84 Costa Rica made specific reference, *inter alia*, to the UNEP Guidelines for the Development of Domestic legislation on Liability, Response Action and Compensation for Damage Caused by Activities Dangerous to the Environment.
85 Article 4 ARISWA.
86 Article 8 ARISWA.
87 Articles on State Responsibility (n 37) 38.
88 Cfr the notion of 'effective control' adopted by the ICJ in the *Nicaragua v US* case (i.e. *Military and Paramilitary Activities in and Against Nicaragua* [1986] ICJ Rep 14) with the 'overall control' test enunciated by the ICTY in the *Tadic case* (*Prosecutor v Dusko Tadic* (Appeal Judgment) [1999] IT-94–1-A). A Cassese, 'The Nicaragua and Tadic Tests Revisited in Light of the ICJ Judgement on Genocide in Bosnia' (2007) 18 European Journal of International Law 649, 653.
89 Case concerning the *Application of the Convention on the Prevention and Punishment of the Crime of Genocide (Bosnia and Herzegovina v Serbia and Montenegro)* (merits) [2007] ICJ Rep 43, para 392.
90 J Brunnée, 'International Legal Accountability through the Lens of the Law of State Responsibility' (2005) 36 Netherlands Yearbook of International Law 3.
91 *Case Concerning the Application of the Convention on the Prevention and Punishment of the Crime of Genocide* (*Bosnia and Herzegovina v. Serbia and Montenegro*) [2007] ICJ Rep 2.

92 By home state, it is meant the state under whose laws a given corporation is incorporated, or in whose territory it has its administrative seat or main place of business. See A Berkes, 'Extraterritorial Responsibility of the Home States for MNCs Violations of Human Rights' in Y Radi (ed.), *Research Handbook on Human Rights and Investment* (Edward Elgar 2018).

93 F Francioni, 'Alternative Perspective on International Responsibility for Human Rights Violations by Multinational Corporations' in W Benedek, K De Feyter and F Marrella (eds.), *Economic Globalization and Human Rights* (CUP 2007). As to the related use of the notion of 'effective control' as a liability determining device, see G Handl, 'State Liability for Accidental Transnational Environmental Damage by Private Persons' (1980) 74 American Journal of International Law 525, 530.

94 F Francioni, 'Exporting Environmental Hazards through Multinational Enterprises: Can the State of Origin be Held Responsible?' in F Francioni and T Scovazzi (eds.), *International Responsibility for Environmental Harm* (Graham & Trotman 1991).

95 Berkes (n 92).

96 Francioni 'Alternative Perspective' (n 93) 245.

97 Ibid. 262.

98 R McCorquodale and P Simons, 'Responsibility Beyond Borders: State Responsibility for Extraterritorial Violations by Corporations of International Human Rights Law' (2007) 70 Modern Law Review 598, 616–617.

99 *Loizidou V Turkey* (Preliminary Objections) (App no. 15318/89) [1997] ECHR 10, 23 March 1995, para 62.

100 *Fadeyeva v Russia* (Application no 55723/00) [2005] ECHR 376, 30 November 2005.

101 *Human Rights and the Environment*, Advisory Opinion OC-23/17, Inter-American Court of Human Rights, 15 November 2017.

102 Ibid., para 78.

103 Ibid., para 72–73.

104 See *UN Guiding Principles on Business and Human Rights: Implementing the United Nations 'Protect, Respect and Remedy' Framework* endorsed by the Human Rights Council in its Resolution 17/4 of 16 June 2011.

105 Council of Europe's Committee of Ministers Recommendation CM/Rec (2016) 3 on Human Rights and Business, 2 March 2016.

106 See with respect to climate change, C Voigt, 'State Responsibility for Climate Change Damages' (2008) 77 Nordic Journal of International Law 1–2, 1; B. Mayer, 'State Responsibility and Climate Change Governance: A Light Through the Storm' (2014) 13 Chinese Journal of International Law 539.

107 ILA, Declaration of Legal Principles Relating to Climate Change, Committee on Legal Principles Relating to Climate Change—Resolution 2/2014. For a commentary see A Zahar, 'Mediated Versus Cumulative Environmental Damage and the International Law Association's Legal Principles on Climate Change' (2014) 4 Climate Law 3–4, 217.

108 See A Nollkaemper and D Jacobs (eds.), *Distribution of Responsibilities in International Law* (CUP 2015).

109 Zahar (n 107).

110 Article 42(b) distinguishes between the case of a breach of an international obligation that specially affected a state and a breach that 'is of such a character as radically to change the position of all the other States to which the obligation is owed with respect to the further performance of the obligation'.

111 M Fitzmaurice, 'International Responsibility and Liability' in *The Oxford Handbook of International Environmental Law* (n 11) 1021.

112 B. Simma, 'From Bilateralism to Community Interest in International Law' in V-250 (1994) *Collected Courses of the Hague Academy of International Law*; J Crawford, 'Responsibility for Breaches of Communitarian Norms: An Appraisal of Article 48 of the ILC Articles on Responsibility of States for Internationally Wrongful Acts' in U

Fastenrath et al. (eds.), *From Bilateralism to Community Interest: Essays in Honour of Bruno Simma* (OUP 2011).

113 See E Brown-Weiss, 'The Changing Structure of International Law' in C Lambrechts and M Prieur (eds.), *Les Hommes et L'Environnement—Quel Droits pour le Vingt-et-Uniemen siècle?* (Frison-Roche 1998) 8.

114 *Whaling in the Antarctic (Australia v Japan: New Zealand intervening)* (Merits) [2014] ICJ Rep 226.

115 Boyle and Redgwell (n 9) 245.

116 E Brown-Weiss, 'Invoking State Responsibility in the Twenty-First Century' (2002) 96 American Journal of International Law 798, 805.

117 Early precedents include the cases of *Trail Smelter*, *Lac Lanoux*, *Gut Dam*. The Corfu Channel case is often cited as a precedent for the no-harm proposition, but this was not at all concerned with environment.

118 PM Dupuy, 'A propos des mésaventures de la responsabilité internationale des Etats dans ses rapports avec la protection de l'environnement' in *Les Hommes et l'Environnement* (n 113) 275.

119 Handl, 'International Accountability' (n 31), 118.

120 PM Dupuy and J Viñuales, *International Environmental Law* (CUP 2018) 300.

121 F Francioni, 'Dispute Avoidance in International Environmental Law' in A Kiss, D Shelton and K Ishibashi (eds.), *Economic Globalization and Compliance with International Environmental Agreements* (Kluwer Law 2003).

122 *Nuclear Tests case* (Australia v France) [1974] ICJ Report, p 253; (New Zealand v France) [1974] ICJ Report 547.

123 *Aerial Herbicide Spraying (Ecuador v Colombia)*, Application Instituting Proceedings (31 March 2008) [37].

124 Ibid. See especially [8.7] and [8.8] where Ecuador highlights the 'need for a more precautionary approach to international risk management' and argues that 'the precautionary principle redefines existing rules of international law on the control of environmental risk and conservation of natural resources'.

125 See the extensive review undertaken by the ILC on this topic: 'Survey of Liability Regimes Relevant to the Topic of International Liability for Injurious Consequences Arising Out of Acts Not Prohibited by International Law: Study prepared by the Secretariat', International Law Commission, 47th session (1995), UN General Assembly, A/CN.4/471, 92. See also R Lefeber, *Transboundary Environmental Interference and the Origin of State Liability* (Kluwer Law International 1996) 112–113.

126 See Handl, 'International Accountability' (n 31) 119.

127 G Handl, 'Catastrophic Nuclear Accidents: Mass Tort Claims in a Transboundary Context' (presentation) <https://cil.nus.edu.sg/wp-content/uploads/2017/08/Presentation-on-Claims-Processing-Gunther-Handl-6-July-2017.pdf> accessed 29 December 2022.

128 A Schwabach, 'The Sandoz Spill: The Failure of International Law to Protect the Rhine from Pollution' (1989) 16 Ecology Law Quarterly 2, 443.

129 See HU Jessurun d'Oliveira, 'The Sandoz Blaze: The Damage and the Public and Private Liabilities', in *International Responsibility for Environmental Harm* (n 94).

130 Ibid. 440.

131 1936 UNTS 269 (adopted on 17 March 1992; entered into force 6 October 1996). Romania is a party to the Convention since 1992.

132 Background Document for the UNECE Workshop (Budapest 2007).

133 See G Handl and K Svendsen (eds.), *Managing the Risk of Offshore Oil and Gas Accidents: The International Legal Dimension* (Edward Elgar 2019).

134 B Doherty, 'Very Hard Life Now: 12 Years after the Montara Oil Spill, Indonesians are Still Fighting to be Heard' *The Guardian* (15 January 2022) < https://www.theguardian.com/environment/2022/jan/16/very-hard-life-now-12-years-after-the-montara-oil-spill-indonesians-are-still-fighting-to-be-heard> accessed 21 March 2023.

135 PB Stephan, 'Privatizing International Law' (2011) 97 Virginia Law Review 1537.
136 E Hey, *Advanced Introduction to International Environmental Law* (Edward Elgar 2016) 109.
137 A Boyle and J Harrison, 'Judicial Settlement of International Environmental Disputes' (2013) 4 Journal of International Dispute Settlement 245, 246.
138 F Francioni, 'Realism, Utopia, and the Future of International Environmental Law' in (The Late) A Cassese (ed.), *Realizing Utopia: The Future of International Law* (OUP 2012).
139 Boyle and Harrison (n 137) 251.
140 Several multilateral environmental treaties have dispute settlement clauses, but they do not establish a compulsory adjudicatory procedure. See for example Article 27(3) of the Convention on Biological Diversity whereby States may express their consent to submit their disputes to the ICJ or to an arbitration procedure.
141 J Harrison, 'Reflection on the Role of International Courts and Tribunals in the Settlement of Environmental Disputes and the Development of International Environmental Law' (2013) 24 Journal of Environmental Law 501, 504.

2 The quest towards an international law framework of states' environmental liability in the work of the ILC

1. State liability as a primary rule of international law

Alongside the law of State responsibility, a distinct concept of international liability started to be considered during the second half of the twentieth century, particularly in connection with technological and industrial expansion and the increased risk of significant transboundary damage caused by such novel technologies. This idea of international liability of States would operate in parallel to the law of State responsibility and would embody a primary obligation for the State to provide compensation for the harmful consequences of acts or activities which are not in contravention to an international law obligation.[1] State liability would therefore be premised upon the mere occurrence of an environmental damage causally linked to activities carried out within the jurisdiction of the State; it would amount in practice to strict liability.

Scholars advocating for the strict liability of States for the accidental damage caused during the operation of hazardous and ultra-hazardous activities took for the most part inspiration from analogous developments occurring in several municipal legal systems, where a standard of strict liability in tort had progressively been established with respect to activities involving a high level of risk. At the basis of these proposals was the belief that a globally applicable regime of 'strict' State liability for transboundary environmental damage would overcome some of the gaps and limitations of the law of State responsibility. In this framework, the identification and codification of certain general principles of State liability applicable to transboundary damage caused by lawful activities has been the object of a prolonged and somehow controversial project carried out by the ILC under the title 'International Liability for Injurious Consequences Arising Out of Acts Not Prohibited by International Law'.[2]

However desirable these proposals might be from a policy point of view, their practical realisation met with significant obstacles, including *in primis* the absence of relevant State practice on which to ground the existence of such duty and the reluctance of most governments to accept the idea of a no-fault State liability for damage caused by private actors. At present, the only clear precedents of strict State liability in international law can be found in certain multilateral treaties related to the operation of specific kind of ultra-hazardous activities, such as the exploration and use of outer space and the launch of space objects.[3]

DOI: 10.4324/9781315676708-4

Additionally, a further mechanism to indirectly engage State liability under international law is the idea of a supplementary liability of the State, or the idea of 'State relay'.[4] An example of this can be found in the 1963 Brussels Supplementary Convention additional to the 1960 Paris Convention on Third Party Liability in the Field of Nuclear Energy.[5]

These conventional liability provisions remain, however, rather exceptional and do not lend support for more extensive generalisation on the applicability of a principle of State liability to other instances of transboundary environmental damage. In this respect, it is significant that even the proposal to introduce a Member State's duty to take environmental remedial measures under the EU Directive on Environmental Liability in case of inaction or insolvency of the polluter was firmly rejected by EU Member States in the Council during the legislative process.[6]

2. Environmental liability in the work of the ILC: from international liability to allocation of losses

The ILC officially started its work on the liability topic in 1978 under the heading of 'International Liability for Injurious Consequences Arising Out of Acts Not Prohibited by International Law'.[7] The decision to split the work related to responsibility and liability stemmed originally from the assumption that most instances of transboundary damage resulting from the activities of industries or businesses could not be easily accommodated within the law of State responsibility.[8]

Work on the liability topic was protracted for several years during which, despite the valuable contributions of the Special Rapporteurs who have succeeded one another in overseeing the project, progress became slow and difficult. At the conceptual level, the project was criticised as being 'fundamentally misconceived'.[9] Further important obstacles were the perceived absence of a consistent State practice on which to ground the existence of a primary international obligation to redress transboundary damage arising independently from the commission of an international wrongful act and the lack of support for this idea by many governments.[10]

In response to the aforementioned concerns, a substantial revision of the ILC's approach was undertaken, leading to a formal scission of the work on the topic of 'liability' from that on 'prevention'. A Special Rapporteur was appointed to lead the work on prevention, which was completed in 2001 with the elaboration of the 'Draft Articles on Prevention of Transboundary Harm from Hazardous Activities'.[11] The work on liability resumed in 2002 under the guidance of the Special Rapporteur Pemmaraju Sreenivasa Rao and was finally completed in 2004 with the 'Draft Principles on the Allocation of Loss in the Case of Transboundary Harm Arising Out of Hazardous Activities' (the 'Principles'). The Principles were eventually submitted to the UN General Assembly in 2006.[12]

For the question of liability, the ILC working group and the Special Rapporteur decided to adopt a pragmatic approach, guided by the belief that the ultimate purpose of a liability regime should be to ensure that the innocent victim is not left to bear entirely the burden of environmental harm.[13] The Principles therefore shifted the emphasis from State liability to the liability of private operators, in line with the general trend emerging within most environmental liability treaties. They put forward a 'privatized approach to risk',[14] while maintaining an important role for the State, which would be responsible for crafting a workable and effective regime capable of ensuring prompt and adequate compensation to the victims of pollution. Features of such a regime may include provisions of strict liability of private operators and the setting up of financial security, such as insurance or industry-wide funding at the national level.[15] Principle 6 outlines the main elements of an international standard of compensation, based on the criteria of promptness, adequacy and effectiveness, 'which affects not only the compensation itself but also the procedures and remedies through which it is to be obtained'.[16] It also reaffirms the importance of a non-discriminatory access to justice, including access to information relevant for the pursuance of remedies.[17]

From an environmental perspective, the inclusion of environmental protection among the main purposes of a prospective regime on compensation and reparation for transboundary damage represents an important advance compared to the initial ILC's work on liability, which was primarily with the protection and compensation of private victims of transboundary harm. However, the Principles remain limited to 'transboundary' damage, excluding damage to the global commons and areas beyond states' territorial jurisdiction.

The Principles only apply to physical damage caused by activities entailing a foreseeable risk of causing significant transboundary harm.[18] As noted, this would arguably mean that, 'like in the decision on strict liability in the *Cambridge Water* case, there will be no liability where damage could not have been foreseen', thereby leaving some damage uncompensated.[19] In that respect, the ILC should perhaps have better clarified the role of the precautionary principle when assessing whether a certain activity may present a risk to the environment.

Overall, the Principles reflect a cautious, yet pragmatic approach of the ILC in dealing with the highly controversial issue of international environmental liability. By proceeding along the line of private operators' liability, the Principles try to balance between private and public responsibilities and reaffirm some fundamental concepts which should inspire national and international developments in the field of environmental liability. In terms of their scope of application, they are 'general and residuary in character' and are aimed to provide appropriate guidance to States with respect of hazardous activities not already covered by specific agreements.[20] They do not preclude the application of the rules relating to State responsibility in cases where damage arises as a direct consequence of the State's breach of its preventive obligations. As explained by the ILC, 'the attachment of primary liability on the operator, does not in any way absolve the State from discharging its own duties of prevention under international law'.[21]

Albeit not formally binding, the Principles on Allocation of Loss together with the Draft Articles on Prevention contribute to clarify the complex web of questions involved in the topic of international responsibility for environmental harm and to better define the relationship between liability, responsibility and prevention. They reaffirm the interrelation between prevention and reparation, which since the beginning informed the ILC's work on this topic.[22] Like the Articles on Prevention, their material scope of application cover activities entailing a foreseeable risk of transboundary harm, although the factual situation to which they apply is considered from a different angle than in the ILC's work on Prevention.[23] Compared to the law on State responsibility, their value consists in being applicable also where environmental damage is not connected to a wrongful act. However, by focusing on private operators' responsibility, they can also apply to damage occurring from an activity for which the source State did not abide by the preventive duties, thereby complementing the Draft Articles on Prevention. In that respect, they reflect the complementarity between the regime of State responsibility in international law and the existence of civil liability and compensation schemes in domestic law.[24]

3. Response measures and *ex post* prevention in the environmental field: between primary and secondary rules?

The relationship between prevention and reparation underlie the ILC's work in this context. This relationship is already apparent from the functional interplay between the ILC's Draft Articles on Prevention and those on State Responsibility. Prevention, however, is also relevant to the topic of international liability. The Principles on Allocation of Loss come into the picture when preventive measures have been taken but failed to avoid the occurrence of the transboundary damage. Furthermore, the Principles reflect the idea of liability as a system of management of risk. As Barboza noted, 'an operator's knowledge that damages will have to be compensated regardless of fault should make him especially careful in handling a hazardous activity'.[25]

A yet further link between prevention and liability emerges from the concept of prevention *ex post*. This notion includes the additional international obligations of notification, consultation, response action and assistance that arise in the immediate aftermath of an accident which creates an imminent threat of significant environmental damage. This concept is reflected in Principle 5 of the Allocation of Loss Principles, which enumerate the duties of prompt notification, response measures, consultation and assistance. These duties have an '*ex post*' preventive nature in that they arise and become relevant in those situations when the incident creates an imminent threat of such damage, but damage has not yet actually occurred.[26] In that sense, these 'emergency response' obligations can be situated conceptually in-between the primary rules on prevention and the rules and principles on liability. There is also a continuum between the response action obligations envisaged in the Principles and the duties of prompt notification and emergency assistance in the Draft Articles on Prevention, which include the obligation of the source State to adopt contingency plans for responding to emergencies and to undertake measures aimed at containing and minimising the harmful effects of the accident.[27]

More generally, the idea of *ex post* prevention is gradually becoming an integral part of a broad concept of liability. There are relevant developments in several international environmental liability treaties, which usually include in the scope of compensable damage the costs involved in the adoption of certain emergency preventive measures taken in the immediate aftermath of the accident. Of relevance is also the Liability Annex to the Antarctic Treaty, in which the notion itself of liability refers to the obligation to take the necessary and appropriate response measures in case of an environmental emergency. A distinction needs to be made, however, between the '*ex ante*' preventive measures taken before an incident occurs and those that are taken afterwards and in response to it. The first category falls within the scope of the Articles on Prevention, and the associated costs would not be part of the concept of damage for compensation purposes. By contrast, response measures—including both clean-up and preventive (mitigation) measures adopted when damage has not yet materialised—can be compensable, and the relevant costs can be recovered, even if 'the damage has not materialised', 'if there was a "grave and imminent threat of pollution damage" '.[28]

4. Conclusions

Despite the absence of a customary principle of strict State liability for transboundary harm, important developments have been taking place in this sense in domestic law and in international treaties establishing the liability of private operators. The ILC Principles on Allocation of Loss are based on this generalised practice. The multiplicity of sectoral regimes on strict civil liability and their convergence with parallel trends in domestic law may in the long term lead to the consolidation of this idea as a general principle of law in the meaning of Article 38(1)(c) of the ICJ Statute.[29] The Principles may also in the long run contribute to consolidate a general international law standard of prompt and adequate compensation for transboundary environmental damage caused by hazardous activities, where such compensation is to be provided through legal and institutional mechanisms found in the source State's domestic law. Although it is difficult to predict the extent to which these principles may one day translate into binding norms, they certainly retain an important normative value in contributing to shape the further development of international law in this field.

Notes

1 J Crawford, *Brownlie's Principles of Public International Law* (8th ed., OUP 2012) 560.
2 This was a longstanding ILC project, which saw different rapporteurs over the years, aimed to explore the topic of States' international liability for transboundary damage occurring during the operation of lawful activities. See DB Magraw, 'Transboundary Harm: The International Law Commission's Study of "International Liability" ' (1986) 80 American Journal of International Law 305.
3 Article VII of the Treaty on Principles Governing the Activities of States in the Exploration and Use of Outer Space ('Outer Space Treaty') (27 January 1967) 610 UNTS 205. A more significant example is Article II of the Convention on International Liability for Damage Caused by Space Objects ('Space Liability Convention') (29 March 1972; 1 September 1972) 961 UNTS 187, which establishes the absolute liability of the launching state to pay compensation for damage caused by its space object on the surface of the earth or to aircraft in flight.

4 This term is borrowed from P Guttinger, 'Allocation of Responsibility for Harmful Consequences of Acts Not Prohibited by International Law' in J Crawford et al. (eds.), *The Law of International Responsibility* (OUP 2010) 516.
5 See further in Chapter 3 of this book.
6 This aspect of the EU directive is discussed more in detail in Chapter 4, text at nn 123–125.
7 ILC, Report of the Working Group on the Topic of International Liability for Injurious Consequences Arising Out of Acts Not Prohibited by International Law, A/CN.4/L.470, 3 July 1992 (available at https://legal.un.org/ilc/documentation/english/a_cn4_l470.pdf). For an overview and summary of the ILC work on the topic, see International Law Commission, Summaries of the Work of the International Law Commission <https://legal.un.org/ilc/summaries/9.shtml>.
8 ILC, (1977) *Yearbook of the International Law Commission*, Vol. II, Part II, Document A/32/10, para 17: '[b]ecause of the entirely different basis of the liability for risk and the different nature of the rules governing it, as well as its content and the forms it may assume, a joint examination of the two subjects could only make them more difficult to grasp'.
9 I Brownlie, *System of the Law of Nations—State Responsibility—Part I* (Clarendon Press, 1983) 50. See also, MB Akehurst, 'International Liability for Injurious Consequences Arising Out of Acts Not Prohibited by International Law' (1985) Netherlands Yearbook of International Law 3; PM Dupuy, 'The International Law of State Responsibility: Revolution or Evolution?' (1989) 11 Michigan Journal of International Law 105, 113; A. Boyle, 'State Responsibility and International Liability for Injurious Consequences of Acts Not Prohibited by International Law: A Necessary Distinction?' (1990) 39 International and Comparative Law Quarterly 11.
10 A Boyle, 'Globalising Environmental Liability: The Interplay of National and International Law' (2005) 17 Journal of Environmental Law 3, 16.
11 ILC, 'Draft Articles on Prevention of Transboundary Harm from Hazardous Activities', adopted by the International Law Commission at its 53rd Session (2001), Report of the International Law Commission on the work at its fifty-third session, *Official Records of the General Assembly, Fifty-sixth session, Supplement No. 10*, UN Doc. A/56/10 (Draft Principles on Prevention).
12 ILC, 'Draft Principles on the Allocation of Loss in the Case of Transboundary Harm Arising Out of Hazardous Activities', adopted by the ILC at its 58th session and published in Yearbook of the International Law Commission (2006) Vol II, Part II, Report of the Commission to the General Assembly, A/CN.4/SER.A/2006/Add.1 (part 2) (Draft Principles on the Allocation of Loss).
13 PS Rao, 'First Report on the Legal Regime for Allocation of Loss in Case of Transboundary Harm Arising Out of Hazardous Activities', (2003) United Nations General Assembly, Doc. A/CN.4/531, 18–19.
14 C Foster, 'The ILC Draft Principles on the Allocation of Loss in the Case of Transboundary Harm Arising Out of Hazardous Activities: Privatizing Risk (2005) 14 Reciel 3.
15 See Principles 3 and 4.
16 A Boyle, 'Liability for Injurious Consequences of Acts Not Prohibited by International Law' in *The Law of International Responsibility* (n 4) 100. Principle 6(1) reads, 'States shall provide their domestic judicial and administrative bodies with the necessary jurisdiction and competence to ensure that these bodies have prompt, adequate and effective remedies available in the event of transboundary damage caused by hazardous activities located within their territory or otherwise under their jurisdiction or control'.
17 Principle 6(5).
18 Principle 2.
19 Boyle, 'Globalising Environmental Liability' (n 10) 17.
20 Draft Principles on the Allocation of Loss, with Commentary (n 12), 111.
21 Ibid. 113.

22 Commentary to Principle 1, Draft Principles on Allocation of Loss (n 12).
23 Draft Principles on the Allocation of Loss (n 12) 118 [6].
24 Boyle 'Liability for Injurious Consequences of Acts Not Prohibited by International Law' (n 16).
25 J Barboza, *The Environment, Risk and Liability in International Law* (Martinus Nijhoff Publishers 2010) 14.
26 Principle 5 reads: 'upon the occurrence of an incident . . . which *is likely* to result in transboundary damage'.
27 Article 16 and 17 of the ILC's Draft Articles on Prevention.
28 PM Dupuy and J Viñuales, *International Environmental Law* (2nd ed., Cambridge University Press 2018) 323, referring to art I(6)-(7) of the 1992 Protocol amending the International Convention on Civil Liability for Oil Pollution Damage.
29 M Montjoie, 'The Concept of Liability in the Absence of an Internationally Wrongful Act' in *The Law of International Responsibility* (n 4) 512.

3 Civil liability for environmental damage in international treaties

1. Introductory remarks

Starting from the second half of the last century, the intensified use of modern and high-risk technologies and the increasing occurrence of industrial accidents characterised by the presence of transnational elements began to raise the international community's attention on the need to harmonise legal frameworks on liability and reparation across different jurisdictions. It became clear that differences in the substantive and procedural legal frameworks across various legal systems would further accentuate the difficulties for private victims to claim compensation and pursue appropriate redress. Therefore, starting from the 1960s, several international agreements were being negotiated and adopted in specific sectors of hazardous activities with a view to set uniform rules of civil liability and compensation for environmental damage to be implemented in the domestic legal systems of the respective contracting parties. With their main focus on private operators' liability, as opposed to State responsibility, those conventional liability regimes represented an alternative to the shortcomings of pursuing redress via interstate litigation at the international level and a potentially more reliable avenue for private victims of environmental harm compared to the uncertainties characterising the application of State responsibility in the environmental context.

The first international liability conventions were adopted in the fields of nuclear energy[1] and marine oil pollution.[2] Additional liability treaties were adopted in the following decades to cover other sectors of hazardous activities, including the carriage of dangerous goods by different means of transport,[3] the transnational movement of hazardous waste or GMOs, as well as damage caused by certain other industrial activities and technologies.

Overall, including treaties not yet in force and the protocols amending some of the original conventional texts, there around 17 international 'environmental liability' instruments. In general, and with the exception of the Council of Europe's Lugano Convention,[4] which applies horizontally to different types of hazardous activities, these liability treaties tend to follow a sector-specific approach, focusing each on a specific type of hazardous activity or substance, or on a specific type of damage. The liability of private operators is articulated slightly differently in the various regimes, being exclusively channelled to a single person or entity in some

DOI: 10.4324/9781315676708-5

of them (i.e. the registered owner of the ship or the operator of the nuclear installation) or spread out across various operators in others.[5] Provisions on State liability, however, remain exceptional and are usually reserved to ultra-hazardous activities characterised by a substantial degree of governmental involvement, such as in the nuclear sector.[6]

The extent to which environmental concerns are embodied within the scope and objectives of these different instruments varies significantly. A distinction can be made between 'first generation' and 'second generation' liability treaties. The former category includes treaties negotiated and adopted during the 1960s and 1970s in the field of nuclear energy and transport of oil or other hazardous substances. While these treaties have been subsequently revised to encompass the environmental dimension of the damage, they remain primarily oriented at ensuring that appropriate compensation is available to private victims for damage suffered to their property or person. 'Second generation' liability treaties are those conceived after the 1992 Rio Conference on Environment and Development. In this category is the Lugano Convention on Liability for Environmental Damage and various liability regimes established by annexes or protocols to multilateral environmental agreements (MEAs), including the Basel Protocol on Liability and Compensation to the Basel Convention on Transboundary Movement of Hazardous Waste and their Disposal;[7] the Protocol on Civil Liability and Compensation for Damage Caused by the Transboundary Effects of Industrial Accidents on Transboundary Water to the 1992 Convention on the Protection and Use of Transboundary Watercourses and International Lakes and to the 1992 Convention on the Transboundary Effects of Industrial Accidents;[8] the Annex on Liability Arising from Environmental Emergencies to the Madrid Protocol to the Antarctic Treaty;[9] and the Nagoya-Kuala Lumpur Supplementary Protocol on Liability and Redress to the Cartagena Protocol on Biosafety to the Biological Diversity Convention.[10] These more recent liability agreements reveal a greater emphasis on environmental concerns, which is reflected in the specific inclusion of damage to the environment and to natural resources in their scope of application. Moreover, the fact that most of them are annexes or protocols to MEAs reflects an understanding of liability as being not only a tool for allocation of losses and compensation between private parties, but also an integral component of environmental protection strategies.[11]

2. The international liability framework for nuclear damage

2.1. The 1960 Paris and 1963 Vienna Conventions

The elaboration of an international legal framework in the field of liability for damage caused by nuclear activities started at the beginning of the 1960s in a climate of increasing interest in the production and use of nuclear energy for civilian purposes.[12] Three conventions were adopted in this period with a view to create a harmonised regime of civil liability for nuclear damage. The first is the Paris Convention on Third Party Liability in the Field of Nuclear Energy (1960 Paris Convention), adopted in 1960. The Convention was negotiated under the auspices of the Organisation for European Economic Co-operation and Development (OECD) formerly Organization for European Economic Co-operation (OEEC), and open to ratification by OECD States. It was complemented by a Supplementary Convention to the 1960 Paris Convention, adopted in Brussels in 1963 (Brussels Supplementary Convention). Finally, the Vienna Convention on Civil Liability for Nuclear Damage was adopted in 1963 (1963 Vienna Convention), within the framework of the International Atomic Energy Agency (IAEA). Compared to the Paris and Brussels OECD Conventions, the Vienna Convention has a global character and scope of application and is today ratified by several Eastern European States. Together, the Vienna Convention and the Paris-Brussels liability regime form what has often been referred as the 'first generation' of nuclear liability treaties.[13]

These liability conventions responded initially to two main concerns. On the one hand, they were regarded necessary to cope with the wide-range and potentially devastating impacts caused by accidents occurring at a nuclear installation or during transport of nuclear material. On the other hand, their adoption coincided with a time characterised by a prevailing sentiment of optimism in the potential benefits deriving from the civilian use of nuclear energy.[14] They were therefore regarded as a way to protect the then still incipient nuclear industry from financially disrupting compensation claims, thereby indirectly trying to encourage (or at least not discourage) further investments in the nuclear power sector.[15]

The structure of the liability regimes under the two Conventions are very similar and reflect the twin rationales outlined earlier.[16] For one side, they create a common legal framework aimed at facilitating the pursuit of compensation by victims of nuclear damage. This is achieved through a set of general principles which have subsequently become the cornerstone of international nuclear liability law. The first is the idea of exclusive jurisdiction on the courts of the contracting party on which territory the nuclear incident occurred.[17] The rationales behind this are both the need to avoid multiple legal proceedings being brought in different countries and leading to divergent decisions on the same issues, thereby undermining consistency, and a concern for the equitable distribution of compensation among the victims, thereby minimising the possibility that funds available for compensating nuclear damage will be exhausted before all claims are considered.[18] A downside of this solution is that claimants may find it more difficult, and more expensive, to bring the claim abroad. In fact, some authors remarked that a more effective protection for victims would have consisted in the adoption of a system similar to that applied in the European Union under the 1968 Brussels Convention on Jurisdiction and Enforcement of Judgements in Civil and Commercial Matters, whereby it is up to the plaintiff to decide where to sue the defendant.[19]

A second feature is the exclusive liability of the operator of the nuclear installation with the exclusion of other potentially liable parties ('legal channelling'). If the incident occurs during transport of nuclear material to or from the nuclear installation, the liability of the installation operator replaces that of the carrier, who would otherwise be liable under common law. A corollary of this is that the nuclear installation operator can only be liable under the terms of the Conventions, with the exclusion of other possible legal grounds on which their liability can be established. Finally, the operator's liability is absolute, with very limited exceptions in case of armed conflict, hostilities, civil war and insurrections and, unless otherwise provided by the legislation of the relevant contracting State in case of damage caused via a grave natural disaster of exceptional character.[20]

From the perspective of private victims, the channelling of liability combined with its almost absolute nature helps with the smooth identification of the responsible actors and to avoid multiple cross-party claims, thereby reducing costs and facilitating an easier recovery of damages. However, this solution is also part of a regime which seeks to facilitate the development of nuclear energy for civilian use. The exclusive channelling of liability on the installation operator exempts all the other parties involved in the development of nuclear energy, including the suppliers of nuclear material.[21] It also potentially enables a 'concentration of insurance capacity', since other actors are exempted from the need to contract insurance for compensation purposes.[22] Moreover, the absolute nature of operator's liability is counterbalanced by its limitation to a specific amount. Under the 1960 Paris Convention, this limit is set to 15 million special drawing rights (SDRs) for each incident, but contracting parties can establish a greater or lesser amount by domestic law, provided that it does not fall below the minimum of 5 million SDRs.[23] The 1963 Vienna Convention does not indicate a maximum liability cap, but it allows States Parties to place a limit on the operator's liability, which cannot be less than US$ 5 million for any nuclear incident. States are also free to impose unlimited liability on the operator. However, very few States have opted for this option, probably because—unless this liability can be covered through public funding—it is usually very difficult to obtain unlimited coverage under insurance.[24] Both Paris and Vienna Conventions require the nuclear installation operator to seek financial security coverage (through either insurance or other forms of financial guarantee as specified by domestic) up to the amount of the liability limit set under the Convention, or under the domestic law of the installation State.[25] The time limit to bring compensation claims under the 1960/63 nuclear liability Conventions is ten years.

Both Paris and Vienna Conventions cover nuclear damage caused by the occurrence of a nuclear incident in a nuclear installation or in the course of transport of nuclear material to or from a nuclear installation.[26] 'Nuclear installations' are defined in broad terms, including reactors and reprocessing, manufacturing or storage facilities, where nuclear fuel, nuclear material and radioactive products are used or reproduced. Territorially, the 1960 Paris Convention expressly excludes from its application incidents occurred, or damage suffered in, the territory of a non-contracting state, unless so provided by the legislation of the contracting State where the installation is located. The 1963 Vienna Convention does not mention this exclusion, thereby implicitly leaving open the possibility to apply also to nuclear damage originating in the territory of a contracting party but suffered by victims resident in a non-party state.[27] Finally, both Vienna and Paris Conventions define nuclear damage narrowly and limitedly to traditional forms of damage (loss of life, personal injury and damage to property), without any references to the possible environmental consequences of the accident.

Both Conventions are in force. The 1960 Paris Convention has 17 European States Parties,[28] some of which host nuclear facilities. The 1963 Vienna Convention comprises 44 States Parties including several States in Central and Eastern Europe[29] and since May 2005 also the Russian Federation.

2.2. The role of the state in the nuclear liability regime

2.2.1. State liability under the 1963 Vienna and 1960 Paris Conventions

A unique feature of the international nuclear liability regime, which implicitly reflects the underlying aim of promoting the nuclear industry,[30] is the coexistence of private operator's liability with supplementary financial guarantees covered by public funds from the installation State. This approach was first introduced under the 1960 Paris Convention, where the additional public financed guarantee was implemented through the 1963 Brussels Supplementary Convention, putting in place a three-layered system of compensation. The first layer consists in the liability of the operator under the 1960 Paris Convention, currently set up to a maximum of 15 million SDRs and guaranteed, up to this amount, by mandatory insurance or other compulsory financial security. To this, the 1963 Brussels Convention establishes two additional layers: one formed by public funds of the territorial State of the nuclear installation, which guarantee compensation up to an amount of 175 million SDRs;[31] and a third layer formed by a fund collectively financed by all the contracting parties to the Supplementary Convention in proportion to their relative gross national product and the relative amounts of thermal power produced by nuclear reactors. This will cover the eventually exceeding amount up to the limit of 300 million SDR.[32]

Unlike the Paris-Brussels regime, the 1963 Vienna Convention did not originally include a second layer of state-funded liability. It did envisage, however, a sort of supplementary and residual State liability in Article VII.1 whereby

> the Installation State shall ensure the payment of claims for compensation for nuclear damage which have been established against the operator by providing the necessary funds to the extent that the yield of insurance or other financial security is inadequate to satisfy such claims, but not in excess of the limit, if any, established pursuant to article V

(i.e. USD 5 million for any one nuclear incident). Therefore, in case where the financial guarantor is bankrupt, or in the hypothesis where the operator's liability is unlimited or set for a higher amount than the amount of financial security, the Convention envisages the intervention by the installation State, albeit only up to USD 5 million.[33] Article VII.2 of the Vienna Convention provides for the case in which the State itself is the operator, in which case the State has to ensure the payment of compensation up to the relevant limit set for nuclear operators' liability.

It is worth mentioning here that a further example of State-funded compensation for nuclear damage can be found in the more recent Supplementary Compensation Convention (CSC), which will be examined in more detail in the following sections.

2.3. Revising and enhancing the international nuclear liability regime

2.3.1. The 1988 linking protocol

The Chernobyl disaster awoke dramatically the international community to the potential disastrous consequences of nuclear accidents for both private victims and the environment.[34] It also highlighted the limitations of the original nuclear liability regimes, raising the need for their substantial revision. A first, albeit modest, step in this direction was the adoption of the 1988 Joint Protocol linking together the 1960 Paris and the 1963 Vienna Conventions with a view to extend their respective geographical coverage by providing reciprocal benefits to the parties to either Convention.[35] Countries that ratify the Joint Protocol are considered as being parties to both conventions, with benefits in terms of access to compensation for their respective nationals. In practice, the effectiveness of this Protocol depends on the number of States Parties and its ratification by nuclear power countries.

More important reforms of the international nuclear liability regime were, however, introduced in 1997 with the adoption, under the auspices of the IAEA, of two international instruments, namely[36] the Protocol amending the 1963 Vienna Convention (1997 Protocol),[37] and the aforementioned Convention on Supplementary Compensation for Nuclear Damage (CSC). A few years later, the OECD undertook similar efforts of revision, which led to the adoption in 2004 of an Amending Protocol to the 1960 Paris Convention (2004 Paris Protocol)[38] and to corresponding amendments to the Brussels Supplementary Convention with respect to the relevant limits of liability and the compensation available.[39]

2.3.2. The 1997 Vienna amending protocol

The 1997 Protocol makes a number of significant changes to the 1963 regime, revealing 'a shift in the nuclear liability policy towards general protection of the public against nuclear damage'.[40] It increases the permitted limit of operators' liability from USD 5 million to no less than 300 million SDRs per incident, albeit with the option for the State party to finance up to 150 million of this amount from public funds—thereby limiting the operator's liability up to 150 million SDRs. The Protocol keeps the possibility for the State to set unlimited liability of the operator, but in these cases, there is a requirement for the operator to maintain a financial security of at least 300 million SDRs. It also extends from 10 to 30 years the period to bring claims for death or personal injury.

From an environmental perspective, the most significant amendment is the wider scope of compensable damage, which now expressly includes damage to the environment, albeit limitedly to the costs of measures for reinstatement which have been actually taken or are to be taken, and the costs of preventive measures and further loss or damage caused by such measures.[41] This notion of environmental damage is based on similar solutions adopted under other international conventions, especially in the field of marine pollution, with which it shares the rationale of limiting compensation to those aspects of environmental damage which are capable of monetary evaluation. The revised notion of compensable damage also includes compensation for economic losses (*lucrum cessans*) arising from the nuclear incident, and these also encompass 'losses of income deriving from an economic interest in any use or enjoyment of the environment, incurred as a result of a significant impairment of that environment'.[42] These types of economic losses are often labelled in tort law as 'pure economic losses', as they are not related to any property damage or personal injury but are suffered by the individuals as a result from the impairment of a natural resource. Moreover, both the definition of nuclear damage and that of nuclear incident have been revised to make clear that the Protocol applies even in the case of a '*grave and imminent threat* of causing [nuclear] damage'[43] (i.e. in the absence of an actual release of radiation) to provide compensation for preventive measures aimed at responding and minimising the damage. However, compensation for the costs of measures of reinstatement of impaired environment and for the costs of preventive measures and economic losses is envisaged only 'to the extent determined by the law of the competent court'.[44] This wording is the result of a compromise reached during the negotiations of the 1997 Protocol with a view to mediate disagreements arising from different conceptions of national tort law with respect to compensation for economic losses and environmental damage, while at the same time maintaining a priority for compensation for personal injury and damage to property.[45]

The 1997 Protocol explicitly clarifies that the Convention applies to nuclear damage 'wherever suffered'.[46] It therefore extends its benefits also to victims in non-contracting States. From a policy perspective, this approach can be seen in line with the principles of non-discrimination and equal access and, especially when damage affects a State that has not itself implemented nuclear energy power, it is in line with fundamental considerations of fairness and justice. A potential drawback of such extension is that adding further claimants from non-contracting States will reduce the share available for those victims in States Parties. To address these concerns, the 1997 Protocol allows contracting parties to exclude from such extension those States that, albeit hosting power installations, do not afford equivalent reciprocal benefits.[47]

At the time of writing, the 1997 Protocol has 24 signatories and 15 ratifications,[48] of which only Argentina has a nuclear reactor. As to its relationship with the 1963 Convention, the two treaties are conceived as two distinct legal instruments independent of each other.[49] This means that any State may accede to the 1997 Protocol even if it is not already a party to the 1963 Convention. As between the States Parties to the Protocol, the Vienna Convention and the Protocol are read and applied together as a single text, which may be referred to as the 1997 Vienna Convention on Civil Liability for Nuclear Damage. For the States Parties to the 1963 Convention, which have not (yet) ratified or acceded to the Protocol, the 1963 Convention will continue to exist and apply until it is terminated.

2.3.3. The 1997 Convention on Supplementary Compensation (CSC)

The Convention on Supplementary Compensation for Nuclear Damage[50] was adopted in 1997 under the auspices of the IAEA as a free-standing instrument,[51] which is open not only to States that are already parties to either the Vienna or the Paris nuclear liability regimes, but also to any country, provided that their national legislation is consistent with the uniform principles on nuclear civil liability laid down in its Annex. Being open to all States, the CSC sets itself as a truly global instrument. It is regarded as an opportunity to develop a harmonised global liability regime in the field of nuclear damage through the alignment of States' domestic legislation to a minimum set of basic nuclear liability principles, without requiring accession to either the Paris or the Vienna regime.[52]

In line with this global aspiration, the CSC sets up an enhanced system of compensation for nuclear damage, which seeks to extend the amount of compensation available beyond that provided by the Vienna and Paris Conventions or by national law for those States who are not parties to either international nuclear liability regime. This enhanced compensation framework was also aimed at attracting the adherence by those non-nuclear countries which had so far been unwilling to join the Paris or the Vienna regimes, as they perceived them as too biased in favour of the nuclear industry and not sufficiently focused on the concerns of those who might instead suffer nuclear damage in the event of an incident.[53]

The solution envisaged under the CSC consists in a two-tier compensation system combining private operators' and States' contributions similar to that of the 1963 Brussels Supplementary Protocol. The first tier of compensation corresponds to the requirement (Article III(1)(a)(i)) that the installation State (i.e. the State on which territory the nuclear installation is situated) shall ensure funds available for a minimum amount of 300 million SDRs. Liability is primarily, and exclusively, placed on the operator. However, to the extent that funds from the liable operator are insufficient, the CSC requires the installation State to make public funds available to cover the difference. For compensation claims exceeding the 300 million SDRs amount, the CSC provides for a second-tier of compensation achieved through an international fund to which contracting parties contribute according to their installed nuclear capacity and on the ratio of their contribution to the United Nations budget. The amount overall available under this international fund is not fixed and depends on the adherence of States and the extent to which these include nuclear power generating states. This international fund supplements the amount of compensation available under national law and is to be used only to the extent that national funds are inadequate. Moreover, Article XI provides that 50% of the funds shall be available to compensate claims for nuclear damage suffered in the territory of the contracting parties, inside or outside the Installation State; whereas the other 50% of the funds shall be available to compensate claims for damage suffered in contracting parties outside the installation State. This explicit consideration of transnational damage may represent a further incentive for non-nuclear States sharing borders with countries hosting nuclear reactors to ratify the CSC.

Some scholars see the involvement of the State in bearing supplementary responsibility in the event of operator's insolvency and/or insufficient financial security under the Brussels Supplementary Convention and the more recent 1997 CSC as one rare example of implicit acceptance of State liability,[54] albeit of a different nature from the kind of strict State liability established under the Space

Liability Convention, whereby the State is the primary liable subject. This financial intervention of the State is a feature almost unique to the nuclear liability regimes and can be interpreted as indicating an implicit acknowledgment of the existence of a residual responsibility of States to compensate for damage caused by nuclear activities where the operator is unable to do so, or where the installation is owned by the State. This rather unique feature reflects the international community's underlying perception of the particularly hazardous nature of nuclear industrial activities and awareness of the devastating effects of accidents. It also reflects the delicate balance between powerful economic actors in the nuclear industry. At the time when these international conventions were negotiated, it became clear that a system merely based on the civil liability of the operator would be inadequate to compensate victims of major nuclear accidents;[55] there was also a concern that further raising the private operators' liability would have severely hampered the possibility to obtain appropriate insurance coverage.[56] Therefore, supplementing the operator's financial liability by public funds was a solution which in part aimed at overcoming these problems, while at the same time making the regime more acceptable for suppliers.[57] On the other hand, when examined from a polluter pays principle perspective, this subsidisation of nuclear liability by means of public fund is questionable. This is particularly the case when combined (as in fact it is under the international regime) with the 'implicit subsidy' created by the placing of a financial cap on the operator's liability, and with the exclusive channelling of liability to nuclear operators, which in practice limits the incentives for other parties to take further preventive measures.[58]

In terms of its substantive provisions and scope of application, the CSC mirrors the 1997 Protocol regarding the definition of nuclear damage, which includes damage resulting from environmental impairment, and the territorial scope of application. Moreover, like the Vienna and Paris Conventions, the CSC adopts the principle of exclusive jurisdiction of the courts of the country where the incident occurs.

The CSC also includes an Annex outlining a list of principles to which any contracting party which is not also a party to either the Vienna or the Paris nuclear liability regime shall adhere. In so doing, it effectively lays down a set of general principles of nuclear liability law. These include, among others: (i) the operator's absolute liability for nuclear damage, with very few exceptions and with the clause, however, that 'the operator shall incur no liability for damage caused by a nuclear incident outside the provisions of national law in accordance with this Convention'; (ii) the possibility to limit the nuclear operator's liability to no less than 300 million SDRs or no less than 150 million SDRs provided that up to 300 million SDRs are made available by the State through public funds; (iii) the operator's requirement to have financial security or insurance covering his liability in the amount specified by the Installation State, complemented by the State's duty to ensure the payments of compensation claims to the extent that such financial security are inadequate.

The CSC entered into force on 15 April 2015, with the number of ratifications growing particularly during 2015–2017, possibly as a result of Fukushima's dramatic reminder of nuclear risk. At the time of writing, it has 22 signatories and

11 ratifications[59] accounting for almost 50% of the operable nuclear reactors in the world,[60] and it is so far the only international nuclear liability treaty that has also attracted ratification by major nuclear powers such as Japan and the United States.[61] Yet, the price paid for the attempt to attract a greater number of States, including nuclear power States and the US, has been a greater flexibility and margin of discretion left to contracting parties in implementing the Convention into their national law, provided that the first-tier liability limit and the main principles set out in the Annex are respected. By way of exception, the United States was permitted to ratify the Convention without amending its national law—the 1957 Price-Anderson Act—which provides for a different criterion of liability attribution based on economic rather than legal channelling. In terms of its impact, the CSC has led, in some cases, to reform of existing legislation towards a more protective framework in favour of victim compensation.[62]

2.3.4. The 2004 protocols amending the Paris and Brussels Conventions

Two Protocols amending the 1960 Paris Convention and the 1963 Brussels Supplementary Convention were adopted in 2004 with a view to improving the position of the victims and enhancing the compatibility of the OECD regime with the IAEA nuclear liability framework.[63] Like the 1997 Protocol amending the Vienna Convention, the 2004 Protocol to the 1960 Paris Convention amended the definition of 'nuclear damage' to include in the scope of compensation certain consequential economic losses and environmental damage in the form of the reasonable costs of measures to reinstate significant environmental impairment. It also explicitly included preventive measures taken after a nuclear accident or even after an event that creates a serious and imminent threat of nuclear damage. Like in the 1997 Protocol, those heads of damage are compensable 'to the extent determined by the law of the competent court'.[64] The 2004 Protocol also extended to 30 years the limitation period to bring claims and expanded its territorial scope to include damage suffered in a non-contracting state, provided that the latter is either a party to the Vienna Convention or the Joint Protocol, or does not have nuclear installation in its territory, or it has in place nuclear legislation affording equivalent reciprocal benefits.

A major improvement introduced by the 2004 Protocol is the increase of operator's liability which is now raised to a *minimum* amount of no less 700 million euros, although it allows contracting parties to fix lower amounts of liability for low-risk nuclear installations and carriages of nuclear substances, provided that these are, respectively, no less than EUR 70 million and EUR 80 million. Like under the 1960 Paris Convention, the operators are required to financially secure their liability for an equivalent amount, but the 2004 Protocol also requires contracting parties to ensure the payment of nuclear damage, up to the liability amount specified in the Convention, where the operator's insurance is unavailable or insufficient. The 2004 Protocol also allows national legislation establishing unlimited operator's liability provided that there is a financial security guarantee of at least 700 million euros. However, acknowledging that insurance or other financial security may not be readily available in the short term to cover the full extent of the increased liability, the Protocol requires States to provide the necessary funds to cover compensation claims for nuclear damage to the extent that this is not satisfied by other financial security.[65]

The increased amount of liability under the 1960 Paris Convention has entailed a corresponding revision of the Brussels Supplementary Convention, which has been amended to increase the installation State's contribution up to € 500 million, and the joint contracting States funds up to € 300 million.[66] Therefore, with the forthcoming entry into force of these revisions, the overall amount of compensation available to victims of a nuclear incident will be not less than € 1.5 billion.

The entry into force of the Protocols is subject to the ratification by two-thirds of the contracting parties to the Paris Convention and by all the contracting parties to the Brussels Supplementary Convention. The ratification process initially proceeded slowly, partly because most contracting parties are also EU Member States and there was a European Commission's decision requiring them to deposit simultaneously their instruments of ratification or accession.[67] Nevertheless, the existence of the EU's exclusive competence on areas covered by these international agreements and the EU's support for Member States' ratification and/or accession to the revised nuclear liability protocols arguably contributed to enhance the prospects of their entry into force.[68] Indeed, the two protocols to the 1960 Paris and 1963 Brussels Conventions eventually entered into force in January 2022.[69]

2.4. The international nuclear liability framework: an assessment

The negotiation and adoption of different international agreements aimed at harmonising the legal framework on liability and compensation for nuclear damage bear witness to the international community's efforts to address the devastating societal, human and financial consequences of nuclear accidents. The comparative analysis of the different regimes allows identifying a few common principles that can be considered as the main features of a sort of 'global' nuclear liability law and that can represent a blueprint for the development of domestic legislation in the field. Most of these principles are now resumed in the CSC. From an environmental law perspective, the amendments introduced by the Protocols to the 1960 and 1963 Paris and Vienna liability regimes demonstrate a discernible trend towards the formal inclusion of environmental impairment and damage to natural resources within the scope of compensable damage, albeit only within the limit of the costs of reasonable measures of reinstatement and to the extent determined by the law of the competent court.

In terms of the widespread coverage of the nuclear liability framework, the recent entry into force of the 2004 revisions to the 1960 Paris liability framework is a promising step forward. Outside Europe, several States hosting nuclear power installations, such as the United States, India, Japan and the United Arab Emirates, have ratified the CSC which is now in force. Yet, there are still very few contracting parties to the Vienna revised protocol, and these do not include nuclear power countries such as South Korea and China. This means that should a nuclear incident happen in an installation on South Korean or Chinese territory, victims in neighbouring countries will not be covered by any of the international regimes.

As far as Europe is concerned, the existence of eight distinct nuclear liability frameworks has *de facto* created a patchwork of conventions potentially applicable in Europe. This in turn may bring uncertainty as to which countries have ratified which treaty and what type of provisions actually apply to a given accident, particularly in case of transfrontier damage.[70] For example, Russia is a party to the 1963 Vienna Convention, but it has not ratified the revised 1997 Protocol, nor is it a party to the Paris regime or the Joint Protocol. The partial and differentiated geographical coverage of the international nuclear liability regimes also creates uncertainty for victims and for the nuclear industry with respect to the applicable framework. Moreover, apart from the substantial increase in compensation achieved in the Paris regime through the 2004 Paris Protocol, both the 1997 Vienna Protocol and in the CSC provide more modest amounts, especially when these are assessed in the light of the potential catastrophic consequences of a nuclear accident.

At a substantive level, the international nuclear liability regime attracted criticism in terms of the approach to the allocation of risks and burdens. It was argued that the limitation of operators' liability (which translates into a decreased amount of insurance premiums) and the supplementary funding provided by the States amount in practice to a public subsidy for the nuclear industry.[71] These limitations of operators' liability, and the exclusion of other actors in the nuclear industry from the liability regime, seem to run against the idea of a full internalisation of costs under the polluter pays principle and risk undermining the preventive impact of liability, leading operators of nuclear facilities to low investments in prevention.[72] Criticism was also directed at the strong financial State intervention in the liability regime, especially given the changed circumstances and societal attitude towards acceptance of the relevant risks involved in the operation of nuclear power installations compared to the 1960s.

From a normative perspective, however, the main features of the Vienna and Paris Conventions have recently inspired the development of a broader series of Principles of Conducts agreed by major vendor companies and exporters of civilian nuclear power plants.[73] These Principles of Conduct agreed by the Nuclear Power Plant Exporters aim to enhance the national and international legal framework by reaffirming and consolidating best practices in the field of nuclear law and governance. They touch on different aspects, including safety, security, non-proliferation and environmental protection. While these principles are in the form of voluntary guidelines or codes of conduct agreed by private actors, they will arguably have a normative impact in buttressing the main features of the international nuclear liability framework, thereby potentially contributing towards its consolidation, widespread acceptance and globalisation.

3. International civil liability regimes for sea pollution damage

3.1. The 1969 civil liability convention and the 1971 fund convention

The maritime transport of dangerous goods was one of the first sectors of hazardous activities for which issues of liability have been regulated by international treaties. The earliest liability conventions in this field are the 1969 International

Convention on Civil Liability for Oil Pollution Damage ('1969 CLC'), subsequently complemented by the 1971 International Convention on the Establishment of an International Fund for Compensation for Oil Pollution Damage ('1971 Fund Convention'). They apply to damage caused by maritime transport of oil and were negotiated and adopted under the aegis of the International Maritime Organization (IMO), following the severe oil spill from the tanker *Torrey Canyon* in 1967, which caused unprecedented environmental damage to the British coastline and highlighted the importance of having in place an appropriate liability and compensation framework.[74] At that time, the only global instrument dealing with the issue of liability for damage caused during the navigation of sea-going vessels was the 1957 International Convention Relating to the Limitation of the Liability of Owners of Seagoing Ships,[75] which established a fault-based regime of shipowner's liability, limiting it to an amount determined according to the tonnage of the ship. With the *Torrey Canyon* disaster, it became clear that the existing framework was inappropriate to cope with the important costs of clean-up entailed by major instances of marine oil pollution. Moreover, an international oil pollution liability regime was regarded as necessary in the light of the global character of the shipping industry and from the perspective of potential victims, which would otherwise receive different levels of compensation depending on the applicable domestic law.

The 1969 CLC applies to oil pollution damage caused by ships carrying oil in bulk as cargo, when damage is suffered in the territory, including the territorial sea, of a contracting State.[76] The place where damage occurs is the main criterion to determine the scope of application of the convention *ratione territori*, thereby rendering the flag State, the nationality of the ship or the place where the incident occurred irrelevant in this respect. Liability is strict and is 'channelled' onto the registered owner of the ship transporting the oil at the time of the incident which caused the damage.[77] Similarly to the nuclear liability regimes, the CLC contains procedural rules on the competent court and the recognition and enforcement of judicial decisions aimed at improving the situation of potential victims of transnational oil pollution damage when claiming compensation.

During the negotiations leading to the adoption of the 1969 CLC, one of the major challenges was to reconcile the position of coastal States, concerned with the high costs of clean-up and restoration of oil pollution damage and generally favourable to strict liability, with the reluctance of shipping industries and States owning major tanker fleets towards a prospective hardening of the applicable liability rules.[78] In that context, limited liability appeared as the necessary political compromise to encourage maritime States to ratify the Convention and to make the idea of strict liability acceptable to the maritime transport sector. Thus, the 1969 CLC limits shipowner's liability, calculated using as a unit of account the special drawing rights, according to the size of the vessel (i.e. 133 SDRs for each ton of the ship's tonnage, up to a maximum ceiling of 14 million SDRs). However, the shipowner cannot limit their liability if the incident resulted from their personal fault or intention. Furthermore, to ensure financial guarantee against a possible shipowner insolvency, the 1969 CLC requires mandatory insurance (Limitation Fund) for an amount equivalent to the shipowner liability for vessels carrying more than 2,000 tons of oil cargo.[79]

The CLC entered into force in 1975[80] and was complemented by the 1971 Fund Convention establishing the International Fund for Compensation for Oil Pollution Damage (1971 IOPC Fund), which provides an additional layer of compensation financed by the oil industry for those cases where compensation under the 1969 Convention does not suffice. Under the 1971 Fund Convention, the amount of supplementary compensation available was initially up to a limit of 30 million SDRs.

3.2. The 1992 revision protocols of the oil pollution liability framework

The 1969 CLC represented a significant first step in the development of an international liability regime for marine pollution damage. Yet, its practical application over the years revealed some major shortcomings related to the low level of compensation available compared to the high costs suffered by the victims of oil pollution damage and by public authorities for clean-up. Moreover, the definition of compensable damage under the 1969 CLC appeared too generic and open-ended. Article 1(6) defined 'pollution damage' as 'loss or damage caused outside the ship carrying oil by contamination resulting from the escape or discharge of oil from the ship, wherever such escape or discharge may occur, and includes the costs of preventive measures and further loss or damage caused by preventive measures'. This wording left the door open for conflicting interpretations by domestic courts in different contracting parties, thereby undermining the objective of establishing uniform criteria for the compensation of oil pollution victims.

A substantial revision of the 1969 CLC was therefore agreed among the contracting States, leading to the adoption of the 1992 Protocol to the Civil Liability Convention.[81] The 1992 Protocol does not simply amend the 1969 CLC, but it creates a new Convention ('1992 CLC') which is intended to eventually replace the 1969 CLC through a mechanism of compulsory denunciation of the 'old' regime by the States Parties that ratify the 1992 Protocol.[82]

The 1992 CLC maintains the basic structure of the 1969 CLC but includes important amendments to better define its scope of application and to strengthen the protection of oil pollution victims. First, to respond to coastal states' concerns regarding the protection and preservation of the marine environment in their respective EEZs,[83] the territorial scope of application is expanded to include damage occurring in the exclusive economic zone (EEZ) of the States Parties, as established under the UNCLOS.[84] The definitions of 'incident' and of 'preventive measures' have been revised to include, in addition to measures taken to minimise damage after an oil spill has taken place, also those undertaken in the immediate aftermath of an incident even if no oil spills occurred, provided that there was a grave and imminent danger of pollution damage.[85] Correspondingly, 'incident' is defined as 'any occurrence or series of occurrences having the same origin, which causes pollution damage or creates a grave and imminent threat of causing such damage'.[86] These amendments reflect the emerging understanding that liability should also apply to response and mitigation measures necessary to prevent damage in situations where the damage has not yet fully materialised but there is a serious and imminent threat thereof. Thus, although the primary goal of the liability regime remains that of offering adequate compensation for losses caused by oil pollution damage, there was also a view that the new liability regime could as well provide incentives for taking the necessary measures to prevent the damage.[87]

3.3. The definition of oil pollution damage

The two most significant amendments concerned the definition of pollution damage and the financial amount of compensation available. As to the first aspect, there were extensive discussions as to whether damage to the environment and to natural resources was to be included in the scope of compensable damage.[88] The general definition of 'pollution damage' in the 1969 CLC had been in the past interpreted by some contracting parties and national courts to encompass pure ecological damage to marine resources. This raised the fear that domestic courts could unilaterally reach different outcomes, thereby leading to a discordant application of the Convention in the States Parties and to different decisions in similar cases. A further concern was that an over-extensive definition of environmental damage might give rise to excessive or disproportionate claims which would disrupt the functioning of the compensation mechanism.[89] To avoid this, the IOPC Fund[90] had consistently rejected compensation claims for ecological damage under the 1969 CLC as well as other economic losses when such damage was not readily quantifiable in economic and monetary terms, or where the amount of compensation claimed was calculated on the basis of abstract or mathematical methods.[91]

To address this problem, the 1992 CLC revised the definition of pollution damage which now includes

> loss or damage caused outside the ship by contamination, resulting from the escape or discharge of oil from ship, wherever such escape or discharge may occur, provided that *compensation for impairment of the environment other than loss of profit from such impairment shall be limited to costs of reasonable measures of reinstatement actually undertaken or to be undertaken*.[92]

The explicit reference to environmental impairment in the new provision confirms the admissibility of this type of damage. However, it also incorporates the IOPC Fund's stance rejecting compensation for the non-quantifiable aspects of environmental harm. Therefore, compensation for this type of damage is limited to quantifiable economic losses sustained in connection with restoration measures. Damage that is not concretely quantifiable in economic terms as well as hypothetical assessments of environmental damage are instead excluded.[93] This formula embodies a pragmatic approach which addresses concerns about the damaged environment, but overall sidesteps the delicate problem of natural resource evaluation. Seen from an environmental perspective, the new definition of compensable damage leaves out the cases of irreparable damage and all the cases where reasonable measures of restoration are not enough to repair effectively the harm suffered by the marine or coastal environment. As such, this solution attracted criticisms[94] and is arguably inconsistent with the effective implementation of the polluter pays principle.[95] Be that as it may, the 1992 CLC's approach to the definition of environmental damage exerted significant influence on how this concept has been defined in subsequent liability regimes.[96]

The 1992 CLC also admits claims for pure economic losses, although it leaves to national courts the task of reasonably delimiting compensation for those type of losses.[97] 'Pure economic losses' include the pure (i.e. not connected to the contamination of claimant's property) economic damage suffered as a result of the incident, such as the economic losses arising for individuals as a result of the contamination and impairment of public natural resources. In many domestic systems, the admissibility of these types of claims clashes with traditional tort law principles limiting compensation to damage connected to a defined and recognised legal right (such as a property right on land). According to the IOPC Fund's established practice, compensation claims for the economic losses suffered by those who depend directly on earnings from coastal or sea-related activities (i.e. fishermen, hoteliers and restaurateurs at seaside resorts, operators of beach facilities located along the coasts, etc.) are admissible, provided that the loss is causally and directly linked to the oil contamination.[98]

3.4. Revising the amount of compensation

The other important aspect of the CLC revision concerned the amount of compensation available. This was initially increased up to 59.7 million SDRs, and subsequently to 89.77 million SDRs through an amendment to the 1992 CLC Protocol adopted in 2000 in the aftermath of the *Erika*'s oil tanker disaster and aimed at raising the liability available by 50%.[99]

These increases, however, were counterbalanced by an enhancement of the shipowners' right to limit their liability and an extension to the range of subjects excluded from the application of the liability regime. Under the 1992 CLC, the shipowner's right to limits its liability can only be lifted upon proof that the 'damage resulted from his personal act or omission, committed with the intent to cause such damage, or recklessly and with knowledge that such damage would probably result'.[100] This aspect was the subject of criticism at the EU level, particularly by the European Commission, which regarded it as undermining the effectiveness of the oil pollution compensation regime.[101] The 1992 CLC also widened the range of subjects exempted from liability to include, besides the servants and agents of the owner, also the pilot and other persons performing services for the ship, the charterer and manager of the ship as well as their servants or agents, and any persons performing salvage operations with the consent of the owner or upon instruction of a competent public authority, and persons taking preventive measures. These subjects, however, lose their exemption from liability if damage results from their personal act or omission committed recklessly or intentionally with the knowledge that such damage would probably result.[102]

3.5. The International Oil Pollution Compensation (IOPC) Fund

The IOPC Fund was established with the aim of providing an additional layer of compensation for victims of oil pollution in case compensation under the CLC is insufficient for various reasons, such as if the shipowner is not liable or is incapable of meeting in full his obligations under the Convention or its insurance is insufficient to satisfy such claims; or if the amount of damage exceeds the limits of shipowner's liability.[103] If the total amount of claims exceeds the amount of compensation available, the compensation payable to each claimant would be reduced proportionately, in accordance with the principle of equal treatment among the various claimants. Compensation under the IOPC Fund is financed by the oil industry through annual contributions required from any subject in a Contracting State (including government authorities, State-owned companies and private companies) who receives more than 150,000 metric tonnes of oil in any calendar year. These oil-receiving subjects are obliged to pay to the Fund a levy calculated according to their national share of international oil receipts.

The creation of the IOPC Fund responds, thus, to a double rationale. It aims, on the one hand, at strengthening the international liability regime by providing a further layer of compensation and facilitating a quick and smooth processing of the relevant claims, including by offering to the victims the possibility to settle their claims out of court and avoid lengthy and often cumbersome judicial proceedings. Although, there often remain instances where extrajudicial settlement through the IOPC Fund is not feasible, for example because controversies arise on the amount of compensation, and the matter is brought before the domestic courts of the State where the damage occurred.

On the other hand, by allocating part of financial burden of liability on the oil processing industry, it represented a way to reconcile the opposing interests of the various States and stakeholders. Indeed, during the negotiations for the establishment of the oil pollution liability regime, the creation of the IOPC Fund was crucial in offering a solution reconciling opposing stances and in overcoming a potential stumbling block among negotiating parties.[104] The first IOPC Fund was established under the 1971 Fund Convention. The1992 Protocol to the International Convention on the Establishment of an IOPC Fund (1992 Fund Protocol) established the 1992 IOPC Fund and increased the amount of supplementary compensation available to 135 million SDRs.[105]

The IOPC Fund is competent for administering compensation claims under the CLC and deciding over their admissibility[106] and has had a central role in the definition of a clear and consistent policy regarding the admissibility of various types of claims under the system. Both the Assembly and the Executive Committee of the IOPC Fund always strived to maintain the uniform interpretation and application of the liability regime in order to ensure the proper functioning of the compensation system and the equal treatment of claimants in different States Parties. Instrumental to this have been the resolutions and decisions adopted by the IOPC Fund Assembly and by the Executive Committee on the interpretation of the provisions of the CLC and Fund Conventions. While not formally binding, these resolutions and decisions express the opinion of contracting parties' governments, acting through their representatives in the Assembly[107] and, as such, they could be arguably regarded as providing an authoritative interpretation of the conventional texts in line with Article 31 the 1969 Vienna Convention on the Law of the Treaties.[108]

3.6. The 2003 Supplementary Fund

The massive environmental and economic damage provoked by certain catastrophic accidents, like those that in the past involved the *Erika* and *Prestige* tankers, and the changing patterns and intensity of maritime carriage by sea combined with growing public perception of the relevant environmental risks, prompted calls for further increases in the amount of compensation available under the CLC and Fund system.[109] Therefore, a Protocol Establishing a Supplementary Fund for Oil Pollution Damage was adopted in 2003 (Supplementary Fund Protocol).[110] This Protocol, the scope of application of which coincides with that of the 1992 CLC and Fund Conventions, creates a supplementary Fund providing an additional tier of compensation for victims of pollution accidents, to be financed by means of annual contributions by oil receivers of amounts exceeding the 150,000 tons. With the setting up and entry into force of the 2003 Supplementary Fund, it is estimated that an additional amount of 750 million SDRs (approximately USD 1 billion) is available in compensation, thereby enabling redress, at least in principle, for almost every case of marine pollution.[111] This should then encourage claimants to rely more on the international liability regime instead of seeking alternative avenues in the foreign jurisdiction of non-contracting parties, and may eventually reduce resorts by claimants to contentious domestic court proceedings.

A fundamental input towards the establishment of the 2003 Supplementary Fund came from pressure from the EU, which had proposed the establishment of a European Supplementary Fund for Compensation for Oil Pollution Damage (COPE Fund) with a ceiling of EUR 1 billion.[112] As almost all EU Member States were also parties to the international oil pollution regime, the prospect of an autonomous EU fund raised concern in the IOPC Fund, which saw it as a threat to the uniform application of the compensation system in contracting parties. This is an example in which a regional initiative triggered or at least sped up moves for the enhancement of the international regime through the prompt establishment of the Supplementary Fund.[113]

3.7. Oil pollution liability treaties in a multilevel context

The 1992 CLC and Fund Convention establish an integrated international legal framework of liability and compensation for damage caused by oil pollution at sea and significantly contributed to improving the situation of oil spill victims. There currently are 141 States Parties to the 1992 Civil Liability and 118 to the 1992 Fund Protocol, whereas 32 States are contracting parties to the 2003 Supplementary Fund Protocol.[114] This is an impressive achievement for an international liability regime if one considers the general reluctance of States towards assuming binding commitments in this area of law. Moreover, since their adoption and entry into force, the 1969/1992 CLC and 1971/1992 Fund Conventions have been extensively applied and continue to represent the primary avenue for the settlement of compensation claims for marine oil pollution damage in contracting parties.[115]

Notwithstanding this progress, a persisting question remains the tension between the importance of preserving the integrity and smooth functioning of the CLC and Fund's compensation mechanism through a uniform interpretation and application in the contracting parties and the challenges raised by certain domestic courts' decisions that, in some cases, have expanded the scope of redress available to claimants beyond the boundaries set by the conventional regime. Moreover, particularly prior to the entry into force of the Supplementary Fund Protocol, both private claimants and public authorities in the affected areas have on various occasions brought proceedings before domestic courts of non-Party States (such as, typically, the United States) in the attempt to rely on the application of a more favourable national law and to tap into a wider and more comprehensive set of remedies. This happened, for example, in the case of the *Amoco Cadiz* incident occurred in 1978[116] and, more recently, in the *Prestige* incident. In the latter case, in addition to criminal action brought against the master of the ship before the Spanish Court of La Coruna, the Spanish government filed a civil liability proceeding before the US courts against the classification society, the American Bureau of Shipping (ABS). This was probably an attempt to avoid the application of the CLC[117] and the consequent channelling provisions, which would exclude ABS liability, and to recover more than $1 billion in compensatory and punitive damages from ABS.

As things stand, the availability of a much larger amount of compensation through the combination of the 1992 IOPC Fund and the 2003 Supplementary Fund might reduce the need of forum shopping litigation strategies towards non-party jurisdictions. However, civil liability proceedings are still being brought before national courts of Contracting States, particularly with respect to disputes concerning the application of the CLC's provisions. A case that epitomises claimants' attempt to rely on the interplay between the international regime and domestic law in order to obtain a more meaningful remedy before domestic courts is the one arising out of the oil spill of the tanker *Erika*, off the coast of Brittany in northern France. Given the magnitude of the damage, in addition to claims filed under the CLC and the IOPC Fund, the case gave also rise to various proceedings before French domestic courts and the CJEU, in which claimants sought to rely on the parallel application of the CLC and of both French and European Law in order to try and overcome the CLC's narrow scope of application *ratione personae* and file an action against a larger number of defendants.[118] In order to understand the legal and procedural context of these decisions, it is important to bear in mind that according to French procedural law, it is possible for claimants to file a civil action for compensation in the context of criminal proceedings—in these cases, the criminal judge is competent to decide on the civil claims and the damage due to the victims. As far as the criminal charges are concerned, the proceedings revolved around three main questions. First, whether French courts could have jurisdiction on the case, given that the incident occurred in France's exclusive economic zone but outside its territorial waters. Second, whether parties other than the shipowner (such as the charterer, the classification society and the shipping management company) could be held liable and ordered to pay compensation. And third, whether civil compensation could also include ecological damage. On all three questions, the final decision was rendered by the Court of Cassation, which is the highest judicial authority in the French legal system.[119] On the first question, the Court found the jurisdiction of France in the EEZ as established under domestic law to be in accordance with international law. The Court noted in particular that UNCLOS confers to coastal States the competence to adopt laws and regulations to prevent, reduce and manage pollution from ships and inferred from that a corresponding competence to enact sanctions against their violations.[120] On the second point, concerning the liability of the shipowner, the president of the management company, the classification society and the ship's charterer, the Court discarded the existence of a conflict with the principle of exclusive liability of the shipowner under the CLC regime. The Court noted that Article III.4 of the Convention bars compensation claims filed against certain persons other than the shipowner unless the damage resulted from their personal act or omission, committed with the intent to cause such damage, or recklessly and with knowledge that damage would probably occur. In the case, the Court noted that the owner of the *Erika* and its technical manager acted negligently by having failed to provide the adequate repairs to the oil tanker in order to ensure its safety and by having nevertheless chartered the *Erika* despite knowing that its conditions were not satisfactory. From this, the Court inferred that they acted recklessly, as they intentionally avoided the necessary maintenance for the ship, to make saving on costs, even knowing that this would have created danger.[121] As for the Total oil company, the charterer of the ship, the Court held that its negligence consisted in having omitted a new control of the ship by the vetting company before allowing the ship to sail, notwithstanding that a previous control performed a year earlier concluded the ship was in a poor condition.[122] On this basis, the Court concluded that these parties could not benefit from the exclusion of liability under the CLC and could therefore be held liable and ordered to pay civil compensation in accordance with domestic law. The third point, concerning the admissibility of compensation for pure ecological damage, is the one that raised most interest, particularly from an environmental law perspective. In a widely acclaimed decision, the Court ruled that pure environmental damage could be compensated. The Court referred to it as the 'direct or indirect damage inflicted on the environment and resulting from the infringement'. A more precise definition can be found in the ruling of the Court of Appeal,[123] which described it as an objective, independent damage, consisting in 'any significant damage to the natural environment, namely, in particular, air, atmosphere, water, soil, land, landscape, natural sites, biological diversity and the interaction between these elements, which is without impact on a particular human interest but affects a legitimate public interest'.[124] At the basis of this recognition stands the finding of inexcusable fault on the part of the defendants. As noted by the Court of Cassation, '[i]t is not fair to give immunity to persons liable through their fault for damage caused to the environment on the pretext that nature does not belong to anyone in particular'.[125] The Court recognised as entitled to compensation for this type of damage some local authorities and associations (especially those that were granted special powers under the law conferring on them particular responsibility for the protection, management and conservation of the territory) and to accredited environmental protection associations.

Of particular relevance in the context of these proceedings is the claim brought by the French municipality of Commune de Mesquer against Total France SA and Total International Ltd for the reimbursement of the clean-up costs following the spill.[126] This claim, which was brought by the Commune de Mesquer before French courts, gave rise to an interesting preliminary ruling of the CJEU on the interplay and combined application of the oil pollution regime and certain provisions of EU secondary law, which will be discussed and examined in more detail in a following chapter of this book.[127]

These decisions rendered in relation to the *Erika* accident represent an example of how the multilevel interaction of different legal orders (national, European and international) and different regimes of liability can be beneficially exploited by claimants in order to achieve a more meaningful redress, while also promoting the implementation of the polluter pays principle and the ends of environmental justice.[128] By relying on national and European legislation, the claimants in the *Erika* legal proceedings managed to sidestep the 1992 CLC with a potentially advantageous outcome under several respects: first, by overcoming the channelling of liability to the registered shipowner, they could target a wider range of potentially liable parties; second, they managed to access to a greater amount of compensation bypassing the financial limitations imposed by the international regime; finally, they could overcome the limitation of the CLC definition of pollution damage and seek compensation for pure ecological damage.[129] With respect to the last point, the ruling of the French Court of Cassation sent an important signal and represents a welcomed step forwards in the progressive official recognition of ecological damage as an established legal category, adding up to relevant statutory and regulatory developments in the US as well as in Europe and in other jurisdictions. With respect to the application of the CLC, the ruling did not formally create a conflict with the conventional regime, since the Court applied French law on civil liability and the defendants could not rely on the provisions of the Convention due to their inexcusable negligence.[130] Yet, concerns were raised in the aftermath of the ruling that, were other jurisdictions to follow the principles put forward in the *Erika* judgement, there would be 'a risk of loss of uniformity in the application of international rules, unless changes were made to international regulations'.[131] Indeed, by officially recognising the admissibility of compensation for pure ecological damage, it highlighted how, despite the revised definition of 'pollution damage' in the 1992 CLC and despite the various IOPC's initiatives aimed at establishing a consistent practice across the contracting parties,[132] the question of the admissibility of claims for natural resources continues to present a challenge to the uniform application of the oil pollution regime. In that respect, the General Secretariat of the Conference of Peripheral Maritime Regions of Europe presented a technical document outlining possible options for reforms improving compensation for ecological damage under the international regime, which could alleviate the risk of challenges posed by unilateral moves at domestic level. The suggested options ranged from proposals to include full recognition of ecological damage in the international framework to the setting up of additional mechanisms at the EU level complementing the international framework and/or encouraging a converging interpretation of international conventions by national courts and legislations in order to foster recognition of ecological damage.[133]

The uniform application of the conventional regime was once again at issue in the legal proceedings brought before the Spanish courts in relation to the *Prestige* incident. Reversing a previous decision of the First Instance court of La Coruna, the Spanish Supreme Court, in two judgments dated 14 January 2016, affirmed that both the master of the ship and the shipowner had engaged, under different respects, in wilful misconduct. This meant that they lost the exoneration from liability (in the case of the shipmaster) and the limitation of liability (in the case of shipowner) under the 1992 Convention and could be held unlimitedly liable under the Convention.

These domestic courts' rulings reveal the underlying tensions between on the one hand the legitimate aspirations of pollution victims towards a more comprehensive coverage and, on the other hand, the need to maintain the sustainability and smooth functioning of a system based on a delicate balance between the interests of those affected by the oil pollution and the different contributions by the actors involved in the oil transport activity and the insurance industry. The IOPC Fund consistently reiterated the importance of promoting a uniform interpretation of the international regime and voiced concerns about the disruptive impact of diverging applications of the Convention in the contracting parties' legal systems. At the same time, past and current practice under the CLC reveals how litigation before domestic courts can play a role in identifying certain limitations or uncertainties of the conventional texts and provide the input for clarifications or revisions. As already noted, the revised definition of pollution damage in the 1992 CLC was in large part a response to various domestic courts decisions interpreting the more generic definition under the 1969 CLC text as admitting compensation also for ecological damage. Particularly relevant in that sense were the cases related to the oil spills caused by the shipwrecks *Patmos* (1985) and *Haven* (1991), in which the Italian courts admitted compensation for ecological damage under the 1969 CLC convention, in contrast with the more conservative approach laid out in IOPC Fund Resolution No. 3.[134] The decision of the Italian Court of Appeal in the *Patmos* case was particularly interesting at the time, as it was one of the earliest rulings recognising the value of the environment for the community and explicitly admitting its compensation for the non-economic and non-market values of natural resources.[135]

Overall, these past and more recent cases offer interesting examples of the scope for multilevel interaction between the international oil pollution regime and national and European law. They demonstrate that such interaction, while often leading to diverging and potentially disruptive interpretation and application by national courts, could also have a positive impact in identifying uncertainties, clarifying the application of the convention[136] and keeping the international regime 'alive' and in line with evolving needs and understanding and emerging challenges.

4. Complementing the oil pollution regime: the HNS and Bunker oil liability conventions

Following the 'model' provided by the oil pollution liability regime, other treaties have been adopted within IMO to address liability for marine pollution. These are the 1996 International Convention on Liability and Compensation for Damage in Connection with the Carriage of Hazardous and Noxious Substances by Sea ('HNS Liability Convention')[137] and the 2001 International Convention on Civil Liability for Bunker Oil Pollution Damage ('Bunker Oil Convention').[138] These treaties aim at filling the gaps left by the CLC, as the latter does not cover damage to the marine environment posed by carriage of hazardous goods and substances other than oil, and it only applies to pollution damage caused by oil carried as a cargo, thereby excluding from its scope of application the different situation of oil used as a fuel for the vessel. Thus, the Bunker Oil Convention covers damage caused by contamination resulting from the escape or discharge of bunker oil from the ship, whereby 'bunker oil' means any hydrocarbon miner oil 'used or intended to be used for the operation or propulsion of the ship and any residues of such oil'.[139]

Both the Bunker and HNS treaties follow the CLC in their structure and scope of application and thus apply to damage caused in the territory and territorial sea of a State Party; to damage by contamination of the environment caused in the EEZ of a State Party; and to preventive measures wherever taken. Like in the 1992 CLC, compensable damage includes compensation for impairment of the environment, albeit limitedly to the costs of 'reasonable measures of reinstatement actually undertaken or to be undertaken'.[140] Both the HNS and Bunker Oil Conventions channel strict liability, with very limited exceptions, primarily on the registered owner of the vessel, combined with its obligation to maintain insurance or other financial security. Under the Bunker Oil Convention, the insurance requirement applies to the registered owner of ships above 1,000 gross tonnage.[141] Moreover, under both the Bunker Oil Convention and HNS Liability Convention the shipowner's liability is limited. However, the Bunker Oil Convention does not contain specific limits to the shipowner's liability, but it refers to the 'applicable national or international maritime regime, such as the Convention on Limitation of Liability for Maritime Claims, 1976, as amended' by the 1996 Protocol.[142] The latter Protocol sets the threshold of shipowner's liability under the Limitation Convention to 3.02 million SDRs for ships not exceeding 2,000 gross tonnage, with additional amounts provided for larger ships.

Finally, like the CLC/IOPC Fund regime, the HNS Liability Convention envisages the establishment of a supplementary HNS Fund financed with the contributions from receivers of HNS cargo. The HNS Fund is at present not operational and will be established once the Convention will enter into force. There is no supplementary fund complementing the Bunker Oil Convention.

The Bunker Oil Convention entered into force in November 2008, and it has currently 100 Contracting States.[143] On the other hand, the HNS regime has so far attracted a low rate of ratification, and this is preventing its entry into force. To address this problem, a Protocol to the HNS Liability Convention was adopted in

2010, containing some amendments aimed at addressing some of the controversial aspects.[144] The entry into force of the 2010 Protocol requires accession by at least 12 States meeting certain criteria in relation to tonnage and annual reported quantity of HNS cargo received. Once in force, the 2010 Protocol will amend the 1996 Convention, and replace it with the official consolidated text of 2010 HNS Liability Convention. So far, only five States have ratified the Convention.[145] In order to support the process of ratification of the Convention, the EU adopted in 2017 Council Decision 2017/769 urging Member States to take the necessary steps to deposit their instruments of ratification or accession to the 2010 Protocol by 6 May 2021. The EU issued a similar request with respect to the Bunker Oil Convention, by adopting Council Decision 2002/762/EC, which eventually led all EU countries to ratify/accede to the convention by 2015.[146] Denmark has been the first EU Member State that ratified the 2010 HNS Liability Convention, but there are prospects that other EU Member States may join in the near future. If and when the 2010 HNS Liability Convention will also enter into force, it will form together with the Bunker and CLC an integrated regime of liability for ship source pollution.

5. The international liability framework and the protection of the marine environment

From a broader international environmental law perspective, the developments in the field of liability for marine pollution damage must be examined in light of the relevant provisions of UNCLOS (or 'Law of the Sea Convention').[147] Part XII of UNCLOS concerning the protection and preservation of the marine environment places upon States Parties a duty to take measures, jointly or individually, to prevent, reduce and control pollution of the marine environment from the potential sources of pollution.[148] Article 235 deals specifically with the question of responsibility, liability and compensation. It confirms the responsibility of States for the fulfilment of their international obligations concerning the protection and preservation of the marine environment. At the same time, it requires States to ensure that recourse is made available in accordance with their domestic legal systems for compensation for pollution damage caused by natural or juridical persons under their jurisdiction. Finally, Article 235(3) endorses the further development of international regimes in the field of liability and compensation for marine pollution damage.

While the marine pollution liability regimes are not in themselves directly related to this UNCLOS provision, they may be considered as an implementation of it, although there are certain divergences between the two instruments, with regard to their respective underlying rationales and context of application. Article 235 is included in Part XII of UNCLOS, which is primarily directed at the protection of the marine environment. The marine pollution civil liability regimes are instead primarily aimed at providing compensation to private victims, with environmental concerns still remaining secondary to that primary objective. Moreover, the current international liability framework only addresses pollution from vessels, while the Law of the Sea Convention covers several types of sources, including land-based and atmospheric sources of pollution.

At present, the proliferation and intensification of offshore facilities and other oil extraction activities prompts the need to reconsider the scope of application of the liability regimes so to include also these other threats to the marine and coastal environment. It seems in fact that while the annual amount of oil spilled from vessels seemed to have registered a reduction over the past decades, also due to the use of safer and structurally improved tankers,[149] the frequency and intensity of offshore accidents has dramatically increased since the late 1970s. Well-known offshore accidents such as the Ixtoc I, BP Deepwater Horizon oil spills, and other perhaps less well-known incidents, such as the Montara blow-out in 2009 off the coast of Western Australia, did not only cause significant and widespread pollution damage in the affected areas, but are also further demonstrations of the gap in the international liability framework. In the EU, offshore oil spill damage is covered by the Environmental Liability Directive[150] (ELD), which was amended by the Offshore Safety Directive[151] to extend the geographical application of the EU liability regime to marine waters, defined in the Marine Strategy Directive as waters, the seabed and the subsurface on the seaward side of the baseline from where the extent of the territorial sea is measured.[152] Furthermore, a European Parliament resolution recently stressed the importance of a European harmonisation of Member States civil liability for bodily injuries and property damage arising as a consequence of an offshore oil spill.[153] Beyond the EU, however, an international legal framework to regulate offshore pollution and liability is still lacking.

Finally, a further limit of the marine pollution liability regimes when compared with the objectives of UNCLOS is the exclusion of marine pollution damage in the high sea. At the moment, work towards the definition of a global regime for Marine Areas Beyond National Jurisdiction has finally led on March 2023 to the conclusion, under the UNCLOS, of a Draft agreement on the conservation and sustainable use of marine biological diversity of areas beyond national jurisdiction (also referred to as the High Seas Treaty).[154] The agreed text does not specifically address liability, but it contains a provision delegating the Conference of the Parties 'to adopt measures in areas beyond national jurisdiction, to be applied on an emergency basis . . . when a natural phenomenon or a human-caused disaster has caused, or is likely to cause, serious or irreversible harm to marine biological diversity of areas beyond national jurisdiction . . .'.

6. 'Second generation' environmental liability agreements

6.1. The 1993 Council of Europe's Lugano Convention

The Convention on Civil Liability for Damage Resulting from Activities Dangerous to the Environment (often referred to as the 'Lugano Convention') is a regional agreement adopted in 1993 under the auspices of the Council of Europe.[155] It is so far the only international civil liability regime applying horizontally to a broad range of environmentally hazardous activities. Although it shares several features with the more traditional civil liability regimes, this Convention embodies a more explicit attention to the environmental dimension of the damage. Article 1 of the

Convention expressly includes among its purposes the 'prevention [of environmental damage] and reinstatement [of the impaired environment]', alongside with the aim of ensuring adequate compensation for victims of damage resulting from dangerous activities. Another unique feature is the inclusion of an explicit definition of 'environment',[156] as including 'natural resources both abiotic and biotic, such as air, water, soil, fauna and flora and the interaction between the same factors; property which forms part of the cultural heritage; and the characteristic aspects of the landscape'. The Convention also broadens the scope of compensable environmental damage which includes not only the 'reasonable measures aiming to reinstate or restore the damaged or destroyed components of the environment', but also those measures necessary 'to introduce, where reasonable, the equivalents of the components into the environment'.[157] This additional element addresses the hypothesis in which natural resources are irremediably destroyed.

As an additional feature compared to the previously examined civil liability regimes, the Lugano Convention contains specific provisions on the role of individuals and NGOs through articles on the access of the public to information held by public authority or the operator,[158] and on the possibility for individuals and environmental associations to request at any time

> the prohibition of a dangerous activity which is unlawful and poses a grave threat of damage to the environment; that the operator be ordered to take measures to prevent an incident or damage; that the operator be ordered to take measures, after an incident, to prevent damage; and that the operator be ordered to take measures of reinstatement.[159]

Despite its progressive features and ambitious scope, the Convention has not entered into force, and it is very unlikely that it will ever enter into force. This is probably due mostly to its broad scope of application, which rendered this instrument not attractive for the industry sectors and its implementation too demanding for the States. From an EU perspective, the adoption of the Environmental Liability Directive might have contributed to further deter or to simply turn away the attention of several EU Member States from ratifying the Lugano Convention,[160] an outcome which might appear surprising given that the Convention itself contained several features aimed at securing the ratification by the EU and that the EU Commission was directly involved in the negotiation of the international agreement.[161] Overall, the Lugano Convention's failure to enter into force illustrates once again the difficulty of setting up a comprehensive and effective regime of environmental liability addressing different types of hazardous activities.[162]

6.2. *The Nagoya-Kuala Lumpur supplementary protocol on liability for biodiversity damage*

6.2.1. *Liability and redress in the framework of the Biodiversity Convention*

The idea of a regime of liability and redress for damage to biological diversity emerged within the framework of the 1992 Convention on the Protection of Biological

Diversity (CBD), in a climate of growing concern for the rapid decline of biodiversity together with ever greater appreciation of its vital importance for the maintenance of ecological systems. The initiatives in this direction proceeded initially along two parallel tracks. On the one side, the elaboration of a liability mechanism for damage to the biological diversity found its basis in Article 14(2) of the Convention, which confers to the Conferences of the Parties (COPs) the task to examine 'the issue of liability and redress, including restoration and compensation, for damage to biological diversity, except where such liability is a purely internal matter'. On the other side, the Cartagena Biosafety Protocol to the CBD conferred a mandate to the COPs to proceed to the 'elaboration of international rules and procedures in the field of liability and redress for damage resulting from transboundary movements of living modified organism'.

Yet, since the beginning there was little agreement on the scope and appropriateness of liability rules under the CBD. Liability is ultimately a limited instrument for addressing the innumerable and different threats posed to the world's biological resources. The definition of damage also proved controversial. The CBD defines biological diversity in terms of the variability between and within genes, species and ecosystems. Pursuant to this definition, in order to constitute damage, the change has to result in an adverse or negative effect and should be measurable.[163] However, the assessment of negative effects of changes occurring in the State of biodiversity would require an in-depth understanding of the interdependencies between the structure and diversity of biotic communities and the functioning of ecosystems.[164] There were also questions on the nature and ultimate purpose of the liability regime, such as whether classic tort law provisions may be suited to tackle harm to biodiversity that is recognised as being 'common concern of mankind'[165] and to what extent the whole spectrum of values attached to biological diversity, as reflected in the CBD's Preamble,[166] can be adequately reflected into a liability regime.[167] Unsurprisingly, given the complexities of issues to be addressed, the negotiations for the elaboration of a liability regime under Article 14(3) of the Biodiversity Convention proceeded very slowly and ultimately stalled. Therefore, the work on liability concentrated on the development of a liability regime for damage caused by genetically modified organisms (GMOs) under the Biosafety Protocol.

6.2.2. Liability for damage caused by LMOs

The negotiations for the elaboration of a regime of liability and redress for damage caused by GMOs under the Biosafety Protocol started in 2005 and lasted almost ten years. There was a general climate of uncertainty surrounding this new technology and its long-term impact on health and environment. Moreover, the negotiation of liability rules with respect to damage caused by GMOs assumed a highly political character in the context of the Northern–Southern countries debate in which both environmental concerns and economic and trade interests were at stake. In this context, the opportunity of introducing liability rules for damage caused by GMOs acted as a catalyst to advance or consolidate different countries' positions in favour or against the commercialisation of GMOs.[168] Thus, besides genuine environmental concerns, the debate on liability also served as the battleground for the discussion on more fundamental issues reflecting diverging opinions on the benefits and risks involved in the trade and utilisation of biotechnologies.[169]

During the negotiation process, these divergences translated into extensive discussions and controversies on the question of the scope and purpose of the prospective liability instrument and its legally binding nature.[170] While several Southern and developing countries—with the exclusion of GMOs exporters such as Brazil—strongly argued for the adoption of a legally binding civil liability regime, many Western countries backed by the biotech industry argued for a completely non-binding instrument. It is in this context that the idea of an administrative type of liability regime started to get traction as a possible way to overcome the resistance against a legally binding civil liability instrument.[171] This public law type of liability was modelled on the EU Environmental Liability Directive and was favoured by many EU Member States. A compromise position was eventually reached at the COP/MOP meeting in 2008 where the negotiating parties finally agreed to work towards a legally binding instrument embodying a regulatory approach to liability for biodiversity and natural resources damage similar to the EU Environmental Liability Directive.[172] It was also agreed that the prospective instrument would feature a provision on civil liability, although the binding nature of such provision was left open for further discussions.[173]

This compromise agreement eventually led to the adoption, in October 2010, of the final text of the Nagoya-Kuala Lumpur Supplementary Protocol on Liability and Redress to the Cartagena Protocol on Biosafety ('Nagoya-Kuala Lumpur Supplementary Protocol' or NKLSP).[174] Consistent with its stated objective of contributing 'to the conservation and sustainable use of biological diversity taking also into account risks to human health',[175] liability under the NKLSP is principally focused on addressing harm to the biological components of biodiversity and to their conservation and sustainable use. 'Damage' is defined as a measurable and significant 'adverse effect on the conservation and sustainable use of biodiversity, taking also into account risks to human health'.[176] Thus, such adverse effect has to be measurable or otherwise observable taking into account, where available, scientifically established baselines recognised by a competent authority that take into account any other human-induced variation and natural variation. The significance of the damage is to be determined on the basis of several factors, including long-term permanent change to biodiversity which cannot be redressed through natural recovery within a reasonable period of time; the extent of the qualitative and quantitative changes adversely affecting biodiversity components and the reduction of the ability of those components to provide goods and services; and the extent of any adverse effects on human health.[177]

In terms of its structure, the NKLSP embodies a primarily administrative approach to the question of liability and compensation for biodiversity damage, which largely evokes the one developed within the EU. States Parties are required to appoint competent authorities which would liaise with the operator in the event of a significant damage. Liability is associated with the operator's primary duty to inform the competent authorities and to take the necessary 'response measures'.[178] The latter are defined as including both 'measures to prevent, contain, mitigate or otherwise avoid damage' and remedial measures aimed at restoring biological diversity.[179] It is also stated that remedial measures should aim at restoring biological diversity 'to the condition that existed before the damage occurred, or its nearest equivalent'; and that where the competent authority determines that full restoration is not feasible, operators are expected to achieve restoration by replacing the loss of biodiversity with species and genetic material that is functionally similar, either at the place where the damage occurred or as appropriate at an alternative location.[180] If the operator fails to take the appropriate response measures, the competent authorities are enabled, but not required, to take the relevant measures themselves, and then recover the costs and expenses from the operator.

In addition to these provisions on administrative liability for damage to biodiversity, which are based on the adoption of 'response measures' and constitute the core of the Nagoya-Kuala Lumpur Supplementary Protocol's liability regime, Article 12 contains a clause envisaging the development, or application (if already available), of civil liability rules for both biodiversity damage and for more traditional types of damage associated with biodiversity damage. Specifically, according to this provision, States Parties *may* include civil liability rules among the norms and procedures that, in addition to response measures, address biodiversity damage;[181] at the same time they *shall* also aim at 'providing adequate rules and procedure in their domestic law on civil liability for material and personal damage associated with [biodiversity damage]'. To that end, Article 12(2) provides that Parties shall either 'continue to apply their existing law on civil liability' or 'develop and apply or continue to apply civil liability law specifically for that purpose' or a combination of both. It was remarked, however, that it is not easy to envision what such 'associated' damage may be.[182] Moreover, Article 12(2) remains rather laconic regarding the specific contents of the civil liability regime. It indicates that parties shall aim at providing 'adequate' rules and procedures on civil liability, but it limits itself to outline the main elements that should be included in such a regime (i.e. a definition of damage; standard of liability; right to bring claims and channelling of liability, where appropriate), leaving any further and more specific details to be determined by the parties through the implementation in their respective domestic systems.

Overall, the text of the NKLSP shows how the negotiating parties' deeply divided positions translated into the compromise language and open-ended formulation of many of its provisions. This agreement has in fact been criticised as reflecting a 'diminished ambition' in the development of international law in the field of environmental liability.[183] When examined from a broader perspective, however, it remains significant under several other respects. It is the first comprehensive and global agreement providing for liability for damage to biological diversity. It contributes to the definition at the international law level of a regulatory approach to liability with an explicit recognition of the importance of adopting liability rules addressing damage to natural resources *per se* considered. It also consolidates an approach to remediation that is primarily focused on the restoration of the environment and natural resources with remedies that go beyond the mere compensation for the cost of reasonable measures of reinstatement. Finally, the NKLSP was significant from a political and normative point of view. Its negotiation and adoption took place at a time when the international community was losing faith in the role of international treaties and multilateral environmental diplomacy as an effective avenue to find solutions for environmental problems.[184] It was also a period characterised by growing scepticism on the appropriateness and 'sensibility' of negotiating further international liability treaties.[185] Both academics and practitioners were in fact looking with disillusionment at the slow and difficult ratification process of other liability treaties adopted during the late 1990s. From this perspective, the NKLSP stands out as a successful example of environmental diplomacy, particularly in the light of the challenging and deeply divisive issues that negotiators had to overcome in order to reach an agreement.[186] The NKLSP entered into force on 5 March 2018 and as of July 2022 has 51 Parties.[187]

6.3. The liability annex to the Madrid Protocol on Environmental Protection

The elaboration of a specific regime on liability for damage to the Antarctic environment was envisaged in a programmatic provision included in the 1991 Madrid Protocol on Environmental Protection to the Antarctic Treaty ('Madrid Protocol').[188] However, it was only in June 2005 that, after more than ten years of negotiations, negotiating parties finally adopted the text of Annex VI on Liability Arising from Environmental Emergencies ('Antarctic Liability Annex'). This is the first environmental liability regime adopted in the framework of the Antarctic Treaty System.[189]

Given the juridical and natural peculiarities of Antarctica, the definition of liability norms for damage to its environment proved especially challenging. For several reasons, the private-municipal law approach retained in the existing civil liability treaties could not provide a useful source of inspiration for the elaboration of a prospective liability framework for the Antarctic environment.[190] First, from a legal perspective, the status of the Antarctic continent is mainly regulated by the 1959 Antarctic Treaty, which freezes current and future sovereignty claims over Antarctica and thus forecloses the exercise of traditional State jurisdiction in this area. It was therefore necessary to search for alternative jurisdictional links between the State and the private person carrying out activities in Antarctica and eventually causing damage to its environment. Because of such unique jurisdictional situation, traditional rules of standing were also hardly applicable.[191] Second, the Antarctic Liability Annex shares with the Madrid Protocol the primary objective of protecting and safeguarding the Antarctic environment and its dependent and associated ecosystems, and this objective was to be adequately reflected in the definition of damage.[192] Third, the remote location of Antarctica and the uniqueness and the fragility of its environment required the elaboration of ad hoc remedial measures. It was also important that clean-up measures follow an assessment of their feasibility to ensure that they would positively boost the natural rate of recovery without risk of further damage.[193] Finally, given Antarctica's unique role for scientific research, the liability regime was to be designed in a way to balance the primary interests of environmental protection with the needs of scientific research.[194]

Considering the unique set of circumstances characterising the Antarctic environment, the adoption of the Liability Annex is an important achievement. However, if compared to the more comprehensive liability framework originally envisaged under the Madrid Protocol, the narrow approach eventually retained in the final text of the Liability Annex appears rather a compromise solution.[195] The Parties had in fact opted, pragmatically, for a step-by-step solution, with the idea that the consensus reached for this first agreement would hopefully pave the way for development of a more comprehensive liability regime in the future.[196]

The Liability Annex embodies a rather original approach to liability and proposes a unique scheme for its implementation and enforcement. First, the remedies are limited to the prompt adoption of effective 'response action' aimed at containing and minimising the harmful impact of an 'environmental emergency'. 'Environmental emergency' is defined as 'any accidental event that has occurred . . . and that results in, or immediately threatens to result in, any significant and harmful impact to the Antarctic environment'. The content of liability therefore amounts to the cost of response action, which is to be paid by the operator to the Party that undertook the response action.[197] The liable entity can be either a State-operator or a non-state/private operator. In either case, the liability is not triggered by the occurrence of an environmental damage, but it only arises from the operator's failure to take response action when faced with an environmental emergency. However, the enforcement mechanism varies depending on whether the liability entity is a State operator or a non-state/private operator. In case of a non-state operator's liability (i.e. failure to take the response action), the Annex envisages a duty on the State Party of the operator to order the latter to take the response action, or alternatively the possibility to itself take the response action.[198] The Annex allows other States Parties to take response action, provided that they previously notify their intention to do so to the State Party of the operator. In that case, the State Party or the other State incurring costs by taking the response action can bring an action for compensation of such costs against the operator in the national courts of the State Party of the operator or the Party where the operator is incorporated or has its principal place of business.[199] In case of an environmental emergency for which none has taken response action, Article 6(2)(b) provides that the operator shall be liable to pay an amount of money which reflects as much as possible the costs of the response action. This is to be paid directly to a Fund established pursuant to Article 12 of the Annex, to the Party of the operator or to any Party that has taken the enforcement action. It was observed that this kind of private operator's liability corresponds in practice to a sort of administrative fine or penalty, whose objective is to deter the operator from escaping from the scene of an environmental emergency.[200] In the case of State operators' liability, and another State intervening in its place to take the response action, the Annex provides instead for an institutionalised mechanism of implementation and compulsory settlement of disputes by arbitration or in the International Court of Justice. In case nobody has taken response action, the liability of the State operator and the costs will be ascertained by the Antarctic Consultative Meeting (ACM). The role of the ACM in the application of the Liability Annex can be of particular significance for a normative perspective. Although the effective strength of this body to intervene in protection of the Antarctic environment in case of 'orphan' damage (i.e. when nobody took response action) will be tested only with the practical application of the Annex, the liability regime established in the Annex can be considered an embryonic example of international administration.

Overall, the Annex's limited scope of application to environmental emergencies came probably as a disappointment for those who had hoped for a comprehensive liability regime for damage to Antarctica. The concept of response action includes preventive measures and may include clean-up provisions, but it excludes the costs for reinstatement measures in case environmental damage occurs.[201] It also leaves uncovered hypothesis of irreparable damage to the environment as well as the case of environmental damage caused otherwise than by an environmental emergency, such as the gradual accumulation of harmful effects or the intentional destruction of habitats. At present, it is doubtful whether a broader liability regime will be negotiated in the future in order to address those limitations,[202] particularly given that, more than 16 years after its adoption, the Annex has still not entered into force, and any decisions on further negotiations have been repeatedly postponed.[203] In spite of these shortcomings, the Annex retains the merit of connecting the concept of liability to the objective of environmental protection. It also signals an important shift in international law towards a public law regime of liability. Its underlying objectives and unique features make it an interesting example and a potential model for a liability regime applicable to public spaces, an aspect still very little explored under public international law.[204]

7. Conventional systems of international liability: a layered framework

The international conventional framework in the field of environmental liability reflects the 'layered' nature that characterises the global scenario concerning the legal responses to transnational environmental harm. This is especially evident in the liability treaties adopted in the field of marine pollution and nuclear damage, where the idea of allocation of loss among the different participants in the operation of the hazardous activity translated into the different levels and forms of financial contribution of those various actors to compensation for the ensuing environmental damage. In the oil pollution regime, a two-tier system of compensation is established, with the liability of the oil tanker owner being supplemented by a further layer of compensation through a fund financed by the oil and shipping industries. In the nuclear liability framework, the liability of the operator of the nuclear installation coexists, and is supplemented, by a second layer of State liability through the public financing of a supplementary fund. These different layers of liability aim essentially at ensuring that an appropriate amount is available to cover the enormous costs of compensation in case of accidents taking place during the operation of these hazardous activities.

The 'layering phenomenon', however, does not only relate to the contributions of different actors at different levels, to the compensation system set up under the international conventions. It is also emerging at the regulatory level through liability frameworks developed by non-state actors, including stakeholders representing the interests of the involved industries. Illustrative examples of this trend were the Tanker Owners Voluntary Agreement Concerning Liability for Oil Pollution (TOVALOP),[205] which came into effect in 1969, and the Contract Regarding Interim Supplement to Tanker Liability for Oil Pollution (CRISTAL), adopted in 1971. These two voluntary agreements were contractually[206] set up by the tanker and oil industries, respectively, in the aftermath of the *Torrey Canyon* accident and in the wake of increasing concern for the hazards related to the maritime transport of oil. They aimed at enhancing the prospects of prompt and effective clean-up and adequate compensation for oil pollution damage, while at the same time representing an indirect avenue for the relevant industries to influence the intergovernmental negotiations towards the development of the international liability framework.[207] These two schemes, and TOVALOP in particular, were instrumental in forging consensus around the establishment of strict liability for oil pollution.[208] They operated in parallel to the intergovernmental regime, although they were not intended to replace it but only to supplement or fill in the gaps where the international framework was not applicable.[209] Both agreements eventually terminated in 1997.

More recently, a voluntary 'Compact' has been established as a Contractual Mechanism for Response in the Event of Damage to Biological Diversity Caused by the Release of a Living Modified Organism.[210] The agreement has been entered into by six biotechnology corporations operating in the agricultural sector with the purpose of creating an accessible, efficient, effective and fair dispute resolution system on which States can rely. By entering into the agreement, the companies are bound to a system of arbitration to adjudicate claims by States in relation to damage to biological diversity allegedly caused by a release of a living modified organism.

Overall, the emergence of these private sector liability schemes is an example of the 'law beyond the state' phenomenon and of the increasing involvement of private actors in the formulation of regulatory and normative solutions at the global level.[211] In the field of liability, these developments illustrate the pluralistic and multi-layered character of this area of the law. From a regulatory perspective, the involvement of relevant industries' stakeholders in the setting of liability and compensation schemes may positively contribute to further societal acceptance for these hazardous and ultra-hazardous activities.

8. Soft law developments in the field of environmental liability

Soft law can play an important role in the progressive development of international law of the environment.[212] Soft law instruments like the 1972 Stockholm Declaration and 1992 Rio Declarations are probably the most significant example of the normative influence of certain non-binding legal instruments in forging gradually the necessary consensus around certain legal principles and their subsequent translation into legally binding rules.[213] While not exclusive to international environmental law,[214] the trend towards the use of soft law or informal type of law-making is particularly prominent in the environmental legal field,[215] as in this context international institutions and non-governmental bodies and organisations have been especially relevant in the elaboration and diffusion of 'soft' normative frameworks.[216] With respect to the field of environmental liability, an example of a soft law/informal law framework is offered by the 1997 Resolution of the Institute of International Law on 'Responsibility and Liability under International Law for Environmental Damage'.[217] While a non-binding document developed by a learned society, mostly composed by academics and distinguished jurists, the resolution can certainly be regarded as having contributed to shape understandings around the concepts of international responsibility and liability for environmental damage. Although subsequent State practice did not endorse one of its legal principles on 'strict responsibility of the State on the basis of harm or injury alone',[218] this document contained nevertheless certain features that are gradually becoming a common item in international environmental liability regimes, such as provisions on response action[219] and on the inclusion of damage to the environment as such in the scope of reparation.[220]

More recently, soft law instruments, especially in the form of guidelines, have been used to contribute to, guide and promote the setting up of liability provisions and legal frameworks at the domestic level. An example of this is the development by UNEP of the Draft Guidelines for the Development of Domestic Legislation on Liability, Response Action and Compensation for Damage Caused by Activities Dangerous to the Environment. The Guidelines, first drafted in 2007 and subsequently revised in 2009, provide a set of recommendations offering guidance to countries—particularly developing countries and countries with economies in transition—in drafting domestic legislation in the field.[221] They constitute implementation of Principle 13 of Rio Declaration which, recognising the importance of domestic legislation on environmental liability, called on States to develop national law in that area. The Guidelines identify key elements of an environmental liability regime for possible inclusion in domestic law, including concepts and approaches that can be found in certain more advanced domestic and regional (i.e. EU) environmental liability regimes, such as the definition of 'environmental damage' and criteria to assess its significance; measures for response action; a standard of strict liability and circumstances excluding liability in exceptional cases (such as act of God, *force majeure* and armed conflicts); and provisions on access to justice and compensation.

The recourse to Guidelines and soft law instrument can represent an interesting and potentially powerful way to indirectly influence prospective legal developments while at the same time overcoming the complexities and obstacles encountered in the attempts to negotiate legally binding liability regimes. In fact, several international environmental conventions contain programmatic provisions on the prospective adoption of appropriate rules on liability and compensation for environmental harm. Yet, in most cases, these '*pacta de contrahendo*' provisions have never been followed up by corresponding legally binding developments.[222] In that respect, particularly arduous was the drafting of liability rules for damage arising from the pollution of the marine environment to be attached or annexed to regional seas conventions.[223] An example are the longstanding discussions on the development of liability rules held in the framework of the 1976 Barcelona Convention for the Protection of the Marine Environment and the Coastal Region of the Mediterranean.[224] Article 12 of the Barcelona Convention mandated the contracting parties to 'cooperate as soon as possible in the formulation and adoption of appropriate procedures for the determination of liability and compensation for damage resulting from the pollution of the marine environment deriving from violations' of the Convention's provisions. A similar provision was included in the Protocol for the Protection of the Mediterranean Sea against Pollution Resulting from Exploration and Exploitation of the Continental Shelf and the Seabed and its Subsoil.[225] Work aimed at implementing these programmatic provisions started already in 1996.[226] Initially, the preferred option was a legally binding instrument, preferably in the form of a Protocol to the Convention.[227] However, the difficulties of reaching consensus after several years of meetings and discussions, and other obstacles related to the need not to conflict with existing international or regional (EU) instruments on liability, led eventually the negotiators to opt for a step-by-step approach and to start by adopting a set of non-binding Guidelines.[228] Hence, the Draft Guidelines on Liability and Compensation for Damage Resulting from Pollution of the Marine Environment in the Mediterranean Sea Area were adopted in 2007 within the framework of UNEP.[229] Despite being non-mandatory, the Guidelines are regarded as a first step to strengthen cooperation among the contracting parties with a view to eventually develop a future, legally binding, international liability regime for damage caused by the pollution of the Mediterranean Sea. The idea is therefore that, at a minimum, these Guidelines will serve to orient the development of domestic relevant domestic law and to promote convergence among the various national approaches on this issue.

The Guidelines are also interesting for the type of approach that they take to the question of liability. Building upon the experience gathered from existing civil liability regimes in international law, and partly taking inspiration from the public law approach to liability that underlines the EU Environmental Liability Directive, they bring together both the public and private dimension of environmental damage in their scope of application.[230] Therefore, they recommend that domestic legislation in contracting parties include provisions to cover both traditional damage (i.e. loss of life or personal injury; loss of or damage to property; loss of income directly deriving from an impairment of a legally protected interest in the use of the marine environment for economic purposes) and environmental damage to the marine and coastal environment of the Mediterranean Sea. The concept of environmental damage has inspired similar notions contained in the more recent liability instruments, such as the EU Environmental Liability Directive or the Nagoya-Kuala Lumpur Supplementary Protocol (NKLSP) and is defined as 'a measurable adverse change in a natural resource or measurable impairment of a natural resource service which may occur directly or indirectly'. Moreover, compared to the majority of international environmental liability treaties, the Guidelines' approach to reparation is more progressive and follows the broader and more advanced model offered by the EU Environmental Liability Directive.[231] Like the Directive, the Guidelines set primary remediation (that it the restoration of the damaged natural resources to the baseline condition) as the main objective, followed as an alternative by complementary remediation, and by compensatory remediation to tackle interim losses in natural resources services occurring from the date of the damage until when the primary remediation has achieved its full effect. Furthermore, the dual dimension of the damage (private and public) covered by the Guidelines is reflected also in the mechanisms to actually implement and enforce liability. In that respect, a two-system approach is envisaged which includes both civil liability for private claimants pursuing compensation for traditional damage and an administrative type of enforcement operated by competent authorities to be designated to this purpose by the contracting parties for environmental damage to the marine environment.

Overall, when examined alongside the Nagoya-Kuala Lumpur Liability Protocol and the Antarctic Liability Annex, the Guidelines reveal a progressive normative diffusion of the administrative/regulatory model of environmental liability. They also represent the yet further confirmation of the legal recognition of ecological damage in international law, thereby revealing a gradual overcoming of the traditional opposition to the idea of including the non-economically quantifiable aspects of the damage in the scope of reparation.

9. Concluding remarks

This overview of international liability treaties and negotiated liability schemes suggests some concluding reflections on the evolving scope and purpose of environmental liability in international law. To start with, the comparative analysis of the various international conventions shows how the scope and structure of environmental liability regimes has been evolving and adjusting to the need to cope with new environmental challenges, as well as with new understandings of environmental harm. This is mainly reflected in the progressive revision of the notion of compensable damage to provide appropriate recognition for damage to the environment and to natural resources. Moreover, traditional schemes of civil liability have in some cases been superseded by the adoption of administrative or regulatory mechanisms of response action and remediation, regarded as either more appropriate to deal with the specificities of harm to natural resources (i.e. Antarctica) or simply more acceptable to the contracting parties (i.e. the Nagoya-Kuala Lumpur Supplementary Protocol).

A further consideration relates to the role and function(s) that liability rules are expected to play in the context of international environmental law. Efforts towards the international harmonisation of rules of environmental liability need to be situated and understood in connection with the increased risks related to new technologies and industries, and the potential transnational dimension of the damage caused by these activities. In that sense, international liability provisions are becoming an important part of many schemes regulating transboundary hazardous activities[232] and an integral component of risk management strategies.[233]

At the conceptual level, international liability regimes contribute to the operationalisation of the polluter pays principle by reconnecting the costs and externalities of the hazardous activities to those who contribute to the creation of risk. The establishment of strict liability, the principle of legal channelling and, in some of the conventional regimes, the setting up of compensation schemes by entities considered as co-creating or co-benefiting from the risks involved in the operation of the hazardous activities feature as some of the constitutive elements of these international liability schemes. This conceptual connection between liability and risk brings international developments in line with parallel trends at the domestic level, displaying similar tendencies towards the objectivisation of liability rules[234] and the 'communitarisation' or 'socialization of risks',[235] via the creation of compensation schemes or other mechanisms aimed at spreading losses across various participants in the risk-creating activity. As Barboza aptly describes it, liability rules are 'part of a regime seeking to regulate certain socially useful but hazardous activities so that they continue being economically viable in spite of the damage they cause—without imposing undue burdens on victims or deteriorating the environment'.[236]

At the same time, more recent developments in this context show that liability provisions are increasingly regarded also as an important element of environmental protection strategies. This is reflected in the gradual inclusion of natural resources damage in the scope of compensable damage under several conventional frameworks, as well as in the elaboration of environmental liability schemes regarded as better tailored to address the public law dimension of the environmental harm. Finally, the incorporation of liability rules in the context of multilateral agreements suggests a somewhat more proactive—as opposed to only reactive and *ex post*—role of liability schemes in support of the objectives of the relevant convention. For example, the adoption of both the Liability Annex to the Protocol to the Antarctic Treaty and the Nagoya-Kuala Lumpur Supplementary Protocol was functional to the protection and safeguarding of natural resources considered a common international concern.

On a less positive note, there remain important difficulties and uncertainties surrounding the development of comprehensive international law regimes on liability and reparation for environmental damage. The lack of widespread State support that characterises the ratification process of many international liability treaties stresses once more the highly sensitive and complex nature of the liability issue and led many authors to question the appropriateness of embarking in costly and lengthy negotiations to elaborate a regime of which the entry into force is uncertain.[237]

When assessed from the point of view of determining the existence of a general extra-conventional principle of international liability, it is clear that in international law the proliferation of harmonised civil liability regimes has superseded the development of direct State liability.[238] States have clearly preferred an approach that de-emphasises their own responsibility either by adopting civil liability schemes and organising international schemes of insurances and financial guarantees or by ensuring equal access to judicial remedies for private parties.[239] Only in exceptional and very specific circumstances related to the operation of ultra-hazardous activities have States accepted to assume directly the burden to financially contribute to compensation (i.e. in the nuclear liability treaties) or even to assume liability (i.e. Space Liability Convention).[240] However, the very special circumstances that surround the inclusion of a positive role of the States in this context—such as in the field of space activities or nuclear energy—impose caution in interpreting those precedents as an implicit acceptance of a general principle of State liability; in most instances, in fact, State liability is rather the result of policy and economic considerations,[241] and it is normally proportionate to the degree of intervention of the State in the regulation and operation of the activity in question.[242]

One may need to reflect on the repercussions of the widespread reluctance of States to accept a principle of State liability for environmental damage. It has been contended that the ILC's dismissal of State strict liability in its work on the Allocation of Loss Principles, even as a potential progressive development of international law, is regrettable.[243] Given the limitations of State responsibility and the fragmented and patchy coverage offered by the sectoral liability treaties, the absence of a general international law framework of State liability arguably leaves an important gap in the availability of remedies for transboundary environmental damage.[244] In that respect, the aforementioned 1997 Institute of International Law's (IIL) Resolution on Responsibility and Liability for environmental damage was more progressive in proposing an integrated approach that combined principles of State responsibility and liability for transboundary environmental harm with elements of private operators' liability in a single overarching framework.[245]

Nowadays, a careful consideration of the role that States can play in this context is all the more needed in light of the increasing environmental challenges posed by the expansion and intensification of hazardous activities and the rising of non-state actors at the global level. In that sense, it has been argued that in spite of the difficulties in affirming the existence of a general international law principle of State liability, the increasing inclusion of civil liability rules in the international regulation of hazardous activities shows the emergence of a new primary obligation for the State to ensure prompt and effective compensation to victims of transboundary environmental harm.[246] This primary rule would respond to basic considerations of fairness and justice whereby the innocent victims cannot be left to bear the burden of the entire loss.[247] However, despite this optimistic outlook to prospective developments, the international legal framework appears still behind the full realisation of such an effective system of environmental justice. This objective would also require combining the principle of adequate and prompt compensation for transboundary pollution victims with the establishment of an international policy framework enabling an effective access to justice.[248]

In light of the aforementioned remarks, it is now appropriate to move the focus to the analysis of how the question of liability for environmental damage and access to remedies have been addressed in the EU.

Notes

1 Convention on Third Party Liability in the Field of Nuclear Energy (adopted 29 July 1960; entered into force 1st April 1968) 956 UNTS 251 (1960 Paris Convention); 1963 Vienna Convention on Civil Liability for Nuclear Damage 1063 UNTS 263 (adopted 21 May 1963; entered into force 12 November 1977) (1963 Vienna Convention); Convention Supplementary to the Paris Convention on Third Party Liability in the Field of Nuclear Energy, 1041 UNTS 358 (31 January 1963; entered into force 4 December 1974)(1963 Brussels Supplementary Convention).

2 International Convention on Civil Liability for Oil Pollution Damage (adoption 29 November 1969; entry into force 19 June 1975) 973 UNTS 3 (1969 CLC); International Convention on the Establishment of an International Fund for Compensation for Oil Pollution Damage (adopted 18 December 1971; entry into force 16 October 1978) 1110 UNTS 57 (1971 Fund Convention).

3 Among these are the Brussels Convention Relating to Civil Liability in the Field of Maritime Carriage of Nuclear Material 974 UNTS 255 (in force 15 July 1975); the Convention on Civil Liability for Damage Caused during Carriage of Dangerous by Road, Rail and Inland Navigation Vessels (CRTD), adopted 10 October 1989 (not yet entered into force); the International Convention on Liability and Compensation for Damage in Connection with the Carriage of Hazardous and Noxious Substances by Sea (HNS Convention) adopted 3 May 1996 (not entered into force), and subsequently amended by the Protocol adopted in 2010 (not yet in force); and the International Convention on Civil Liability for Bunker Oil Pollution Damage (Bunker Oil Convention) (adopted 23 March 2001; entered into force on 21 November 2008).

4 Convention on Civil Liability for Damage Resulting from Activities Dangerous to the Environment, 32 ILM 1228 (1993).

5 The 2001 Bunker Fuel Convention makes the shipowner, charterer, manager and operator jointly and severally liable. A similar approach is adopted by the 1999 Basel Protocol on Liability and Compensation for Damage Resulting from Transboundary Movements of Hazardous Waste and Their Disposal (adopted on 10 December 1999, not in force) and by the Nagoya-Kuala Lumpur Supplementary Protocol (adopted 15 October 2010, entered into force 5 March 2018).

6 DL Shelton and A Kiss, 'Strict Liability in International Environmental Law' in TM Ndiaye and R Wolfrum (eds.), *Law of the Sea, Environmental Law and Settlement of Disputes: Liber Amicorum Judge Thomas A Mensah* (Brill Academic Publishers 2007). Rules on direct or supplementary state liability can be found in the nuclear liability conventions and in the Antarctic Liability Annex, see further infra text at nn 198–200; R Lefeber, 'The Prospects for an Antarctic Environmental Liability Regime' in D Vidas (ed.), *Implementing the Environmental Protection Regime for the Antarctic* (Springer 2000).

7 Adopted 10 December 1999; not in force. Text available at http://archive.basel.int/meetings/cop/cop5/docs/prot-e.pdf (Basel Liability Protocol).

8 Doc ECE/MP.WAT/11-ECE/CP.REIA/9 (adopted 21 May 2003, not in force).

9 Adopted 14 June 2005 (not in force). Text <www.ats.aq/e/liability.html>

10 UNEP/CBD/BS/COP-MOP/5/15 (adopted 15 October 2010; entered into force 5 March 2018).

11 J Brunnée, 'Of Sense and Sensibility: Reflections on International Liability Regimes as Tools for Environmental Protection' (2004) 53 International and Comparative Law Quarterly 351. See also A Daniel, 'Civil Liability Regimes as a Complement to Multilateral Environmental Agreements: Sound International Policy or False Comfort?' (2003) 12 Reciel 225.

12 T Ghering and M Jachtenfuchs, 'Liability for Transboundary Environmental Damage: Towards a General Liability Regime?' (1993) 4 European Journal of International Law 92, 99–100.

13 M Faure and T Van den Borre, 'Compensating Nuclear Damage: A Comparative Law and Economic Analysis of the US and International Liability Schemes' (2008) 37 William and Mary Environmental Law and Policy Review 219.

14 A Boyle, 'Nuclear Energy and International Law: And Environmental Perspective' (1989) 60 British Yearbook of International Law 257, 301.

15 L De La Fayette, 'Towards a New Regime of State Responsibility for Nuclear Activities' (1992) 50 Nuclear Law Bulletin 7, 14.

16 See for example the Preamble to the 1960 Paris Convention.

17 If the nuclear incident occurred outside the territory of any contracting Party, or where the place of the incident cannot be determined with certainty, jurisdiction over such

actions shall lie within the courts of the installation state of the operator liable (Article XI of the Vienna Convention and Article 10 of the Paris Convention).

18 DB Davies, 'Convention on Supplementary Compensation for Nuclear Damage and Participation by Developing Countries: A South African Perspective' (2014) 93 Nuclear Law Bulletin 25, 29.

19 P Galizzi and P Sands, 'The 1968 Brussels Convention and Liability for Damage' (1999) 64 Nuclear Law Bulletin 7.

20 The natural disaster defence is no longer available in the revised text of the Vienna Convention as amended by the1997 Protocol.

21 Ghering and Jachtenfuchs (n 12) 99. Under the Paris Convention, the nuclear installation operator has a right to recourse in specific circumstances so provided in the Convention.

22 J Liu and M Faure, 'Compensation for Nuclear Damage: A Comparison Among the International Regime, Japan and China' (2016) 16 International Environmental Agreements: Politics, Law and Economics 165, 169.

23 Article 7 and Article 7(b) of the 1960 Paris Convention. It has been noted that the legislation of some contracting parties, such as Sweden or Germany, set higher limits than those provided under the Paris Convention; Liu and Faure, 'Compensation for Nuclear Damage' (n 22) 170.

24 IAEA, 'The 1997 Vienna Convention on Civil Liability for Nuclear Damage and the 1997 Convention on Supplementary Compensation for Nuclear Damage—Explanatory Texts' (2020) International Law Series No 3, 13 (hereafter 'VC Explanatory Texts'). So far, very few countries provide for unlimited liability in their national law: these include Germany, Switzerland and Japan (source Nuclear Energy Agency (NEA) <www.oecd-nea.org/jcms/pl_31319/nuclear-liability> accessed 10 July 2022.

25 Article 10 Paris Convention, Article VII Vienna Convention.

26 Article II of the Vienna Convention.

27 International agreements are in principle binding only on States Parties and cannot therefore create obligations for non-States Parties; however, this limitation on the reach of the obligations does not preclude an interpretation which allows to extend some benefits of an international treaty to non-contracting states. The preparatory works to the Vienna Convention reveals, however, a certain opposition against the idea that non-contracting parties may benefit from liability regime. S. Cigoj, 'International Regulation of Civil Liability for Nuclear Risk' (1965) 14 International and Comparative Law Quarterly 809, 816.

28 As of June 2022, States Parties include Belgium, Denmark, Finland, France, Germany, Greece, Italy, Luxembourg, Netherlands, Norway, Portugal, Slovenia, Spain, Sweden, Switzerland, Turkey and United Kingdom (www.oecd-nea.org/jcms/pl_31798/paris-convention-latest-status-of-ratifications-or-accessions).

29 A list of contracting parties to the Vienna Convention can be found here: <https://www.iaea.org/sites/default/files/22/06/liability_status.pdf> accessed March 2023.

30 Ghering and Jachtenfuchs (n 12) 99.

31 Article 3(b, i) of the Supplementary Convention.

32 3 (b, ii).

33 VC Explanatory Texts (n 24) 13.

34 See M Politi, 'The Impact of the Chernobyl Accident on the State's Perception of International Responsibility for Nuclear Damage' in F Francioni and T Scovazzi (eds.), *International Responsibility for Environmental Harm* (Graham & Trotman 1991).

35 Joint Protocol relating to the application of the Vienna Convention and the Paris Convention (21 September 1988; entered into force 27 April 1992).

36 See N Pelzer, 'Concept of Nuclear Liability Revisited: A Post-Chernobyl Assessment of the Paris and Vienna Conventions' in P Cameron et al. (eds.), *Nuclear Energy Law After Chernobyl* (Graham & Trotman 1988).

37 Protocol to Amend the Vienna Convention on Civil Liability for Nuclear Damage (1997) 36 ILM. 1462 (adopted 12 September 1997; entered into force 4 October 2003).

38 Protocol of 12 February 2004 to Amend the Paris Convention on Third Party Liability in the field of Nuclear Energy (adopted 12 February 2004; entered into force 1 January 2022).
39 Protocol of 12 February 2004 to Amend the Brussels Convention Supplementary to the Paris Convention of 29 July 1960, as amended (entered into force on 1 January 2022).
40 X Hanqin, *Transboundary Damage in International Law* (Cambridge University Press 2003) 35.
41 Article 2(2) of the 1997 Protocol, amending Article 1 (1) (k) of the 1963 Vienna Convention.
42 Ibid.
43 Article 2(3) 1997 Protocol amending Article 1(i) 1963 Vienna Convention [emphasis added].
44 Ibid.
45 See VC Explanatory Text (n 24) 33.
46 Article 3 of 1997 Protocol adding Article I A to the 1963 Vienna Convention.
47 Article 3 of the Protocol.
48 Ratifying countries include Argentina, Belarus, Benin, Bosnia and Herzegovina, Ghana, Jordan, Kazakhstan, Latvia, Montenegro, Morocco, Niger, Poland, Romania, Saudi Arabia and United Arab Emirates (situation as of 22 February 2021).
49 VC Explanatory Text (n 24) 21.
50 (1997) 26 ILM 1473 (adopted 12 September 1997; entry into force 15 April 2015).
51 B McRae, 'The Compensation Convention: Path to a Global Regime for Dealing with Legal Liability and Compensation for Nuclear Damage' (1998) 61 Nuclear Law Bulletin 25.
52 B McRae, 'The Convention on Supplementary Compensation for Nuclear Damage: Catalyst for a Global Nuclear Liability Regime' (2007) 79 Nuclear Law Bulletin 17.
53 McRae, 'The Compensation Convention' (n 51) 26.
54 De la Fayette, 'Towards a New Regime' (n 15), who considers the third layer of liability as a form of collective responsibility for having contributed to the risk of nuclear damage.
55 L De La Fayette, 'Nuclear Liability Revisited' (1992) 1 Review of European Community and International Environmental Law 443.
56 Ghering and Jachtenfuchs (n 12) 100.
57 G Doeker and T Ghering, 'Private or International Liability for Transnational Environmental Damage—The Precedents of Conventional Liability Regimes' (1990) 2 Journal of Environmental Law 3, 9.
58 Liu and Faure, 'Compensation for Nuclear Damage' (n 22) 184.
59 As of 22 February 2021, ratifying States include Argentina, Benin, Canada, Ghana, India, Japan, Montenegro, Morocco, Romania, UAE and USA.
60 J Bellamy, 'Civil Liability for Nuclear Damage in Countries Developing Nuclear New Build Programmes' (2019) 12 Journal of World Energy Law and Business 108.
61 United States ratified on 21 May 2008, and Japan on 15 January 2015.
62 See for example in Canada, where a new Nuclear Liability and Compensation Act entered into force in 2017 to replace the older Nuclear Liability Act and brought the domestic system in line with the basic principles set forth in the CSC. The new law increases the liability limits and provides a longer timeframe to bring the claims.
63 F Nocera, *The Legal Regime of Nuclear Energy* (Intersentia 2005) 413.
64 Article I (A) of the 2004 Protocol amending Article 1 of the 1960 Paris Convention.
65 Article 10 (c) of the Paris Convention as amended by the 2004 Protocol.
66 2004 Protocol to Amend the Brussels Convention Supplementary to the Paris Convention on Third Party Liability in the Field of Nuclear Energy (signed 12 February 2004; entry into force 1 January 2022).
67 RJ Heffron, SF Ashley and WJ Nuttal, 'The Global Liability Regime Post-Fukushima Daiichi' (2016) 90 Progress in Nuclear Energy 4. On the simultaneous ratification

requirement and the scope of EU's involvement in the international nuclear liability framework, see further in Chapter 6 of this book.

68 See further in Chapter 6, section 9, of this book.

69 As of 11 July 2022, the 2004 Paris Protocol has been ratified by Belgium, Denmark, Finland, France, Germany, Greece, Italy, Netherlands, Norway, Portugal, Slovenia, Spain, Sweden, Switzerland, Turkey and United Kingdom.

70 See Heffron and others (n 67).

71 MG Faure and K Fiore, 'An Economic Analysis of the Nuclear Liability Subsidy' (2009) 2 Pace Environmental Law Review 419.

72 Ibid.

73 The Nuclear Power Plant Exporters Principles of Conduct: <https://carnegieendowment.org/publications/special/misc/nppe/#:~:text=The%20Nuclear%20Power%20Plant%20Exporters,exportation%20of%20nuclear%20power%20plants> accessed 20 June 2022.

74 M Goransson, 'Liability for Damage to the Marine Environment' in A Boyle and D Freestone (eds.), *International Law and Sustainable Development: Past Achievements and Future Challenges* (Oxford University Press 1999) 346–347.

75 International Convention Relating to the Limitation of the Liability of Owners of Sea-going Ships (adopted in Brussels, 16 October 1957), (1968) UK Treaty Series, No. 52. This convention was replaced by the Convention on Limitation of Liability for Maritime Claims (LLMC) (adopted on 19 November 1976 and entered into force on 1 December 1986) 1456 UNTS 221 and its 1996 Protocol.

76 Article II of 1969 CLC.

77 Article III of 1969 CLC.

78 TA Mensah, 'Civil Liability and Compensation for Vessel-Source Pollution of the Marine Environment and the United Nations Convention on the Law of the Sea' in N Ando et al. (eds.), *Liber Amicorum Judge Shigeru Oda*, Vol. II (Kluwer Law International 2002) 1398–1399.

79 Article V (3) of 1969 CLC.

80 As of July 2022, it has 33 contracting parties given that many of the original contracting parties have denounced it in correspondence to their accession to the 1992 amending Protocol.

81 Protocol of 1992 to Amend the International Convention on Civil Liability for Oil Pollution Damage (adopted 27 November 1992; entered into force 30 May 1996). Many of the amendments to the 1969 Civil Liability Convention introduced by the 1992 Protocol had been already envisaged in a previous Protocol, adopted in 1984. The 1984 Protocol, however, never enter into force because of the strict ratification requirements and the United States' unwillingness to ratify it.

82 The 1992 Civil Liability Convention is a consolidated version of the 1969 CLC as amended by the 1992 Protocol. Article 11 of the 1992 Protocol provides that both instruments are to be read and interpreted together as a single instrument.

83 M Mason, 'Transnational Compensation for Oil Pollution Damage: Examining Changing Spatialities of Environmental Liability', (2002) *LSE Research Papers in Environmental and Spatial Analysis* (No. 69) <http://eprints.lse.ac.uk/570/> accessed on July 2022, 12.

84 Article 3 of the 1992 Protocol.

85 Article 3(4) of the 1992 Civil Liability Protocol defines 'incident' as 'any occurrence, or series of occurrences having the same origin, which causes pollution damage or creates a grave and imminent threat of causing such damage'.

86 Article 3(4) 1992 CLC.

87 Mensah (n 78) 1414.

88 See L De la Fayette, 'The Concept of Environmental Damage in International Liability Regimes' in M Bowman and A Boyle (eds.), *Environmental Damage in International and Comparative Law: Problems of Definition and Valuation* (Oxford University Press 2002) 155–159.

89 M Mason, 'Civil Liability for Oil Pollution Damage: Examining the Evolving Scope for Environmental Compensation in the International Regime' (2003) 27 Marine Policy 1, 3.
90 See further infra at section 3.5.
91 In 1980, the IOPC Fund adopted Resolution No. 3—'Pollution Damage' (October 1980), FUND/A/ES.1/13, paragraph 11 (a) and Annex I, where it clarified. 'the assessment of compensation to be paid by the International Oil Pollution Compensation Fund is not to be made on the basis of an abstract qualification of the damage calculated with theoretical models'.
92 Article 1(6)(a) 1992 CLC [emphasis added].
93 De La Fayette, 'The Concept of Environmental Damage' (n 88) 156.
94 D Wilkinson, 'Moving the Boundaries of Compensable Environmental Damage Caused by Marine Oil Spills: The Effect of Two New International Protocols' (1993) 5 Journal of Environmental Law 71, 73.
95 D Ong, 'The Relationship between Environmental Damage and Pollution: Marine Oil Pollution Laws in Malaysia and Singapore' in *Environmental Damage in International and Comparative Law* (n 88) 201.
96 De La Fayette (n 88) 155.
97 M Jacobsson and N Trotz, 'The Definition of Pollution Damage in the 1984 Protocols to the 1969 Civil Liability Convention and the 1971 Fund Convention' (1986) 17 Journal of Maritime Law and Commerce 467.
98 IOPC Fund Claims Manual (2019 Edition).
99 Resolution adopted by the IMO Legal Committee on 18 October 2000 LEG.1(82), 'Adoption of Amendments of the Limitation Amounts in the Protocol of 1992 to Amend the international Convention on Civil Liability for Oil Pollution Damage, 1969'. No formal ratifications were required, and the amendment came into force automatically in 2003.
100 Article V(2) 1992 Protocol.
101 European Commission, Communication from the Commission to the European Parliament and the Council on the Safety of the Seaborne Oil Trade, COM (2000) 142 final, 35. On this, see also further discussion in Chapter 6 text at nn 189 ff.
102 Article II(4).
103 M Jacobsson, 'Oil Pollution Liability and Compensation: An International Regime' (1996) 2 Uniform Law Review 260, 263.
104 Ghering and Jachtenfuchs (n 12) 98.
105 Protocol to Amend the International Convention on the Establishment of an International Fund for Compensation for Oil Pollution Damage, 27 November 1992 (27 November 1992; entry into force 30 May 1996). The 1992 Fund Convention is a consolidated version of the 1969 Fund Convention as amended by the 1992 Protocol. Article 27 of the 1992 Protocol provides that both instruments are to be read and interpreted together as one single instrument. D. Wilkinson (n 94) 71–90.
106 See Jacobsson (n 103).
107 J Nichols, 'Admissibility of Claims: Development of the IOPC Funds' Policy' in IOPC Fund (ed.), *The IOPC Funds' 25 Years of Compensating Victims of Pollution Accidents* (2003) 118.
108 In this sense, A Bianchi, 'Harm to the Environment in Italian Practice: The Interaction of International Law and Domestic Law', P Wetterstein (ed.), *Harm to the Environment: The Right to Compensation and the Assessment of Damages* (Clarendon Press 1997).
109 M Faure and H Wang, 'The International Regimes for Compensation of Oil Pollution Damage: Are They Effective?' (2003) 12 Review of European Community and International Environmental Law 242.
110 Protocol of 2003 to the International Convention on the Establishment of an International Fund for Compensation for Oil Pollution Damage, 1992 (London, 16 May 2003;

entry into force, 3 March 2005). As of 30 September 2021 the Supplementary Protocol has 32 State Parties, see https://iopcfunds.org/wp-content/uploads/2021/10/explanatory-note_e.pdf> accessed 17 July 2022.

111 See M Faure and H Wang, 'Smart Mixes of Civil Liability Regimes for Marine Oil Pollution' in J Van Erp and others (eds.), *Smart Mixes for Transboundary Environmental Harm* (CUP 2019) 289.

112 See S Poli, *La Responsabilitá per Danni da Inquinamento Transfrontaliero nel Diritto Comunitario e Internazionale* (Giuffré 2006) 127. On the relationship between EU developments and international law, see further in Chapter 6.

113 Faure and Wang, 'Smart Mixes' (n 111) 299; G Gonsaeles, 'The Impact of EC Decision-Making on the International Regime for Oil Pollution Damage: The Supplementary Fund Example' in F Maes (ed.), *Marine Resource Damage Assessment, Liability and Compensation for Environmental Damage* (Springer 2005) 85.

114 Data as of February 2021, from <imo.org/en/About/Conventions/Pages/StatusOfConventions.aspx>.

115 See IOPC Fund (ed.), *The IOPC Fund's 25 Years of Compensating Victims of Oil Pollution Incidents* (IOPC Fund, 2003).

116 The spill caused massive environmental damage to French coast. French claimants took the position that the most favourable US law should apply to the case. L Rosenthal and C Raper, 'Amoco Cadiz and Limitation of Liability for Oil Spill Pollution: Domestic and International Solutions' (1985) 5 Virginia Journal of Natural Resources Law 259.

117 See Fund Doc. IOPC/OCT09/3/5.

118 N De Sadeleer, 'Liability for Oil Pollution Damage Versus Liability for Waste Management: The Polluter Pays Principle at the Rescue of the Victims' (2009) 21 Journal of Environmental Law 299.

119 *Cour de Cassation, Chambre Criminelle*, 25 Septembre 2012, 10–82.938.

120 MP Camproux-Duffrène and D Guihal, 'Pollution Maritime. Naufrage de l'Erika. Responsabilité Pénale. Loi du 5 juillet 1973. Convention MARPOL. ZEE. Responsabilié civile pour Dommages Causés à l'Environnement par des Hydrocarbures en Mer. Réparation du prejudice écologique pur' (2013) 3 Revue Juridique de l'Environnement 457, 460.

121 See the analysis of the decision by V Rebeyrol, 'The Erika Case: An Incitement to Rewrite the CLC' (2013) European Energy and Environmental Law Review 33.

122 Ibid 37.

123 Cour d'Appel de Paris, No RG 08/02278 *Clemente et a. c./Conseil Général de la Vendée et a*, arret du 30 mars 2010.

124 Translation from N Hervé-Fournerau, 'National Report FRANCE' (Avosetta Meeting, Helsinki 2013).

125 As reported in the document submitted to the IOPC Fund by the Conference of Peripheral Maritime Regions of Europe (CPMR), IOPC/APR13/3/3/2, 28 March 2013, 5.

126 See J Adshead, 'The Application and Development of the Polluter-Pays Principle across Jurisdictions in Liability for Marine Oil Pollution: The Tales of the "Erika" and the "Prestige"' (2018) 30 Journal of Environmental Law 425, 437.

127 Chapter 7, text at nn 94–109.

128 De Sadeleer (n 118) 299; cfr Adshead (n 126).

129 B Soyer, 'Emergence of EU and Maritime Law' in D Patterson and A Sodersten (eds.), *A Companion to European Union and International Law* (Wiley and Blackwell 2016) 430.

130 IOPC Fund, 'Incidents Involving the IOPC Funds—1992 Fund—Erika', document submitted by France, 28 March 2013, IOPC/APR13/3/1.

131 See Technical Paper from the General Secretariat of Conference Des Regions Périphériques Maritimes d'Europe (CPMR), 'Following the "Erika" Ruling by the French Court of Cassation, What Steps Should be Taken at European and International Level?', 16 May 2013, 2.

132 See in particular the Claims Manual, initially adopted by the 1992 Fund Assembly in 1998 and since them regularly updated and amended by the 1992 Fund Administrative Council. The Manual seeks to offer a practical guide to presenting claims against the 1992 and provides clarity on the interpretation of the compensation criteria under the Convention. The Claims Manual is available at https://iopcfunds.org/publications/iopc-funds-publications/> accessed 15 December 2021.

133 Ibid., Annex II.

134 See A Merialdi, 'The *Patmos* and *Haven* Cases: Recent Developments' (1994) 9 International Journal of Marine and Coastal Law 389.

135 Court of Appeal of Messina, *Ministero della Marina Mercantile e Ministero dell'Interno v. Patmos Shipping Co. et al.*, 24 December 1993 reproduced in (1994) 9 Rivista Giuridica dell'Ambiente, 683–94. In that case, the Court quantified environmental damage on the basis of equitable criteria. For a commentary see MC Maffei, 'The Compensation for Ecological Damage in the *Patmos* case' in F Francioni and T Scovazzi (eds.), *International Responsibility for Environmental Harm* (Graham & Trotman 1991) 381–394.

136 See, for example, J Harrison, 'Conflicting Interpretations—The Slops Incident and the Application of the International Oil Pollution Liability and Compensation Regime to Offshore Storage and Transfer Operations' (2008) 20 Journal of Environmental Law 455.

137 IMO Document LEG/CONF.10/8/2

138 IMO Document LEG/CONF.12/DC/1.

139 Article 1(5) Bunker Oil Convention.

140 De La Fayette (n 88) 155–156.

141 Article 7 Bunker Oil Convention.

142 Article 6 Bunker Oil Convention.

143 Data as of February 2021.

144 IMO Legal Committee, 'An Overview of the International Convention on Liability and Compensation for Damage in Connection with the Carriage of Hazardous and Noxious Substances by Sea', >hnsconvention.org/the-convention>.

145 Canada, Denmark, Norway, Turkey and South Africa (source: www.hnsconvention.org/status/> accessed 20 July 2022.

146 See further in Chapter 7 of this book.

147 United Nations Convention on the Law of the Sea (10 December 1982; 16 November 1994) 1833 UNTS 397.

148 See Articles 194 and 207–212 UNCLOS.

149 Y Yang, 'Liability and Compensation for Oil Spill Accidents: International Regime and Its Implementation in China' (2017) 57 Natural Resources Journal 465, 469.

150 See further on the ELD in Chapter 4 of this book.

151 Directive 2013/30/EU on safety of offshore oil and gas operation (Offshore Safety Directive) OJ L 179.

152 Directive 2008/56/EC establishing a framework for community action in the field of marine environmental policy, OJ L 164, Article 3.

153 European Parliament Resolution of 1 December 2016 on liability, compensation and financial security for offshore oil and gas operations, P8_TA(2016) 0478, OJ C 224/157.

154 UNGA Resolution of 24 December 2017, International legally binding instrument under the United Nations on the Law of the Sea on the conservation and sustainable use of marine biological diversity of areas beyond national jurisdiction, A/RES/72/249. For the text of the High Seas Treaty as agreed in March 2023, see https://www.un.org/bbnj/sites/www.un.org.bbnj/files/draft_agreement_advanced_unedited_for_posting_v1.pdf

155 Convention on Civil Liability for Damage Resulting from Activities Dangerous to the Environment, Lugano, (21 June 1993; not in force) (1993) 32 I.L.M. 1228.

156 Article 2(10). See B Sandvik and S Suikkari, 'Harm and Reparation in International Treaty Regimes: An Overview' in *Harm to the Environment: The Right to Compensation and the Assessment of Damages* (n 108) 60.
157 Article 2(8) of the Lugano Convention, 'Definitions—measures of reinstatement'.
158 Article 13 to 16 of the Lugano Convention.
159 Article 18.
160 See Chapter 6, section 7.2, of this book.
161 D Wilkinson, 'The Council of Europe Convention on Civil Liability for Damage Resulting from Activities Dangerous to the Environment: A Comparative Overview' (1993) European Law Review 130, 134.
162 See M Fitzmaurice, 'International Responsibility and Liability' in D Bodansky, J Brunnée and E Hey (eds.), *The Oxford Handbook of International Environmental Law* (Oxford University Press 2007) 1032. See, however, B Sen, 'Civil Liability for Injurious Consequences of Potentially Hazardous Activities—The Need for Uniform Law' (1996) Uniform Law Review 453, asserting the need of uniform liability rules applicable generally in the field of hazardous activities.
163 See UNEP/CBD/COP/8/27/Add.3, para. 19.
164 Conference of the Parties to the Convention on Biological Diversity, *Synthesis report on technical information relating to damage to biological diversity and approaches to valuation and restoration of damage to biological diversity as well as information on national/domestic measures and experiences*, Bonn, 19–30 May 2008, UNEP/CBD/COP/9/20/Add.1.
165 See Preamble to the CBD defining the protection of biological diversity as 'common concern of mankind'; similarly, the Preamble to the 1979 Bern Convention on the Conservation of European Wildlife and Natural Habitats 'recognises that European wildlife constitutes a natural heritage'.
166 The CBD's Preamble comprehensively refers to the 'intrinsic value of biological diversity and of the ecological, genetic, social, economic, educational, cultural, recreational, and aesthetic values of biological diversity and its components'.
167 See M Bowman, 'Biodiversity, Intrinsic Value, and the Definition and Valuation of Environmental Harm' in Bowman and Boyle (eds.), *Environmental Harm in International and Comparative Law: Problems of Definition and Valuation* (OUP 2002).
168 See KL Holtby, WA Kerr and JE Hobbs, *International Environmental Liability and Barriers to Trade—Market Access and Biodiversity in the Biosafety Protocol* (Edward Elgar 2007).
169 See K Cook, 'No Liability, No Protocol' in C Bali, R Falkner and H Marquand (eds.), *The Cartagena Protocol on Biosafety: Reconciling Trade in Biotechnology with Environment and Development?* (Royal Institute of International Affairs 2002).
170 S Jungcurt and N Schabus, 'Liability and Redress in the Context of the Cartagena Protocol on Biosafety' (2010) 19 Reciel 2.
171 R Lefeber and J Nieto Carrasco, 'Negotiating the Supplementary Protocol: The Co-Chairs' Perspective' in A Shibata (ed.), *International Liability Regime for Biodiversity Damage: The Nagoya-Kuala Lumpur Supplementary Protocol* (Routledge 2014).
172 *Proposed Operation Texts on Approaches and Options Identified Pertaining to Liability and Redress in the Context of Article 27 of the Biosafety Protocol,* Addendum to the Final Report of the Ad Hoc Working Group of Legal and Technical Experts on Liability and Redress in the Context of the Cartagena Protocol on Biosafety, UNEP/CBD/BS/COP-MOP/4/11/Add.1. The text was further discussed by the COP/MOP during its meeting in Mexico City, in February 2009.
173 D Tladi, 'Civil Liability in the Context of the Cartagena Protocol: To Be or Not to Be (Binding)?' (2009) 10 International Environmental Agreements 15.
174 UNEP/CBD/BS/COP-MOP/5/17 of 15 October 2010. Supplementary Protocol adopted on 15 October 2010, entered into force 5 March 2018.
175 Article 1 of the Nagoya-Kuala Lumpur Supplementary Protocol.

176 Article 2(2)(b).
177 Article 2(3).
178 Article 5 of the Supplementary Protocol.
179 Article 2.
180 Article 2.2 (d).
181 Article 12(1).
182 GS Nijar, 'Civil Liability in the Supplementary Protocol' in *International Liability Regime for Biodiversity Damage* (n 171).
183 C Foster, 'Diminished Ambitions? Public International Legal Authority in the Transnational Economic Era' (2014) 17 Journal of International Economic Law 355.
184 See A Shibata, 'The Nagoya-Kuala Lumpur Supplementary Protocol on Liability and Redress' in *International Liability Regime for Biodiversity Damage* (n 171) 2.
185 J Brunnée, 'Of Sense and Sensibility' (n 11).
186 Shibata (n 184).
187 <https://bch.cbd.int/protocol/supplementary/> accessed 18 July 2022.
188 (1991) 30 ILM 1455.
189 Liability rules were originally also envisaged by the 1988 Wellington Convention on the Regulation of Antarctic Mineral Resources Activities (subsequently superseded by the Madrid Protocol), which was the first international law agreement establishing the operator's liability for damage to the environment *per se*: De La Fayette, 'The Concept of Environmental Damage' (n 88) 178.
190 F Francioni, 'Liability for Damage to the Common Environment: The Case of Antarctica' (1994) 3 Reciel 223.
191 Ibid. 228.
192 Article 2 of the Madrid Protocol.
193 Hanqin (n 40) 234.
194 M Johnson, 'Liability for Environmental Damage in Antarctica: The Adoption of Annex IV to the Antarctic Environmental Protocol', (2006–2007) 19 Georgetown International Environmental Law Review 33.
195 P Vigni, 'A Liability Regime for Antarctica' (2006) The Italian Yearbook of International Law 214.

Article 2 of the Madrid Protocol. See also S Voneky, 'The Liability Annex to the Protocol on Environmental Protection to the Antarctic Treaty' in D Doing, P Tobias Stoll and R Volker (eds.), *International Law Today: New Challenges and the Need for Reform?* (Springer 2008).

196 See D MacKay, 'The Proposed Antarctic Treaty on Environmental Damage' (1999–2000) ILSA Journal of International and Comparative Law 473.
197 Article 6(1) of the Annex.
198 Article 5(3, lett. a).
199 Article 7(1) of the Annex.
200 A Shibata, 'How to Design an International Liability Regime for Public Spaces: The Case of the Antarctic Environment' in T Komori and K Wellens (eds.), *Public Interest Rules of International Law* (Routledge 2009) 363–364.
201 Ibid. 354–358.
202 Johnson (n 194).
203 AD Hemming, 'Liability Postponed: The Failure to Bring Annex VI of the Madrid Protocol into Force' (2018) 8 The Polar Journal 315.
204 Shibata (n 220) 366.
205 ILM (1969) 8, 497.
206 What was voluntary is the decision of the relevant companies to participate or not in the agreement. Once they decided to become parties, they were subject to contractual obligations to respect the terms and conditions of the applicable agreement.
207 J Harrison, 'Regime Pluralism and the Global Regulation of Oil Pollution Liability and Compensation' (2009) 5 International Journal of Law in Context 379, 386.

208 C de La Rue, 'TOVALOP and CRISTAL—A Purpose Fulfilled' <www.colindelarue.com/publications/> accessed 16 December 2021.
209 Ibid.
210 Information about and the text of the Compact are available at <www.biodiversitycompact.org/> accessed 16 December 2021.
211 Harrison (n 207).
212 PM Dupuy, 'Soft Law and the International Law of the Environment' (1991) 12 Michigan Journal of International Law 420.
213 See A Boyle, 'Soft Law in International Law Making' in MD Evans (ed.), *International Law* (5th ed., OUP 2018).
214 Boyle (n 213); J Pauwelyn, RA Wessel and J Wouters, 'When Structures Become Shackles: Stagnation and Dynamics in International Law-Making' (2014) 25 European Journal of International Law 733.
215 E Orlando, 'Principles, Standards and Voluntary Commitments in International Environmental Law' in E Techera and others (eds.), *Routledge Handbook of International Environmental Law* (2nd ed., Routledge 2020).
216 Dupuy (n 212).
217 *Yearbook of the Institute of International Law* (1997) vol. 67, Part II, session of Strasbourg, 486. See Chapter 4.
218 Ibid., Article 4.
219 Ibid., Article 14.
220 Ibid., Articles 22–24.
221 UNEP Governing Council, 11th special Session, Environmental Law: Report by the Executive Director (Addendum), 3 December 2009, UNEP/GCSS.XI/8/Add.1.
222 T Scovazzi, 'State Responsibility for Environmental Harm' (2002) 12 Yearbook of International Environmental Law 43, 44.
223 T Scovazzi, 'The Mediterranean Guidelines for the Determination of Environmental Liability and Compensation: The Negotiations for the Instrument and the Question of Damage that Can Be Compensated' in A Von Bogandy and R Wolfrum (eds.), *Max Planck Yearbook of United Nations Law*, Vol 13 (Martinus Nijhoff Publishers 2009) 183.
224 Entered into force on 12 February 1978; amended in 1995.
225 Adopted 14 October 1994; entry into force 24 March 2011.
226 Scovazzi 'The Mediterranean Guidelines' (n 223) 188.
227 Ibid.
228 Ibid. 196–198.
229 Draft Guidelines on Liability and Compensation for Damage Resulting from Pollution of the Marine Environment in the Mediterranean Sea Area, UNEP (DEPI)/MED WG. 319/3, June 2007.
230 E Orlando, 'Public and Private in the Law of Environmental Liability' in F Lenzerini and AF Vrdoljak (eds.), *International Law for Common Goods: Normative Perspectives on Human Rights, Culture and Nature* (Hart 2014).
231 Scovazzi (n 223) 206.
232 A Boyle, 'Globalizing Environmental Liability: The Interplay of National and International Law' (2004) 17 Journal of Environmental Law 1, 12.
233 J Barboza, *The Environment, Risk and Liability in International Law* (Martinus Nijhoff 2011) 9–15.
234 See, among others, RL Rabin, 'Some Thoughts on the Ideology of Enterprise Liability' (1996) 55 Modern Law Review 1190, 1198; G Brüggemeier, 'Enterprise Liability for Environmental Damage in German Law and EC Law' in G Teubner, L Farmer and D Murphy (eds.), *Environmental Law and Ecological Responsibility: The Concept and Practice of Ecological Self-Organization* (Wiley & Sons 1994); RB Bush, 'Between Two Worlds: the Shift from Individual to Group Responsibility in the Law of Causation of Injury' (1986) 33 UCLA Law Review 1473.

235 G Teubner, 'The Invisible Cupola: From Causal to Collective Attribution in Ecological Liability' in *Environmental Law and Ecological Responsibility* (n 234) 17.
236 Barboza (n 233) 3.
237 Daniel (n 11).
238 R Lefeber, *Transboundary Environmental Interference and the Origin of State Liability* (Kluwer Law International 1996) 230.
239 PM Dupuy, 'A Propos des Mésaventures de la Responsabilité International de l'État Dans Ses Rapports Avec la Protection International de l'Environnement' in M Prieur and C Lambrechts (eds.), *Les Hommes et l'Environnement: Quels Droits pour le Vingt-et-unième Siècle? Études en Hommage à Alexander Kiss* (Frison-Roche 1998) 271.
240 A Rosas, 'Issues of State Liability for Transboundary Environmental Damage' (1991) 60 Nordic Journal of International Law 29, 38.
241 See Doeker and Ghering (n 57).
242 PM Dupuy, *La Résponsabilité Internationale des Etats Pour les Dommages D'Origine Technologique et Industrielle* (Pédone, 1976) 155–156.
243 See, e.g., G Handl, 'International Accountability for Transboundary Environmental Harm Revisited: What Role for State Liability?' (2007) 37 Environmental Policy and Law 12.
244 Ibid.; also G Handl, 'Environmental Security and Global Change: The Challenge to International Law' in W Lang, H Neuhold and K Zemanek (eds.), *Environmental Protection and International Law* (Graham & Trotman 1991).
245 F Orrego Vicuna, 'Responsibility and Liability for Environmental Damage under International Law—Final Report Prepared for the Eight Committee of the Institut de Droit International' (1998) 10 Georgetown Environmental Law Review 279, 287.
246 Lefeber (n 238) 229–232.
247 PS Rao, *First Report on the International Legal Regime for Allocation of Loss in Case of Transboundary Harm Arising Out of Hazardous Activities,* International Law Commission, UNGA Doc., A/CN.4/531, 19.
248 Ibid. 19. Lefeber (n 238) 230.

Part 2

Harmonising environmental liability in the EU

Substantive and procedural legal aspects

Part 2 of this book moves the analysis from the examination of the international legal framework in the field of environmental liability to relevant developments within the EU. The establishment of harmonised legal standards across the various Member States is one of the main features characterising the normative action of the EU, although of course harmonisation at the EU level may occur in different forms and to different degrees.[1] In the field of environmental liability, the most remarkable instance of harmonisation of substantive standard of environmental liability at the EU level is represented by the EU Environmental Liability Directive, which is examined in great detail in Chapter 4. There are, however, also other EU secondary law instruments on conflict of laws and jurisdiction that by harmonising the legal principles applicable for the identification of the competent court and the law applicable have been especially relevant in the pursuit of environmental claims through transnational tort litigation. Chapter 5 illustrates these developments with a view to explore the extent to which those EU developments are contributing to enhance environmental claimants' pursuit of legal redress in a transnational context.

Overall, the two chapters in Part 2 aim to offer an overview and an assessment of the value of regional efforts of harmonisation in the field of environmental liability and to prepare the ground for the analysis of the interaction between EU and international law, which is developed in Part 3.

DOI: 10.4324/9781315676708-6

4 The EU approach to environmental liability

The 2004/35 environmental liability directive

1. Introduction

In the European Union, the question of environmental liability has been primarily addressed through the adoption of the *2004/35 Directive on Environmental Liability with regard to the Prevention and Remedying of Environmental Damage* (hereinafter 'Directive' or 'ELD').[2] With the aim to fill the gaps left by the application of traditional civil liability rules to environmental harm,[3] the Directive sets up a distinct public law-based scheme of environmental liability aimed at the prevention and remediation of damage to the natural environment. To this end, it provides duties of preventative and remedial action for operators and envisages a central role of the public competent authorities in the enforcement of such duties. Although the lengthy period of gestation leading to its adoption has somehow altered the final outcome with respect to earlier proposals, this Directive overall reflects the main concerns which prompted the European Commission's initiative in this area, namely to reinforce environmental protection in Europe by ensuring restoration of environmental damage and to improve private operators' compliance with environmental standards. Conceptually, the ELD is based on the polluter pays principle, which is one of the main principles of EU environmental policy.[4] Adopted in 2004, the ELD has recently undergone a process of revision also in the light of the findings emerged from the Commission's systematic review of its implementation and application in the various Member States, as formerly provided by its Article 18.[5]

2. Historical background

For a long time, EU environmental law did not feature specific provisions on environmental liability. During the 1980s and beginning of the 1990s, EU environmental law was characterised by a major focus on prevention and on the maintenance of good 'environmental quality'. Accordingly, aside from isolated initiatives providing for a prompt response to industrial accidents, the question of serious environmental harm caused during the operation of hazardous activities did not find a comprehensive and systematic regulation at the EU level and was instead dealt with mainly at the domestic level, through national rules of civil liability or, where available, through ad hoc legislation concerning specific aspects of environmental damage.

DOI: 10.4324/9781315676708-7

This gap in the EU environmental legal framework became evident especially after the occurrence of a number of devastating industrial accidents, which prompted the Council and the Commission to consider the adoption of new measures to ensure 'prompt clean-up and restoration, coupled with arrangements for liability and compensation by the polluters for any damage caused'.[6] Thus, after stillborn attempts to introduce rules on liability for damage caused by waste,[7] the process leading towards the elaboration of an EU-wide system of environmental liability started officially with the adoption of two consultation papers, namely the European Commission's Green Paper on Remedying Environmental Damage adopted in 1993[8] and the White Paper on Environmental Liability adopted in 2000.[9] The latter put forward concrete proposals for an EU intervention in the field, including a combined system of civil liability rules for traditional forms of damage to property and persons and rules on environmental liability for environmental damage to biodiversity and site contamination.[10] The discussions emerging from the White Paper led in 2002 to a draft Proposal for a directive on environmental liability,[11] the main features of which were subsequently maintained in the final text of the ELD. Compared to the White Paper, the Directive's Proposal operated a radical shift from civil liability to a regulatory/administrative type of liability characterised by a central role of the competent administrative authorities in the enforcement process; it also discarded any references to civil liability for traditional damage, maintaining instead an exclusive focus on damage to natural resources (i.e. natural habitats, damage to water and land contamination).

It is appropriate to remark at this point that during the 1990s, the debate around environmental liability in the EU was influenced in various ways and degrees by a number of parallel developments at the international level and in domestic jurisdictions. At the international level, the 1993 Lugano Convention played a major role in determining the course of action of relevant EU initiatives and was initially regarded as a possible model for a future EU intervention in the field.[12] The White Paper prospected in fact the EU accession to the Convention as one of the possible options for the harmonisation of liability rules across the Member States. Meanwhile, domestic legal systems in various EU Member States and in other OECD countries were converging towards the acceptance of strict liability as the preferred standard for damage to persons, property and the environment caused by dangerous activities,[13] while an administrative type of liability started to emerge in a few Member States to address land contamination and historical land pollution. In addition to these European developments, a further major influence in the crafting of an EU-wide environmental liability regime came from across the Atlantic. In 1980, the United States federal government adopted the Comprehensive Environmental Response, Compensation, and Liability Act (CERCLA), otherwise known as 'Superfund'.[14] This liability statute consisted in an administrative scheme of enforcement, imposing liability to a wide range of responsible parties and tackling the most hazardous sites. It was particularly innovative at the time of its adoption as it embodied a totally different approach from the classic tort law system.[15] The Superfund was followed in 1990 by the Oil Pollution Act (OPA) providing specific rules on liability and clean-up procedures in the case of oil spills.[16] These new models of liability and remediation of environmental damage played a significant role in the definition of the Directive's environmental liability regime and in guiding the definitive shift towards a public law system of liability.

3. The underling regulatory and policy rationales

While environmental liability is primarily a tool to achieve reparation for environmental damage, the EU's decision to legislate in the field was also connected to important policy and regulatory goals. During the 1990s, the so-called command and control regulation, which in the EU still represented the predominant form of environmental regulation, started to be subjected to considerable criticism.[17] The 1992 Fifth Environmental Action Programme[18] therefore encouraged the search for more flexible and efficient instruments, such as the use of economic and market-based instruments to influence actors' behaviour in addition to prescriptive commands from regulatory bodies.[19] In this context, the development of a liability instrument seemed to fit with the Commission's commitment to diversifying its regulatory approaches, as liability was viewed as providing a clear economic incentive for management control of risk, pollution and waste[20] while also allowing a more effective implementation of the polluter pays principle.[21] Thus, the idea of liability as a tool to improve compliance with environmental standards started to gather increasing support in the discussions towards the elaboration of an EU environmental liability regime[22] and became gradually one of the primary underlining rationales of the Directive. During the negotiations of the text of the ELD, questions of implementation and enforcement of EU environmental law had become a strategic priority,[23] while the existing enforcement tools available under the EU treaties, through the role of the European Commission and the CJEU, were perceived insufficient, of themselves, to fill the implementation gap which was affecting the effectiveness of EU environmental law.

Against this background, the shift from the initial idea of a harmonised civil liability regime to the development of an administrative law approach to liability with an exclusive focus on natural resources damage seem to mirror this renewed stance on the topic. First, in terms of the underlying rationales, the harmonisation of civil liability rules was no longer felt necessary to improve the internal market (an earlier concern underlying previous civil liability proposals in the field of waste), while the need to strengthen compliance with EU environmental standards was acquiring an ever-increasing importance within EU policies.[24] Second, the departure from the civil liability approach was also a pragmatic choice to render the new instrument more acceptable to the EU Member States. The latter, in fact, proved particularly resistant to initiatives that 'touched upon their national systems of tort law that had been built up and shaped by jurisprudence over decades and even centuries'.[25] Moreover, 'differences between common law and civil law approaches added to the difficulties of achieving a common approach'.[26] Third, from an environmental law perspective, a public-law/regulatory approach to liability appeared as more appropriate to the pursuit of publicly oriented environmental goals. The idea of vesting administrative enforcement powers against polluters would help to overcome some of the inherent limits and difficulties of private litigation,[27] while also tackling concerns over the narrow private and individual law focus typical of civil liability.[28] At the same time, a liability regime exclusively concerned with natural resources damage represented a response to growing concern for the protection of the environment, both in terms of devising appropriate strategies to promote compliance and of setting up effective mechanisms to ensure the remediation of environmental damage. These twin rationales of improving compliance and promoting environmental remediation are now reflected in the ELD's almost exclusive focus on the ecological dimension of the damage and in its scope of application, which is for the most part defined through direct reference to EU secondary legislation.

4. The Directive's main elements and scope of application

The application of the ELD is defined by the concept of environmental damage and by the definition of the liable person or entity—i.e. the 'operator'—in combination with the type of activities to which the liability regime applies. Moreover, the Directive also covers instances of 'imminent threat of environmental damage' defined as a situation in which the damage has not yet occurred but there is 'a sufficient likelihood' that it will occur in the near future.[29]

4.1 Definition of 'environmental damage'

The concept of environmental damage has a pivotal role in the operation of the ELD. This concept consists of two elements. The first is represented by the notion of 'environmental damage', defined in Article 2(1) by reference to the natural resources covered by the liability regime—i.e. protected species and natural habitats, water and land—and the indication of the respective significance thresholds. Except for land contamination for which so far there is no specific EU legislation, the natural resources to which the Directive applies are purportedly defined through reference to existing EU environmental directives. This reflects the ELD's aims to act as a horizontal, cross-cutting environmental law instrument that complements and supports the pursuit of important goals under sectoral EU environmental legislation, including the objective of halting biodiversity loss and improving the quality of European freshwaters under the Water Framework Directive.[30]

The second element of the concept is represented by the autonomous notion of 'damage' in Article 2(2), defined as 'a measurable adverse change in a natural resource or measurable impairment of a natural resource service which may occur directly or indirectly'. Article 2(13) defines 'natural resources services' as the functions performed by a natural resource for the benefit of another natural resource or the public'.

The respective thresholds of significance in the separate heads of natural resources damage (i.e. damage to water, natural species and habitats, and land contamination) together with the notion of damage in Article 2(2) make clear that the application of the Directive, at least with respect to the operator's duty to remediate environmental damage, is only triggered when damage exceeds a certain threshold of significance. An important concept in determining the significance of the damage is that of 'baseline condition' defined in Article 2(14) as 'the condition at the time of the damage of the natural resources and services that would have existed had the environmental damage not occurred, estimated on the basis of the best information available'. Although the Directive refers to baseline condition only to determine the significance of damage to protected species and habitats, this concept is relevant in the assessment of the significance of damage to the other natural resources covered by the ELD.[31] Moreover, the recently approved Commission Guidelines on providing a common understanding of the term 'environmental damage' clarify that determining the occurrence of a significant damage 'involves comparing the condition of natural resources and services *before* the damaging occurrence took place with the condition *after* the occurrence took place'.[32] Carrying out this comparison necessitates inevitably the availability of relevant information concerning the baseline condition. Therefore, gathering information concerning the baseline and making it available to operators and to competent authorities is, according to the Commission, one of the priority actions to ensure a proper and effective implementation of the Directive.[33] With respect to natural habitats and species, however, relevant information useful to determine the baseline can also be gathered through the requirement for the Member States to provide information on the status of these resources for their designation as Natura 2000 sites as well as to monitor the conservation status of these habitats and species.[34] Moreover, specific biodiversity databases are in place in some Member States, while at the EU level a Register of Biodiversity Baseline Information Sources has been established to provide information on sources and methodological approaches to determine the baseline conditions for damage to natural resources.

The reference to the 'impairment of a natural resource service' in the definition of damage indicates that the Directive is concerned not only with the physical destruction or impairment of a natural resource, but also with the loss of its ecological functions and of its recreational or aesthetic functions.[35] It reaffirms the idea of natural resources being considered as 'public' goods and evaluated not on the basis of their economic or market value, but by taking into account also their value for the ecosystem maintenance and their collective and recreational values for the public. This explicit consideration of losses of natural resources services within the Directive sets the EU liability regime apart from most international environmental liability frameworks. In fact, this head of damage is not even provided in the Nagoya-Kuala Lumpur Supplementary Protocol, which so far represents the international liability agreement with greater similarity to the ELD.

The expression 'directly or indirectly' in relation to the occurrence of the adverse changes refers to the causal link between the damaging event and the specific adverse effects on the natural resource or its services.[36] An indirect causal link may occur when polluting emissions from an occupational activity adversely affect a specific natural resource through the intermediation of air, water or land, such as in the case where a habitat is adversely affected by contaminated nutrients passing through land. In that respect, paragraph 4 of the Directive's Preamble clarifies, 'environmental damage caused by airborne elements' is included 'as far as they cause damage to water, land or protected species or natural habitats'.

In terms of scope of application, the Directive's exclusive focus on damage to environmental resources has two important implications. The first is the exclusion of traditional forms of damage from the ELD's coverage so that this instrument cannot be used to claim compensation for personal or property damage or to give private parties a right to compensation for other losses related environmental damage. Article 3(3) indicates, however, that these types of damage are still recoverable under national legislation, typically through tort provisions or civil liability. The second consequence is that the legal status of the affected natural resources becomes totally irrelevant, so that the Directive applies regardless of whether the affected natural resources are privately or publicly owned or are, instead, unowned.[37]

4.2. The natural resources covered

4.2.1. Damage to 'biodiversity'

The inclusion of damage to natural habitats and species in the liability framework is one of the ELD's main innovations and added values. Prior to the ELD, several countries already had liability rules in place addressing contamination of land and groundwater, but only a few provided specific liability schemes for damage to natural elements, such as habitats and species. The inclusion of this category of damage also reaffirms the idea of liability as an independent and additional means to enhance the effectiveness of EU nature conservation legislation and to protect biodiversity resources in Europe.[38]

The concept of biodiversity retained in the Directive is, however, a rather narrow one, especially when compared to the broader and more holistic definition available in relevant international environmental instruments, in particular the CBD. The Directive does not cover biodiversity as such, but it only addresses damage to protected species and natural habitats as defined through reference to the European legislation on nature conservation, namely the 79/409/EEC Directive on the conservation of wild birds (hereinafter the 'Birds Directive') and 92/43/EEC Directive on the conservation of habitats and semi-natural habitats and of wild fauna and flora (hereinafter the 'Habitats Directive').[39] It is accepted, however, that the ELD should not be interpreted as being limited to 'Natura 2000' sites.[40] Moreover, when transposing the Directive into national law, Member States had the option to include in the environmental liability regime any other habitat, site or species which is not covered by the Habitats or Birds Directives, provided that these are covered by equivalent national legislation for the protection and conservation of nature. According to a report on the implementation of the Directive, at least 16 Member States have decided to make use of this option.[41] Moreover, the reference to the Habitats Directive and Birds Directive also extends the application *ratione loci* of the ELD to include damage to habitats and species situated within the exclusive economic zone and on the continental shelf, thereby allowing addressing important marine habitats situated within these areas.[42]

There is a close relationship between the ELD and the Habitats and Birds Directives, which is not limited to the identification of the natural resources included in the scope of 'natural resource damage' but extends to the adoption and use of concepts relevant to the determination of 'significant damage'. An example is the concept of 'favourable conservation status'. This is a pivotal concept in determining the adoption of nature conservation or prevention measures under the Habitats Directive, and it is also relevant under the ELD in order to assess the threshold of significance of the harm to natural resources necessary to trigger the application of the liability regime.[43] Under Article 2(1)(a), the Directive applies to damage having 'significant adverse effects on reaching or maintaining the favourable conservation status of habitats and species' as defined in the Birds and Habitats Directives.[44] The significance of such effects is to be determined with respect to changes to the baseline condition,[45] on the basis of 'measurable data' and taking into account the criteria to assess the significant thresholds set out in Annex I to the ELD. The wording 'reaching or maintaining a favourable conservation status' indicates that the ELD also applies to harm to natural species and habitats that are *not yet* in a favourable conservation status. As explained in the Commission's Draft Guidelines on Environmental Damage, 'adverse effects on a protected species or natural habitat in unfavourable status cannot be treated as lying outside the scope of damage . . . on the sole ground that the species or habitat is already in a poor condition'.[46]

The application of well-established concepts under other EU environmental legislation has the advantage that competent authorities are familiar with them and can count on data and experience regarding their implementation, which they could then use in the evaluation and assessment of the significance of the damage.[47] In that respect, records of data and information gathered or even measures taken to implement other EU or national environmental legislation may prove useful in the application of the ELD liability regime. For instance, the CJEU recently clarified that the expression 'normal management of the site' in Annex I of the ELD must be determined in the light of the necessary measures that Member States must adopt under the Habitats and Birds Directives for the conservation of the species and habitats present on that site.[48] The ELD also contains provisions aimed at maintaining coherence and coordination with relevant EU legislation on nature conservation. For example, it excludes from its definition of damage to natural resources the adverse effects on protected species and natural habitats 'which result from an act by an operator which was expressly authorised by the relevant authorities in accordance with provisions implementing article 6(3) and (4) of the [Habitats Directive] or article 9 of the [Birds Directive]'.

Notwithstanding the aforementioned, a study on the implementation of the ELD reported that the main challenges for implementing the ELD with respect to biodiversity damage are due to the fragmented application of this liability instrument in relation to the Habitats Directive and especially in the non-harmonised interpretation across the various Member States of the 'significant damage' threshold as applied under the ELD and under the Habitats Directive, respectively. Specifically, while under Article 6(2) of the Habitats Directive a disturbance is considered significant when it affects the conservation status of habitats or species, under the ELD the damage must have significant effect on the *favourable* conservation status. This led in practice to inconsistent application of the two legislative instruments in the various Member States, with some Member States dealing with potential ELD cases through nature conservation legislation. This meant that preventive or protection measures had to be adopted by public authorities, according to Article 6 of the Habitats Directive, instead of being required from the operators responsible for the potential harm under the ELD.[49] In that respect, the study stressed the need for greater guidance at the EU level on the coordination between the ELD and the Habitats Directive, particularly with respect to the interpretation and application of the respective significance thresholds.[50] A further, related, issue is the need to further clarify the significance threshold for ecological damage under the ELD in order to dispel the widespread perception that such threshold necessarily corresponds to a very high level of harm, thereby limiting the scope of application of the Directive.[51]

In order to address these concerns, the Commission has promoted studies and initiatives aimed at achieving a common understanding of the Directive's main concepts and scope of application, and which also address the question of natural resources damage.[52] It is in this context that the Commission very recently enacted the aforementioned Guidelines for a common understanding of the term 'environmental damage' under the ELD.[53]

4.2.2. Damage to water

Damage to water under the Directive corresponds to damage to the waters covered by the Water Framework Directive (WFD),[54] including surface waters, groundwater, transitional waters and coastal and inland waters. The achievement or maintenance of good water quality is one of the main objectives under the WFD and a key objective of the EU environmental policy. Prior to the ELD, some Member States already had in place legislation addressing groundwater contamination, usually within the framework of legislation concerning contaminated land. The ELD's contribution and added value is, however, to have introduced a specific category of 'damage to waters' and provided a common EU framework for its determination, assessment and reparation.[55]

As with damage to natural habitats and species, the definition of damage to water under the Directive is qualified by concepts that are crucial to the implementation of the WFD. Under Article 2 (1)(b) ELD, damage to water is 'any damage that significantly adversely affects the ecological, chemical and quantitative status and/or ecological potential [of these waters] as defined in Directive 2000/60'. There are ELD provisions bringing coherence between the liability regime and the WFD. For example, the ELD specifies that adverse effects covered by the derogation provided by Article 4(7) of the WFD do not constitute water damage. According to Article 4(7) WFD, a Member State is not in breach of the WFD when failure to achieve good water status or to prevent deterioration is the result of new modifications to the physical characteristic of a surface water body or alteration to the levels of groundwater bodies or are the result of new sustainable human development activities, provided that specific conditions are met, including that all practicable steps to mitigate the adverse impacts have been taken and that the reasons for those modifications or alterations are of overriding public interest. The CJEU clarified the scope of application of this exception with respect to the application of the ELD in the *Gert Folk* case.[56] In that decision, it indicated that the derogation under Article 4(7) WFD cannot be used to exclude automatically and generally that damage to water, which has significant adverse effect on the ecological, chemical or quantitative status or ecological potential of the water in question, be categorised as 'environmental damage' under the ELD, simply on the mere basis that it is covered by an authorisation under national law.[57]

In principle, the conceptual linkages between the ELD and the WFD can lead to positive and mutually reinforcing outcomes, allowing the ELD to complement the WFD and to contribute to the attainment of the WFD's objectives. For example, data from the monitoring and classification of different waters under the WFD can be used to determine the baseline condition to identify and assess the occurrence of significant water damage under the ELD. The Commission, however, indicated that when cross-cutting concepts between the two instruments (such as the concept of ecological, chemical and/or quantitative status and/or ecological potential) are used in the context of the ELD, they have to be interpreted and applied to enable the effective implementation of the ELD's environmental liability regime.[58] This means that whereas within the WFD these concepts are principally used for the purpose of achieving the long-term objectives of non-deterioration and attainment of good ecological status, in the ELD they have to be employed to serve a different purpose, namely to prevent and remediate 'localised, often accidental or sudden, damage'.[59]

Geographically, one of the limitations of defining water damage based on the WFD is that the scope of application of the WFD does not cover marine pollution but is confined to coastal areas.[60] This limit is now partially overcome with the adoption of the 2013 Offshore Safety Directive (OSD), which extends the definition of 'water damage' under the ELD to include damage to marine waters as defined in the Marine Strategy Framework Directive 2008/56/EC.[61] The territorial scope of the ELD has accordingly been extended beyond coastal waters to include waters within Member States' EEZ or continental shelf, up to 370 km from shore.[62] This amendment to the ELD is accompanied by the provision of strict liability for offshore operations. As a result of these amendments to the ELD, the liability and remediation of environmental damage caused by oil and gas offshore operations and activities covered by the OSD is regulated by the ELD insofar as damage falls within the ELD definition of environmental damage. However, pursuant to Article 7 of the OSD, such liability is channelled to the licensee of the offshore activities rather than generally to the 'operator'.

4.2.3. Damage to land

The Directive includes damage to land in the form of land contamination.[63] At present, land contamination is not covered by apposite EU legislation or strategy, although the issue is indirectly regulated by a number of parallel legislative measures.[64] However, in various Member States, the clean-up of contaminated land was already an important part of administrative liability regimes preceding the ELD.[65]

When compared with some of these domestic law developments, the ELD's definition of land contamination appears rather restrictive, as it is limited to damage which 'creates a significant risk of human health being adversely affected'. This theoretically means that even if there is a high level of contamination threatening significant harm to species and living organisms other than human beings, the ELD may not apply unless a significant risk of an adverse impact on human health can be proven. This predominance of the human health element appears at odds with the ELD's proclaimed concern with and focus on the 'environment' as such. The implementation of the ELD's definition also risks narrowing down the scope of application of domestic legislation on land contamination, which in several Member States is triggered when the environment, and not only human health, is also at risk of being adversely affected.[66] A further difference between the ELD and some of the earlier domestic statutes on land contamination in various Member States is that the Directive's lack of retrospective application and its requirement that a clear causal link between the activity and the damage is established. Both features can be problematic in cases of land contamination, given the often long latency of the damage and the fact that such contamination often results from the concurrence of more than one substance.[67] It was also noted that the Directive would rarely lead to establish liability for land damage caused by agricultural activities and other non-Annex III activities, as only fault or negligence liability applies to these activities and the Directive does not regulate liability for non-Annex activities other than for natural resources damage.[68] In practice, these discrepancies and limitations have in some cases led Member States to apply their own existing legislation to instances of soil contamination, as this was considered to be more stringent than the Directive. This aspect raises in turn important considerations on the need to better coordinate the interplay between EU and existing domestic law in this field, particularly with a view to ensure an effective added value of the ELD with respect to damage to soil.

4.3. A limited approach to environmental damage?

The progressive approach to environmental liability characterised by a central focus on natural resources damage is in part undermined by the limited notion of 'environment' that implicitly emerges from the Directive and which limits its application to a restricted selection of natural resources. First of all, unless unilaterally extended by the Member States, 'damage to protected species and natural habitats' only covers a limited part of the European territory. This limitation arguably bears potential implications on the usefulness of the ELD to address damage related to the use of GMOs. Annex III to the Directive includes the deliberate release of GMOs into the environment among the 'occupational activities' to which strict liability applies. Additionally, fault liability applies to damage to natural habitats caused by non-listed activities related with the use of GMOs. Therefore, the Directive establishes a mechanism whereby the operator could be held accountable in respect of environmental damage caused by the escape of GMOs. However, the definition of environmental damage given by the Directive is not likely to fully address all the potential adverse environmental and biodiversity impacts caused by widespread cultivation of GM crops, since for example other territories than protected habitats, such as farmlands, seem to be excluded.[69] As the ELD represents so far the main legal framework for the EU implementation of the Nagoya-Kuala Lumpur Supplementary Protocol on liability and redress for GMO-related biodiversity damage, this limitation may also raise questions on the effectiveness of the EU's implementation of that international law agreement.[70] A further potential discrepancy between the ELD and the Nagoya-Kuala Lumpur Supplementary Protocol concerns the Directive's notion of 'biodiversity damage', which comprehends only damage to protected species and habitats in contraposition to the wider and more holistic definition of biodiversity retained by the Convention on Biological Diversity and applicable under the Nagoya-Kuala Lumpur Supplementary Protocol.

Further questions concerning the limited scope of application and narrow definition of damage under the ELD may be raised in relation to damage to water. Despite the amended territorial extension introduced by the OSD, which included damage to the EEZs caused by offshore activities, the ELD limits its application to EU territorial waters and does not extend to the marine environment. In principle, this approach is in line with the territorial scope of application of the Environmental Liability Directive and may be justified in the light of jurisdictional considerations. However, given the growing range of initiatives of the European Union in the field of marine protection and maritime pollution prevention, there may be scope to explore the role of the EU in fostering further developments, if not through the ELD then at the international level addressing questions of liability and compensation for damage to the marine environment and to biodiversity beyond national jurisdiction.

There are other important components of the environment that the Directive only addresses in a limited and indirect manner. Air, for example, is a fundamental component of the environment, intended as a whole. It is also an important sector of European Community environmental policy. However, the Directive does not deal with air as a distinct and essential element of the environment, but only insofar as air pollution will in turn cause significant damage to water, land or protected species and natural habitats.[71]

The Directive also omits an explicit consideration for damage to landscape. The latter may be indirectly and limitedly addressed through the concept of damage to 'natural habitats'. However, the ELD's definition of environmental damage still leaves outside impairment to the aesthetic and cultural features of landscapes or natural sites that are a significant expression of European cultural heritage. From an EU law standpoint, potential negative impacts on landscape are taken into consideration in other pieces of EU secondary legislation, such as the Waste Framework Directive and the Environmental Impact Assessment Directive. Landscape and cultural heritage can be considered as a collective resource providing services to the general public particularly in terms of amenities and recreational value. Their inclusion would be in line with the public law approach and the policy objectives retained by the Directive. From an international law perspective, many EU Member

States are parties to the Council of Europe European Landscape Convention[72] and to the 1972 UNESCO Convention concerning the Protection of the World Cultural and Natural Heritage.[73] The former is expressly directed to the protection of European landscapes, while the UNESCO Convention has included 'cultural landscapes' responding to certain defined criteria within the type of cultural and natural sites eligible for inclusion in the World Heritage List. The European Union, as such, is not party to either convention. However, the inclusion of damage to landscape in the scope of application of the Directive would have opened the way for potential synergies with the relevant international instruments.

4.4. The notion of operator and the activities covered

Ratione personae, the scope of application of the Directive, is defined by the notion of 'operator', the concept of 'occupational activity' and, with respect to the application of the strict liability regime, by the list of activities in Annex III. Unlike many international liability conventions, the Directive does not focus on a single sector of hazardous activity, but it applies to a broader range of economic activities. Article 2(7) ELD defines 'occupational activity' as 'any activity carried out in the course of an economic activity, a business or an undertaking, irrespectively of its private or public, profit or non-profit character'. The term 'occupational' refers to 'operational' activities 'carried out in an occupational context', 'as opposed to activities operated in a purely domestic or personal context', and regardless of whether they are 'market-related or competitive in nature'.[74] It may therefore include not only economic activities carried out by private persons but also 'activities carried out in the public interest pursuant to a statutory assignment of tasks'.[75]

A distinction is established between activities included in Annex III, which lists potentially hazardous activities already regulated by secondary legislation, and other types of economic activities. Pursuant to Article 3 ELD, strict liability applies to damage to protected species and habitats, water damage and land contamination caused by Annex III activities. Fault-based liability applies to damage caused by other occupational activities non-listed in Annex III, but only in case of damage to protected species and natural habitats.

'Operator' is broadly defined as 'any natural or legal, private or public person who operates or controls the occupational activity'; furthermore, where provided by national law, operator can also be considered the natural or legal, private or public person to whom 'decisive economic power over the technical functioning of such an activity has been delegated, including the holder of a permit or authorization for such an activity and the person registering or notifying such an activity'.[76] Thus, the key issue in identifying the 'operator' is the concept of control. The Directive does not explain what it exactly means by 'control', but it was suggested that the wording of Article 2(6) indicates a deeper relationship with the activity than merely immediate contact with it.[77] The 'operator' would therefore be the subject who has an effective, rather than merely formal, control of the risk of the activity causing the damage.

The ELD's definition of operator is based on the definition provided by the Industrial Emissions Directive (IED)[78] and other EU environmental legislation.

It also recalls the notion of operator in the Council of Europe's Lugano Convention, which refers to 'the person who exercises the control of a dangerous activity'. The idea of channelling liability to the person or entity who is best suited to control the activity giving rise to environmental damage is a common trend under many international liability conventions.[79] Compared to the almost exclusive channelling under the oil pollution and nuclear liability regimes, however, the ELD's concept of 'operator' is framed in a more open-ended manner and reflects the reality that an installation may be operated by two or more persons or companies.[80] For example, Article 4(3) IED allows Member States to opt for a permit that covers several parts of an installation operated by different operators, albeit requiring in such case that the permit specifies the responsibilities of each operator. Arguably, in this hypothesis the allocation of responsibilities under the permit may be relevant in attributing the relevant liability under the ELD.

In principle, the broader and open-ended notion of operator may have the advantage of expanding the range of potentially liable subjects, but this comes at the expense of potentially creating uncertainties and ambiguities. The concept of 'control', which represents the basis for the identification of the potentially liable entity under the Directive, may in fact lend itself to different interpretations, which may in turn result into divergences in the application of the Directive across the various Member States. It was noted, 'although the core focus is on control, the definition . . . may also cover persons that are not normally regarded as operators and do not exercise any direct operational control, such as a notifier of a waste shipment'.[81] This consideration arguably points to the appropriateness of having a more coordinated approach at the EU level regarding the definition and identification of potentially liable subjects.

4.5. The Directive's temporal scope of application

The Directive does not apply retroactively[82] and therefore it does not cover environmental damage caused by an emission, event or incident that took place before the Directive's date of transposition.[83] It also excludes environmental damage that becomes evident after 30 years have passed since the emission, incident or event.

However, in the case *Raffinerie Mediterranee ERG*, one of the first cases on the application of the ELD, the CJEU had the opportunity to clarify that the 'Directive 2004/35 applies to damage caused by an emission, event or incident which took place after 30th April 2007 where such damage derives either from activities carried out after that date *or activities which were carried out but had not finished before that date*'.[84] The case in question concerned land contamination of the littoral area in the south of Sicily as a result from the operations of numerous hydrocarbon and petrochemical companies which succeeded one another in the region. Since the polluting activities started in the early 1960s, it was likely that most of the contamination was caused by activities that started operating much earlier than the ELD's transposition date.

The CJEU was again confronted with a situation of historic land contamination in the case of *Fipa Group and Others*.[85] The case concerned significant contamination caused by economic activities undertaken by former owners of the land. However, in contrast with the factual situation at stake in the aforementioned ruling in *Raffinerie Mediterranee ERG*, where there was continuity between past activities and present pollution, in the *Fipa* case the activities could be regarded as having been completed before the date of entry into force of the ELD. The CJEU therefore held that if the assessment of the national court indicates that the activities were brought to completion before the entry into force of the ELD, the latter shall not apply and the situation would be governed instead by relevant national law if applicable with due observance of the rules of the treaty and without prejudice to other secondary legislation. The CJEU's reasoning was based in this case on the polluter pays principle, on which the ELD is based, and which would require to exclude the Directive's application where the respondents (i.e. the owners of the land affected by land contamination) did not contribute to the pollution and could not therefore be considered responsible for it.[86]

Yet, in the subsequent case of *Gert Folk* concerning water damage, the CJEU found the ELD to be applicable to damage to water resulting from the operation of a hydroelectric power plant authorised and brought to operation before the Directive's entry into force.[87] To reach that conclusion the CJEU based its reasoning on the fact that the incident (the stopping of the turbine) causing the damage took place after the Directive entered into force. In so doing it implicitly highlighted the temporally relevant distinction between the 'activity', which may have commenced its operation before entry into force of the ELD, and the 'incident' which caused the damage and which, in order to trigger the Directive's application, should occur after the ELD's entry into force.

4.6. Exceptions and defences under the Directive

Pursuant to Article 4, the application of the ELD is excluded in case of damage, or imminent threat thereof, caused by an act of armed conflict, hostilities, civil war or insurrection as well damage caused by natural phenomena of exceptional, inevitable or irresistible character. It is also excluded in cases of environmental damage arising from an incident in respect of which liability or compensation falls within the scope of a number of international civil liability conventions listed in Annex IV and V to the Directive.

Article 8 envisages various defences that may be available to the operator allowing him to 'escape' liability when certain conditions are met. These defences can be differentiated between 'mandatory' and 'optional'. 'Mandatory' defences[88] are those already provided by the ELD and exempt the operator from sustaining the costs of preventive and remedial measures in case of damage caused by a third party or resulting from compliance with a mandatory order or instruction emanating from a public authority.

More controversial is the availability of the 'permit defence' and the 'state-of-the-art defence' envisaged in Article 8(4). Their inclusion in national law is left to Member States' discretion when transposing the Directive (hence, 'optional' defences). The permit defence would allow operators to be exempted from bearing the costs of remedial measures in case of damage caused by an emission or event that was expressly authorised pursuant to applicable national laws and regulations implementing EU legislative measures and was fully in accordance with the conditions of the permit. The state-of-the-art defence allows the operator not to bear the costs of remedial action if the emission or activity was not considered likely to cause environmental damage 'according to the state of scientific and technical knowledge at the time when the emission was released or the activity took place'. Both 'defences' only apply to the costs of remedial actions and do not cover preventive measures, and in both cases the operator bears the burden of proving the absence of fault or negligence on his part. Moreover, some authors suggested that the expression 'shall not be required to bear the costs' is to be interpreted as limiting the operator's exemption only to the costs, without excluding *in toto* his liability.[89]

The inclusion of those defences was however quite controversial. For example, one of the shortcomings of the ELD is that the availability of the permit defence is not counterbalanced by corresponding provisions placing on competent authorities the responsibility for bearing the costs of the remedial measures.[90] As to the state-of the art defence, it is arguably aimed at not deterring the development and use of new technologies and products,[91] but may in practice result in less pressure on the operators to carefully ponder the eventual harmful effects of innovations.[92] Arguably, an interpretation of these defences in the light of the precautionary principle—for example in assessing the operator's absence of negligence or fault—might help to attenuate these potential shortcomings and their impact on limiting the scope of application of the liability regime.[93]

4.7. Questions of causation and plurality of responsible parties

A major limitation in the use of liability to recover damage to the environment consists in the difficulty of establishing a clear causal link between the adverse effects and the specific activities involved. Article 4(5) deals with the application of the Directive to damage caused by diffuse pollution, by providing that such damage is recoverable 'only when it is possible to establish a causal link between the damage and the activities of the operators'. The Directive does not exclude *a priori* its applicability to diffuse forms of air pollution, but these are covered indirectly, and only to the extent that airborne pollution causes environmental damage to water, land or protected species and natural habitat,[94] and that a causal link can be established between the activity causing air pollution and the environmental damage.[95] Besides these situations, there are also cases of 'environmental damage' to habitats, water contamination and soil pollution that, while not properly sharing the same characteristics of the earlier described type of diffuse pollution, are caused by several different sources or installations operating in the area. In those situations, having clear rules governing the attribution of liability in case of multiparty causation could provide some guidance.

The Directive leaves it open to national law to adopt specific provisions on cost allocation in case of multiparty causation—for example whether through joint liability schemes or proportionate attribution.[96] It also does not provide indications on how causal link is to be established. In a preliminary ruling delivered in the previously mentioned case *Raffinerie Mediterranee* ERG,[97] the CJEU considered the application of the ELD to situations of land contamination caused by multiple potentially liable operators. In this case, the identification of the liable entities was made difficult by the time factor and the multiplicity of actors involved and succeeding one another in the region since the 1960s so that it was 'not only impossible but also pointless to determine each individual's share of responsibility'.[98] The CJEU addressed the question concerning the allocation of responsibilities and liability for the historical contamination of the land by interpreting the ELD in the light of the 'polluter pays principle'. It start by acknowledging that the ELD leaves discretion to the Member States in determining the criteria to establish causation between the activity and the damage. It then noted that in accordance with the 'polluter pays principle', the obligation to take remedial measures under the ELD is to be imposed on the operators on the basis of their contribution to the creation of pollution or of the risk of pollution. However, according to the CJEU, this does not preclude a domestic law that operates *a presumption* of a causal link between the pollution and the activities of operators whose installations are located on the polluted site, provided that 'the competent authority has plausible evidence capable of justifying such presumption, such as the fact that the operator's installation is located close to the pollution found and that there is a correlation between the pollutants identified and the substances used by the operator in connection with his activities'.[99]

The relationship between the polluter pays principle under the ELD and the determination of the causal link between the operator and the damage was also at stake in the *Fipa Group* case concerning the imposition of specific emergency safety measures relating to properties contaminated by various chemical substances in the Italian province of Massa Carrara.[100] The question concerned whether, on the basis of the polluter pays principle as set out in Article 191(2) TFEU and in the Directive 2004/35, the national administrative authorities are required to impose on owners of polluted land, who are not responsible for the pollution, the obligation to implement the emergency safety measures referred in the domestic legislation transposing the Directive. In answering that question, the Court reiterates that the proper application of the polluter pays principle requires that liability under the ELD is attributed on the basis of an established causal link, and that the competent authority must establish such link both in the context of strict liability with respect to Annex II activities and fault-based liability. However, the CJEU also held that if 'no causal link can be established between the environmental damage and the activity of the operator, the situation falls to be governed by national law', 'with due observance of the rules of the Treaty and without prejudice to other secondary legislation'.[101] This ruling essentially reaffirms that the scope of application of the ELD is and must be defined by the actual possibility to establish the causal link between the operator's activity and the damage. In the absence of such causal link, or where such link cannot be proved, the situation would fall outside the Directive, although it could eventually be covered by national law.

Subsequently, in the *Túrkevei Tejtermelő* case, the Court held that, although the causal link requirement under the Directive applies to both instances of strict and fault-based liability, the Directive does not preclude the possibility for Member States to adopt more stringent measures under domestic law which lead to the identification of additional activities and additional responsible parties to be subject to the prevention and remediation requirements in the Directive.[102] Accordingly, the ELD does not preclude the identification of an additional category of persons who share joint and several liability for environmental damage—in that case, the owner of the land where a different operator carried out an activity emitting toxic fumes and contaminating air took place, provided that such legislation complies with the general principles of EU law, the relevant provisions of the treaties and of acts of secondary law.[103] In reaching this conclusion the Court also noted that the domestic law in question, in expanding the category of liable person and in imposing fines in addition to remediation duties, was actually aimed at strengthening the mechanism set out in the ELD, by promoting diligence on the part of the owners of the land and encouraging them to adopt measures and develop practices to minimise the risk of environmental damage.[104]

5. Enforcing environmental liability

5.1. Combining prevention and reparation for environmental harm

A distinctive feature of the Directive compared to classic tort law and to the majority of the international liability regimes is that liability fits within a comprehensive system of response actions aimed at addressing potential damaging effects as soon as possible and remedial measures. The coexistence of prevention and reparation in the Directive is reflected in the Preamble, which states that the financial liability attached to operators whose activity caused environmental damage or imminent threat thereof, will '*induce operators to adopt measures and develop practices to minimize the risk of environmental damage* so that their exposure to financial liabilities is reduced' [emphasis added]. Therefore, prevention and liability are considered two complementary aspects of a single reality within the ELD.

Article 5 adds a further dimension to this general preventive function of liability by establishing a duty for the operator to adopt 'preventive measures' in case of 'imminent threat of damage'. Preventive measures are defined broadly as 'any measures taken in response to an event, act or omission that has created an imminent threat of environmental damage, with a view to preventing or minimising that damage'.[105] Furthermore, the definition of imminent threat of environmental damage indicates that these are measures to be taken 'without delay' whenever there is 'a sufficient likelihood that environmental damage will occur in the near future'.[106] The ELD does not specify the content of those preventive measures, but the link with the concept of 'environmental damage', where a significance threshold is required, indicates that these 'are only triggered when it is likely that a non-action would result in a significant environmental damage'.[107] It has been suggested that preventive measures would also 'cover those actions that prevent any damage from becoming significant' under the ELD.[108] Accordingly, Article 5 would refer to measures to be taken where there is a sufficient likelihood that damage will occur in the near future, including both measures to prevent the occurrence of a future significant damage and those necessary when the event or incident itself has already occurred and measures are needed to prevent the damage from becoming significant.[109] In any case, the Commission indicated that this threshold of significance for the application of preventive measures must be interpreted in the light of the precautionary principle, and therefore scientific certainty that the damage will exceed the threshold of significance is not required, but a reasonable belief would be sufficient to trigger the duty to take preventive measures.

By envisaging preventive measures as an integral part of the liability system, Article 5 adds a third layer of prevention in the overall EU environmental law framework,[110] the first two being represented by the ordinary measures to be taken in order to limit pollution during the normal operation of industrial activities[111] and the higher preventive standards imposed by EU law to ultra-hazardous activities and specifically aimed at preventing industrial accidents.[112] A similar trend can be found in certain international liability conventions. For example, the marine oil pollution regime includes preventive measures in the scope of compensation. According to the IOPC Fund Claims Manual, these measures would include reasonable measures to combat oil at sea and protect vulnerable resources which have been taken 'even if no pollution occurs, provided that the incident created a grave and imminent threat of causing pollution damage'.[113]

Within the context of EU environmental law, the requirement for operators to prevent an imminent threat of damage has been regarded as an important added value of the ELD since it covers a gap for those sectors where current European legislation does not establish an emergency system to prevent the damage.[114] Research also highlighted that the provision of preventive measures may allow addressing certain situations of environmental harm which might otherwise escape the application of the remedial measures under Article 6.[115] This is because preventive measures also cover damage that has not yet reached the threshold of significance. Furthermore, unlike remedial measures, the operator is not exonerated from the duty to take preventive measures in the event that the activity is covered by a permit or authorisation under Article 8(4), as the permit defence would not apply.[116]

In the ELD, the inclusion of 'imminent threat of damage' contributes to shape this liability regime more as a sort of comprehensive response system than classic civil liability. Indeed, the Directive is not only about imposing financial liability on operators to pay compensation for the costs of preventive or restoration measures; it also directly imposes on them a primary and self-executing obligation *to take* all the prescribed actions to prevent and/or repair environmental damage, including specific duties of notification and management of environmental harm.[117] These duties are placed directly on operators independently from administrative command.[118] In that sense, this instrument can be regarded as laying down a sort of 'responsibility' for environmental harm,[119] an aspect which was welcomed by commentators as contributing to the promotion of 'an entrepreneurial culture which takes environmental protection as a matter of self-responsibility rather than exclusive bureaucratic command'.[120]

While Article 5 applies to the imminent threat of damage and requires the operator to immediately take the necessary preventive measures and to inform the competent authority as soon as possible in case the preventive measures are not sufficient to dispel the damage,[121] Article 6 applies when environmental damage actually occurs. This provision requires the operator to inform without delay the competent authority, to immediately take all necessary and 'practicable steps to control, contain, remove or otherwise manage the relevant contaminants', and to take the necessary remedial measures.

A distinction is made between measures to be taken immediately after the event in order to contain or prevent further damage and 'long term' remedial measure. The former represent a sort of 'response action' or 'emergency remedial measures' consisting in immediate action designed to stop the incident, minimise and contain the environmentally harmful effects and prevent further damage and would include measures to clean up the damage.[122] 'Long-term remedial measures' referred to in Article 6(1)(b) are instead the measures taken with the aim of restoring the natural resource that has been affected by the damage to the baseline conditions. These measures are to be identified by the operator in accordance with the guidelines provided by Annex II to the Directive and subject to the approval of the competent authority.[123] Thus, while clean-up measures may still be broadly considered part of primary remediation, they do not necessarily restore the damaged natural resources. In fact, if the delicate situation of the environmental ecosystem is not carefully considered, preventive measures, including measures to clean up pollution, may even cause further damage and thus ultimately be incompatible with the primary remediation objective. In international law, the civil liability convention for marine oil pollution damage takes this eventuality into account when it includes within the scope of compensable damage the cost of 'preventive measures' as well as 'further loss or damage caused by preventive measures'.

5.2. *The competent authorities and the enforcement of the ELD's liability regime*

Competent authorities have a crucial role in the implementation and enforcement of liability under the Directive. When compared to the more decentralised tort law approach, where enforcement action is primarily left to the initiative of the injured party, this centralised enforcement mechanism reflects the administrative law nature of the ELD. Pursuant to Article 11, Member States are required to designate the competent authorities 'responsible for fulfilling the duties provided for in the Directive'. In line with the principles of subsidiarity and of 'procedural autonomy', the ELD leaves each Member State free to decide the relevant institutional arrangements concerning the nature and status of the competent authority insofar as compatible with the achievement of the Directive's objectives. The powers of competent authorities are spelled out in Articles 5, 6 and 7. Articles 5 and 6 provide the competent authorities with specific powers vis-à-vis the polluter, namely to require the operator to provide supplementary information and data necessary about the damage and to take the necessary preventive and/or remedial measures as the case may be. Article

11 provides public authorities with important duties to identify the operator who caused the damage or the imminent threat thereof, assess the significance of the damage, approve the restoration measures proposed by the operator and determine whether and which additional remedial measures are to be taken.

The operational mechanism of the Directive is centred on the relationship between the operator and the competent authority. The ELD places specific duties on the operator to inform the competent authority and to proceed with them in the identification and implementation of the remedial measures. In that sense, the ELD seems to envisage a dynamic relationship of dialogue, consultation and cooperation between the State (the public bodies) and the operator. While it vests public authorities with the power to enforce liability against the polluter, the ELD also seems to replace the rigid adversarial approach typical of command-and-control regulation, with more flexible forms of dialogue and consultation between the regulators and the private subjects.

At the same time, the Directive does not place on the public authorities a specific responsibility to act and take the necessary remedial measures. Instead, in cases in which the operator fails to comply with the 'order' to take the measures, or if he cannot be identified, it merely provides that the competent authority 'may' take the preventive and restoration measures itself as a 'means of last resort'.[124] The failure to provide for supplementary responsibility of public authorities in case of the operator's inaction is a step back from the 2002's Commission Proposal. The Proposal contained in fact a more imperatively worded provision for the competent authorities, disposing that where 'environmental damage has occurred' or 'there is a threat of such damage occurring, 'the competent authority shall either require the operator to take the necessary restorative [or preventive] measures *or shall itself take such measures*'.[125] Such a provision was particularly relevant to ensure that damaged 'orphan sites' (i.e. natural areas affected by the damage for which liability cannot be properly implemented because the polluter cannot be identified or is insolvent) might be restored.

The absence of a competent authorities' supplementary responsibility arguably leaves an important gap in the current environmental liability regime. If provided, it would have contributed to strengthening the ELD's underlying idea of the public bodies as 'guardians' of the environment. It would have also promoted greater environmental awareness on the part of public authorities, acting as an incentive for them to be more cautious when granting permits or authorising development projects, thereby potentially counterbalancing the existence of the permit defence. As previously noted, liability is not applicable when the harmful emission or event causing the damage has expressly been authorized under national law implementing EU law in relation to one of the activities listed in Annex III to the ELD.[126] Moreover, the provision of a supplementary responsibility of the competent authorities in addition to private operators' liability would not be necessarily in conflict with the polluter pays principle, especially if the competent authority is afterwards entitled and enabled to recover the costs from the operator.

Finally, the availability of financial coverage is an important aspect in an environmental liability regime. On this point, while it is not possible to address the complex issue of financial mechanisms for environmental damage in this work, it must be recalled that Article 14 ELD touches upon the question of insurance. According to this provision, Member States shall take measures to encourage the development of financial security instruments and markets, including financial mechanisms in case of insolvency, in order to enable them to cover their responsibility under the Directive. At present, the question of developing financial insurance mechanisms under the ELD is under further study at the European Commission. In the light of developments at national level, ad hoc studies and analyses have been carried out to provide an examination and update of the current situation of financial security for the ELD liabilities in the Member States and investigate how to make financial securities for liability under the Directive more effective.[127]

6. Remedies

Taking inspiration from the US natural resources liability statutes (i.e. CERCLA and OPA), and in particular from the Natural Resource Damage Assessment Regulations under OPA,[128] Annex II to the ELD provides detailed guidance for operators and public authorities when determining the type and scale of remedial measures for environmental damage and the criteria for assessing natural resources damage. This is a distinctive feature of the ELD when compared to relevant international liability treaties and previous legislation in place in most EU Member States.[129]

Annex II distinguishes remedial measures for damage to natural habitats and species and those to remedying land contamination. For damage to water and to natural habitats and species, it identifies between three different levels of remediation, namely (i) primary remediation, which is the priority and consists in the restoration of the natural resources and natural resources services to their baseline conditions; (ii) if this option is not feasible, 'complementary remediation' is to be undertaken, whereby restoration of the environment is achieved through the introduction of a similar level of natural resources, even at an alternative site; finally (iii) compensatory remediation constitutes an additional layer aimed at compensating 'interim losses' of natural resource services pending recovery. Both complementary remediation and the idea of compensating for interim losses are innovative when compared to earlier liability frameworks adopted at the international law level, as well as to some domestic law regimes. In principle, if primary remediation is possible, the feasibility of achieving restoration of the environment through natural recovery shall first be considered.[130] As to complementary and compensatory remedial measures, these are to be identified first by following a resource-to-resource or service-to-service approach,[131] and if this is not possible, alternative equivalence techniques may be used.[132] The inclusion of complementary remediation is important because it may enable to address 'irreparable' damage. Underlining this approach is the idea of interdependency of the ecosystems and a holistic approach to the restoring damage to natural habitats and waters.

Compared with the detailed provisions for remediation of damage to natural habitats and species and to waters, the guidance for remediation in case of land contamination appears more limited. Decontamination of soil is foreseen only until it no longer poses any significant risk of adversely affecting human health, with the presence of such risks to be evaluated by taking into account the current use of the land at the time of the damage or its approved future use. Moreover, the criteria for remediation of land damage appear to be less stringent than those provided for water and biodiversity,[133] and arguably such differentiation may cause further uncertainty for competent authorities particularly in those cases (such as in the case of groundwater contamination) where it is difficult to determine whether a given environmental harm is to be classified as land damage or water damage.[134]

7. Issues of access to justice under the ELD

The question of the proper role for environmental associations, NGOs and other individuals and interested private parties to act in defence of the environment was largely debated in the discussions about the prospective development of a European Union environmental liability regime. The importance of granting individuals adequate avenues to defend environmental interests before a court of law cannot be overstated. Access to justice is an essential instrument in a democratic society in order for citizens to effectively confront violations of the law and ensure its enforcement. This is especially important when breaches of environmental law are at stake, since the environment cannot defend itself.[135] Access to justice in environmental matters therefore means giving a voice to the environment. Moreover, since breaches of environmental law are often not adequately prosecuted, public involvement in the enforcement process, through access to justice mechanisms, becomes an important implementation tool.

The ELD presents two distinct avenues for the involvement of private parties and NGOs. First, pursuant to Article 12 of the Directive, interested individuals and environmental NGOs may activate the environmental liability mechanism by informing the competent authority of the occurrence of an environmental damage or of an imminent threat thereof and require the authority to take the appropriate action against the polluter. This provision acknowledges the public's important role in support to the monitoring functions of the public authorities, since the latter may not always be aware of actual or potential instances of environmental damage. Moreover, this same provision provides that the competent authority must inform the requesting parties of its decision and, whether it accepted or refused their request, to state the reasons for it.

Second, Article 13 of the Directive provides NGOs and interested parties with a right to apply for judicial review in case of competent authorities' failure to act. In order to be entitled to exercise their rights under Articles 12 and 13 ELD, both natural and legal persons and environmental NGOs must fulfil certain qualifications, namely they must be 'affected or likely to be affected by environmental damage' or 'have sufficient interest in environmental decision making relating to the damage'. Furthermore, when it is so required by administrative law of the Member State concerned, they must also 'allege the impairment of a right'; however, the same provision specifies that a non-governmental organisation that promotes environmental protection and meets the requirements under national law is automatically considered to have standing under the Directive.[136]

The provision of a right of interested parties and NGOs to request action and invoke legal review in case of inaction of the competent authorities provides individual persons and environmental NGOs with an important opportunity to enforce the Directive's liability mechanism. From a comparative perspective, it has been observed that although some Member States' legislation already allows for this type of third party intervention,[137] this right was never codified so explicitly as in the ELD.[138] Furthermore, comparative research shows that in some EU countries, NGOs or interested parties do not have the right to request legal review under legislation regulating Annex III activities or under the Habitats Directive.[139] In that sense, the ELD's provisions on access to judicial review may be regarded as an important added value.

As to the effectiveness of the ELD's access to justice provisions, it may be appropriate to examine them in the light of the standards laid down in the Aarhus Convention on Access to Information, Public Participation in Decision-Making and Access to Justice in Environmental Matters.[140] Under the Aarhus Convention the right of access to justice pertains to three different types of situations. Articles 9 (1) and (2) of the Convention, respectively, define the right of access to justice as a procedural right to judicial review, which is ancillary to the protection of the rights of access to information and public participation that are granted under the other two pillars of the Convention. These first two 'prongs' of Article 9 envisage an approach to the right of access to justice that is very similar to the one in Article 13 ELD in that it concerns a means for having erroneous administrative decisions on environmental issues corrected by a court or another independent and impartial body established by the law.[141] Article 9(3) of the Aarhus Convention adds, however, another dimension that concerns the possibility to challenge, before an administrative or a judicial body, 'acts or omissions by private parties and by public authorities which contravene provisions of its national law relating to the environment'. This provision defines access to justice as a general means available to the public to challenge acts of private and public bodies violating environmental law.

Being a general international agreement, the Convention leaves the States Parties with a wide discretion in the choice of the procedural means to render effective the exercise of this right by the individuals. Such discretion, however, finds a limit in Article 9(4) imposing on States Parties an obligation to make available 'effective remedies, including injunctive relief, which are fair, equitable, timing and not prohibitively expensive'. Additionally, Article 9(5) requires States to consider the establishment of 'appropriate assistance mechanisms to remove or reduce financial and other barrier to access to justice'. Together, these two provisions lay down substantive standards for an 'effective' access to justice, which would include, on the one hand, the removal of procedural and economic barriers associated with legal proceedings that may act as a deterrent for private parties to bring legal actions on behalf of the environment and, on the other, also remedies which are effective both in terms of their type and quality, including the possibility to ask for injunctive relief.

Compared to the Aarhus Convention, Article 13 ELD does not go into much detail on the procedural rules related to access to justice, which are instead mostly left to domestic law. Moreover, as to the question of actionable remedies available for NGOs and private interested parties, this is limited under the ELD to the possibility to request the competent authority to order the liable operator to take the necessary preventive and/or remedial measures. The availability of other remedies, such as the possibility to ask the competent authority or the competent judicial body for an injunction ordering the cessation of the harmful activity, is arguably left to be determined under the applicable national law.

In general, a complete harmonisation of Member States' procedural rules on access to justice may not be easily achieved and EU action on this may need to be balanced with the principle of Member States procedural autonomy.[142] Nevertheless, as the EU is a party to the Aarhus Convention, the latter may be relevant in the interpretation and application of the access to justice provisions in the ELD. It can also be submitted that, where relevant, the CJEU's case-law on the interpretation and application of the Aarhus Convention can be taken into account when interpreting and applying the ELD. This could have an important impact particularly concerning the practical (i.e. procedural and financial) barriers imposed under existing national legislation. In that respect, an interpretation of the Directive in the light of the effectiveness requirement under the Aarhus Convention may entail, if not the overruling and setting aside of the conflicting national procedural law, at least an interpretation of that domestic law in a way that it is as far as possible consistent with the objective of wide and effective access to justice. Translated into more concrete terms, it may entail to interpret the domestic legislation which is relevant to the implementation and application of the Directive in a way not to render 'excessively difficult' the rights and remedies provided by Articles 12 and 13 of the Directive.

With specific regard to legal standing, the CJEU clarified the interpretation of standing requirements under the Directive and, implicitly, on the relationship between the Directive and the Aarhus Convention, in the *Gert Folk* case.[143] The question in this case concerned the rights of persons holding fishing rights to have access to environmental review procedures before the competent administrative authority in case of damage affecting those rights. The challenged national provision at stake in the domestic judicial proceeding restricted the possibility to lodge an environmental complaint only to natural or legal persons whose rights may be violated by the environmental damage. The national court interpreted this provision restrictively as excluding persons holding of fishing rights. The CJEU, however, held that Articles 12 and 13 of the ELD must be regarded as enumerating the three categories of natural or legal persons which, alternatively and autonomously considered, have standing.[144] Thus, the ELD 'establishes three independent paths to the procedures referred to articles 12 and 13'.[145] In reaching this conclusion, the CJEU followed the opinion of the Advocate General in which a comparison was made between the wording of Article 12(1) ELD regarding the NGOs and private individuals entitled to enjoy the relevant rights laid down in the Directive and the access to justice provisions under the Aarhus Convention. Unlike the Convention, the Directive does not present Member States with alternative options from which they can choose when implementing the relevant provisions in their domestic law.[146] Instead, the Directive 'lays down three alternatives in terms of qualifying the individual situation (i.e. (i) affected or likely to be affected by environmental damage; (ii) have sufficient interest in the decision making relating to the damage'; (iii) alleging the impairment of a right), all of which shall be implemented by national law'.[147] Moreover, while the ELD provides Member States with discretion in the interpretation of sufficient interest and impairment of a right requirement under Article 12(1) (b) and (c), the individual situation in Article 12(1)(a) (i.e. affected or likely to be affected by environmental damage) is not subject to any similar qualification. The Advocate General also pointed out that the ELD's provisions on access to justice in Articles 12 and 13 must be read in conjunction with Article 47 of the EU Charter of Fundamental Rights, the EU law principle of effectiveness and Article 9(3) of the Aarhus Convention. These EU legal principles and international provisions would support a broader interpretation and application of the relevant national provisions implementing Article 12(1)(a) of the ELD and would also qualify the margin of discretion of Member States in the interpretation of sufficient interest and impairment of a right. This reading of the access to justice requirement for NGOs and the public under Articles 12 and 13 ELD is interesting as it highlights how, at least for what it concerns the rights to standing of private persons and association, the ELD seems to provide a slightly more stringent guarantee. At the same time, the decision also reveals the potential for positive interaction between the Convention and the ELD, whereby the former can contribute to reinforce the ELD's rights of access to justice for private persons and NGOs.

8. Harmonising environmental liability in the EU: assessing the ELD and its potential added value

The overall assessment of the ELD and its added value needs to take into account a few factors, including the extent to which its provisions are strengthening or filling gaps in existing Member States' legislation on environmental liability, the relationship and coordination of this instrument with other EU secondary legislation, and the extent to which it contributes to the achievement of EU's environmental protection objectives.

With respect to the first aspect concerning the impact of the ELD on Member States' existing legislation, one of the studies prepared for the European Commission pursuant to former Article 18 of the Directive[148] identified it in the establishment of strict liability for natural resources damage caused by the hazardous activities listed in Annex III and the setting up of a liability regime specifically addressing damage to protected species and natural habitats and to freshwater resources.[149] Further important features of the ELD are identified in the provision of preventive and emergency response measures, the inclusion of primary remediation as the main restoration objective and the articles on access to justice for NGOs and private interested parties.[150] It must also be reminded that, in accordance with the principle of subsidiarity[151] and the minimum harmonisation character of EU legislation in the environmental field,[152] Article 16 of the ELD stresses that the Directive 'shall not prevent Member States from maintaining or adopting more stringent provisions in relation to the prevention and remedying of environmental damage, including the identification of additional activities to be subject to the prevention and remediation requirements of this Directive and the identification of additional responsible parties'.

At the same time, as with most EU legislation in the field of environmental protection, the harmonisation impact of the ELD and its implementation in the various Member States' domestic systems meets with a double challenge. First, the division of powers between the EU and the Member States in the environmental field and the existence of shared competence imply that legislative harmonisation would often be at a lower level. Environmental measures adopted at the EU level usually aim at establishing a minimum common environmental standard across the Member States, leaving them with a relatively wide margin of discretion in the implementation and application. Furthermore, as the environment is an area of shared competence, subsidiarity plays a key role in determining not only the need for but also the scope of EU's intervention and the relevant degree of harmonisation, with possible impacts on the form of the legislative instrument adopted to regulate a certain matter, i.e. whether by directive or regulation.[153] Second, the very nature of environmental protection implies that complex interdependencies and interrelationships between the environmental media and the local geographical conditions must be taken into account when drafting legislative measures that apply to the territory of different Member States. In the field of environmental policy, the treaty makes clear that the pursuit of the two main EU objectives of environmental protection and regulatory integration must be balanced with the need to take into account the diversity of environmental, social and economic conditions of the various European 'regions'.[154] The introduction of a threefold reference to the concept of 'regions' can therefore be explained with the legitimate concern of orienting European policy according to the environmental problems of different regions or geographical areas.[155] Environmental legislation must also reflect and adapt to a constantly changing state of knowledge, thereby entailing regulatory flexibility and scope for adaptation and changes of approaches.

Both aspects are reflected in the text of the Directive, which aims to lay down a minimum common framework across the European Union in the field of environmental liability, while at the same time leaving flexibility to the Member States. The framework nature of the Directive and the margin of discretion left to Member States means that its scope of application and real effectiveness are ultimately depending on its transposition in domestic law and its practical application at the domestic level to concrete cases. For example, differences have been reported in the type of natural resources included in the definition of environmental damage, with some Member States going beyond the fairly limited conceptualisation of environmental damage under the Directive and including in the scope of application also damage to air or to the atmosphere.[156] Member States' discretion is also inbuilt in the wording of several ELD provisions, such as those concerning the application of the permit and state of the art defences; to decision on how to apportion joint and several liability; and whether to extend the provisions on biodiversity damage beyond the sites covered by the Habitats Directive so as to include national protected areas.

The comparative studies undertaken on behalf of the European Commission on the Directive's implementation in the various Member States reveal that in some cases the flexibility left to domestic law in terms of options and exceptions responded to pragmatic reasons related to either questions of EU competence[157] or concerns about placing greater financial burdens on operators.[158] However, these studies also suggest that this differentiated implementation had in some cases a negative impact on ELD's effectiveness.[159] It was found for example that the availability of the permit and state-of-the-art defence undermined the incentives provided by strict liability in promoting investment in risk-minimising technologies or undertaking additional precautionary measures. Moreover, the development of financial security and insurance options for environmental damage, which is left to the Member States, remains a problem, especially when operators cannot be identified or are insolvent and particularly for accidents causing large-scale losses. The question therefore arises as to whether the EU should take a coordinating and supporting role in this context.

Finally, an often overlooked but not less significant issue relates to terminological (in)consistency, and the impact that multilingualism in the EU, combined with 'ambiguous terminology' and 'poorly defined concepts', has on the harmonisation process.[160] This issue is apparent in the different understandings and interpretations of the 'significance threshold' for ecological damage under the ELD, which according to some studies is a main reason for its uneven application across the EU and one of the factors undermining its effectiveness.[161] For example, in those Member States where a high severity threshold is applied to evaluate the significance of the damage,[162] many cases of environmental damage were considered as falling outside the Directive's scope of application and were therefore addressed by means of domestic law or other sectoral legislation.[163]

The overall conclusion that can be drawn from the aforementioned analysis is that while the ELD's objective remains relevant, its ability in achieving a high level of environmental protection and in preventing and remedying environmental damage in the EU is often undermined by significant lack of clarity, uniform application and diverging interpretations of key concepts, as well as by 'underdeveloped capacities and expertise'.[164]

In paving the way forward to address these challenges, the Commission underlined the need to gather increasing empirical data in order to improve the evidence base for the evaluation of the ELD and having a clearer picture about its functioning.[165] The envisaged strategy at the moment would be to primarily rely on collaborative efforts between the Commission and the Member States in improving the ELD's implementation and on parallel efforts aimed at clarifying key terms and promoting their uniform application in Europe, rather than embarking in more drastic measures and introducing significant amendments to ELD.[166]

Finally, the Directive must be examined within the broader context of the institutional structure and governance of EU environmental law and in light of the role and work carried out by the Commission, which retains a pivotal position in the implementation of EU environmental law. The centralised governance and institutional structure of the EU as a regional model of integration is quite distinctive compared to the decentralised and somewhat fragmented framework of international environmental governance. Harmonisation of environmental legislation is to some extent slightly easier to achieve at the EU level, although this is not without compromises and difficulties, as the ELD's negotiating history and its current implementation demonstrate. The enforcement and implementation of EU environmental law can also benefit from greater support and institutional structures. Member States retain primary responsibility for the implementation and enforcement of EU environmental legislation, in accordance with the principle of sincere cooperation in Article 4(3) TEU, whereby they shall take 'any appropriate measure' to ensure the fulfilment of their treaty obligations and 'to facilitate the achievement of the Union's tasks'. Nevertheless, they are not left totally on their own in this task but they can benefit from comparative studies and support activities put in place at the EU level, primarily by the Commission. Improving the implementation of EU environmental law and enhancing regulatory integration and policy coherence were among the priorities identified in the EU 7th Environmental Action Programme, which guided EU environmental action until 2020.[167] Renewed efforts to enforce and implement EU environmental legislation were also a central part in the European Green Deal,[168] and are currently reiterated in the 8th Environmental Action Programme (EAP) as one of the enabling conditions for the achievement of the EAP's priority objectives.[169] To this end, besides traditional enforcement tools and the use of infringement proceedings, the accent has been placed on the importance of facilitating compliance with EU legislation, including through targeted actions aimed at making it simpler and easier to comply with. Thus, in line with the objectives of the Better Regulation Agenda, the Commission has launched the REFIT exercise, which also covers the ELD and which aims at gathering information and experience on the Directive's implementation with a view to evaluate its effectiveness, coherence and consistency and how it can be improved. The philosophy behind these actions reflects a slight change in the approach to environmental implementation and compliance, based on the idea that improving the clarity of legislation and making it simpler and more user-friendly will in turn have a positive effect on compliance.[170]

9. Concluding remarks

This chapter sought to show that despite the various challenges and shortcomings, the adoption of the ELD has been an important achievement. This Directive introduced for the first time a European common framework in the field of environmental liability, with specific focus on damage to natural resources. In so doing, it has certainly contributed to raising awareness of the need to tackle the ecological and natural resources dimension of the damage caused by environmental pollution. Other important features of the Directive are its remediation standards and the provisions on public participation and access to justice.

For the future, it is to be hoped that the process of reviewing of the ELD will allow capitalising and maximising on the achievements, while at the same time addressing the outstanding challenges. Harmonising legislation in the field of environmental liability is not an easy task, as demonstrated by the difficulties encountered by similar initiatives at the international level. In Europe, the ELD remains a first important step towards the development of an EU law framework on environmental liability and environmental remedies. Its operation and impact must therefore be examined also in connection with other legislative developments addressing relevant aspects. Worth mentioning are the adoption of Directive 2008/99 on the protection of the environment through criminal law, which seeks to lay down common standards in the application of sanctions and criminal liability to breaches of EU environmental legislation,[171] and recent initiatives aimed at strengthening access to justice in environmental matters in the EU.

Notes

1 See M Klamert, 'What We Talk About When We Talk about Harmonisation' (2015) 17 Cambridge Yearbook of European Legal Studies 360.
2 Directive 2004/35 of the European Parliament and of the Council of 21 April 2004 on environmental liability with regard to the prevention and remedying of environmental damage, 30 April 2004, OJ L 143/56; subsequently amended by Directive 2006/21/EC on the management of waste from extractive industries and 2009/31/EC on the geological storage of carbon dioxide.
3 C Clarke, 'Updated Comparative Legal Study on Environmental Liability' (Study Contract No 201919/MAR/B3, 2001) <https://ec.europa.eu/environment/legal/liability/pdf/legalstudy_full.pdf> accessed 16 December 2021.
4 Article 191(2) TFEU.
5 Following the adoption of Regulation (EU) 2019/1010 on the alignment of reporting obligations in the field of legislation related to the environment, OJ L 170, Article 18 ELD is now replaced with a new requirement for the Commission to collect information from Member States on the experience gained in the application of the Directive, with special focus on the 'data regarding the type of environmental damage, date of occurrence and/or discovery of the damage', and the 'description of the activity in accordance with Annex III'.
6 [1986] EC Bull. 11, pt 2.1.146.
7 S Poli, 'Shaping the EC regime on Liability for Environmental Damage: Progress or Disillusionment?' (1999) 8 European Environmental Law Review 299.
8 European Commission, *Green Paper on Remedying Environmental Damage*, COM (93) 47.
9 European Commission, *White Paper on Environmental Liability*, COM (2000) 66.
10 Ibid. 16.
11 COM (2002) 17 final.
12 P Thieffry, 'Environmental Liability in Europe: The European Union's Project and the Convention of the Council of Europe' (1994) 29 International Lawyer 1083.
13 For a partial review of these trends, see Clarke (n 3).
14 42 US Code 9601 et seq.
15 L Burlington, 'Valuing Natural Resources Damages: A Transatlantic Lesson' in G. Betlem and E.H.P. Brans (eds.), *Environmental Liability in the EU—The 2004 Directive Compared with US and Member States Law* (Cameron May 2006).
16 33 US Code, Chapter 40.
17 See J Golub, 'New Instruments for Environmental Policy in the EU: An Overview' (1998) EUI Working Paper RSC No 98/12 (European University Institute 1998).

18 European Commission, *Fifth Environmental Action Programme (EAP)* 'Towards Sustainability: A European Community Programme of Policy and Action in Relation to the Environment and Sustainable Development', COM (92) 23 final.
19 Golub (n 17).
20 (n 18).
21 *White Paper on Environmental Liability* (n 9) 14; a similar idea is expressed in the Explanatory Memorandum to the Proposal for a Directive on Environmental Liability and in the Preamble of the current version of the Environmental Liability Directive.
22 *White Paper* (n 9) 14: 'If liability exerts the preventive effect described earlier . . . it should also improve compliance with EC environmental legislation'.
23 Decision 1600/2002 of the European Parliament and the Council, of 22 July 2002, laying down the Sixth Environmental Action Programme, [2002] OJ L 242/1, Article 3.
24 L Kramer, 'Directive 2004/35 on Environmental Liability' in G Betlem and E Brans (eds.), *Environmental Liability in the EU* (Cameron & May 2004).
25 G Winter et al., 'Weighing Up the EC Environmental Liability Directive' (2008) 20 Journal of Environmental Law 163, 165.
26 Ibid.
27 MS Grieve, 'The Private Enforcement of Environmental Law' (1990) 65 Tulane Law Review 339.
28 M Lee, 'From Private to Public: The Multiple Faces of Environmental Liability' (2001) 7 European Public Law 375, 385.
29 Article 2(9).
30 European Commission, Staff Working Document—*REFIT Evaluation of the Environmental Liability Directive*, accompanying the document 'Report from the Commission to the European Parliament and to the Council pursuant to Article 18(2) of Directive 2004/35/EC on environmental liability with regard to the prevention and remedying of environmental damage', SWD (2016) 121 final ('Commission REFIT Evaluation'), 10.
31 H Josefsson, 'The Environmental Liability Directive, The Water Framework Directive and the Definition of 'Water Damage' (2018) 20 Environmental Law Review 151.
32 European Commission, Commission Notice, Guidelines Providing a Common Understanding of the Term 'Environmental Damage' as defined in Article 2 of Directive 2004/35/EC on environmental liability with regard to the prevention and remedying of environmental damage ('ELD Environmental Damage Guidelines') (C/2021/1860) OJ C 118, p 14 (para 64).
33 Commission REFIT Evaluation (n 30) 43.
34 Articles 4, 11 and 17 of the Habitats Directive.
35 A Klaphake, 'The Assessment and Restoration of Biodiversity Damages—Some Remarks on Environmental Damages under the Directive 2004/35' (2005) 4 Journal of European Environmental & Planning Law 268, 270.
36 See ELD Environmental Damage Guidelines (n 32) p 10, para 45.
37 EH Brans, 'Liability for Damage to Public Natural Resources under the 2004 EC Environmental Liability Directive—Standing and Assessment of Damages' (2005) 7 Environmental Law Review 90, 95–96.
38 M Petersen, 'The Environmental Liability Directive—Extending Nature Protection in Europe' (2009) 11 Environmental Law Review 5, 8.
39 Article 2(3); note that although the text of the Directive refers to the original version of the Birds Directive, the latter has been amended in 2009 and became Directive 2009/147/EC.
40 EH Brans, 'The Environmental Liability Directive: Legal Background and Requirements' in L Bergkamp and B Goldstein (eds.), *The EU Environmental Liability Directive. A Commentary* (OUP 2013) 33.
41 Stevens & Bolton LLP (2013), 'The Study on Analysis of Integrating the ELD into 11 National Legal Frameworks', Final Report Prepared for the European Commission—DG Environment, 49.

42 Case C-6/04 of 20 October 2005; European Commission, 'Guidelines for the Establishment of the Natural 2000 Network in the Marine Environment. Application of the Habitats and Birds Directive' (May 2007) 14–18.
43 See Milieu Ltd./IUCN, 'Experience Gained in the Application of ELD Biodiversity Damage', Final Report for the European Commission—DG Environment (Brussels 2014) ('Milieu Ltd/IUCN Report').
44 See Article 1 (e) and (i) of the Habitats Directive.
45 Article 2(1)(a) combined with Article 2 (14) of ELD.
46 ELD Environmental Damage Guidelines (n 32) p 21, para 105.
47 Milieu/IUCN Report (n 43) 14.
48 Case C-297/19, *Naturschutzbund Deutschland—Landesverband Schleswig-Holstein e.V.v Kreis Nordfriesland*, 9 July 2020, EU:C:2020:533.
49 Milieu Ltd/IUCN Report (n 43) 20–25.
50 Ibid.
51 V Fogleman, 'The Threshold for Liability for Ecological Damage in the EU: Mixing Environmental and Conservation Law' in H Schoukens et al. (eds.), *The Habitats Directive in Its EU Environmental Law Context* (Routledge 2015) 210.
52 Milieu Ltd (2017) 'Towards a Common Understanding of ELD Key Terms and Concept—support in the implementation of REFIT actions for the ELD—phase I', DOC5–05/10/2017.
53 ELD Environmental Damage Guidelines (n 32).
54 Directive 2000/60/EC of the European Parliament and of the Council establishing a framework for the Community Action in the field of Water Policy.
55 BIO Intelligence Service (2014), 'ELD Effectiveness: Scope and Exceptions, Final Report prepared for European Commission—DG Environment', 69.
56 Case C-529/15 *Gert Folk*, ECLI:EU:C:2017:419.
57 Ibid [34].
58 ELD Environmental Damage Guidelines (n 32) para 144.
59 Ibid.
60 Article 2 WFD defines coastal areas as the surface waters distant one nautical mile from the baseline from which the breadth of the territorial sea is measured.
61 Directive 2013/30/EU on the safety of offshore and gas operations, OJ L 178, Article 38.
62 S Baughen, 'Environmental Damage and UK Offshore Operations: Uncertain Liabilities in Deep Waters' (2016) 28 Journal of Environmental Law 497, 498.
63 ELD, Article 2(1)(c).
64 Soil protection is indirectly achieved in the EU by means of other EU policies. A proposal for a Soil Framework Directive was drafted but subsequently withdrawn: European Commission, Proposal for a Directive of the European Parliament and of the Council establishing a framework for the protection of soil and amending Directive 2004/35/EC, Article 1(2), COM (2006) 232 final.
65 G Betlem and M Faure, 'Environmental Toxic Torts in Europe—Some Trends in Recovery of Soil Clean-Up Costs and Damages for Personal Injury in Belgium, England, Germany and the Netherlands' (1998) 10 Georgetown International Environmental Law Review 855.
66 BIO Intelligence Service (2014) (n 55) 95.
67 Ibid.
68 Ibid.
69 Further problems concern limiting the Directive to 'significant harm'; see M Lee, 'Regulatory Solutions to GMOs in Europe: The Problem of Liability' (2003) Journal of Environmental Law and Practice 311.
70 This question was raised in the context of the European Commission's REFIT Evaluation of the ELD (n 30), at p 56, where it was noted, 'there were no incidents of environmental damage caused by GMOs in the EU within the reporting period' and 'no reason for any modification to the ELD on the ground of experience with its application to environmental damage caused by genetically modified organisms has been identified'.

71 ELD Preamble: 'Environmental damage shall include damage caused by airborne elements, as far as they pose damage to water, land or protected species and natural habitats'.
72 ETS No. 176, adopted 20 October 2000; entered into force on 1 March 2004.
73 1037 UNTS 151, adopted 16 November 1972; entered into force 17 December 1975.
74 CJEU, C-297/19, *Naturschutzbund Deutschland*, 9 July 2020, ECLI:EU:C:2020:533, para 76.
75 Ibid.
76 ELD, Article 2(6).
77 B Mullerat, 'European Environmental Liability: One Step Forward' (2005) 16 International Company and Commercial Law Review 26.
78 See Article 3(15) of Directive 2010/75/EU of the European Parliament and of the Council of 24 November 2010 on industrial emissions (integrated pollution prevention and control) (IED), OJ L 334.
79 See Chapter 3 in this book.
80 European Commission DG Environment, 'Answers Given by DG Environment on the Implementation of the Industrial Emissions Directive—Chapter 1', 'Definition of "Operator"' <ec.europa.eu/environment/industry/stationary/ied/implementation.htm> accessed July 2022.
81 L Bergkamp, 'The Environmental Liability Directive and Liability of Parent Companies for Damage Caused by Their Subsidiaries (Enterprise Liability)' (2016) 13 European Company Law 183.
82 Article 17 ELD.
83 See, for example, the exclusion of the Directive from the discussion concerning the applicable legal framework in the case concerning maritime pollution caused by the shipwreck of the oil tanker *Erika*, ECJ, Case C-188/07 *Commune de Mesquer v Total France SA and Total International Ltd*, Opinion of the Advocate General Kokott, 13 March 2008 [90–91].
84 Case C-378/08, *Raffinerie Mediterranee ERG and others v Ministero Sviluppo Economico and others* ECLI:EU:C:2010:126 [39–41] [emphasis added].
85 Case C-534/13, *Ministero dell'Ambiente e della Tutela del Territorio e del Mare and Others v Fipa Group and Others*, ECLI:EU:C:2015:140 [44].
86 Ibid. [57–60].
87 *Gert Folk* (n 56).
88 Article 8(3) ELD.
89 G Betlem, 'Scope and Defences of the 2004 Environmental Liability Directive: Who Is Liable for What?' (2005) 6 ERA Forum 376.
90 See further text at n 126.
91 L Kramer, 'Directive 35/2004 on Environmental Liability' (n 24) 43.
92 P Wenneraas, 'Permit Defences in Environmental Liability Regimes—Subsidizing Environmental Damage in the EC', (2005) 4 Yearbook of European Environmental Law 149.
93 Ibid.
94 Recital 4 of the Directive's Preamble.
95 See on the causal link under the ELD, Case C-129/16, *Túrkevei Tejtermelő Kft v Országos Környezetvédelmi és Természetvédelmi Főfelügyelőség*, ECLI: EU:C:2017:547.
96 Article 9 ELD.
97 Case C-378/08 *Raffinerie Mediterranee* (*ERG*) (n 84).
98 Ibid. [27].
99 Ibid., para 56–57.
100 *Ministero dell'Ambiente v FIPA Group* (n 85).
101 Ibid. [4] and [57]–[59].
102 *Túrkevei Tejtermelő Kft* (n 95).
103 Ibid. [63].

104 Ibid. [58].
105 Article 2(10).
106 Article 2 (9).
107 Commission REFIT Evaluation (n 30) 13.
108 See Milieu (2017) 'Towards a Common Understanding' (n 52), 33 ff.
109 Ibid.
110 M Prieur, 'La Responsabilité Environnementale en Droit Communautaire' (2004) 2 Revue Juridique de l'Environnement 5.
111 See the provisions on pollution prevention and control in Directive 2010/75/EU (Industrial Emissions Directive).
112 See Directive 2012/18/EU on the control of major-accident hazards involving dangerous substances (Seveso III).
113 It is to be noted, however, that the oil pollution convention includes clean-up measures as preventive measures, whereas clean-up operations are part of the Directive emergency remedial measures in Article 6.
114 Milieu Ltd/IUCN Report (n 43) 65.
115 V Fogleman, 'The Duty to Prevent Environmental Damage in the Environmental Liability Directive; A Catalyst for Halting the Deterioration of Water and Wildlife' (2020) 20 ERA Forum 707.
116 Ibid.
117 V Fogleman, 'Enforcing the Environmental Liability Directive: Duties, Powers and Self-Executing Provisions', (2006) 4 Environmental Liability 127.
118 Ibid. 130.
119 Prieur (n 110) 12.
120 Winter et al. (n 25) 169.
121 A more stringent duty is provided in the transposing legislation of some Member States—Denmark, Finland, the Netherlands and Hungary—requiring the operator to notify the competent authority whether preventive measures have dispelled the threat, source: Stevens & Bolton (2013) (n 41) 79.
122 EFTEC (2013), 'Environmental Liability Directive: Training Handbook and Accompanying Slides' prepared for European Commission—DG Environment, 11.
123 Article 7(1) of the Directive.
124 Articles 5(4) and 6(3).
125 Proposal for a Directive of the European Parliament and of the Council on Environmental Liability with regard to Prevention and Remedying of Environmental Damage, COM (2002) 17 final, Article 4(1) and Article 5(1).
126 See earlier text at n 90.
127 See study prepared for the European Commission by V Fogelman, 'Improving financial security in the context of the Environmental Liability Directive' (May 2020) <https://ec.europa.eu/environment/legal/liability/pdf/Final_report.pdf> accessed 10 January 2022.
128 Burlington (n 15).
129 BIO Intelligence Service (2013), 'Implementation challenges and obstacles of the Environmental Liability Directive', Final Report prepared for European Commission—DG Environment, 118.
130 ELD, Annex II, point 1.2.1.
131 A resource-to-resource approach or service-to-service approach consists in providing resources or services of a level and quality comparable to those lost due to the incident (ELD, Annex II, point 1.2.2).
132 Such an approach consists in an evaluation, even in monetary terms, of the complementary and compensatory remedial measures necessary or, where it is not possible, valuation of the lost resources and services; in the latter case, the authority may prescribe remedial measures whose cost is equivalent to the estimated monetary value of the lost natural resources or services (ELD, Annex II, point 1.2.3).

133 BIO Intelligence Service (2014), 'ELD Effectiveness: Scope and Exceptions', Final Report prepared for European Commission—DG Environment, 68.
134 Ibid.
135 L Kramer, 'The Environment and the Ten Commandments' (2008) 21 Journal of Environmental Law (Forewords) 5, 6.
136 ELD, Article 12(1).
137 See, for instance, K de Graaf and J Jans, 'Liability of Public Authorities in Cases of Non-Enforcement of Environmental Standards' (2007) 24 Pace Environmental Law Review 377.
138 Winter et al. (n 25).
139 Milieu Ltd/IUCN Report (n 43).
140 UNTS vol. 2161, 447 (adopted 25 June 1998; entry into force 30 October 2001).
141 J Ebbeson, *Access to Justice in Environmental Matters in the EU* (Kluwer Law International, 2002).
142 A communication was adopted by the European Commission in 2020 on 'Improving access to justice in environmental matters in the EU and its Member States', COM (2020) 643 final.
143 (n 56).
144 Case C-529/15, *Proceedings brought by Gert Folk*, ECLI:EU:C:2017:419.
145 Opinion of Advocate General Bobek delivered in proceedings brought by *Gert Folk*, para 72.
146 AG opinion, para 74.
147 Ibid., para 75.
148 Note that this article has been updated in order to adjust the date for the submission of the relevant information by the Member States (compare ELD version from 2004 and current version as lately amended in 2019).
149 Milieu Ltd/IUCN (n 43) 64 ff.
150 Ibid.
151 Article 5(3) TEU.
152 Article 193 TFEU.
153 C De Burca, 'Legal Principles as an Instrument for Differentiation' in B De Witte, D Hanf and E Vos (eds.), *The Many Faces of Differentiation in EU Law* (Intersentia 2001).
154 Article 191(2) TFEU.
155 L Kramer, 'Differentiation in EU Environmental Policy' in *The Many Faces of Differentiation in EU Law* (n 153) 91.
156 BIO Intelligence Service (2014), 'ELD Effectiveness' at 85, reporting Italy and Hungary as having adopted this approach.
157 Milieu Ltd/IUCN (n 43) 43.
158 The Commission considered the extension of strict liability to include also non-Annex III activities but because of potential significant draw-backs in terms of additional financial burdens on operators, it ultimately decided not to amend the ELD on this point. Source: Commission REFIT Evaluation (n 30) 39.
159 Report from the Commission to the Council and the European Parliament under Article 18(2) of Directive 2004/35/EC on environmental liability with regard to the prevention and remedying of environmental damage, COM (2016) 204 final, 5.
160 B Pozzo, 'The Environmental Liability Directive and the Problem of Terminological Consistency' in F Ruggieri (ed.), *Criminal Proceedings, Languages and the European Union: Linguistic and Legal Issues* (Springer 2014) 123.
161 Report from the Commission to the Council and the European Parliament under Article 18(2) of Directive 2004/35 on environmental liability with regard to the prevention and remedying of environmental damage, COM (2016) 204 final, 5.
162 Milieu Ltd/IUCN Report (n 43) 48.
163 Ibid.

164 Commission REFIT Evaluation (n 30) 60. Concerns about the weaknesses and (in)effectiveness of the Directive were also voiced in a Resolution of the European Parliament, titled 'Implementation of the Environmental Liability Directive, European Parliament resolution of 26 October 2017 on the application of Directive 2004/35/EC', P8_TA-PROV(2017)0414.

165 Article 18(1): 'The Commission shall collect information from Member States . . . and as far as available on the experience gained in the application of this Directive. That information shall cover the data set out in Annex VI to this Directive and be collected by 30 April 2022 and every five years thereafter'.

166 Article 18(3) ELD envisaging the adoption of Guidelines for a common definition of environmental damage.

167 Decision No 1386/2013/EU of the European Parliament and of the Council of 20 November 2013 on a General Union Environment Action programme to 2020 'Living well, within the limits of our planet', OJ L 354, 28.12.2013.

168 Communication from the Commission, 'The European Green Deal' COM (2019) 640 final.

169 Decision (EU) 2022/591 of the European Parliament and of the Council of 6 April 2022 on a General Union Environmental Action Programme to 2030, OJ L 114, 12.4.2022, Article 3.

170 S Kingston, 'Mind the Gap: Difficulties in Enforcement and the Continuing Unfulfilled Promise of EU Environmental Law' in S Kingston (ed.), *European Perspectives on Environmental Law and Governance* (Routledge 2012).

171 A proposal for a revision of this Directive has recently been put forward by the European Commission, in December 2021: Proposal for a Directive of the European Parliament and of the Council on the protection of the environment through criminal law and replacing Directive 2008/99/EC, COM (2021) 851 final.

5 Transnational harm in Europe and the potential for a harmonised legal framework

1. Introduction

It is a well-acknowledged fact that pollution knows no frontier. Contaminants released in water or air are quick to propagate into the environment and especially if discharged in large quantities, such as in cases of serious industrial accidents, they can often spread across the territory of more than one state. The problem of how to provide appropriate remedies for transboundary environmental damage has thus remained one of the oldest and still highly relevant challenges for environmental legal scholars. In Europe, two main legal frameworks are applicable to transboundary damage. The first, and older one, consists in the transnational application of domestic law. As substantive rules on civil liability or tort law are usually considered as remaining within the remit of domestic legislation, harmonisation at a supranational level has consisted in coordinating frameworks that concern issues of access to justices and procedural aspects concerning the competent jurisdiction and the recognition and enforcement of judicial decisions. In the EU, the harmonisation of private international law rules regarding the competent court and applicable law and ensuring the mutual recognition and enforcement of judicial decisions have proven to indirectly benefit the pursuit of environmental liability claims in a cross-national context. These legislative instruments do not directly address the substantive aspects of environmental liability but are limited to the harmonisation of the procedural and conflict of law aspects. However, as further illustrated in the following pages, there is a close interrelation between procedure and substance, and the questions concerning the determination of the competent court and applicable law can have an important impact on the outcome of the case.

The second framework that is relevant to transnational environmental liability litigation in Europe is represented by EU endeavours to harmonise substantive standards of environmental liability and their application in a transboundary or transnational context. In this respect, this chapter will examine the application of the Environmental Liability Directive to transboundary environmental damage, as well as the recent debates at the EU level,[1] and in various domestic jurisdictions, concerning the inclusion and role of liability provisions in the context of legal frameworks establishing mandatory standards of due diligence for human rights environmental harm.

DOI: 10.4324/9781315676708-8

2. The harmonisation of conflict of law in Europe

The growing globalisation of legal transactions, and the correlated need to litigate in foreign courts or enforce judgments in other jurisdictions, brought increased attention on the question of the harmonisation of civil procedures.[2] The existence of significant differences in the rules of civil procedure across various legal systems may create obstacles which jeopardise access to justice for litigants in a transnational context. Furthermore, in a regional context of economic integration, such as the EU, the existence of extensive differences in the civil procedural rules of the various Member States might have negative implications on the uniform application and implementation of EU legislation.[3]

Within the EU, the interest in regulating private international law issues dates back to the origin of the European Economic Community (EEC), when the need for coordinating the autonomous national procedures of Member States in cross-border settings was perceived as functional to the establishment and functioning of the internal market. Absent a specific competence of the EEC in the area, it was for the Member States to negotiate among them with a view to regulate certain cross-border aspects of private law 'for the benefit of their nationals'.[4] Accordingly, the first steps towards the unification of civil procedure were represented by the adoption of private international law agreements among Member States aimed at harmonising their conflict of law provisions. Thus, the 1968 Brussels Convention on Jurisdiction and Enforcement of Judgements in Civil and Commercial Matters ('Brussels Convention')[5] and the parallel 1988 Lugano Convention,[6] which applies also to EFTA countries, laid down uniform principles determining the competent jurisdiction and the mutual recognition and enforcement of judicial decisions. With the entry into force of the Treaty of Amsterdam in 1999 and the extension of EU competence in the field of judicial cooperation in civil matters, the EU could finally adopt its own secondary legislation on specific aspects of private international law and procedure. The Brussels Convention was therefore replaced by Council Regulation (EC) 44/2001 on Jurisdiction and the Recognition and Enforcement of Judgements in Civil and Commercial Matters[7] ('Brussels I Regulation') and more recently by Regulation (EU) 1215/2012 (Recast Brussels I Regulation). These Regulations maintained the Brussels Convention's approach with respect to the identification of the competent court and the recognition of judicial decisions across the EU. Additionally, the newly acquired competence on civil cooperation allowed the EU to intervene in 2007 on the question of applicable law to non-contractual obligation, with the adoption of Regulation 864/2007 ('Rome II Regulation').[8]

3. The Brussels I Regulation and its application to transboundary environmental damage

The Brussels Convention and the two subsequent EU Brussels Regulations apply to civil and commercial matters and to non-contractual liability, and therefore they also cover the area of environmental torts. Their relevance for the question of transboundary environmental harm became already apparent in one of the first preliminary rulings rendered by the CJEU in this context in the case of *Bier v Mine de Potasse d'Alsace*.[9] The dispute concerned the claim of Dutch gardeners complaining about damage to agricultural irrigation caused by the high salinity of the Rhine River waters, which was due to the discharges from a French potassium mine. Since the case involved a cross-border civil liability claim, the Court was asked to give a preliminary ruling on the interpretation of Article 5 of the Brussels Convention containing specific exceptions to the general rule allocating jurisdiction according to the domicile or residence of the defendant (*forum rei*). In particular, with respect to matters of torts, delict or quasi-delict, Article 5(3) allowed the plaintiff to bring the case before the courts of 'the place where the harmful event occurred'. In its ruling, the CJEU clarified that in transboundary environmental cases, the expression 'place where the harmful event occurred' must be interpreted 'in such a way as to acknowledge that the plaintiff has an option to commence the proceedings in either the place where the damage occurred or the place of the event giving rise to it'.[10] In other words, plaintiffs in transboundary environmental liability cases have the option to choose whether to bring the action in the courts of the place where the defendant company is located, according to the general *forum rei* principle, or to instead sue the defendant company in their own domestic courts. Since an analogous provision to Article 5(3) of the Convention is contained in Article 7(2) of the Brussels I Regulation—whereby the defendant can be sued 'in the courts for the place where the harmful event occurred or may occur'—the interpretation given by the Court in the *Bier* ruling remains valid also with respect to the Regulation.

For the victims of transboundary damage, the possibility to choose the most appropriate forum presents several advantages. Environmental litigants may have good reasons to prefer litigation in their domestic courts. They can avoid the higher costs and the complexities involved in pursuing litigation in a foreign court. Moreover, home courts may be more concerned with the harm suffered by the population in their territory and consequently be more sympathetic with the situation of the plaintiffs.[11] More generally, the development of common jurisdictional rules applicable across EU Member States may also enhance predictability in the determination of the competent court and the recognition of foreign judicial decisions.

To better understand the relevance of these procedural harmonisation endeavours, it should be recalled that questions of competent jurisdiction and applicable civil procedure have been traditionally regarded as 'deeply embedded in national (legal) culture'[12] and intrinsically connected with ideas of sovereignty. As such, they have been usually considered as a matter to be left to national law. In this respect, the harmonisation brought forward by the Brussels Regulations represented an important step forward. At the same time, the strong entrenchment of jurisdictional and procedural rules on national law explains the limitations in the scope of application of these instruments. The Brussels Regulations only cover jurisdictional rules applicable to cross-border cases within the EU, with the consequence that national procedural rules continue to apply to purely domestic cases.[13] Moreover, the extent of harmonisation only concerns purely jurisdictional issues related to the competent court and the enforcement of judicial decisions, and not the realm of civil procedure and civil justice more generally. Thus, questions regarding standing and access to justice in relation to private law claims remain a matter for the autonomous systems of the Member States, although some trends towards alignment around certain procedural principles is discernible at the EU level,[14] particularly with respect to question of access to justice in environmental matters.[15] Finally, the Brussels Regulation applies to defendants domiciled in the EU, and therefore its applicability to environmental harm occurring outside the jurisdiction of the EU Member States encounters certain limitations. This, however, has not precluded it being used to tackle some harmful conduct taking place outside the EU territory, as the following discussion concerning litigation against transnational corporate actors in European courts will demonstrate.

4. Rome II regulation and the determination of applicable law

Albeit important, an approach based on the jurisdictional aspects of access to justice and allowing foreign claimants to have their case heard in European courts is only the first step in the process. A further question concerns the substantive law applicable to the case and the size of any eventual damages award. Different rules and standards of liability and different types and levels of remediation may apply in different countries. Therefore, the choice of the applicable law can be crucial as it may have a direct bearing on the final outcome of the case. While rules of private international law usually apply the law of the competent forum to the procedural aspects, the applicable law for the substantive aspects is open to a variety of approaches.[16] This means that the choice to bring the action in the defendant's State does not necessarily imply that the legislation of the forum State will also be applicable to the substantial merit of the decision.

The EU intervened on the question of the applicable law with the adoption of the Rome II Regulation[17] that harmonises the conflict of laws rules among the EU Member States. Pursuant to Article 4(1) of the Regulation, the general principle to determine the law applicable to non-contracting obligation arising out of a tort is the law of the country in which the damage occurs (*lex loci damni*). In cases of personal injury or damage to property, this would be the country where the injury or damage is suffered. However, with specific respect to claims related to 'environmental damage', Article 7 follows a trend that emerged in the conflict of laws of various European states[18] and offers the plaintiff the possibility to choose between the law of the place where the damages occurred (as per Article 4(1)) or 'the law of the country in which the event giving rise to damage occurred'.[19] The inclusion of a specific provision for the case of environmental damage and the application of the 'principle of ubiquity'[20] with respect to these types of claims has been regarded by some as a recognition of the regulatory and public policy role of private international law.[21] Providing environmental claimants with a choice of the most favourable law would indirectly foster the prevention of environmental harm, for example 'by reducing incentives for a State with high protective standards to locate new polluting facilities near the border with a State with laxer regulation'.[22] This understanding finds recognition in the Regulation Preamble according to which an approach that discriminates in favour of the person sustaining the damage would be fully justified by Article 191(2) TFEU and by the EU objective of attaining a high level of environmental protection.[23]

The question is what is to be regarded as 'environmental damage' for the purpose of applying Article 7. Recital 24 of the preamble defines environmental damage as meaning 'adverse change in a natural resource, such as water, land or air, impairment of a function performed by that resource for the benefit of another natural resource or the public, or impairment of the variability among living organisms'. Read in conjunction with the wording of Article 7—which expressly mentions both 'environmental damage and damage sustained by persons or property as a result of such damage', this definition suggests that the plaintiff's possibility to choose among two different approaches with respect to the substantive law applicable to the case extends to both ecological damage and the more traditional type of damage indirectly arising in connection with environmental pollution.[24]

It is worth mentioning that Article 17 of the Regulation provides that 'in assessing the conduct of the person claimed to be liable, account shall be taken, as a matter of fact and in so far as is appropriate, of the rules of safety and conduct which were in force at the place and time of the event giving rise to the liability'. In the environmental field, this provision would allow the court to consider the relevant public regulations and safety standards of the place where the polluting conduct has taken place. This is particularly relevant in situations governed by the law of the place of injury, although Article 17 only requires the courts to 'take into account' those public rules and standards, without a specific obligation to apply them to the situation at hand.[25] The wording of this provision also leaves unclear as to whether it applies only to 'prescriptive rules', excluding administrative permits or authorisations that the polluting company might have obtained in the source state.[26] This issue was indirectly addressed in a ruling concerning the potential nuisance caused by ionising radiation arising from the Czech CEZ nuclear power plant at Temelin and potentially affecting agricultural land in Austria. In its ruling, the CJEU concluded that a Member State (in this case Austria) may not categorically refuse to recognise the preclusive effect of a foreign authorisation on the liability of a company located in another Member State.[27] The CJEU noted in particular that Austrian law provided that an industrial undertaking situated in Austrian territory which has been officially authorised by the competent Austrian authorities could not, in principle, be subject to an action for an injunction to prevent an actual or potential nuisance caused by that installation to neighbouring properties. Thus, according to the CJEU, allowing an action for injunction against an industrial installation located in another EU Member State would lead to a difference in treatment between domestic and foreign undertaking and thus violate the EU cardinal principle of non-discrimination on grounds of nationality.[28]

5. Transnational corporate litigation before domestic courts in Europe

Although both Rome II and Brussels I Regulations were designed to apply within an intra-EU context, they proved relevant in a transnational context involving litigants from third countries and in relation to environmental litigation against transnational corporations. In particular, the provisions of the Brussels Regulation combined with their interpretation by the CJEU, enabled foreign (non-EU) plaintiffs wishing to bring an action against the parent company to have access to the domestic courts of the corporation's home state. This has been possible thanks to a consistent line of case-law in which the CJEU clarified that Article 4(1) of Brussels Regulation must be interpreted as applying to defendants domiciled in Europe regardless of the nationality of the plaintiff, and including where plaintiffs have their domicile in a third country.[29] This interpretation aims to prevent disparities between two sets of civil actions against the same EU-based defendant brought by plaintiffs respectively located in an EU Member State and in a third country.[30] The same approach applies when the EU-based defendant is a company or a legal entity. In particular, the combined reading of Article 4(1) with Article 63(1)—which specifies that in the case of companies or legal persons, their domicile is determined by the country where they have their statutory seat, central administration or principal place of business—meant that foreign victims based outside of the EU could bring an action before the courts of an EU Member State directly against the EU-domiciled parent company for damage caused through the operation of its subsidiary established in a third country.[31]

Over the past years, a number of cases brought by third country residents in the courts of England and the Netherlands offer a good illustration of this scenario. In *Akpan v Royal Dutch Shell*, a group of Nigerian farmers were able to file lawsuits in the courts of the Netherlands against the Dutch-based parent company Royal Dutch Shell (RDS) and its Nigerian subsidiary Shell Petroleum Development Company of Nigeria (SPDC) for the severe environmental oil pollution and damage caused by the operation of the company's subsidiary in the Nigerian territory.[32] In a first interlocutory judgment on jurisdiction, rendered in 2010 and confirmed on the merits, the Hague District Court affirmed its jurisdiction over RDS, citing the Brussels Regulation 44/2001 (Articles 2(1) and 60(1)). The District Court's findings were reaffirmed by the Court of Appeal of the Hague. The Dutch courts' ruling was also significant as it was enacted at a time where it had become clear that US courts—traditionally among the preferred forums for foreign victims of human rights abuses and environmental pollution perpetrated by corporations—had significantly narrowed down the prospects of access to justice for third country claimants under the Alien Tort Statute (ATS).[33]

The introduction of the harmonised EU jurisdictional provisions has proved particularly impactful on those European common law–based jurisdictions, such as notably the UK, in which the doctrine of *forum non conveniens* was applicable. According to this doctrine, courts having jurisdiction are given substantial discretion as to whether to stay or dismiss the proceedings in favour of an available more appropriate forum. It should be noted that already in a line of personal injury cases decided during the 1990s and involving third country plaintiffs, English courts had adopted an interpretative approach which prevented the courts from declining their jurisdiction in favour of a foreign court when this would have amounted to a denial of justice for the plaintiffs.[34] However, the final turning point for the demise of the *forum non conveniens* principle in the UK, and within the EU more generally, was the CJEU's ruling in *Owusu v Jackson*.[35] According to the CJEU, application of the *forum non conveniens*, by allowing the national court wide discretion regarding the more appropriate forum for the trial, would undermine the predictability of the jurisdictional rules laid down by the Brussels Convention and thus the principle of legal certainty which is at its basis.[36] Translated in the context of environmental liability claims against multinational corporations, the *Owusu* decision effectively widened the door for overseas claimants to start proceedings against English-based and generally EU-based parent companies before EU courts.[37] Whether Brexit, by discontinuing the application of the Brussels Recast Regulation, will mean a reinstatement of the *forum non conveniens* doctrine remains to be seen; it will, presumably, also depend on the possible UK accession to the Lugano Convention.[38]

Akpan and a series of recent cases in UK courts show that the assertion of jurisdiction over the EU-domiciled parent company may have further collateral advantages for the claimants, as they can use the EU-domiciled defendant as an 'anchor' to extent the jurisdiction of EU courts also on the connected claims against a foreign-based subsidiary. In the UK, a significant example of this approach is represented by the litigation in the case of *Lungowe v Vedanta*.[39] The case concerned the claim of Zambian citizen living in the Chingola region of Zambia for the alleged personal injury and property damage, as well as loss of amenity and enjoyment of the land as a result of the pollution and other environmental harm caused by discharges of harmful substances from the copper mine into local waterways. The claims were based on the tort of negligence, although the claimants also alleged breaches of applicable Zambian environmental laws. In that case, English courts, from the High Court to the UK Supreme Court, affirmed their jurisdiction not only on the UK-based parent company, Royal Dutch Shell, on the basis of Article 4(1) Brussels, but also on the Nigerian-based subsidiary SPDC.

In practice, whether or not the court of an EU Member State will assert its jurisdiction over the foreign subsidiary will ultimately depend on the national procedural law. Article 6 of Brussels Regulation leaves it to domestic law to determine the court jurisdictionally competent over defendants not domiciled in an EU Member State. In case of a plurality of defendants, national procedural law usually allows, under certain circumstances, the national court to hear claims on a foreign co-defendant when there is a connection with the claim made against the defendant over which the court has jurisdiction. In the English cases of *Vedanta*[40] and *Okpabi*,[41] for example, the jurisdiction of the UK courts over the foreign subsidiary of a UK-based parent company was based on domestic law, i.e. rule Civil Procedure Rule (CPR) 6.36, 6.37 and Practice Direction 6B (Service out of the jurisdiction), according to which English courts can hear claims against a co-defendant outside the jurisdiction where it can be proved, *inter alia*, that the foreign co-defendant is a necessary and proper party to the proceeding; that there is an arguable case on the merit against the anchor defendant; and that England is the proper place to bring the claim against the foreign subsidiary. On that last point, a decisive factor in asserting English courts' jurisdiction over the case was the existence of a real risk that substantial justice could be denied in Zambia. Similarly, in *Akpan*, the jurisdiction of the Hague District Court and Court of Appeal to hear the case against the subsidiary (SPDC) was based on a combination of the Brussels I Regulation regime, which allowed claims to be brought in the Netherlands against the parent company, and Article 7(1) of the Dutch Code of Civil Procedure that allows the joint hearing of claims, including if one of the defendants is not within the jurisdiction of the court, for reasons of efficiency when there is a close connection between the rights of actions against the two defendants.[42] In *Akpan*, this provision permitted the Dutch District Court and subsequently the Court of Appeal to affirm their jurisdiction over the claims against the Nigerian-based subsidiary.

Overall, the aforementioned cases offer a vivid illustration of the positive impact that Brussels I Regulation exerted in improving the position of third country victims of pollution seeking redress for environmental harm suffered abroad. Its relevance in the context of transnational private litigation is especially evident when confronted with the narrower stance more recently adopted by US courts. Arguably, following the more stringent reading adopted by the US Supreme Court on the extraterritorial scope of application of the Alien Tort Claim Act (ATCA), European courts might represent a promising and attractive alternative venue for developing countries' victims of EU-based corporations.[43] This seems demonstrated by the recent human rights case brought before Dutch courts against Shell and its daughter companies by four widows of the nine Ogoni environmental activists who were sentenced to death and executed.[44] The proceedings were initiated in the Dutch courts following failure by the United States Supreme Court to accept jurisdiction under the ATCA in the *Kiobel* case.[45]

Nevertheless, and despite being an important step forward in improving the position of third country victims of pollution seeking redress in European courts against European-based companies, the Brussels Regulation regime does not always guarantee that the claim involving a foreign defendant will be tried in EU courts. For while EU law makes it mandatory to sue EU-based defendants, regardless of their nationality, in the courts of the Member State where they have their domicile or seat, for foreign (extra-EU) defendants—i.e. where the claim of the parent company is connected to a claim against the foreign subsidiary—the assertion of jurisdiction by the court of an EU Member State is determined by the law of the Member State. As noted, in England, service out of the jurisdiction under Article 6 CPR depends on a series of factors, including whether the foreign defendant is a necessary and proper party to the proceeding and the existence of a real issue to be tried against the 'anchor' (UK-based) defendant. Thus, in *Okpabi*, the High Court and the Court of Appeal had initially dismissed the claim of Nigerian farmers against Royal Dutch Shell and its subsidiary for the significant damage and ongoing pollution caused by the defendants' oil pipeline on the basis that there was no arguable case that RDS owed the claimants a duty of care.[46] This approach can be confronted with the more open, and arguably more plaintiff-friendly, attitude of the Dutch District Court in *Akpan*. In its 2013 ruling,[47] the court clarified its assertion of jurisdiction over the claims against SPDC on the basis that it was *foreseeable*, given the closely connected nature of the claim with that against RDS, that it would have jurisdiction.[48]

Of course, the identification of the competent forum and the possibility to have the case heard by a domestic court in an EU Member State are only one step in the context of complex transnational litigation proceedings. A further important question is to identify the law that is applicable to decide on the substantive aspects of the case. With respect to actions brought by foreign plaintiffs in an EU jurisdiction, what remains unclear is whether the most favourable law principle embodied in Article 7 of the Rome II Regulation is limited to the case of transboundary environmental damage occurring locally between two EU countries, or whether it extends to cover the tortious conduct of EU-based actors (i.e. the EU-based parent company) that results in environmental damage in third (outside-EU) countries. Arguably, a broader interpretation of the Rome Regulation's provision as being applicable also to the damage caused extraterritorially would be more in line with the environmental aims stated in the Preamble of the Regulation.[49] Moreover, policy recommendations and reports by international bodies and associations, such as the Permanent Bureau of the Hague Conference on Private International Law[50] and the International Law Association,[51] have noted the increasing support for the principle of the law more favourable to the injured party. With respect to the Rome II Regulation, this would mean an interpretation of Article 7 of the Regulation so that, in case of environmental damage, plaintiffs may opt for the law of the place of the tortious conduct. Such an approach would be particularly relevant in the case of claims brought against the EU-based parent company of a multinational group for the environmental damage caused by the company's local subsidiary located in a foreign jurisdiction. Extending the application of Article 7 of the Rome Regulation to these claims, when brought against the EU parent company, would allow the foreign plaintiffs to benefit from the application law of the place where the parent company is domiciled. In the cases of *Akpan*, such an approach would have allowed the assessment of the parent company liability on the basis of Dutch law, rather than Nigerian common law.[52] This could have potentially improved the position of the plaintiff since under Dutch law the 'parent company RDS could have been held liable for not preventing or reacting to the risks created by its Nigerian subsidiary'.[53]

6. Jurisdictional aspects, corporate liability and duty of care

Beyond the relevant jurisdictional aspects, the recent wave of transnational environmental tort cases brought in European courts has contributed to clarify some of the legal issues regarding the liability of EU-based parent companies for the environmental damage caused during the operations of their foreign-based subsidiaries. The company law doctrine of corporate separate personality represented for a long time a major stumbling block for plaintiffs trying to connect the liability of the parent company to the injuries caused by the operations of the subsidiary. In that respect, the harmonisation of jurisdictional rules facilitating the pursuit of transnational tort liability claims against the EU-based parent company for the environmental damage caused by the foreign-based subsidiary may help to close the 'regulatory gap in international corporate accountability'.[54] These foreign direct liability cases seek to establish the direct liability of the parent company for breach of the duty of care it owes to the foreign claimant. Therefore, the claim focuses on the conduct (i.e. acts and/or omissions) of the parent company, rather than that of the subsidiary,[55] and as such this approach may allow to bypass the obstacles posed by the separate legal personality doctrine.

In fact, these types of negligence-based liability cases against parent corporations are not a novelty. A trend in this sense already emerged during the 1990s through a series of tort claims against corporations based in the UK and other common law jurisdictions.[56] Most of these claims concerned health and safety issues related to the company's use of hazardous substances, such as asbestos and other unsafe production practices. Despite most of these claims not eventually reaching the merit stage, the relevant proceedings were significant in building up a narrative around a parent company's tort liability in relation to harm occurring outside the parent's home State jurisdiction, and they laid the ground for the subsequent pursuit of more environmentally focused cases.

In the UK, a seminal decision opening the way for using the common law duty of care as a standard in transnational corporate liability claims against UK-based parent companies was the Court of Appeal's decision in *Chandler v Cape*.[57] This case concerned once again asbestos exposure injuries. However, its significance compared to previous cases lies in the fact that the domestic court, almost for the first time, outlined the set of circumstances in which a parent corporation may be regarded as having assumed a direct duty of care for the health and safety of its subsidiary's employees. These circumstances included the fact that 'the business of the parent and subsidiary are in a relevant aspect the same'; that the parent has, or ought to have, superior knowledge on some relevant aspects of health and safety in the particular industry; that the subsidiary's system of work is unsafe as the parent company knows or ought to have known, and the parent knew or ought to have foreseen, that the subsidiary or its employees would rely on its using that superior knowledge for the employee's protection. The ruling was highly significant, and the criteria for parent company's duty of care laid down therein were subsequently relied upon in other transnational tort proceedings concerning environmental harm, although they did not always lead to a favourable outcome for the foreign plaintiffs.[58]

More recently, a number of corporate liability cases, such as those of *Akpan*, *Vedanta* and the recent UK Supreme Court's decision in *Okpabi*,[59] went a step further in the definition of a legal framework of transnational corporate accountability, and they are significant under at least two main respects. First, these cases reveal a greater sensitivity of domestic courts towards the need of facilitating access to justice for foreign claimants who are victims of human rights and environmental abuses, often extending their jurisdictional reach to encompass the activities of the subsidiaries. In particular, in the *Okpabi* case, the UK Supreme Court established a lower threshold for the scrutiny of one of the jurisdictional requirements—namely whether the claimants had a real issue to be tried against an English-based parent company—asserting that the lower courts had erred in law when engaging in a proper mini-trial of the claimants' arguments. The second aspect concerns the normative implications of these rulings with respect to the definition of the parent company's duty of care. In that respect, the rulings reveal a trend towards a greater degree of scrutiny by the domestic court into the relationship between the parent and the foreign subsidiary. In *Vedanta*, for example, the UK Supreme Court, while formally basing its decision on classic common law principles of tort liability and negligence and rejecting the claimants' argument concerning the existence of a 'special' doctrine of corporate liability in tort, had nevertheless engaged in a more in-depth analysis of the relationship between the parent company and the subsidiary. As this decision is still related to the jurisdictional phase of the proceedings, the court's assessment was mainly directed at ascertaining whether there was a real issue to be tried against the parent company as the anchor defendant; therefore, the court's assessment of the parent company's duty of care did not go as in depth as it would when adjudicating on the merit. Nevertheless, the court's approach suggests an increased willingness of the judges to go beyond the formalistic structures that link together the different entities in a corporate group, and to examine the substantive level of intervention of the parent company into the activities of the subsidiary in order to conclude that there was a real case to be tried against the parent. The Court held in fact that a sufficient level of intervention of the parent company into the activities of the foreign subsidiary could be evinced from the published material in which the parent company 'may fairly be said to have asserted its own assumption of responsibility for the maintenance of proper standards of environmental control over the activities of its subsidiaries . . . and not merely to have laid down but also implemented those standards by training, monitoring and enforcement'.[60] Arguably, such an approach, which focuses on the parent company's policies of corporate responsibility and on its degree of supervision over the activities of its subsidiaries, goes in the direction of expanding the scope of parent companies' accountability for hazardous practices put in place by their subsidiaries in third countries. Yet, it was noted that it may also have a 'perverse effect' of discouraging corporations from conducting human rights and environmental due diligence.[61]

All in all, the aforementioned precedents show how the combination of harmonised procedural rules on jurisdiction with the definition of substantive law standards of corporate's duty of care may enhance the prospects of access to justice and reparation for the foreign victims of transnational environmental harms, by allowing these victims to bring direct tort liability directly against the European-based parent company. From a transnational law perspective, these decisions are to be read in the light of the United Nations Guiding Principles on Business and Human Rights (UNGPs). Based on the work done by UN Special Rapporteur John Ruggie, the UNPGs are articulated around three interrelated pillars, namely (i) the State duty to protect human rights; (ii) the corporate responsibility to respect human rights; and (iii) access to remedy. Seen in this perspective, the decisions of domestic courts asserting the possibility for parent companies to be held accountable, in tort and civil liability, for human rights violations and environmental harm caused by the operations of its subsidiaries can be regarded as a way to implement and realise the principles of corporate responsibility and access to justice embodied in the UNGPs. This scenario also shows how the interplay between different regulatory frameworks, at the domestic, supranational and international levels, can contribute to implement environmental liability, broadly conceived as including both elements of corporate accountability and access to remedies. Whether the current legal framework, and in particular the level of harmonisation so far realised at the EU level, is adequate to achieve effective environmental justice and affirm cross-border corporate accountabilities is, however, something that needs further assessment in the light of other factors, as will be discussed further in the next section.

7. The harmonisation of EU private international law rules: an assessment

As the previous discussion has sought to demonstrate, the establishment at the European level[62] of a common private international law framework on jurisdiction and conflict of laws aspects and its application to environmental torts has contributed to facilitate the pursuit of environmental justice in situations involving multiple legal and jurisdictional systems. Furthermore, the possibility to extend European courts' jurisdiction to cases involving foreign claimants against corporate defendants domiciled in Europe increases the prospects for environmental victims in developing countries to have their case heard in a European court without fear of protracted legal battles on jurisdictional grounds.[63]

Furthermore, at the normative level the harmonisation of jurisdiction and conflict of law rules could also have the effect of bringing the realm of private international law beyond its traditional territorial focus and deference to municipal law. In particular, the establishment of a harmonised jurisdictional and conflict of laws framework in EU, by means of the Brussels and Rome II Regulations, may have an important regulatory potential.[64] By providing victims of transboundary environmental torts with the option of choosing the forum in which to bring the claim and the law applicable, it may contribute to remove the shields that protect companies when de-locating in countries with less stringent standards.[65] In that sense, the application of jurisdictional and conflict of law rules to transnational environmental liability claims provides a further illustration of private law's regulatory potential and its 'basic role . . . in addressing transnational regulatory gaps'.[66]

In practice, however, the extent to which the EU private international law rules can also perform a public policy and regulatory function, by contributing to enhance environmental protection standards and promoting environmental justice in a transnational context, needs to be assessed against two sets of considerations. The first is the extent to which these rules can be open to incorporate public values, for example by integrating public law and environmental standards in the assessment of liability under tort law. Second, in a situation where the impact of environmental harm and the perpetrators of such harms increasingly have a transnational and global dimension, the role and effectiveness of private international law in enhancing the opportunities for victims to obtain justice depend on the substantive law applicable and the standards and rules of liability. Harmonised rules on jurisdiction and conflict of law serve essentially to coordinate the application of the substantive regulatory frameworks of the various legal systems. Therefore, whether and to what extent Article 4(1) of the Brussels Regulation and Article 7 of the Rome II Regulation by providing foreign claimants with, respectively, access to EU-based courts and a choice in the possible applicable laws are adequate to strengthen a company's accountability for transnational environmental harm will ultimately depend on the quality of the substantive legislation that is available. In the absence of a common legal framework governing substantive law issues of corporate environmental liability, the question concerning the parent company's duty of care and the remedies available remain governed by the domestic rules of the applicable legal systems. Therefore, harmonisation of procedural law through private international law instruments may not be able to completely fill the gaps left by the absence of a global framework on environmental liability and corporate accountability.

Moreover, although an action based on tort law may well secure redress for individual victims, there is no guarantee that it will also address the harm suffered by the environment as such. There are inherent limitations in the private law of civil liability to address harm to common natural resources, which can also stand in the way of using transnational tort litigation to claim redress for the degradation of a natural habitat or the destruction of an ecosystem unrelated to injury to private individual rights. Not every country has a specific legislation addressing damage to natural resources, although in the EU the adoption of the ELD has contributed considerably to fill this legal gap. The question, however, is whether and how an administrative liability regime like the ELD can operate and be enforced in a transboundary context.

Finally, a private international law-based approach is only one piece of the complex legal edifice that needs to be put in place to achieve an appropriate system of environmental justice at the transnational level, capable of securing adequate redress both for victims of environmental torts and for the environment. Besides questions concerning the applicable law and competent forum, there are substantive and procedural law issues which form an equally essential component of a proper and effective access to justice, and which often play an important role in claimants' decision regarding the choice of forum. These include the availability of legal assistance, the cost of litigation, the possibility of obtaining legal aid or funding to bring the lawsuit, the availability of discovery and rules concerning evidence and so on. At a procedural law level, standing is a further important component to be considered in environmental cases. Particularly where the claim involves damage to the natural environment or to public natural spaces, the question arises as to whether NGOs and other private interested individuals can have standing to claim compensation under tort law. Different jurisdictions may have different approaches to this question. Neither Rome II nor Brussels address procedural law applicable to standing, which is therefore left to the single domestic court—in transnational cases, this is usually the law of the forum. Thus, in *Akpan*, both the District Court and the Appeal Court ruled that the NGO Milieudefensie could be regarded as having legal standing on the basis of Dutch procedural law.[67]

8. Transboundary environmental liability litigation in Europe: perspectives after the ELD

The need to address transboundary environmental damage was among the reasons initially put forward by the Commission in support of the EU intervention in the field of environmental liability. Moreover, from an EU law perspective, extending the scope of application of the ELD to cover transboundary harm between two or more neighbouring Member States offers a further justification for adopting a harmonised legal framework in the light of the principle of subsidiarity.

The ELD addresses the hypothesis of transboundary damage to natural resources affecting two or more Member States in Article 15, according to which the Member States affected by the damage 'shall cooperate, including through the appropriate exchange of information, with a view to ensuring that preventive action and, where necessary, remedial action is taken in respect of any such environmental damage'.[68] The following two indents of this provision outline the respective duties and rights of, respectively, the source State and the victim State. Specifically, the State in which the damage originates has a specific duty to provide sufficient information to potentially affected State(s),[69] whereas Member State(s) affected by damage may report the issue to the Commission and to the other Member States concerned and may make recommendation for the adoption of preventive or remedial measures. Finally, Article 15(3) envisages the possibility that the Member State affected by an environmental damage which does not originate within its jurisdiction may seek, in accordance with the Directive, to recover the costs it has incurred in relation to the adoption of preventive or remedial measures.

From the text and wording of this provision, it seems that the ELD is envisaging two parallel sets of action that may take place in the case of transboundary environmental damage. On the one hand, Article 15 promotes cooperation between Member States' authorities with respect to the prevention and/or reparation of environmental damage. On the other hand, the ELD envisages the possibility that public authorities may in parallel initiate cross-border civil actions for the recovery of environmental-related costs against an operator situated in another EU Member State. Two considerations, then, stem from the analysis of this provision. First, that even in the case of transboundary damage, the Directive avoids envisaging a direct State liability for damage caused by the operation of private hazardous activities. Following an approach analogous to the one envisaged at the international level in the ILC's Principles on the Allocation of Loss, Article 15 ELD only imposes on the source State specific duties of notification, exchange of information and cooperation, but it does not expressly envisage the liability of the State for transboundary damage. The situation might be different where it can be proved that the State origin of the damage has violated environmental standards or prescriptions established under EU environmental legislation. In this case, there is a possibility under Article 259 of the TFEU that the victim State may bring an action against the source State before the CJEU for failure to conform to EU law. However, this type of interstate enforcement is realistically a rather remote possibility, as States tend to avoid interstate litigation before the CJEU.[70]

The second consideration relates to the legal position of the affected State with respect to the right to recover damages under Article 15(3). Considering that the ELD is essentially a public law system of liability, it is plausible to think that this provision refers to potential actions brought by public authorities against foreign operators for the recovery of costs sustained through action of prevention or remediation of the damage. The Directive does not provide details on the procedural mechanism for bringing such actions, which are therefore left to be regulated by Member States' domestic law and procedure.[71] Nevertheless, as Article 3(2) ELD States that the Directive shall apply 'without prejudice to Community legislation containing rules on conflicts of jurisdiction', the question arises as to the relationship between the ELD and the rules contained in the Brussels I Regulation. In principle, the application of Brussels I regulation to cross-border actions between competent authorities for the recovery of costs under Article 15(2) ELD would presuppose that the latter can be regarded as falling within the concept of 'civil matters'. With respect to this, it can be noted that civil law claims brought by public authorities to recover the costs of clean-up have become an established practice especially in the field of oil spills at sea. For example, the 1992 CLC explicitly includes States and public bodies among potential claimants in transnational civil liability claims concerning the reimbursement of the costs of restoration of environmental damage. In the EU, the CJEU contributed to clarify the meaning of civil and commercial matters for the purpose of applying Brussels I Regulation. While in older rulings the Court appeared to adopt a more restrictive interpretation,[72] more recent pronouncements reveal a more open approach, in which the CJEU pays greater attention to whether the public authority actually exercised powers that go beyond those existing under the rules applicable to relationships between private individuals,[73] and consider more closely 'the basis and the detailed rules governing the bringing of the action' (for example, whether the action is based on domestic civil law or private law provisions of non-contractual liability).[74] In the light of this, it can be argued that cross-border actions by public authorities against foreign operators in another Member State for the recovery of costs related to environmental damage might fall under the scope of Brussels Regulation, particularly if they are based on civil liability or tort law.[75] If this finding is correct, it may also be argued that, based on the previous remarks concerning the definition of environmental damage under the Rome II Regulation, the latter instrument would also be applicable to damage to natural resources covered by the Directive, thereby allowing public authorities in cross-border cost recovery claims under civil law to avail themselves of the possibility to select the most favourable applicable law under Article 7 of Rome II.

There are other aspects concerning the transboundary application of the Directive that do not find explicit regulation in its text. These include the rights and legal position of interested parties and NGOs to access judicial review procedures in a foreign court against the foreign public authorities' failure to take action in the case of transboundary harm originating by a private economic activity located in another Member State. In other words, the question is whether Articles 12 and 13 of the ELD, which regulate the rights and role of private interest parties and NGOs, may also apply in a transboundary context.

An interesting comparative law precedent in this respect is provided by the US case of *Pakootas v Teck Cominco Metals Ltd.*[76] The case, which in many aspects resembled the well-known *Trail Smelter* dispute, involved severe cross-border pollution across Washington State originating from the dumping of heavy metals and other substances by the Canadian smelter operated by Teck Cominco Metals Inc. After unfruitful attempts by the US Environmental Protection Authority (EPA) to have the matter solved extrajudicially, and following Teck Cominco's refusal to comply with EPA's administrative order for a remedial/feasibility study under section 9606 of the Comprehensive Environmental Response, Compensation and Liability Act (CERCLA), members of the indigenous community in the Colville Reservation decided to take up the case in civil courts as a matter of private enforcement against the company pursuant to the citizens' suit provisions of the CERCLA.[77] In their rulings, both the District Court of Eastern District of Washington and the Court of Appeal issued decisions that, albeit on different grounds, had the effect of extending the reach of CERCLA to the Canadian company causing pollution in the United States.[78] This case is often cited as an interesting, and yet controversial, example of how a public law environmental statute could be applied in a cross-border context. However, unlike CERCLA, the ELD does not contemplate the possibility of a direct citizens' enforcement action against the polluter, and it is therefore difficult to operate a straightforward 'transplant' of the US approach to the EU. Nevertheless, it may be possible to envisage the application of the rights of intervention and judicial review provided in Articles 12 and 13 of the ELD. Although the ELD's provisions offer NGOs and private parties a more indirect and limited role compared to the US citizens' suit approach, they can arguably be interpreted as applicable also in a transboundary context, given that the ELD's scope of application extends across the whole EU territory, and that this instrument aims to provide a common framework across the different EU Member States. Such an approach would also be in line with the spirit of the Aarhus Convention, to which the EU is a contracting party, and according to which 'the public shall have . . . access to justice in environmental matters without discrimination as to citizenship, nationality or domicile'.[79]

9. The new proposal for a directive on corporate sustainability due diligence

The foregoing discussion on the questions of duty of care and environmental liability in a transnational context would not be complete without an express mention of an important recent development at the EU level, represented by the presentation by the European Commission of a Proposal for a Directive on Corporate Sustainability Due Diligence.[80] Pressure for EU action on this topic came from civil society as well as from the European Parliament, which, in a Resolution of 10 March 2021, provided a set of recommendations to the Commission on corporate due diligence and corporate accountability and called upon the Commission to propose EU rules for a comprehensive corporate due diligence framework.

From an EU perspective, the proposal represented also a response to the emergence over the past years of specific legal frameworks on corporate due diligence in some EU Member States. While those initiatives reflect the growing importance of ensuring that business conduct respects human rights and the environment, from an EU law point of view they also 'bring fragmentation and risk undermining legal certainty and a level playing field for companies in the single market'. The idea of adopting EU legislation on corporate sustainability due diligence therefore finds justification under the principle of subsidiarity also in the need to harmonise the field and avoid fragmentation of the market resulting from unilateral actions by the Member States.

The proposal aims at setting out a horizontal framework to foster the contribution of business operating in the single market to the respect of human rights and environment in their own operations and through their value chains. Recalling the approach to due diligence in the UNGP and the six steps in the due diligence process as defined by the OECD Due Diligence Guidance for Responsible Business Conduct, the Directive proposal envisages specific duties for companies to integrate due diligence in their policies and management system; to identify, prevent and mitigate, monitor and account for their adverse human rights and environmental impacts and to have adequate governance mechanisms in place to this end; and to provide remediation.

The proposal's scope of application is quite broad in that it covers both companies[81] acting through their subsidiaries and those within a supply chain, imposing due diligence obligations for the potential human rights and environmental adverse impacts arising in relation to the companies' own operations, the operations of their subsidiaries and the value chain operations carried out by entities with whom the company has an established business relationship.

The proposal complements the companies' due diligence duties with the provision of dissuasive, proportionate and effective sanctions for infringement of measures implementing this Directive and with specific provisions on civil liability aimed at ensuring compensation of victims of adverse impacts. Moreover, the proposed Directive also contains provisions related to the enforcement, including the establishment at Member States' level of apposite supervisory authorities, and provisions on criminal and civil liabilities. In particular, the Directive Proposal envisages the liability of companies to pay damages if they failed to comply with the obligations related to the prevention of adverse impacts and to ensure that those impacts are brought to an end or at least minimised, and as a consequence of such failure, damage has occurred. The Directive Proposal does not define damage, and thus there is no express indication as to whether it only covers damage to persons occurred as a consequence of the adverse human rights and environmental impact or whether it also includes damage to the environment as such. However, the fact that the recital refers to compensation claims to be brought by victims of human rights and environmental harms,[82] that it envisages civil liability provision, and that it explicitly states that this civil liability regime is without prejudice to the application of the ELD seems to suggest that 'damage' includes mostly damage suffered by private victims as a result of the adverse impacts.

If adopted, this Directive will stand by other parallel initiatives which, under different aspects, are seeking to promote more responsible business practices and to reduce the environmentally harmful impacts of EU companies, and of EU production and consumption, in third countries and globally.[83] It will also sit in parallel to the ELD, thereby prompting interesting research questions on the relationship between these two instruments in a transnational context. At the moment of writing, the Proposal, whose adoption follows the ordinary legislative procedure of co-decision, is at the stage of first reading in the European Parliament.

Notes

1 Among more recent EU initiatives, see European Parliament resolution of 10 March 2021 with recommendations to the Commission on corporate due diligence and corporate accountability, with the annexed Recommendation for Drawing up a Directive of the European Parliament and of the Council on Corporate Due Diligence and Corporate Accountability, P9 TA (2021) 0073; followed by the Proposal for an EU Directive on Corporate Sustainability Due Diligence, COM (2002) 71 final.
2 See XE Kramer and CH van Rhee (eds.), *Civil Litigation in a Globalising World* (Springer 2012).
3 Ibid. 2.
4 Article 220 of the 1957 Treaty Establishing the European Community.
5 Brussels Convention on Jurisdiction and Enforcement of Judgements in Civil and Commercial Matters, 27 September 1968 reprinted in (1990) 29 ILM 1413.
6 Convention on Jurisdiction and the Enforcement of Judgments in Civil and Commercial Matters done at Lugano on 16 September 1988, OJ L 319, 25.11.1988, p 9. This Convention has now been superseded by the 2007 Lugano Convention and therefore only remains relevant for proceedings commenced before the applicable date of the entry into force of the 2007 Lugano Convention in the relevant state of origin.
7 Council Regulation (EC) No. 44/2001 of 22 December 2000 on jurisdiction and the recognition and enforcement of judgments in civil and commercial matters, OJ L12.
8 Regulation (EC) No 864/2007 of the European Parliament and of the Council of 11 July 2007 on the law applicable to non-contractual obligations (Rome II), OJ L199/40.
9 Case C-21/76 *Handelskwekerij Bier v Mines de Potasse d'Alsace*, EU:C:1976:166, [1976] ECR 1735.
10 Ibid. [19].
11 M Faure and G Betlem, 'Applying National Liability Law to Transboundary Pollution: Some Lessons from Europe and the United States' in M Faure and Y Song (eds.), *China and International Environmental Liability, Legal Remedies for Transboundary Pollution* (Edward Elgar 2008) 129.
12 A Nylund and M Strandberg, 'Introduction' in A Nylund and M Strandberg (eds.), *Civil Procedure and Harmonisation of Law: The Dynamics of EU and International Treaties* (CUP 2019) 1.
13 W Hau, 'Europeanization of Civil Procedure: Overcoming Follow-Up Fragmentation through Bottom-Up Harmonisation?' in Nylund and Strandberg, *Civil Procedure and Harmonisation of Law* (n 12) 61.
14 Kramer and van Rhee (n 2).

15 In Europe, an important role in this sense has been played by the Aarhus Convention on Access to Information, Public Participation in Decision-Making and Access to Justice in Environmental Matters (adopted 25 June 1998) to which the EU is a contracting party.
16 M Anderson, 'Transnational Corporations and Environmental Damage: Is Tort Law the Answer?' (2002) 41 Washburn Law Journal 399, 415. U Baxi, 'Mass Torts, Multinational Enterprise Liability and Private International Law' in *Collected Courses of the Hague Academy of International Law*, vol. 276 (Martinus Nijhoff 1999) 370.
17 Regulation 864/2007 of the European Parliament and the Council on the law applicable to non-contractual obligations (Rome II), OJ L199, 40.
18 A Rest, 'The Most Favourable Law Principle in Transfrontier Environmental Law. A Means of Strengthening the Protection of the Individual?' (E. Schmidt 1980).
19 For an analysis of the Rome II Regulation, see W Posch, 'Some Observations on the Law Applicable to Transfrontier Environmental Damage' in M Hinteregger (ed.), *Environmental Liability and Ecological Damage in European Law* (CUP 2008) 33–51.
20 M Bogdan, 'The Treatment of Environmental Damage in Regulation Rome II' in J Ahern and W Binchy (eds.), *The Rome II Regulation on the Law Applicable to Non-Contractual Obligations: A New International Litigation Regime* (M Nijhoff 2009) 221.
21 H Van Loon, 'The Global Horizon of Private International Law: Inaugural Lecture, Private International Law Session' in *Collected Courses of the Hague Academy of International Law*, Vol 380 (Brill 2015) 86.
22 E Rehbinder, 'Extra-Territoriality of Pollution Control Laws from a European Perspective' in G Handl, J Zekoll and P Zumbansen (eds.), *Beyond Territoriality: Transnational Legal Authority in an Age of Globalization* (Brill 2012) 148.
23 Para 25 of the Preamble to the Rome II Regulation.
24 In this sense, Bodgan (n 20); and T Kadner Graziano, 'The Law Applicable to Cross-Border Damage to the Environment' (2007) *Yearbook of Private International Law* 71.
25 Rehbinder (n 22) 151.
26 On this case see Rehbinder (n 22) 149–154.
27 Ibid. 154.
28 Case C-115/08, *Land Oberosterreich v CEZ*, ECLI:EU:C:2009:660, para 93–95. The Court also found that disparity of treatment is not justified.
29 Relevant CJEU's case-law where this principle was first presented refer to the corresponding provisions under the Brussels Convention. See Case C-281/02 *Owusu v Jackson* ECLI:EU:C:2005:120, where the CJEU extended the application of the Brussels regime to claims brought by foreign plaintiffs located in a non-EU Member States and explicitly ruled out the compatibility of the *forum non conveniens* doctrine in situations falling within the scope of application of the Brussels Regulation.
30 Faure and Betlem (n 11).
31 Case C-412/98 *Group Josi Reinsurance Company SA v Universal General Insurance Company* (UGIC), ECLI:EU:C:2000:399. See H. Ward, 'Securing Transnational Corporate Accountability through National Courts: Implications and Policy Options' (2001) 24 *Hasting International and Comparative Law Review* 451.
32 District Court of the Hague, 30 January 2013, *Akpan and others v Royal Dutch Shell plc and Shell Petroleum Company of Nigeria Ltd* (2013) LJN BY9854 (Netherlands).
33 See *Kiobel et al. v Royal Dutch Petroleum Co et al.*, 569 US (2013), where the US Supreme Court relied on a presumption of extraterritoriality to exclude the application of the ATS to human rights violations committed in other countries, unless there is a strong connection with the US. R Meeran, 'Tort Litigation against Multinational Corporations for Violation of Human Rights: An Overview of the Position Outside the United States' (2011) 3 City University of Hong Kong Law Review 1, 1.
34 *Connelly v RTZ Corp Lpc (No 2)* [1998] A.C. 854; *Ngcobo v Thor Chemicals Ltd* [1995] 10 WLUK 81; *Lubbe v Cape plc* [2000] 1 E.L.R. 1545.
35 *Owusu v Jackson* [2005] QB 801.
36 Ibid. [41]–[46].

37 See Court of Appeal in *Lungowe v Vedanta Resources Plc* [2017] EWCA Civ 1528, [34]: 'The effect of the ECJ decision in Owusu v Jackson is that Article 4 of the Recast Regulation precludes the English Court from declining what is a mandatory jurisdiction where the defendant is a company domiciled in England and Wales'.

38 Post-Brexit, the UK has also lost its membership of the Lugano Convention. While it has applied to join the Convention, its accession requires the unanimous support from all the contracting parties to the Convention.

39 [2019] UKSC 20.

40 *Lungowe v Vedanta* (n 37).

41 *Okpabi v Royal Dutch Shell Plc* [2021] UKSC 3.

42 For an analysis, see L McDonnel, Case note 'Establishing Liability for Multinational Oil Companies in Parent/Subsidiary Relationship' (2014) 16 Environmental Law Review 50.

43 Meeran (n 33). But see C Ryngaert, 'Tort Litigation in Respect of Overseas Violations of Environmental Law Committed by Corporations: Lessons from the Akpan v Shell Litigation in the Netherlands (2013) 8 McGill International Journal of Sustainable Development Law and Policy 245, 253 who notes that even the plaintiff-friendly approach of the Dutch Court in *Akpan* may be far apart from the more liberal rules of personal jurisdiction in the US.

44 District Court of the Hague C/09/540872/HA ZA 17–1048, ECLI:NL: RBDHA: 2019: 4233.

45 *Kiobel v Royal Dutch Petroleum* Co 621 F 3d 111 (2d Cir 2010). In this decision, the US Second Circuit Court of Appeal held that customary international human rights law does not recognise the liability of corporations and therefore such actions cannot be brought under the ATCA.

46 *Okpabi and others v Royal Dutch Shell Plc and another* [2018] EWCA Civ 191. Note that this decision was overturned by the Supreme Court, which applying the approach laid down in its previous ruling in Vedanta ([2019] UKSC 3) concluded that there can be a real issue to be tried against RDS, [2021] UKSC 3.

47 District Court of The Hague, 30 January 2013, *Akpan and others v Royal Dutch Shell and Shell Petroleum Development Company of Nigeria, Ltd* (2013) LJN BY 9854.

48 See C Ryngaert (n 43) 251. Interestingly, such an approach based on the foreseeability criterion reflect the case-law of the CJEU regarding the scope of the Brussels I Regulation (see CJEU decision in Case C-145/10 ECLI:EU:C:2011:798 [2011] ECR I-0007 (*Painer*).

49 Recital 25 Rome II Regulation. L Enneking, 'Judicial Remedies: The Issue of Applicable Law' in J Alvarez Rubio and K Yannibas (eds.), *Human Rights in Business: Removal of Barriers to Access to Justice in the European Union* (Routledge 2017) 50.

50 Hague Conference on Private International Law, 'Should the Hague Conference revisit the scope and nature of possible work in the field of Civil Liability for Environmental Damage?', HCCH Prel. Doc. No 12, February 2010.

51 ILA Resolution on Transnational Enforcement of Environmental Law No 6/2006.

52 See on the question of applicable law the arguments brought by the claimants in *Okpabi and others v Royal Dutch Shell plc and another*, Queen's Bench Division, 26 January 2017 [2017] EWCH 89 (TCC) [50–56].

53 Ryngaert (n 43) 256.

54 E Aristova, 'Tort Litigation against Transnational Corporations in the English Courts: The Challenge of Jurisdiction' (2018) 14 Utrecht Law Review 2.

55 Ibid. 7.

56 See among others, *Connelly v RTZ Corporation Plc* [1998] AC 854; *Dagi and Others v Broken Hill Proprietary Company Ltd (BHP)* [1997] 1 VR 428 (pollution claim against the Australian parent company, BHP, in relation to the damage caused by the mining activities of its subsidiary, Ok Tedi Mining Ltd, in Papua New Guinea); *Sithole v Thor Chemicals Holding & Desmond Cowley* (mercury poisoning of South African workers,

case brought in England) 2000 WL 1421183; *Lubbe v Cape Plc* (again, involving asbestos related injuries suffered by South African workers) [2000] 1 WLR 1545; also Meeran (n33); P Nygh, 'The Liability of multi-national corporations for the torts of their subsidiaries' (2002) 3 *European Business Organization Law Review* 1, 51.

57 [2012] EWCA Civ 525.

58 See, for example, the rulings of both the High Court and the Court of Appeal in *Okpabi & Others v Royal Dutch Shell plc and Shell Petroleum Development Company in Nigeria*, [2017] EWHC 89 (TCC) and [2018] EWCA Civ 191, and the Court of Appeal in *AAA & Others v Unilever Plc & Unilever Tea Kenya Ltd* [2018] EWCA Civ 1532, which found that there was no arguable case that a duty of care existed since there was insufficient proximity between the UK parent company and the Nigerian claimants. Similarly in *Akpan*, the Dutch District court—relying on English common law precedents arguing that these constituted persuasive authority for the interpretation of Nigerian common law—considered that the situation at stake in *Akpan* was rather different from the scenario in *Chandler*, in that 'the duty of care of a parent company in respect of employees of a subsidiary that operates in the same country only comprises a relatively limited group of people, whereas a possible duty of care of a parent company of an international group of oil companies in respect of the people living in the vicinity of oil pipelines . . . would create a duty of care in respect of a virtually unlimited group of people in many countries', District Court of The Hague, C/09/337050/HA ZA 09–1580 (30 January 2013), para 3.29.

59 *Okpabi v Royal Dutch Shell Plc* [2021] UKSC 3.

60 *Vedanta Resources Plc v Lungowe and others* [2019] UKSC 20, [61].

61 In this sense, N Bueno and C Bright, 'Implementing Human Rights Due Diligence Through Corporate Civil Liability' (2020) 69 International & Comparative Law Quarterly 4.

62 The previous discussion has made reference also to UK courts' cases, as the EU-derived private international law rules also applied in the UK before Brexit.

63 E Blanco and B Pontin, 'Litigating Extraterritorial Nuisances under UK Common Law and UK Statute' (2016) 6 Transnational Environmental Law 285, 300.

64 O Boskovic, 'The Law Applicable to Violation of the Environment—Regulatory Strategies' in F Cafaggi and H Muir Watt (eds.), *The Regulatory Function of European Private Law* (Edward Elgar 2009) 188, 196.

65 U Grusic, 'International Environmental Litigation in EU Courts: A Regulatory Perspective' (2016) 35 Yearbook of European Law 1, 180.

66 R Wai, 'Transnational Liftoff and Juridical Touchdown: The Regulatory Function of Private International Law in an Era of Globalization' (2002) 40 Columbia Journal of Transnational Law 208, 253.

67 Article 3:305 (a) Civil Code of the Netherlands provides that a foundation or association with legal personality can file a legal action pertaining to the protection of similar interests of other person, provided that it protects these interests on the basis of its statute.

68 Article 15(1).

69 Article 15(2).

70 G Butler, 'The Court of Justice as an inter-state court' (2017) 36 Yearbook of European Law 179.

71 A study on the implementation of the Directive reveals indeed that most Member States' legislation specifies the procedures to take in the event of damage originating from outside the national border. See Stevens & Bolton LLP (2013), 'The Study on Analysis of Integrating the ELD into 11 National Legal Frameworks', Final Report prepared for the European Commission—DG Environment.

72 Case C-814/79 *Netherlands State v Ruffer* [1980] ECR 3807.

73 T Kadner Graziano, 'The Law Applicable to Cross-Border Damage to the Environment' (2008) Yearbook of Private International Law 71, at 82–83. See, Case C-420/07, EU:C:2009:271, *Apostolides*, paragraph 44 and the case-law cited, where the Court

excludes from Article 1(1) Brussels Regulation cases where one of the parties ' exercises powers falling outside the scope of the ordinary legal rules applicable to relationships between private individuals'. See more recently Case C-641/18, *LG v Rina SpA and Ente Registro Italiano Navale*. ECLI:EU:C:2020:349.

74 See, in this sense, AG Spuznar Opinion in LG v Rina SpA, para 35. See also judgments of 11 April 2013, Sapir and Others, C-645/11, EU:C:2013:228, paragraph 34 and the case-law cited, and of 12 September 2013, Sunico and Others, C-49/12, EU:C:2013:545, paragraph 35 and the case-law cited).

75 M Faure and G Betlem, 'Applying National Liability Law to Transboundary Pollution: Some Lessons from Europe and the United States' in M Faure and Y Song (eds.), *China and International Environmental Liability, Legal Remedies for Transboundary Pollution* (Edward Elgar 2008) 129.

76 *Pakootas v Teck Cominco Metals*, 452 F. 3d 1066 (9th Cir. 2006).

77 Section S.9659 of CERCLA.

78 For a comment on this case, J Ellis, 'Extraterritorial Exercise of Jurisdiction for Environmental Protection: Addressing Fairness Concerns' (2012) 25 Leiden Journal of International Law 394.

79 Article 3(9) Aarhus Convention.

80 COM (2022) 71 final.

81 The proposal, however, applies only to companies above a certain threshold established therein.

82 Recital 61 of the Preamble to the Directive Proposal.

83 These include, among others, Directive 2014/95/EC (Non-Financial Reporting Directive (NFRD)); Regulation (EU) 2019/2088 on sustainability-related disclosures in the financial services sector; EU Regulation 2017/821 laying down supply chain due diligence obligations for Union importers of so-called conflict minerals. Moreover, a Commission's proposal is currently under examination for a Regulation on deforestation-free supply chains, COM (2021) 706 final.

Part 3

Exploring the interactions between EU law and international law

Following the examination of the various endeavours aimed at the harmonisation of substantive and procedural norms applicable in the context of environmental liability, Part 3 of this book moves the discussion to the analysis of the multi-level interaction between different legal orders and regulatory frameworks, focusing in particular on the relationship between EU law and international law. This part is articulated in two chapters, each exploring different aspects of the interplay between EU law and international law in the field of environmental liability. Chapter 6 mostly focuses on the external relations aspects of EU environmental law and policy and examines how the EU may contribute to international law-making, both through its direct participation in the negotiation and adoption of international agreements and, more indirectly, by influencing and promoting developments at the international level. Chapter 7 shifts the analysis instead to the 'substantive' dimension of the interplay between EU and international law. It examines how international law provisions penetrate and display their effects in the EU legal order and interact with EU primary and secondary legislation. The analysis aims in particular at assessing whether the combination and interaction of EU and international law can have a positive impact in enhancing effectiveness of the responses to environmental harms. Thus, albeit with different focus and perspective, each chapter aims to explore the scope and potential for a synergic and mutually supportive interaction between EU and international law in the field of environmental liability and the extent to which the combination and interplay between the two legal orders can eventually lead to a strengthened legal framework in the field of liability and remedies for environmental harm.

DOI: 10.4324/9781315676708-9

6 The EU's contribution to international law-making in the field of environmental liability

1. Introduction

As part of its ambition to act as a global leader in the environmental field, the EU has put in place a variety of approaches to contribute to and to influence the further development of international law. These include both direct forms of involvement in international law-making, primarily through its participation in the negotiation and adoption of international environmental treaties, and other mechanisms and initiatives through which the EU indirectly influences and promote developments at the international level. This chapter examines the EU's contribution to international law-making in the field of environmental liability. It starts by focusing on the EU's direct involvement in international treaty-making, through an analysis of the rules and legal principles governing the EU's participation in the negotiation and conclusion of international agreements in the field of environmental liability. The second part of the chapter, however, acknowledges the existence of further normative interactions between EU and international law that may also significantly concur to forge the international environmental liability regimes and their scope of application within the EU legal order.

Methodologically, the analysis relies on a doctrinal approach. As such, it takes a primarily legal perspective to the study of the interplay between the EU external relations law and international law. From this angle, the chapter discusses how certain EU's external relations principles, applicable to the relationship between the EU and the Member States and aimed at preserving the effectiveness and consistency of the EU legal order and of EU's action on the international sphere, may also have an important role in determining the respective EU's and Member States' positions during the negotiation and application of international environmental liability agreements. In this respect, it will be suggested that while the EU seeks to actively play a role on the international level and to promote international law developments, its interaction with international law and its influence on international law-making is also in part defined by concerns related to its consolidation as an effective international actor and to the integrity and unity of its legal system.

DOI: 10.4324/9781315676708-10

2. The EU's participation in international agreements: general remarks

One of the primary avenues through which the EU contributes to international law-making is through its external relations competences and its capacity to enter into international agreements. The EU is currently a contracting party to numerous MEAs, it has member or observer status in several international organisations dealing with environmental issues, and it has been extensively engaging and cooperating with international institutions in shaping solutions to global environmental problems. The analysis of the legal rules and principles governing the EU's involvement in international treaty-making and the scope and extent of such involvement is, therefore, relevant to assess its contribution to the further development of international law, including in the specific field of environmental liability.

The EU treaties (both TEU and TFEU) contain a few provisions on the external relations of the EU and its participation to international agreements. Particularly relevant are Article 47 TEU, asserting that the EU has legal personality under international law,[1] and Article 218 TFEU, which lays down the procedure for the EU negotiation and conclusion of international agreements.[2] According to the latter provision, the Council decides by qualified majority[3] whether to authorise EU participation in the negotiations and conclusion of an international agreement on the basis of a recommendation submitted by the Commission. This procedure also applies to decisions regarding the position to be adopted on behalf of the EU in the context of bodies set up in the context of the international agreement—such as the Meetings of the Parties (MOPs) or Conferences of the Parties (COPs) to MEAs—when these bodies adopt acts having legal effects.[4] Moreover, since the entry into force of the Lisbon Treaty, and except for matters falling under the Common Foreign and Security Policy, the Union is represented externally by the Commission in the context of international agreements and at the meetings of the COPs or MOPs under MEAs.[5] According to some, the Commission's explicit mandate to represent the EU in its external relations is one of the most important innovations introduced by the Lisbon Treaty, as it is regarded as potentially strengthening and streamlining the EU position and representation in international negotiations.[6] In reality, there still appears to be room for the previous informal practice of involving the rotating Council presidency in the negotiations and external representation of the EU in cases of shared competences and mixed agreements.[7]

3. The principle of conferral and EU's external competence

3.1. *Express external competences*

Besides specific treaty provisions on the EU participation in international treaty-making, general principles of EU law also apply to the field of external relations.[8] Among these, the principle of conferred powers (Article 5(2) TEU), a cardinal tenet of the EU's internal action, is also a fundamental pillar of the EU's external relations. In that respect, a distinction must be made between express and implied external competences. 'Express' external competences are those explicitly stated in the EU treaties. Originally, the Treaty of Rome in 1957 only granted to the then European Economic Community two express competences to conclude international agreements, namely in the field of trade (currently resumed under the common commercial policy) and with respect to the conclusion of association agreements with third States or group of States.[9] Since then, however, the external powers of the EU have expanded on an increasingly wider array of policy areas, both by means of subsequent treaty amendments, which have added new express legal basis for EU external powers, and through the proactive judicial interpretation of the CJEU. In the field of environment, a specific external competence was introduced in the 1986 Single European Act (SEA). The relevant provision, which corresponds to current Article 191(4) TFEU, stated, 'within their respective sphere of competences, the Union and the Member States shall cooperate with third countries and with the relevant international organizations'.

3.2. The doctrine of implied external powers

In addition to competences expressly conferred in the treaties for specific policy sectors, Article 216 TFEU codifies, or attempts to codify, the longstanding case-law of the CJEU on implied external powers by identifying three circumstances in which the EU may implicitly acquire treaty-making competences. Specifically, pursuant to this provision, '[t]he Union may conclude an agreement with one or more third countries or international organisations' not only 'where the Treaties so provide' but also 'where the conclusion of the agreement is necessary in order to achieve, within the framework of the Union's policies, one of the objectives of the Treaties, or is provided for in a legally binding Union act or is likely to affect common rules or alter their scope'.

The implied powers doctrine, developed by the CJEU, had a pivotal role in shaping and further consolidating the EU's treaty-making capacity. It is possible to distinguish in that respect two distinct rationales which underline the relevant rulings in which the CJEU identifies the existence of EU implied external powers in specific areas.[10] The first rationale is linked to the existence of EU common rules in the same field covered by the international agreement. The assertion of EU's external competence in this case is aimed at avoiding that Member States may autonomously enter into international agreements and assume commitments conflicting with existing EU provisions. This reasoning emerges clearly from the Court ruling in the well-known AETR case, which is also the decision were the implied external powers doctrine was first laid down.[11] The case concerned the negotiation and conclusion by the Member States of an agreement concerning the work of crews of vehicles engaged in international road transport. The Community had already adopted legislation in that sector, namely through the adoption of a Council regulation. In its ruling, the CJEU adopted a purposive interpretation of the treaty provisions regarding the European Community's international legal personality and concluded that the Community competence to enter into international agreements was not limited to those cases where there was an express provision for external action, but 'it may equally flow implicitly from other provisions of the Treaty and from measures adopted, within the framework of those provisions, by the Community institutions'.[12] It also clarified that the emergence of the EU implied external competence in this case was based on 'pre-emption', that is the adoption and pre-existence of EU common rules which may be affected by the international provisions and which, therefore, pre-empted Member States from acting autonomously at the international level. In other words, in this case the assertion of the existence of implied external powers was immediately complemented by the definition of the exclusive character of those powers. The Court indeed stated,

> [e]ach time the Community, with a view to implementing common policy envisaged by the Treaty, adopted provisions laying down common rules, whatever form these might take, the Member States no longer had the right, acting individually or collectively, to undertake obligations with third countries which affected those rules. . . . As and when such common rules come into being, the Community alone is in a position to assume and carry out contractual obligations towards third countries affecting the whole sphere of application of the Community legal system.[13]

From an EU law perspective, the AETR principle appears as the external relations counterpart of the pre-emption principle embodied in Article 2(1) TFEU and which determines the boundaries between EU's and Member States' internal regulatory powers in areas where competence is shared. Similarly to Article 2(1) TFEU's pre-emption, the exclusivity of EU external competences is in this case based on the need to avoid normative conflicts which may affect the uniform application of EU legislation across the Member States. As we shall see, concerns about preserving the uniformity, integrity and effectiveness of the Union legal system are an important theme that characterises the modalities of EU engagement with international law, including in the specific field of environmental liability.

Subsequent CJEU rulings have elaborated further on the circumstances in which the EU can acquire implied external competences and on the nature and extent of such competences. In particular, the CJEU added a further rationale to the doctrine of implied powers[14] in the *Kramer* case,[15] concerning the North-East Atlantic Fisheries Convention on the conservation and exploitation of marine resources, and in Opinion 1/76 on the compatibility with Community law of a draft agreement intended to regulate over-capacity on the Rhine and Moselle,[16] where the CJEU made a connection between the conferral to the EU of internal powers for the achievement of a defined Union's objective ('*effet utile*' principle) and the existence of a corresponding implied external competence. In particular, in *Kramer* the Court noted that the Union 'had at its disposal, on the internal level, the power to take any measure for the conservation of the biological resources of the sea', concluding that 'it follows from the very duties and powers which Community law has established and assigned to the institutions of the Community on the international level that the Community has authority to enter into international commitments for the conservation of the resources of the sea'.[17] Similarly, in Opinion 1/76 it held, 'whenever Community law created for those institutions powers within its internal system for the purpose of attaining a specific objective, the Community had authority to undertake international commitments necessary for the attainment of that objective even in the absence of an express provision to that effect'.[18] The Court subsequently clarified that this is the case when 'the conclusion of the international agreement [is] necessary in order to attain objectives of the Treaty that cannot be attained by establishing autonomous rules'.[19] Therefore, while in the AETR case the existence of external competence was based on pre-emption (i.e. the existence of EU legislation covering the field) and was linked to the exclusive nature of such competence, these subsequent rulings clarified that the EU can also have external competence to enter into international agreements that are necessary to achieve one of its objectives in areas where it has competence to legislate internally. In this case, however, the existence of implied external powers is independent from the prior adoption of internal common rules harmonising the field and is therefore independent from whether these competence are exclusive to the EU or shared with the Member States.[20] Accordingly, even in policy sectors where competence is shared, the EU can act at the international level as soon as there is a connection with the achievement of one of the treaty objectives in a given policy area.[21]

Thus, through its case-law the CJEU 'progressively develop[ed] the doctrines of implied powers and exclusivity in a characteristically incremental manner'.[22] Subsequent and more recent CJEU case-law provided additional elucidation on the doctrine of implied external powers and on the circumstances and rationales for exclusive powers on the basis of the AETR principle.[23] First, the CJEU clarified that a risk that common EU rules may be adversely affected by the international commitments, so as to trigger the EU exclusive competence, arises not only when the provisions of the international agreement and the existing Union legislation coincide fully, but also potentially where the international commitments 'are concerned with an area which is already covered to a large extent' by EU rules'.[24] Moreover, the CJEU confirmed that in order to ascertain the existence of a potential normative conflict, it is necessary to take into account 'not only the current state of Community law in the area in question but also its future development, insofar as that is foreseeable at the time of that analysis'.[25] This case-law seems also to suggest that an explicit normative conflict between the international commitments and the EU law provision is not required to affirm the exclusive competence of the EU on the basis of AETR doctrine, since the CJEU went on to say, 'EU rules may be affected by international commitments even if there is no possible contradiction between those commitments and the EU rules'.[26] That said, the Court also made clear that on the basis of the principle of conferred powers, a finding of EU exclusive competence

> must have its basis in conclusions drawn from a comprehensive and detailed analysis of the relationship between the envisaged international agreement and the EU law in force . . . [taking] into account the areas covered by the EU rules and the provisions of the agreement envisaged, their foreseeable future development and the nature and content of those rules and those provisions, in order to determine whether the agreement is capable of undermining the

uniform and consistent application of the EU rules and the proper functioning of the system which they establish.[27]

Overall, this line of case-law has the effect of expanding the impact of the AETR principle. On this, a ruling rendered in an infringement proceeding launched by the Commission against Greece (*Commission v Greece* case) [28] illustrates well the potentially far-reaching implications of the AETR exclusivity and how it may limit the scope for Member States' autonomous action. The case at hand concerned a Greek government's submission of a proposal to the IMO Maritime Safety Committee concerning the monitoring of compliance with the Convention for the Safety of Life at Sea (SOLAS) and the International Ship and Port Facility Security Code (ISPS Code). The EU is not a member of IMO. Both the relevant SOLAS Convention provisions and the ISPS Code were already subject of an EU Regulation[29] that implemented them in the EU legal order, and were therefore covered by EU exclusive competence. The question consequently concerned the impact of these EU exclusive powers on the scope and modalities of a Member State's participation in international organisations. Greece did not seem to dispute that the EU had exclusive competence in this area. However, it argued that the AETR doctrine is limited to the conclusion of international commitments and does not extend to other initiatives of participation in an international organisation.[30] The CJEU reached instead a different conclusion and held Greece in violation of its obligations under the treaty. The CJEU based its decision on the fact that although Greece was not directly entering into an obligation which could affect the EU Regulation, it nevertheless, through its unilateral submission of a national proposal to IMO, 'initiated a procedure which could lead to the adoption by the IMP of new rules', which would in turn have an effect on the EU Regulation.[31]

With this ruling the CJEU had in practice extended the application of the AETR doctrine beyond the conclusion and ratification of international treaties to cover also other acts and initiatives which are not *per se* immediately legally binding, such as the adoption by a Member State, within the framework of an international organisation (i.e. the IMO) to which it is a member, of an autonomous national position on specific subject matters, to the extent that these unilateral initiatives may have legal effects in the EU legal order and therefore potentially 'affect' EU rules.[32] An author noted that by expanding the AETR exclusivity principle to cover also 'future possible legislative developments at the international law level' and their 'hypothetical' impact on EU law, the CJEU has essentially transformed 'the effect based test [of the AETR] into a "hypothetical compatibility" test'.[33] Moreover, especially relevant for the CJEU's decision seems to have been the fact that the EU is not a member of IMO, thereby implying that Member States' obligation to refrain from independent action applies even more strongly where the EU is not able to represent itself directly on the international sphere.[34] Overall, the ruling consolidated the principle that in areas covered by exclusive competences the Member States must abstain from acting independently at the international level, for example by adopting national positions on matters falling in areas of exclusive EU powers, and may instead take initiatives only in the framework of the EU (typically, through the adoption of a common position).[35]

Overall, the prior discussion demonstrates how the CJEU has played a significant role in expanding the scope of EU external competences in a wide range of policy areas, including the environment. With respect to the latter, the idea of a parallelism between EU external powers and its internal competences and objectives has been particularly relevant in defining the legal basis for the EU's competence to participate and conclude international environmental agreements. In fact, while Article 191(4) already provides the EU with an express external competence in the environmental field, the wording of this provision appears limited to cooperation agreements. Therefore, in its Opinion 2/00 concerning the EU's accession to the Cartagena protocol on biosafety, the CJEU found that Article 192(1), which is the article representing the legal basis for the adoption of internal legislation in the environmental field, is the most appropriate legal basis also for the participation of the EU in international environmental agreements which go beyond merely establishing arrangements for cooperation regarding environmental protection.[36] Since then, Article 192(1) has become the default legal basis for EU participation in international environmental treaties. Arguably, this has implications on the balance and division of external powers between the EU and the Member States. This is because the wording of the second subparagraph of Article 191(4) can be read to imply that 'an engagement of the Union based on shared competence would not prejudice Member States' competence to negotiate in international bodies and to conclude international agreements'.[37] By contrast, the CJEU's case-law on the use of Article 192(1) as legal basis for external action in the environmental field seems to confirm that the AETR doctrine does apply to such measures.[38]

Building on this extensive, and not always linear, jurisprudence, the Treaty of Lisbon has made a notable attempt to codify the CJEU's case-law regarding EU (implied) external competences, including by systematising the distinction between the different categories of competences. Therefore, while Article 3(1) TFEU provides an exhaustive list of areas where the EU has *a priori* exclusive competence, Article 3(2) TFEU seeks to transpose the CJEU's case-law on the circumstances under which the EU may acquire exclusive external competence and identifies three situations in which the EU becomes exclusively competent to conclude international agreements on areas where competences were previously shared. These three situations are also referred to as 'conditional exclusivity',[39] to indicate the fact that in these cases the exclusive treaty-making power of the EU is linked to three conditions, namely (1) when the conclusion of an international agreement is provided for in a legislative act of the Union, (2) when it is necessary to enable the Union to exercise its internal competence, or (3) insofar as the conclusion of the agreement may affect common rules or alter their scope.[40] The third condition mentioned in this provision reflects the CJEU's case-law on AETR implied exclusive competences. There is admittedly a certain overlap between Article 3(2) and 216, but the two provisions relate to two distinct aspects: Article 216(1) is concerned with the existence of EU competence, whereas Article 3(2) concerns the exclusive nature of that competence.[41] That said, the Court's case-law, including its pre-Lisbon case-law, continues to retain its validity and therefore its relevance in the interpretation of these treaty provisions.[42]

3.3. Choosing the appropriate legal basis

Closely linked to the question of Union competences is the choice of the legal basis for the Council decisions authorising the EU to participate in an international environmental treaty, as well as decisions authorising Member States to enter into the international treaty on behalf of the EU. The CJEU reiterated in various occasions that the choice of legal basis has constitutional and institutional significance,[43] as it not only is important from a constitutional perspective (i.e. as a recognition that the EU is acting within the remit of its conferred powers), but also is relevant in determining the kind of acts that may be adopted, the procedures to be followed, including the role of the European Parliament and the relevant voting procedure in the Council, and the 'relative scope of different policies and how they interrelate'.[44] If an agreement is concluded on a legal basis which the CJEU subsequently finds to be incorrect, the relevant Council decision authorising the conclusion of the agreement must be readopted on the correct legal basis, although this does not affect the binding nature of the agreement in international law.[45] The choice of the legal basis may also serve to signal to the other contracting parties to the international agreement the extent of the Union competence and the division of competence between the EU and the Member States for the implementation of the agreement within the EU legal order.[46] In a ruling concerning a Council decision establishing the position to be adopted on behalf of the EU with regard to proposals submitted during the COPs to the Convention on International Trade in Endangered Species (CITES), the CJEU established that Council decisions which produce binding legal effects, such as the one at stake in this case and which established the EU position at the 14th meeting of the COPs to CITES, should not only indicate their procedural basis (that is usually Article 218 TFEU), but also should have as substantive legal basis the relevant treaty provision empowering the EU to take that measure.[47]

As for the determination of which treaty provisions would be the appropriate legal basis for a given agreement, the CJEU consistently held that the choice of the legal basis must be grounded 'on objective factors which are amenable to judicial review and include in particular the aim and content of the measure'.[48] The CJEU also developed the so-called centre of gravity test whereby if a measure appears to have a twofold purpose or component, including a primary purpose or component and another that is merely incidental, the measure must be grounded on a single legal basis, namely the treaty provision corresponding to the external relations power required by the primary component.[49] A joint legal basis is possible only exceptionally in those cases where 'the measure simultaneously pursues several objectives which are inseparably linked without one being secondary and indirect in relation to the other'.[50] In any case, a measure cannot be adopted on a dual legal basis where the relevant provisions entail different procedures that are incompatible with each other—such as different voting rights in the Council or a different representation by the European Parliament.[51]

In practice, and despite the CJEU's efforts to define objective legal criteria assisting the EU institutions in the choice of the appropriate legal basis, it is not infrequent that discussions arise on the appropriate legal basis for a given measure, and these discussions are often charged of political significance since that choice may have further implications on the EU's posture in the negotiation process and in relation to the management and implementation of the agreement. For example, the choice of one or another legal basis may signal a correspondingly different type or extent of EU competence in relation to a certain international agreement.[52] From an EU perspective, it is usually considered preferable to choose a legal basis leading to an EU exclusive competence over all or most aspects covered by the agreement, particularly as this would avoid the complexities and uncertainties arising from mixed agreements.[53] On the other hand, Member States sitting in the Council usually prefer to ground the agreement on a legal basis which recognises their shared competence, as this may pave the way to conclude the agreement in a mixed format where both EU and Member States participate.[54]

In the environmental field, a case that epitomises the political controversies surrounding the choice of legal basis are the disputes between the Commission and the Member States in relation to the conclusion by the EU of two international agreements at the intersection between trade and environment, namely the Cartagena Protocol on Biosafety and the Rotterdam Convention on Prior Informed Consent Procedure for certain hazardous chemicals and pesticides in international trade.[55] In both cases, the Commission launched an action for annulment of the respective Council decisions by arguing that these should have been based either on Article 207 TFEU (formerly, Article 133 EC) which grants exclusive competence to the EU in the field of common commercial policy, or jointly on Article 207 TFEU and Article 192 TFEU, and not solely on Article 192 TFEU on environment. In both cases, it was clear that the question of the choice of the legal basis was closely interlinked with concerns regarding the scope of EU competence and the role of the EU, and of the Commission, in the management of the agreement. In its request for a CJEU opinion on the conclusion of the Cartagena Protocol, the Commission argued, 'the exercise of shared competence is always a source of difficulty' in terms of the management of the Protocol and the exercise of voting rights[56]—however, the CJEU dismissed this argument as irrelevant to the determination of the appropriate legal basis.[57]

These institutional disputes involving international agreements at the intersection between two policy areas, such as typically trade and environment, and more recent litigation,[58] demonstrate that especially in the case of multilateral treaties which cut across different policy sectors and pursue different objectives, it may be difficult to identify a predominant objective and, thus, to determine the most appropriate legal basis according to the centre of gravity test. Arguably, sticking to the rule of a single legal basis may therefore not always be possible or appropriate.[59]

Interestingly, inter-institutional discussions between the Commission and the Council concerning the appropriate legal basis have recently arisen also in relation to the adoption of the Council Decision to authorise the signature and ratification by the Member States in the interest of the EU, of the 2010 Protocol to the International Convention on Liability and Compensation for Damage in Connection with the Carriage of Hazardous and Noxious Substances at Sea.[60] These types of discussions show both the difficulty to separate and distinguish among the closely connected treaty objectives and the close ties between the choice of legal basis and the related question of the nature and scope of EU external competence.

4. The practice of EU external relations

4.1. Mixed agreements

Although both the treaty and the case-law of the CJEU contributed to lay down the main legal principles governing the law of EU external relations, the reality of EU participation in international agreements is also normatively shaped by the practice of EU institutions and of the Member States. Of special relevance is the practice of the so-called mixed agreements, namely the joint negotiation and conclusion of international agreements by the EU institutions and the Member States. This is a phenomenon that does not find explicit regulation in the treaties but that has become an integral part of EU external relations[61] especially in those areas, such as environmental policy, where competences are shared between the EU and the Member States. In theory, the legal justification for mixed agreements is that the competences of the EU do not cover the entirety of the agreement, and thus the co-participation of the Member States is necessary to 'fill the gap' and complement the EU competence.[62] In practice, the decision whether to recur to a mixed agreement is often a political decision, and a great majority of international treaties are concluded in mixed format, including those treaties covering policy areas, such as transport and environment, where both the EU and the Member States share competences and where, in principle and at least according to a certain scholarly opinion, the EU would have the competence to conclude the agreement as an EU-only treaty, independently on whether it has exercised that competence internally in the sense of Article 3(2).[63]

The phenomenon of mixed agreements represents therefore a pragmatic response to a reality in which very few treaties fall entirely within the exclusive competence of the EU, while at the same time Member States are reluctant to leave completely the scene of international relations. Whether a treaty is concluded by the EU alone, as an EU-only treaty, or as a mixed-agreement with the participation of the Member States has procedural consequences. Specifically, while EU agreements are concluded pursuant to Article 218 TFEU, and therefore in most cases on the basis of a qualified majority voting in the Council, mixed agreements need to be ratified by all the Member States, and therefore their ratification require *de facto* unanimity. Therefore, from the perspective of the Member States, mixed agreements appear the preferable option for various reasons, including a feeling that it gives Member States greater international visibility and greater control over the assumption of international commitments, while at the same time also allowing to preserve a certain degree of domestic democratic scrutiny.[64]

4.2. Member States acting as 'trustees' of the EU[65]

If from an EU perspective the capacity to enter into international agreements depends on it having the relevant authority and competence to do so, from an international law standpoint it is necessary that such capacity is accepted by the potential treaty partners. In the environmental field, many MEAs explicitly accommodate EU participation through the inclusion of a provision allowing Regional Economic Integration Organisations (REIOs) to join the treaty alongside its Member States. However, there are still a wide majority of international treaties that are only open to States, for example because the treaty is adopted under the auspices of international organisations to which the EU is not (or not yet) a member.[66] In the field of environmental liability, this scenario is quite frequent given that most liability treaties in the field of marine pollution are negotiated and adopted in the framework of the International Maritime Organization (IMO), which does not yet admit EU membership. Similarly, the International Atomic Energy Agency (IAEA) and OECD conventions in the field of nuclear liability do not envisage EU participation. Therefore, a situation may arise whereby the EU has exclusive powers over all or parts of an international agreement, but it cannot be a party to it. In principle, if Member States conclude the agreement without formal EU participation, the treaty is only part of the national law of the Member States that have concluded them and does not become part of the EU legal order.[67] Yet, the agreement may also bear consequences for EU law, especially if it governs aspects that are covered by EU competence. Thus, in the case of an international treaty which falls entirely or in part within the exclusive competence of the EU but which does not allow participation by the REIOs, the solution found in practice is that the EU participates in the treaty through the medium of its Member States acting in the interest of the EU. The presence of EU exclusive competence, even only on some parts of the treaty, implies that in these cases Member States' participation in the negotiation and conclusion of the agreement must be authorised by the EU. This usually occurs by means of a Council decision authorising the Member States to negotiate, sign and ratify the agreement on behalf of the EU.[68] In some cases, the Council authorisation decision includes a provision whereby Member States commit themselves to use their best endeavours to secure an amendment to the international convention in order to allow the EU to become a contracting party. From an EU perspective, the fact that the EU is not itself a party to the agreement or to the relevant international organisation does not affect the existence of its external competences to decide on the positions to be adopted with regard to these instruments. In the field of environmental liability, these type of Council decisions have been adopted to allow Member States to ratify the Bunkers Convention on civil liability for oil pollution damage,[69] the 2003 Protocol to the 1992 International Convention on the Establishment of an International Fund for Compensation for Oil Pollution Damage,[70] the 1996 and 2010 HNS Liability Convention, and the 1997 Protocol to the Vienna convention and the 2004 Protocol to the Paris Convention on liability for nuclear damage.

5. The duty of cooperation and its impact on Member States' external action

EU membership bears important implications on Member States' position at the international level. As the CJEU famously stated, 'the founding treaties of the EU, unlike ordinary international treaties, established a new legal order . . . for the benefit of which the Member States thereof have limited their sovereign rights, in ever wider fields'.[71] In the field of external relations, the limitation of Member States' sovereign rights resulting from the transfer of powers to the European Union means that, while they formally remain sovereign entities under international law, their actual margin of independent action on the international plane is redefined as a consequence of their EU membership.[72] In that respect, the categories of shared and exclusive competences as defined and systematised in the Lisbon Treaty offer a partial reflection of the dynamics that characterise the transfer of powers from the Member States to the EU in the field of external relations. As the previous discussion has illustrated, both the nature and scope of EU external competences develop and evolve in connection with the EU's internal legislative developments and objectives. Therefore, shared and exclusive competences are not abstract and static categories in which the respective roles and scope of action of the Union and the Member States can be crystallised.[73]

In that perspective, the principle of loyal cooperation represents a useful legal and conceptual tool to understand the dynamic relationship between EU and Member States in the field of external relations and the impact of EU membership on Member States' external powers and their scope of independent action at the international level. The duty of sincere cooperation finds its conceptual legal basis on the principle of loyalty enshrined in Article 4(4) TEU. Pursuant to this provision, '[t]he Union and the MS [Member States] shall in full mutual respect, assist each other in carrying out tasks which flow from the treaties'. Moreover, Member States shall take all the appropriate measures 'to ensure fulfilment of the obligations arising out of the Treaties' and 'shall facilitate the achievement of Union's tasks', refraining 'from any measure which could jeopardize the attainment of the Union's objectives'. The wording of this provision and the way it is interpreted and applied by the CJEU make clear that both the principle of loyalty and the duty of sincere cooperation are functionally linked to the protection and pursuit of the EU's interest.[74]

The duty of cooperation becomes especially relevant in the context of EU external relations, where it translates into a series of substantive and procedural obligations which guide, and even constrain, Member States' action in a way to ensure the fulfilment of the EU's interest or the achievement of its objectives. From the analysis of the CJEU's external relations case-law, it is possible to distinguish two dimensions of this duty—an internal and an external one—which are related to the different facets and manifestations of the EU interest in the various contexts. The internal dimension is typically reflected in the AETR doctrine of supervening exclusivity[75] and is concerned with protecting the substantive unity, integrity and effectiveness of EU law and the EU legal order. The external dimension is concerned instead with the effectiveness of the EU action and the protection of its actorness on the international level.[76] In the CJEU's rulings, this aspect is often expressed in terms of the 'requirement of the unity of external representation', which reflects the concern of ensuring the cohesion and coherence of the EU's external action and of presenting the EU as a unified system to the outside world despite its inherent multilevel and composite structure. This external dimension of the duty of cooperation recurs particularly in the management of mixed agreements where it translates into a series of procedural obligations of reporting and consultation, and in a duty for both the EU and its Member States to exercise the respective competences in a way to ensure the unity of external representation.[77] On this, the CJEU consistently stated,

> '[w]here it is apparent that the subject-matter of an agreement or convention falls partly within the competence of the Community and partly within that of its Member States, it is essential to ensure close cooperation between the Member States and the Community Institutions, both in the process of negotiation and conclusion and in the fulfilment of the commitments entered into.[78]

This duty of close cooperation applies even more strongly in those situations where the Member States are called to act on the international plane on behalf of the EU.[79] It is also interesting to note that Article 4(3) TEU refers to the principle of loyalty as a reciprocal principle which binds not only the Member States but also the EU institutions.[80]

In its jurisprudence, the CJEU has made ample use of the duty of cooperation in order to consolidate the unity and effectiveness of EU's external action and to avoid that Member States' independent action at the international level might hamper the coherence and unity of EU law. There are several CJEU decisions that illustrate how the duty of cooperation may impact upon and constrain their margin of independent action even in areas of shared competences and even in the absence of a specific legislative or regulatory action at the EU level. In particular, in two infringement proceedings brought by the Commission respectively against Luxembourg and Germany in the field of transport policy, the CJEU held that, even in an area where competence is shared 'the start of a concerted action at EU level', reflected in the fact that the Commission had started to negotiate an agreement with third States, requires

> if not a duty of a duty of abstention on the part of the Member States, at the very least a duty of close cooperation between the latter and the Community institutions in order to facilitate the achievement of the Community tasks and to ensure the coherence and consistency of the action and its external representation.[81]

The cases concerned the negotiation and conclusion by Germany and Luxembourg of bilateral agreements for inland waterways transport with non-EU central European Member States. However, soon after but prior to the ratification of these agreements, the Commission was mandated by a Council decision to start the negotiations for a Community agreement with the same states.

In the environmental field, an illustrative example is the ruling against Sweden concerning a proposal of the Swedish government to include perfluoroctane sulfonates (PFOS) in the list of persistent organic pollutants (POPs) to be regulated under the Stockholm Convention on POPs.[82] A proposal for a Council decision regarding the inclusion of certain chemicals in a relevant Annex to the Stockholm Convention was presented in 2004 by the Commission, but PFOS were not covered by it. According to the facts of the case, part of the reason for this omission was linked to concerns raised by the Council Presidency for the economic consequences of the inclusion of PFOS, as it might result in a call for additional financial aid on the part of developing countries which are contracting parties to the Convention.[83] Therefore, after having previously raised the issue with the Commission, and in the absence of common action on this subject at EU level, the Swedish government decided to act unilaterally by submitting a proposal for the inclusion of PFOS under the Convention regime. According to Sweden, since the EU had not yet adopted measures related to PFOS and since there had been no agreement in that respect at the EU level, the Member States retained the competence to propose the listing of that substance under the Convention.[84] The CJEU, however, found for the Commission and held that Sweden's unilateral submission of the proposal violated the duty of loyal cooperation. In its reasoning, the CJEU, echoing the conclusion reached in the previous decision against Greece,[85] reiterated that the duty of cooperation binds the Member States not only in the context of conclusion of international agreements, but also with respect to other activities stemming from their participation in international fora, such as when they independently put forward proposals in the framework of an international environmental agreement. However, unlike in the case of *Commission v Greece*, where the measures proposed by the Greek government in the context of IMO fell within the scope of EU exclusive competence, Sweden's proposal in this case fell squarely in the area of environmental law (i.e. an area of shared competence) and touched a subject matter on which there was no previous EU legislative action.[86] Yet, in this case, at the basis of the CJEU's strict approach to the question of Member State's margin of independent action were a range of factors—such as the presence of several measures indicating the existence of a Union coordinated strategy, although not yet formalised through the adoption of a common position, and the specific voting requirements for decision-making under the Convention—which indicated that Sweden's unilateral proposal might in practice have legal consequences for the Union.[87]

The PFOS ruling also touched the other debated question of the external scope of Article 193 TFUE and namely the extent to which Member States can unilaterally promote the adoption of more stringent international environmental measures. On this point, the ruling clarifies that although Article 193 TFEU allows Member States to unilaterally introduce more stringent measures domestically (provided that they are compatible with the internal market), they may not do so at the international level, when the proposed measures may potentially have binding effects on the EU.[88]

This case is overall very interesting for an analysis of the implications of the interplay between EU law and international law on the environment. Like the case *Commission v Greece*, this decision shows how certain internal dynamics concerning the division of powers between the EU and its Member States and related concerns about preserving the integrity and cohesiveness of Union law may indirectly impact on legislative or regulatory developments at the international level. Indeed, both cases are examples of how the expanding scope of EU powers, including through the interpretation and application of the duty of loyal cooperation, may impose constraints on Member States' autonomous law-making action at the international level, even when such action is aimed at the pursuit of more advanced environmental standards.[89] A similar remark can be made, albeit in a different context and with respect to a very different set of issues, with respect to the implications arising from the CJEU's ruling in the *MOX Plant* case involving a dispute between Ireland and the United Kingdom.[90] The case stemmed factually from Ireland's environmental concerns related to the UK decision to authorise the construction and operation of a plant to make mixed oxide fuel (MOX). Proceedings were brought before an arbitral tribunal under the UNCLOS and the ITLOS and before the CJEU. The case before the CJEU was an infringement proceeding brought by the Commission and concerning EU external competence with respect to UNCLOS, to which the EU is a Contracting Party, and the implication of that competence in terms of the exclusive jurisdiction of the CJEU. According to the Commission, Ireland, by submitting its controversy with the UK to dispute settlement bodies instituted under the UNCLOS, would have failed to respect the exclusive jurisdiction of the CJEU under Article 292 EC. In its ruling, the CJEU declared that by instituting arbitral proceedings within the framework of UNCLOS on matters falling in areas of EU competence, Ireland infringed not only its treaty obligation of having recourse to the CJEU for the settlement of intra-EU Member State disputes (Article 344 TFEU) but also the duty of cooperation. Thus, like in *Commission v Sweden*, the *MOX Plant* ruling also reveals how at the basis of the CJEU reasoning there are primary concerns about preserving the autonomy of EU law, which were arguably competing with the underlying environmental concerns raised by Ireland about marine pollution.

6. Reflections on the relationship between the EU legal order and international law

The preceding remarks prompt a reflection on how the CJEU frames the relationship between EU and international law with respect to the balancing between, on the one hand, the EU's interest in the effectiveness of EU law and of its external action and, on the other hand, the universal interest in the protection of the environment. The PFOS ruling, for example, shows how in some cases the preservation of the EU's interest, most notably through the application and interpretation of the duty of cooperation, may compete with, and even override, the pursuit of more ambitious environmental objectives at the international level.[91] There are, however, other cases in which the interaction with the EU legal order may contribute to enhance the effectiveness of international law. As discussed more in detail in the next chapter, the fact that the EU is a contracting party to international environmental treaties has important consequences on the legal status of the international provisions in the EU legal order, as these provisions become an integral part of EU law. This, in turn, bears implications also in terms of the jurisdiction of the CJEU over the interpretation of the agreement, thereby enabling some rather progressive interpretation by the CJEU of the provisions of international environmental agreement read in conjunction with norms and principles of EU law.[92] Moreover, the participation of the EU to international agreements combined with the application of the duty of cooperation may enhance the effectiveness of the international law provisions by subjecting them to the enforcement procedures available in the EU legal order.[93] This is possible thanks to the wording of Article 216 TFEU according to which agreements concluded by the EU are binding on the EU institutions and its Member States. The CJEU interprets this provision to the effect that it is incumbent upon the EU institutions as well as upon the Member States to ensure compliance with the obligations arising from such agreements.[94] The duty of cooperation plays a role in this as the CJEU frequently states that in ensuring respect for commitments arising from an agreement concluded by the EU institutions, the Member States fulfil an obligation not only in relation to the non-member countries concerned but also and above all in relation to the EU which assumed responsibility for the due performance of the agreement.[95]

The duty of cooperation is particularly relevant in the context of mixed agreements. The CJEU relied in several cases on this principle to assert its enforcement jurisdiction in infringement proceedings concerning Member States' failure to comply with the provision of the agreement falling under the competence of the EU.[96] Furthermore, it has been argued that the duty of cooperation may also play a role with respect to Member States' ratification of mixed agreements, extending its impact also on those parts which fall under Member States' competences.[97] This is because mixed agreements need to be ratified by all participating Member States, and it is common for the Council to wait until all the participating Member States have ratified the agreement before formally concluding the agreement on the part of the EU.[98] Thus, although in principle the Member States retains their sovereignty under international law and cannot be bound to ratify the agreement, there is arguably an interest on the part of the EU in the expeditious entry into force of the agreement which it has ratified.[99] Therefore, even though the duty of cooperation 'cannot be stretched as to oblige Member States to ratify a mixed agreement', it could still be read as a best effort 'obligation to initiate the national ratification procedure, but without influencing the outcome of this procedure'.[100] According to some scholars, the previous considerations would apply *a fortiori* to international agreements to which the EU, despite having exclusive competence over all or parts of the agreement, can only participate through the medium of its Member States acting in the EU's interest.[101] The CJEU has restated on various occasions that the duty of cooperation between the EU and the Member States 'is all the more necessary' in view of the fact that the former cannot itself conclude the international agreement.[102] This potential impact of the duty of cooperation on Member States' ratification process finds reflection also in the not infrequent practice to include, either in the provisions or in the Recital of the Council decision approving the conclusion of an international (mixed) agreement, a formula encouraging the Member States to proceed to the ratification of the treaty in an expeditious manner.[103] Moreover, the relevant Council Decision that authorises the ratification of and/or accession to the agreement may even, in some cases, impose certain conditions on the Member States in order to preserve the EU interest, such as to use their best endeavours to facilitate amendments to the agreement in question so to allow the EU to become a contracting party, or to make a declaration that ensures the continued application of EU law in the relation between them instead of the provisions of the agreement which are conflicting with existing secondary EU legislation.[104]

In the light of these remarks, the following sections of this chapter will examine more closely the issues surrounding the EU participation in international environmental liability treaties and their implications from the point of view of the further development of international law in this field. The analysis will seek to assess in particular the extent to which the direct or indirect involvement of the EU in the negotiation, conclusion or ratification of international liability treaties may have positive impacts for the development of international norms in this field.

7. The participation of the EU in international environmental liability agreements

At a general level, the legal principles and practice of EU external relations examined so far also apply to the EU participation in international treaty-making in the field of environmental liability. Yet, when examining the EU involvement in this particular field of international law, it is also important to bear in mind that environmental liability agreements do not form among themselves a homogeneous category. There are significant differences between them in terms of their scope of application, the policy areas involved and the goals and objectives that they each intend to pursue, including the relevance granted to environmental protection concerns. These differences may have an impact on the extent and modalities of the EU's participation in each agreement, since the agreement's underlying aims and objectives and their subject matter are relevant to determine the legal basis on which to ground EU action and consequently also the extent and the nature of the EU's external competence. In general, the existence of the EU's external powers in the environmental field is undisputed thanks also to the conferral of explicit external competence in Article 191(4) TFEU and the acceptance of Article 192(1) TFEU as a default legal basis for external EU environmental action.[105] Less clear is, however, the scope of the EU's external powers in other policy areas which may be relevant to the international regulation of environmental liability. This is the case, for example, of nuclear liability. The existence of an EU competence on this subject has been under debate, including with respect to whether any such competence to legislate internally should be based on the TFEU or Euratom.[106] A further aspect that may impact on EU standing and participation in environmental liability treaties is whether they allow participation by non-State entities and regional organisations such as the EU.

In the light of this, the following sections examine the involvement and contribution of the EU to international law-making in the field of environmental liability by focusing the analysis on the two sets of liability regimes where the normative interaction between EU and international law proves particularly interesting. Specifically, it will discuss the EU's direct participation as a contracting party to the Nagoya-Kuala Lumpur Supplementary Protocol and its indirect involvement in the civil liability treaties in the field of marine pollution.

7.1. Liability agreements with an environmental dimension: the Nagoya-Kuala Lumpur Supplementary Protocol

The Nagoya-Kuala Lumpur Supplementary Protocol on Liability for damage caused by the transboundary movement of LMOs (NKLSP) offers probably the most straightforward example of how EU participation may contribute and influence the formation of international liability regimes. Compared to the classic civil liability treaties that characterised international law developments in the field of marine pollution, nuclear energy and the transport of other hazardous substances, the NKLSP distinguishes itself for its predominant environmental protection objectives linked to the protection and restoration of biodiversity. From an EU law perspective, the existence of the EU's external competence to negotiate and conclude this agreement is linked to the achievement of EU environmental policy objectives, which include the promotion of measures at the international level to deal with regional or worldwide environmental problems.[107] The EU participation in the NKLSP is therefore based on the Environmental Title of the TFEU, and specifically in Article 192(1) TFEU in conjunction with Article 218(6) (a) TFEU.[108] Moreover, Article 18 of the NKLSP expressly admits participation by the European Union as a contracting party.

Since the subject matters regulated by the NKLSP fall in a realm of shared competences, the agreement has been concluded as a mixed agreement. As it is common practice for mixed MEAs to be open to participation by REIOs, a Declaration of Competence was annexed to the relevant Council Decision, with a view to outline the internal division of competences between the EU and its Member States over the provisions of the agreement.[109] Yet, the precise legal relevance of these type of declarations is debated.[110] They are often worded in very general terms in order to account for the dynamic and evolving nature of the relevant EU competences, thereby not being particularly informative as to which specific issues fall under the respective scope of competence and responsibility. The Declaration annexed to the Council Decision related to the conclusion of the NKLSP limits itself to link the EU competence over the agreement to the achievement of the EU environmental policy objectives under Article 191 TFEU, affirming that the EU 'is responsible for the performance of the obligations resulting from this Supplementary Protocol which are covered by Union law in force'. In practice, the question of Member States' responsibility for the proper performance of the obligations arising from the NKLSP may find enforcement at the EU level on the basis of the duty of cooperation.[111]

Within the EU legal order, the NKLSP is primarily implemented through the ELD, to which it was largely inspired. The NKLSP is now in force. It is suggested that the EU's political support for this agreement, and its participation as a Contracting Party to it, may have had a role in promoting its ratification by the Member States.[112] Recital 8 of the NKSPL's Preamble states, '[t]he Union and its Member States should endeavour to deposit as soon as possible their instruments of ratification, acceptance or approval of the Supplementary Protocol'.

From the perspective of the EU relationship with international law, the Protocol offers a very interesting case-study of the normative influence that developments at the EU level may have internationally. During the final stages of the negotiation process leading to the drafting and subsequent adoption of the final text of the NKLSP, the ELD represented an important source of inspiration.[113] The final version of the NKLSP reflects in most respects the administrative approach to liability embodied in the Directive. The direct involvement of the EU in the negotiation process was probably an important factor in asserting the ELD as a model for the definition of an international liability regime in the field of biodiversity damage. It must be recalled that the nature of the prospective biodiversity liability instrument and the possible inclusion of civil liability provisions raised controversies and tensions during the negotiations. While certain Southern countries advocated strongly for a civil liability framework for environmental damage caused by GMOs, this was not an attractive prospect for the EU and other countries, such as New Zealand and Australia.[114] In the EU there was already a rather comprehensive legislation in the field of biosafety, and concerns were raised about having to make substantial reforms.[115] Thus, at the EU level, support for a public law approach during the negotiations of the NKLSP was also driven by internal dynamics. Both the EU and its Member States wanted to avoid entering 'into obligations that reached further than their current systems'.[116] Indeed, as reported in the Explanatory Memorandum to the Commission Proposal for a Council Decision on signing the NKLSP, the negotiating directives clearly 'instructed the Commission to ensure that the results of the negotiation [were] consistent with relevant Union legislation and with the basic principles of Member States' law on liability and redress and that they could be implemented in the EU without introducing or amending substantive rules on civil liability'.[117] As previous experience with the negotiation and drafting of the ELD had shown, Member States are usually protective of their own domestic rules on civil liability and reluctant towards attempts at harmonising the field. Thus, although the EU delegation initially refrained from proposing the adoption of an administrative approach, and thus to 'export' the ELD on the international level, due to the lack of experience regarding the application of the ELD,[118] the EU presence arguably had a role in steering the negotiations in that direction. In any event, the move towards the option of an administrative approach to liability was crucial in 'saving' the negotiations and opened the way towards reaching an agreement over the text of the Supplementary Protocol.[119]

7.2. Disrupting interaction?

From the perspective of the interplay between EU and international law, the case of the NKLSP can be regarded as an example of synergic interaction. Not only was the ELD a source of inspiration for the international biodiversity liability regime, but the final decision to opt for a public law approach to liability contributed significantly to move the negotiation process towards the successful adoption of the NKLSP. The analysis of the EU's role in the context of the NKLSP negotiations also illustrate the subtle dynamics at play in the interaction between the EU internal legal frameworks and the relevant international law developments. The existence in the EU of a harmonised liability regime for natural resources damage and of other instruments applicable in the field of biosafety, and of domestic rules on tort and civil liability in the legal orders of the Member States, bore influence in framing the EU position in the negotiation process.

There are, however, other contexts where these internal dynamics of interplay between internal EU developments at the level of secondary legislation and the international legal system led to less positive outcomes. An interesting example are the discussions concerning the possible accession of the European Community to the Council of Europe Lugano Convention on Civil Liability for Damage Resulting from Activities Dangerous to the Environment. The Commission's White Paper on environmental liability initially listed the EU accession to the Convention as one of the possible options for the development of an EU-wide environmental liability regime. Yet, a number of factors internal to the EU, including the firm opposition by some of the Member States and doubts surrounding the EU's legal competence to accede to this agreement in the absence of pre-existing secondary legislation in the field, contributed to hamper the pursuit of this option.[120] Eventually, the EU's decision to regulate liability by means of the ELD resulted in the *de facto* demise of the Lugano Convention, which never entered into force.[121] Thus, in this case, the presence of legislative developments at the EU level in the field of environmental liability, including the decision to regulate the field through the adoption of an EU directive, have eventually held back progress at the international level.

A more recent instance of 'disruptive interaction'[122] between EU and international law is represented by the EU's decision not to proceed with the ratification of the Kiev Protocol on Civil Liability and Compensation for Damage Caused by the Transboundary Effects of Industrial Accidents on Transboundary Waters to the 1992 Convention on the Protection and Use of Transboundary Watercourses and International Lakes and to the 1992 Convention on the Transboundary Effects of Industrial Accidents.[123] The Protocol, adopted within the framework of United Nations Economic Commission for Europe (UNECE), was signed in 2003 by 24 States, including several EU Member States as well as countries which gained EU membership after the 2005 and 2007 enlargement. In the same year, the Commission adopted a proposal for a Council decision on the signature of the Protocol on behalf of the European Community.[124] The Proposal was based on Article 191 TFEU related to the environment and on former Article 67 EC Treaty related to the cooperation on civil and judicial matters, which reflected the EU's exclusive competence on the Protocol's provisions regulating jurisdiction and recognition and enforcement of judicial decisions in civil and commercial matters. Given the environmental protection objectives of the liability regime laid down by the Kiev Protocol, the Proposal motivated the appropriateness of EU accession based on the Protocol's contribution to the pursuit of the Union's environmental policy objectives and to the 'effective application' of the EU environmental principles.[125] Moreover, the EU was a contracting party to both the UNECE Conventions on the Protection and Use of Transboundary Watercourses and International Lakes, and the Convention on the Transboundary Effects on Industrial Accidents, which both had a provision requesting the contracting parties to support appropriate international efforts to elaborate rules in the field of liability.[126] This notwithstanding, the subsequent adoption of the ELD in 2004 eventually smothered the EU's interest in acceding to the Protocol, which was deemed as almost redundant or even 'antagonistic' to the EU liability regime.[127] In its REFIT evaluation report, the Commission explains,

> the issues addressed by the Directive continue . . . to require action at EU level because in particular transboundary damage needs to be addressed not only in relation to the transfrontier transport of genetically modified organisms . . . but also for other categories of transboundary environmental damage, such as transboundary water damage *where the ELD was a relevant justification for the EU and its Member States not to accede to the Kiev Protocol.*[128]

It seems that, at least from an EU perspective, action at the EU level was regarded as preferable in addressing transboundary water damage. Thus, in this case the EU's decision to refrain from the signature and ratification of the Kiev Protocol might have impacted on the destiny of that international agreement. Moreover, it is arguable that the adoption of the ELD, which contains provisions that may overlap with the scope of application of the Kiev Protocol's liability regime, would preclude EU Member States to independently decide to sign or ratify the Protocol outside the EU institutional framework. Although the ELD and the Kiev Liability Protocol take a different approach to the regulation of liability, with the latter focusing on the harmonisation of civil liability provisions, there still remain substantial elements of overlaps between the two instruments, particularly with respect to their application in the event of transboundary damage to transboundary waters occurring between two or more EU Member States.[129] While it can be debatable whether these overlaps are such to give rise to an AETR effect,[130] it may be argued, in the light of the previously examined CJEU's case-law and its far-reaching reading of the duty of cooperation, that in case the Member States decide to accede to the Kiev Protocol they are at least under a duty to notify and consult with the Commission.

From an environmental law perspective, the EU's decision not to sign the Kiev liability agreement is regrettable given that there is a good potential for positive synergies and complementarity between the two liability regimes.[131] As noted in Chapter 6, although the Directive does apply to transboundary damage occurring between two Member States, its provisions with respect to the cooperation between competent authorities and the recovery of costs in cross-border situations remain very general and often leave to the individual Member State the regulation of the details. On that aspect, the Protocol would provide competent authorities with clearer indications regarding the applicable procedures as well as more legal and financial certainty in terms of their ability to recover the costs of the response and reinstatement measures.[132] Furthermore, the harmonisation of civil liability rules applicable to transboundary water damage would contribute more legal certainty for private parties and operators. Most importantly, the signing and ratification of the protocol by the EU and its Member States would also fill the legal gap currently arising from the absence of a specific liability regime for transboundary water damage originating in non-EU Member States, or caused outside the EU by activities taking place within the territory of EU Member States.[133] The ELD does not apply to this type of damage, which therefore is at present only addressed through the transnational application of domestic tort or civil liability rules.

7.3. The EU's involvement in international civil liability treaties on marine pollution and nuclear damage

7.3.1. The external relations implications of Brussels I Regulation

Compared to the direct participation in the negotiation and conclusion of the international liability regime for biodiversity damage, the EU's involvement in the more 'traditional' civil liability agreements in the field of marine pollution and nuclear energy followed a different trajectory. First of all, most of these treaties are adopted in the context of international organisations, such as the OECD, the IAEA and the IMO, which do not envisage EU membership.[134] The relevant liability conventions do not provide an REIO clause allowing the EU to become a Contracting party. Additionally, some of the earlier civil liability treaties, such as the 1969 CLC and the 1960/1963 Paris and Vienna Conventions on nuclear liability, were negotiated and ratified by the EU Member States at a time when the EU did not have a preponderant regulatory presence in the field of maritime transport, nor was there a specific EU legislation in the field of liability. Hence, the first trigger for the EU involvement in these international civil liability regimes was the adoption of the 2001/44 EU Brussels I Regulation, whose provisions on jurisdiction and the recognition of judicial decisions overlapped with and were thus affected (in the AETR meaning) by the relevant norms contained in the nuclear and marine civil liability regimes, thereby giving rise to an EU exclusive competence with respect to those provisions.[135] In particular, an important difference between the EU Regulation and the international conventional framework is the flexibility concerning the competent court in relation to tort actions. Whilst the EU Regulation allows the plaintiff to choose whether to sue the polluter in the court of his/her home country (i.e. the place where the damage was suffered), such possibility is not available in the international marine and nuclear damage conventions, which usually mandate the exclusive jurisdiction of the State party where the pollution damage or the nuclear incident occurred. A further discrepancy concerned the rules on recognition and enforcement of judicial decisions. According to the Brussels Recast Regulation, a judgement given in a Member State shall be recognised and enforced in the other Member States without any special procedure being required, whereas the relevant provisions in the Bunker and HNS liability treaties allow the judgments to be enforced in each Contracting State 'as soon as the formalities required in that State have been complied with'.[136]

As the EU Regulation was adopted in 2001, the impact of EU exclusive competence did not affect those treaties to which Member States were already contracting parties, such as the 1969 and 1992 CLC and the 1971 and 1992 IOPC Fund Conventions, and the 1960 Paris and the 1963 Vienna Conventions on nuclear liability. In that respect, Article 71 of the Regulation also provided, '[t]his Regulation shall not affect any conventions to which the Member States are parties and which in relation to particular matters govern jurisdiction or the recognition or enforcement of judgments'. More recent civil liability treaties were however impacted by the new supervening exclusive competence, including the 2001 Bunker Oil Convention, adopted in April 2001[137]; the 2010 Convention on Liability for Damage in connection with the Carriage of Hazardous and Noxious Substances by sea ('2010 HNS Liability Convention'), adopted in April 2010; the Protocol establishing an International Oil Pollution Compensation Supplementary Fund, adopted in May 2003 ('2003 Supplementary Fund Protocol'); and the two Protocols adopted in 1997 and 2004 and amending respectively the Vienna and Paris Conventions on civil liability for nuclear damage (the '1997 Protocol' and the '2004 Protocol').

Given that none of these liability treaties are open to participation by regional or international organisations, the exclusive competence of the EU was acknowledged by requiring Member States to be authorised, 'exceptionally', by means of Council decisions to sign and ratify the relevant agreement 'in the interest of the Community'.[138] From the point of view of the Member States, the elaboration of these decisions, which resulted from coordinated meetings between the EU institutions and the Member States, reflect their acknowledgment of the implications and constraints stemming from EU exclusive competences and the corresponding obligation to address the relevant matters within the EU institutional framework rather than individually.[139] Moreover, while the Council emphasises the exceptional nature of this practice, this is by no means an unusual phenomenon.[140] Indeed, only in the field of liability and compensation for pollution damage is possible to count at least six of these Council decisions.

It is also worth mentioning that the Council decisions related to the accession or ratification of the 2001 Bunker Liability Convention and that concerning the 2003 Supplementary Fund Protocol contain a provision requiring the Member States to use, at the earliest opportunity, their best endeavours to ensure that the relevant agreements are amended to allow the Union to become a contracting party to it. No similar statement is included in the Council decisions related to the accession to the 2010 HNS Liability Convention and in those concerning accession to the Protocols to the Vienna and Paris Conventions on nuclear liability. Nevertheless, when present, these clauses can be regarded as concrete expressions of the duty of cooperation in addressing the EU interest in its effective participation in the agreements.

7.3.2. The impact of the ELD on the EU's participation in the marine pollution civil liability regime

While the EU involvement with the international civil liability conventions in the field of marine pollution and nuclear damage was initially confined to jurisdictional and civil procedural issues, the subsequent adoption of the ELD and the concomitant intensification of EU policy and regulatory action in field of maritime transport[141] raised the question of the impact of these internal legislative developments on the nature and extent of EU's external competence with respect to the international maritime liability conventions. These questions emerged in relation to the Council decisions authorising the Member States to ratify in the interest of the Union the 2010 Protocol to the HNS Liability Convention (the '2010 HNS Liability Protocol').[142] It must be noted that in this case, two distinct Council decisions authorising the ratification and accession of Member States to the 2010 HNS Liability Protocol were necessary[143] in order to account for the fact that pursuant to Protocol 22 to TFEU, Denmark is exempted from the application of Title V of Part Three TFEU (Areas of Freedom Security and Justice) and thus not bound by the Brussels Regulation on judicial cooperation on civil matters; this in turn led to diverging voting procedures in the Council in relation to the respective parts of the Decision authorising the Member States to ratify on behalf of the EU the 2010 HNS Liability Protocol. Moreover, the expanding scope of EU competence to cover also the substantive matters of the 2010 HNS Liability Protocol determined the need to ground the relevant Council Decision(s) authorising Member States' ratification and/or accession on two legal bases: one related to the aspects of judicial cooperation on civil matters (i.e. Article 81 TFEU) and the other related to the substantive liability aspects of the 2010 HNS Liability Protocol.[144]

As to the relationship between the 2010 HNS Liability Protocol and the ELD, the Commission argued that the adoption of the ELD and the significant overlap between the scope of application of the ELD and the HNS liability regime, combined with the already exclusive competence of the EU over the provisions on jurisdiction and the recognition and enforcement of judicial decisions, would lead to an exclusive EU competence over the entirety of the international agreement.[145] It noted in particular that the ELD's definition of environmental damage (in combination with Article 3(1) of the Marine Framework Directive), while not identical to that of the HNS liability regime, does cover damage to marine natural resources located in the territorial sea and the EEZ of the Member States, thereby overlapping with the definition of pollution damage under the 2010 HNS Liability Convention. It also pointed to a significant 'key conflict'[146] between the ELD's provisions and the conventional framework with respect to the allocation of liability among the various actors involved. Specifically, Article 7(4) of the HNS Liability Convention, which precludes any claims for damage against the shipowner other than according to the Convention, would affect, and limit, the personal scope of the Directive since the latter cannot apply in addition to the Convention insofar as the shipowner's liability for HNS damage is concerned.[147]

In practice, the extent to which the adoption of the ELD determines an EU exclusive competence with respect to the HNS liability regime remains open to discussion, although the CJEU's case-law suggests a rather expansive approach to the application of the AETR doctrine, including cases where there is not necessarily a contradiction or a conflict between the international provisions and the relevant EU law. In any event, the argument of an EU exclusive competence over the whole

2010 HNS Liability Convention met with opposition in the Council, leading to several discussions and to an attempt of mediation by the European Parliament.[148] The final text of the Council decision, while acknowledging the partial overlap between the subject matter of the Directive and the 2010 HNS Liability Convention, affirms clearly that 'Member States retain their competence for aspects of the 2010 HNS Convention which do not affect common rules'.[149]

As it is often the case, the inter-institutional dispute between Commission and Council on the existence and scope of EU competence over the HNS 2010 Liability Convention also extended the discussion concerning the appropriate legal basis on which to ground the Council Decision aimed at authorising Member States to ratify, or accede to, on behalf of the Union, the 2010 HNS Liability Protocol *with the exception of aspects related to judicial cooperation in civil matters*. The Commission, reflecting the asserted EU exclusive competence over the HNS Convention's environmental liability provisions, proposed Article 192(1) TFEU on environment, in conjunction with Article 218 TFEU,[150] as the appropriate legal basis on which to adopt the relevant Council decision. The Council insisted instead in grounding the decision on Article 100(2), concerning EU policy in the field of transport. The Council Decision was eventually based on Article 100(2) and Article 218(6)(a)(v).[151] In principle, Article 100(2) or 192(1) appear equivalent in terms of voting and decision-making procedure and the overall inter-institutional balance. Nevertheless, the distinct positions of the Commission and the Council, respectively, on the choice of the legal basis can be explained in light of the 'internal' function of the legal basis as an indication of the extent of the EU competence in relation to the Convention. Hence, these inter-EU institutional controversies demonstrate once again how in the field of EU external relations the determination of the legal basis is not merely a procedural aspect, but it may have implications on the scope of the EU involvement in the management of the international agreement and on the division of competences between the EU and the Member States in its implementation. From the Commission's point of view, the proposal of Article 192(1) as legal basis would also have represented an official recognition of the alleged overlap of the Convention's provisions with the ELD and provided a further signal of the asserted EU exclusive powers on the substantive parts of the Convention.[152]

7.4. EU's and Member States' ratification of international liability conventions

From the point of view of the contribution of the EU to the development of international law, a further aspect to consider is whether the EU participation in international treaties has an impact on their effectiveness and implementation, and in particular, whether it may play a role in enhancing their prospects of being ratified by EU Member States. This is not a purely theoretical question. From an international law perspective, promoting the ratification by States of international liability agreements is a desirable goal as it would not only enhance the prospects of entry into force of these agreements, but would also strengthen their impact and effectiveness. Maximising the adhesion of Member States to the international conventions is also desirable from an EU perspective. In the field of environmental liability, an asymmetric participation of the Member States in the various international liability regimes or even significant time delays between each Member State's ratification of the agreement may result in different regimes applicable within the EU with consequences in terms of legal certainty and effectiveness, as well as equal access for private claimants to the available remedies.[153] Therefore, an expeditious ratification of the liability treaties would not only improve the situation of victims of environmental damage but would also avoid the risk of divergences at the level of the law applicable across the EU Member States. In that respect, a common practice is the inclusion in Council Decision authorising the ratification and/or accession of the international agreement by the Member States a provision requiring the latter to 'take the necessary steps' or to 'endeavour' to become contracting parties to the relevant convention by depositing the necessary instrument of ratification or accession 'within reasonable time' and if possible by the specific date indicated in the Decision.[154]

The question remains of the precise legal value and enforceability of such provisions, and the legal force of the duty of cooperation in this respect. It was noted that especially for those parts of the international agreements falling within the competence of the Member States, the duty of cooperation is more appropriately regarded not so much as an absolute duty, but rather as a best effort obligation to take the necessary steps to initiate the ratification process. It has nevertheless been argued that the impact of this duty would be stronger in those cases where the EU cannot directly participate in an international agreement.[155] The Court consistently stressed that cooperation between the EU institutions and the Member States is all the more necessary in those situations in which the Union cannot itself conclude the convention and must do so through the medium of the Member States. In these situations, Member States' efforts to ratify the relevant convention would not only protect the interest in the 'integrity of the legal order', but it would also enable, albeit indirectly, the participation of the EU on the international plane. On this point, Allan Rosas argues,

> a decision to authorize *all* the Member States to adhere "in the interest of the Union" creates a presumption of acceptance of the instrument as part of the Union legal order, at least with respect to those provisions of the instrument that belong to the area of the Union's exclusive competence . . . This is particularly so if, as it the case with the Council authorizations mentioned above, they are based on article 218 TFEU, which concerns the conclusion of agreements on behalf of the Union and seem to imply, for the Member States, not only an authorization but also an obligation to adhere, or at least to seek to adhere, to the respective convention.[156]

It was also suggested that 'the stronger and more specific' is the interest of the Union in the expeditious entry into force of the agreement concerned, the stronger is the obligation to ratify, which on the basis of the principle of loyalty, is imposed on the Member States.[157]

In practice, however, it is difficult to formulate a conclusive answer as to whether the EU's direct and indirect involvement in the conclusion of international environmental liability treaties has an impact on their ratification prospects. The reasons that push States to ratify or not ratify an international agreement are manifold, and an inquiry on this question should also take into account other aspects, such as treaty design or domestic institutional hurdles hampering the ratification process, that cannot be properly captured through a mere legal or doctrinal analysis.[158] Nevertheless, looking at current practice, positive examples in this sense are the Nagoya Protocol on Liability, the Bunker Oil Convention, which have been ratified by all EU Member States, and the 2003 Supplementary Fund Protocol, to which most EU Member States are contracting parties. Most recently, the 2004 Protocol to the Paris Convention on liability and compensation for nuclear damage also entered into force on 1 January 2022.[159] As the entry into force of the Protocol required the ratification by two-thirds of the contracting parties to the Paris Convention, it was estimated that ratification by EU Member States which are signatory to the 1960 Paris Convention was sufficient to bring the Protocol into force.[160]

By contrast, the ratification status of HNS Liability Convention seemed so far to proceed at a much slower rate. The Convention's entry into force had indeed been a recurrent problem, and the 2010 Liability Protocol was developed in part to respond to those issues. At present, Denmark is the only EU Member State that ratified the agreement. However, an EU Ministerial declaration presented at the High Level Ministerial maritime conference held in Opatija in 2020 highlighted once more the importance of ratification by EU Member States of a number of international maritime convention, including those on liability. Meanwhile, some EU Member States, including Belgium, Estonia, France and Germany, are reportedly making progress towards ratification of the agreement.[161]

8. Interaction and coordination between liability regimes in a multilevel context

8.1. The practice of disconnection and non-affect clauses

One of the issues arising from the expansion of EU secondary legislation on matters covered by international agreements concerns the coordination and management of potential normative conflicts between the two applicable legal regimes. While judicial interpretation can go some way in reconciling *ex post* the potential normative conflicts, there are in EU law-making practice various techniques that may allow to address *ex ante* (that is, prior to the conclusion of the relevant agreements by the Member States) potential issues of coordination between EU law and international agreements.[162] First, on a more general level, Article 351 TFEU regulates potential conflicts between pre-accession treaties of the Member States and their obligations under EU law by granting priority to agreements concluded by the Member States with one or more third countries before the entry into force of the EU treaties (in 1958) or prior to their date of accession. This provision, however, leaves unaddressed the situation of 'posterior' treaties concluded by the Member States after joining the EU. The question of a *mutatis mutandis* application of this provision in a situation where an international treaty obligation of a

Member State conflicts with a subsequently agreed measure of a secondary EU law was raised, incidentally, by Advocate General Kokott in its Opinion in the *Commune de Mesquer* case.[163] In examining the relationship between a provision of the 1969 Civil Liability Convention, to which France was a party, and Article 15 of the Waste Framework Directive, the AG considered that an interpretation of Article 351 TFEU giving priority to the international conventions could be conceivable, but found it not applicable to the case at hand.[164] In any event, Article 351 TFEU only applies to pre-existing international commitments of the Member States and therefore, even in the broader interpretation envisaged by the Advocate General, is not applicable to international conventions which Member States have not yet ratified prior to the adoption of the EU regulation.

In addition to this general treaty provision, it is not unusual that EU secondary legislation contains provisions aimed at regulating its relationship with potentially overlapping rules contained in international conventions to which Member States are contracting parties. An example is Article 71 of the Brussels I Recast Regulation (which finds correspondence also in Regulation 44/2001). This norm establishes a 'non-affect' clause whereby precedence is granted to international conventions to which Member States became parties prior to the date of entry into force of the Regulation and which, '*in relation to particular matters*, govern jurisdiction or the recognition or enforcement of judgments'. The prevalent opinion is that the expression 'particular matters' is to be interpreted as referring to conventions which lay down harmonised rules on a specific issue of international law—such as the international conventions on liability for damage caused by international transport of hazardous goods or those in the field of nuclear energy—and which also contains norms on jurisdictional competence and the recognition of judgments.[165] As for the temporal scope of application of this provision, the combined reading of Article 71 with Recital 35 of the Regulation suggests that this non-affect clause refers to conventions and international commitments assumed by the Member States prior to the date of entry into force of the 44/2001 Regulation (i.e. before 1 March 2002).[166] As such, this provision arguably cannot apply to the more recent civil liability treaties, including the Bunker Liability Convention, the 2010 HNS Convention and amendments to questions of jurisdiction and enforcement of decisions eventually introduced by the 1997 and 2004 Protocols to the Vienna and Paris Conventions in the field of nuclear liability.

In the law and practice of EU external relations, we can nevertheless discern two further mechanisms that are available to address those coordination problems *ex ante*. First, the application of the AETR principle ensures that the EU acquires exclusive competence when the provisions of an international agreement are likely to affect existing norms of EU law, thereby precluding Member States from entering into international commitments potentially conflicting with EU law. This doctrine can indeed be regarded as a sort of judicial technique for conflict prevention.[167] Second, a frequent practice in the context of EU external relations with respect to situations of potentially conflicting commitments between the provisions of an international agreement and existing EU legislation is the inclusion of the so-called disconnection clauses. These are a sort of conflict-of-law rules designed to protect the autonomy (and primacy) of the EU legal order by providing that as between EU Member States that are parties to an international agreement, the relevant provisions of EU law shall apply.[168] Accordingly, the international provisions touched by the disconnection clause will continue to apply but only limitedly to the relationship between a contracting EU Member State and the non-EU contracting parties or within the relationship between non-EU contracting parties. Disconnection clauses are different from the so-called non-affect or without prejudice clauses, in that 'they operate automatically and are peremptory'; therefore, they 'do not merely allow the Member States to apply EU law instead of the Convention's rules but require them to do so'.[169] In some mixed agreements to which the EU is a party, these clauses are agreed during the negotiation phase and included in the text itself of the international agreement. This has been the case with the Kiev Protocol on Civil Liability and Compensation for Damage caused by the Transboundary Effects of Industrial Accidents on Transboundary Waters, whose Article 20 provides specific norms on the relationship between the Protocol and the rules of EU law on jurisdiction and recognition and enforcement of judgments, providing, '[i]n their mutual relations, Parties which are members of the European Community shall apply the relevant Community rules instead of articles 15 and 18', respectively concerning the question of *lis pendens* and the mutual recognition of arbitral awards and judicial decisions. The same article also provides,

> '[t]he courts of Parties which are members of the European Community shall apply the relevant Community rules instead of article 13 [concerning the competent court], whenever the defendant is domiciled in a member State of the European Community, or the parties have attributed jurisdiction to a court of a member State of the European Community and one or more of the parties is domiciled in a member State of the European Community'.

A slightly different solution was adopted in the case of the marine pollution and nuclear liability treaties. As these treaties do not envisage EU participation, the solution consisted in requesting the Member States, when ratifying or acceding to the relevant conventions, to make a reservation, whereby they declare to give prevalence to the relevant EU rules over the relevant convention's provisions on specific subject matters falling within the exclusive competence of the EU. These declarations amount effectively to a sort of 'disconnection clause' giving primacy to the rules of the Brussels Regulation over the corresponding provisions of the convention. With respect to the international liability treaties in the field of oil pollution and nuclear damage, these reservations aim at addressing the discrepancies between the rules on the mutual recognition and enforcement of judicial decisions, thereby ensuring that judgments on matters covered by the Convention given by a court of an EU Member State shall be recognised and enforced in another EU Member State in accordance with the relevant EU rules on the subject.[170] At present, these declarations can be found annexed to the Council decisions authorising Member States to sign and ratify/accede, in the interest of the Union, the Bunker

Liability Convention, the HNS 2010 Liability Convention and the 1997 Protocol to the Vienna Convention on nuclear liability.[171]

As to the contents of this reservation, it was deemed appropriate to take a differentiated approach for the rules regulating the competent jurisdiction as compared to the rules on the recognition and enforcement of judgments.[172] It was felt in particular that the Brussels Regulation's provisions on mutual recognition and enforcement of judicial decisions should continue to apply with respect to the relationship between EU Member States (except Denmark) and also to incidents falling within the scope of the two international liability conventions, thereby superseding the norms of the international conventions. This is because these EU law provisions are considered essential to ensure the free circulation of court rulings within the EU and to preserve 'unity in the Community judicial area', 'without involving repercussions on the effective implementation of the Convention nor fundamental implications on non-EU State Parties to it'.[173] Conversely, the international conventions' rules on exclusive jurisdiction and competent court were maintained. According to the Commission, this solution would avoid forum shopping while presenting advantages in terms of the sound administration of justice since it would avoid the setting up of multiple proceedings in different courts in several jurisdictions.[174] Moreover, the principle of exclusive jurisdiction was best apt to the specific situation governed by these liability conventions insofar as it contributes to ensure a fair distribution of the compensation funds available between the victims,[175] while at the same time 'ensuring that victims of accidents can benefit from clear procedural rules'.[176]

To some extent, this differentiated solution shows the potential for integration and complementarity in the application of provisions of EU and international law. Yet, one commentator raised criticism towards the prevalence granted to the international conventions' principle of exclusive jurisdiction over the relevant provisions of the Brussels Regulation,[177] as the latter contains a more progressive approach towards the rights of victims of environmental damage, allowing them the option to sue in their home courts. According to this scholar, this option would be particularly valuable in the case of nuclear incidents, given that nuclear damage is, for its very nature, likely to have a transboundary dimension. Under the Vienna and Paris nuclear liability Conventions and amending protocols, claimants have no choice but to bring their action in the courts of the place where the incident occurred. While this approach is regarded as more advantageous from the point of view of enhancing the effectiveness of the compensation system and facilitating the pursuit of claims, it also deprives victims from the right to claim in their own courts.[178] To this must be added that under the Vienna amending protocols, the competent forum is also relevant to determine the law applicable to matters that the Convention leaves to the discretion of the national law; these include, among other things, questions concerning the admissibility of compensation for environmental impairment, which are left to be determined by the applicable domestic law.

It must finally be noted that in the EU there are five Member States that are not contracting parties to either the Paris or the Vienna Convention: Austria, Ireland, Luxembourg, Cyprus and Malta. As the jurisdictional provisions of these conventions are not as protective for the victims, these countries—which have no nuclear installations on their territory—may well refrain from joining the international legal framework and instead continue to apply the relevant rules of Brussels Regulation concerning the competent court. Issues may arise, however, in those cases concerning the enforcement of judicial decisions rendered by courts of those Member States not parties to the conventions in the territory of a contracting party.[179]

8.2. Coordinating the ELD and the liability conventions on marine pollution and nuclear damage

The question of coordination and overlap between EU law and the international legal framework was also object of discussion during the negotiations and drafting of an EU-wide environmental liability regime. When the text of the Directive was discussed, several environmental liability conventions were already in force and applicable in many of the EU Member States, to which the EU liability regime would also apply. This included in particular the IMO Civil Liability Convention on oil pollution damage, to which all EU Member States are parties; and the 1960 Paris and 1963 Vienna Conventions on nuclear liability, which were ratified by several EU Member States. Furthermore, the EU is actively promoting Member States' ratification of the 2010 HNS Liability Protocol and of the amending protocols to the Paris and Vienna nuclear liability regimes, which may in turn increase the prospects of an EU-wide membership also with respect to those international treaties.

Geographically, both the IMO and nuclear liability conventions apply to transboundary environmental damage within the territory (including territorial sea) of the contracting parties. As for marine pollution damage, the CLC and the Bunker Oil Convention applies to damage occurring to the territory of the contracting parties, including their territorial sea and their exclusive economic zone. This coincides in most part with the territorial scope of application of the Directive, which, especially since the entry into force of Offshore Safety Directive, extends beyond what was already covered under the Water Framework Directive to include also damage occurring beyond Member States' coastal waters. It has been noted for example that many EU Habitats (i.e. Natura 2000 sites) are located close to the coasts or in marine waters;[180] therefore, should a major oil spill occur and impact such a site, the incident could in principle fall under both the IMO oil pollution civil liability convention and the environmental damage definition of the ELD.[181]

The hypothesis of a concurrent application of the ELD and the oil pollution regime is particularly illustrative of the set of problems that may arise from the coexistence and overlap of two applicable liability frameworks. While both the ELD and the international liability conventions share the common aim of harmonising liability rules applicable to environmental damage, there are also important differences in their underlying rationales and objectives. Most civil liability conventions are private international law instruments, which focus primarily on transboundary or transnational type of environmental damage with the objective to facilitate procedurally and substantively the pursuit of civil liability claims and compensation recovery procedures in a cross-national context. Environmental concerns occupy a secondary role, although admittedly the compensation available under the CLC and Fund Conventions has played an important part in addressing some considerable environment-related claims.[182] The ELD is, by contrast, a primarily environmental law measure. Although it also applies to transboundary damage between two or more EU Member States, its main objective is the establishment of an EU-wide minimum common framework in the field of liability and remediation for damage to natural resources *per se* considered. Traditional forms of damage to property or persons are in fact notably excluded from its remit.

These differences in the scope and objectives underpinning the two liability regimes are mirrored in the definition of environmental damage and in the relevant standards of remediation. Under the international liability regimes, the remedies available for environmental damage are limited to the reasonable measures of restoration of the impaired natural resources.[183] Consolidated practice under the IOPC Fund is that these are measures that can be translated in economic terms. Moreover, these measures must be 'technically and objectively reasonable' and there must be proportionality between the costs incurred and the benefits deriving from the remedial measures.[184] Pure ecological damage is as a result excluded from compensation under the IMO Conventions. The Directive recognises too the notion of reasonableness. This is implicitly included in Annex II, which provides criteria that the Member States' competent authorities must take into account when determining the remedial measures and allowing the authorities to take cost consideration into account in the determination of the remedial measures.[185] However, it also provides for complementary and interim loss remediation, which is not usually covered under the IMO Conventions, although more recently the Fund may exceptionally agree to compensate complementary remediation measures where there is a clear link between the measures and the damaged components of the environment.[186] Thus, at least insofar as damage to water and to natural habitats and species is concerned, the Directive's remedial options are broader than the marine liability conventions. Differences exist also between the Directive and the nuclear liability conventions. Even though the 2004 and 1997 Protocols to the Paris and Vienna Conventions extended the scope of compensable damage to include environmental impairment and the cost of preventive measures, the extent to which environmental harm is actually included remains uncertain, particularly because the extent of compensation for those heads of damage is left to be determined by the law of the competent court.[187]

Further, and more significant, discrepancies between the ELD and the international frameworks concern the personal scope of application and the criteria for the allocation of liability. A feature of the international liability frameworks in the field of maritime transport and nuclear damage is the channelling of liability onto specific actors, these being the shipowner or the operator of the nuclear installation. This is usually complemented by specific provisions precluding liability claims against these actors other than in accordance with the relevant convention's provisions. Compensation claims against other actors are also excluded, except under specific circumstances.[188] This approach stands in contrast with the more open-ended notion of operator under the Directive. While the Directive too channels liability onto a single person, i.e. the operator, this is defined more broadly, thereby allowing liability to be potentially allocated on the party who can be regarded as the main 'responsible' for the operation of the activity.

In principle, the more open-ended notion of operator under the Directive has advantages in terms of 'fairness' in the allocation of responsibility, as in theory it impacts on the actor primarily responsible for the operation of the activity. Moreover, the almost exclusive channelling of liability onto a single subject under the nuclear and maritime liability conventions was also subject to criticism at the EU level (particularly with respect to the marine oil pollution liability regime)[189] and by scholars. It was argued, in particular, that such an approach which excludes from liability other actors, who are involved in the relevant hazardous activity and may therefore also contribute to the risk, would eventually undermine the deterrent impact of the liability regime and 'limit the incentives of others who could equally take measures to prevent' the occurrence of an accident.[190] At the same time, however, it was also noted that the ELD's definition of operator as the liable party might be problematic in some contexts since it would create uncertainties in the identification of the liable entity. This would be especially in the case of maritime transport of oil, which is a sector characterised by the involvement of various actors, who are also often 'difficult to trace in an international context'.[191] In fact, one of the justifications provided for the channelling of liability onto a very well defined subject, under the international regimes, is the need to facilitate the identification of the liable entity in order to streamline the pursuit of compensation claims by the victims of an accident.

8.3. Article 4 of the ELD

Given the differences existing between the approach and scope of application of the EU liability regime and the international conventions, the questions arising in these cases concern how to address the relationship between the two legal frameworks. The solution eventually retained consisted in the inclusion in the text of the Directive of a provision excluding the application of the Directive itself in case of environmental damage addressed by certain international conventions listed in Annex IV and V. Thus, Article 4 ELD deals with the question of the relationship with the international liability treaties in terms of 'exceptions' to the application of the Directive. Specifically, Article 4(2) excludes the application of the ELD with respect to 'environmental damage or any imminent threat of such damage arising from an incident in respect of which liability and compensation falls within the scope of' selected international civil liability conventions in the field of, that are listed in Annex IV and 'which [are] in force in the member States concerned'. Annex IV lists five conventions dealing with the transnational transport of oil and other hazardous substances. These include the 1992 Civil Liability Convention for Oil Pollution Damage and the 1992 Fund Convention, the 2001 Convention on Bunker Oil pollution damage, the 1996 HNS Liability Convention and its 2010 amending protocol, and the 1989 Convention on Civil liability for damage caused during carriage of dangerous goods by road, rail and inland navigation vessels. Moreover, paragraph 3 of the same article maintains the operators' (i.e. the owner of the ship and the salvors) right to limit their liability pursuant to the application of national law implementing the LLMC Convention and the CLNI, where these are applicable.

Article 4(4) concerns instead the relationship between the Directive and various international nuclear liability regimes listed in Annex V. These include the 1960/63 conventions establishing the Paris/Brussels and Vienna nuclear liability regime, the 1988 Joint Protocol, the 1997 Supplementary Convention, the 1971 Brussels Convention on civil liability for the maritime carriage of nuclear material as well as any amendments to the aforementioned treaties—thereby including also the 1997 and 2004 Protocols to the Paris and Vienna Conventions. Moreover, pursuant to this provision, the Directive's application is excluded in the case of

> nuclear risk or environmental damage or imminent threat of such damage as may be caused by the activities covered by the Treaty establishing the European Atomic Energy Community or caused by an incident or activity in respect of which liability or compensation falls within the scope of any of the international instruments listed in Annex V.

So, unlike Article 4(2), the exclusion of the ELD's applicability in case of overlap with the relevant nuclear liability treaties is absolute (i.e. it operates independently on whether the relevant conventions are or are not in force in the Member State concerned).

Overall, Article 4 aims at coordinating the contents of the Directive with the relevant international regimes with a view to prevent potential normative conflicts that may arise in the case of overlapping application. In this sense, this provision can be considered as part of the legal tools used by the EU for the *ex ante* prevention of normative conflicts. A similar approach can be found in Article 71(1) of the Brussels I Regulation, according to which the rules provided therein 'shall not affect any conventions to which the MS are parties and which, in relation to particular matters, govern jurisdiction or the recognition or enforcement of judgments'. Compared to Article 71(1) Brussels, however, Articles 4(2) and 4(4) ELD are framed in a slightly more peremptory language and are not limited at simply preserving the priority of the international agreement in the case of a possible conflict, but they explicitly exclude the ELD's application insofar as its scope overlaps with that of the selected international liability conventions.

The question of the relationship between the ELD and the international civil liability conventions in the field of marine pollution and nuclear damage was again touched upon in occasion of the Commission's review of the ELD in accordance with former Article 18(2).[192] The Commission eventually concluded that ELD's exemptions for both the IMO and the nuclear liability conventions should be maintained for the time being, although it acknowledged the need for further work in order to close the gaps in terms of the environmental remediation standards.[193]

One possible exception is represented by the HNS Liability Convention, for which the Commission indicated the possible lifting of the Article 4 ELD exemption in case there are not enough ratifications of this agreement by the Member States.[194]

As to the civil liability conventions in the field of nuclear damage, the decision to exempt this type of damage from the scope of application of the Directive was also linked to uncertainties regarding the existence and scope of EU competence in the field, and specifically whether the subject matter of the nuclear liability conventions fall within the remit of the Euratom treaty, which is the treaty providing legislative competences in the field of nuclear energy, and not under the TFEU.[195] The main difference between the Euratom and the TFEU is that, while the latter also include environmental protection among the EU legislative competence and objectives, the Euratom has remained anchored to the original rationale of promoting nuclear energy.[196] Thus, the concern was that insofar as nuclear liability and not environmental protection is to be regarded as the dominant objective of the international nuclear liability regime, the application of the TFEU could lead to controversial consequences in terms of legislative competences.[197]

9. Environmental policy and governance perspectives on the interaction between the ELD and international law

Besides the more 'technical' questions concerning the scope of EU external competences and the multilevel coordination between the different applicable legal frameworks, the analysis of the relationship between EU law and international law in the field of environmental liability also presents an interesting governance dimension related to the question of the most appropriate level of regulatory intervention (i.e. EU or international) in this context and on the modalities and scope of the intervention at EU level.

Considerations about the value of regulating environmental liability at the international level had implicitly played a role in the EU's decision to support Member States' ratification and accession to the international civil liability treaties for marine pollution and nuclear damage. Indeed, while the EU's involvement in these international conventions was initially prompted by its exclusive competence on the conventions' jurisdictional provisions overlapping with the regime established by the Brussels I Regulation, the interest of the EU in the ratification of these treaties is also partly related to their scope and underlying objectives. For example, the Preambles to the Council decisions authorising Member States' signature and ratification or accession to some of the civil liability agreements in the field of maritime transport of hazardous substances and nuclear energy[198] stress the importance of these international regimes, as they contribute an 'improved protection of the victims of damage' arising in connection with these hazardous activities.[199] Moreover, international regulation is regarded particularly appropriate in those areas, such as the international trade and maritime transport of oil or other industrial substances, which are characterised by the transnational nature of the actors and stakeholders involved and global scale of the activities. As stated in the Explanatory Memorandum to the Council Decision on Member States' ratification or accession, in the interest of the EU to the 2010 HNS Liability Protocol, '[u] sing an international regime rather than regional solutions for these purposes better suits the nature of shipping as a global business and the cross-boundary impact such accidents are likely to have'.[200] Interestingly, this reasoning seems to almost recall the EU law principle of subsidiarity, albeit this time applied in the multilevel relationship between EU and international law.

Arguably, recognition of the value of international regulation in certain sectors of hazardous activities, combined with concerns about not disrupting the application of international regimes to which many Member States are contracting parties,[201] also played a role in the decision to frame the international conventions in the field of oil pollution and nuclear damage as exemption from the application of the ELD.[202]

Yet, support for international regulation does not necessarily mean that parallel EU action in the field is altogether excluded. The Commission's Explanatory Memorandum to the Proposal for the Environmental Liability Directive seems, in fact, to suggest that at least with respect to the relationship between the prospective environmental liability directive and the international conventions in the fields of oil pollution and nuclear damage, action at the EU level was to be regarded as complementary and supportive of international initiatives and developments. The Commission seems to suggest that at least 'as far as these conventions display shortcomings', EU action should aim at improving 'the existing international arrangements', in accordance with the EU tasks under Article 191(1) TFEU of promoting measures at international level to deal with regional and worldwide environmental problems.[203]

This type of approach also emerges from certain EU's initiatives in the field of maritime safety and marine oil pollution prevention, which offer a very interesting case-study to discuss the regulatory implications interplay between EU and international law. At the end of the 1990s, around the same time when discussions where ongoing at the EU level on the elaboration of an EU-wide liability regime, the question of oil pollution damage was very high on the Commission's agenda, prompted especially by the environmental disasters caused by the *Erika* and the *Prestige* shipwrecks. Thus, in the immediate aftermath of the *Erika* disaster, the Commission proposed two ambitious packages of legislative measures in the field of maritime safety with specific respect to seaborne trade (also known as *Erika I*[204] and *Erika II*[205] packages). While the focus of these measures was primarily on shipping safety and oil pollution prevention, liability was since the beginning an important component of the package. According to the Commission's assessment of the international legal framework in the field of oil pollution liability at sea, the latter presented important shortcomings that needed to be addressed. These were in particular: (i) the limited amount of compensation available under the international oil pollution regime; (ii) the limited extent to which rules on the channelling of liability could effectively stimulate the oil operators' compliance with tanker safety standards;[206] and (iii) the narrow definition of pollution damage.[207]

In examining the scope and modalities of EU action to address these shortcomings, concerns at the EU level were raised about not disrupting the international liability framework on oil pollution damage (i.e. the CLC and IOPC Fund Conventions), which already provided a uniform and worldwide available regime that had proved to work in providing compensation to victims of oil spills.[208] It was therefore considered that any shortcomings of such international regime—such as the CLC provisions on the immunity from liability for certain actors other than the shipowner—were best addressed through a coordinated action at the international level, rather than by adopting EU legislation imposing individual liability on those actors, since the latter option would have created conflicts with Member States' international commitments, thereby potentially disrupting the optimal functioning of the international framework.[209]

Similar concerns related to the need to coordinate EU law developments with the liability regimes already set up at the international level seem to have influenced the decision to exclude pure environmental damage from the scope of compensation under the international marine liability conventions. This aspect was more recently reconsidered as part of an assessment of the relationship between the ELD and the international marine pollution liability conventions undertaken in occasion of the Commission's overall review of the ELD.[210] As part of an assessment on the appropriateness of maintaining the exemption in Article 4 ELD, the Commission concluded that the issue concerning the differences in the definition of environmental damage and in the remediation standards between the ELD and the international conventions could be better addressed 'by non-legislative means, in particular through working towards a common understanding closing the gaps between the Conventions and the ELD in this regard'.[211] This could be achieved, for example, by extending practices for compensation claims or through the guidelines included in the IOPC Fund Claims Manual. It was noted, in particular,

> the IOPC Funds have revised their 'Claims Manual' in 2008 to include under 'environmental damage' measures to re-establish a biological community in areas affected by an oil spill in order to enhance the natural recovery, as well as the cost of post- spill studies, and similar developments are envisaged under other conventions.

According to the Commission, 'these developments are encouraging with a view to bridging the current gap as regards the level of the remediation standards between the conventions and the ELD'.[212] Arguably, they may also be regarded as a further example of positive reciprocal interaction between EU and international law, and of how initiatives at the regional level may interact with and thus influence developments at the international law level.

By contrast with the more deferent stance towards international law with respect to the criteria of allocation of liability and the question of remediation of pure environmental damage, the EU took more decisive steps with respect to the need to raise the compensation amount for the victims of oil pollution damage. According to the Commission, this aspect represented one of the most pressing concerns.[213] Accordingly, as part of the *Erika II Package*, it proposed a Regulation establishing a European supplementary fund, the COPE Fund, for the compensation of victims of oil spill in European waters.[214] The rationale behind this was to provide appropriate compensation to victims whose claims were considered justified, but who were still unable to obtain full compensation by the international regime due to the inadequate compensation limits. Given that the EU Fund aimed at complementing the international regime, it had a similar geographical scope of application and was based on the same principles as the international fund system but provided a higher compensation threshold.[215] This EU initiative received a lot of attention at the international level and gave impetus for further discussions within the IOPC Fund on the need to improve the existing international regime. Thus, although the COPE Fund was eventually not adopted, the EU's proposal prompted further steps within the IMO, which led to the creation in 2003 of an international Supplementary Fund.[216] The new Supplementary Fund is very similar to that proposed by the EU in both the substance and the amount of compensation.[217] From the IOPC Fund perspective, taking action at the international level in order to guarantee the uniform application of the international conventions was clearly preferable to having a separate regional regime.[218] As noted by Faure, 'without the activism of the European Union, the Supplementary Fund would not have been so quickly adopted at the international level'. In this case it was the EU unilateral initiative, and the corresponding fear by the IOPC Fund of potential disruption to the international regime, that 'initiated, or at least sped up, decision-making at the international level to change the Fund convention and eventually adopt the 2003 Supplementary Fund Protocol'.[219] From the point of view of the relationship between EU and international law, this shows how, in some circumstances, impact at the international law level can be achieved not only through the EU direct participation to international negotiations and conclusion of international agreements, but also indirectly through internal policy developments.

10. Concluding remarks

This chapter started by exploring the relationship between internal dynamics and legal principles governing the relationship between the EU and its Member States in the field of external relations and the EU position towards international law. The analysis sought to show how those internal EU dynamics concerning the definition of the respective powers of the EU and its Member States 'are very relevant when defining the institutional and constitutional space for EU external action'.[220] Building upon this, the focus then moved to examine the legal issues surrounding the EU's involvement in the development and ratification of international environmental liability agreements. The findings demonstrated how in some cases the adoption of EU secondary legislation in this field did not only have relevance from the point of view of the allocation of competences, but may also impact more substantively on developments at the international level. It was discussed, for example, how the adoption of the ELD informed the position of the EU within international negotiations concerning the international liability regime for biodiversity damage caused by the transboundary movements of LMOs. It was then discussed how the indirect involvement of the EU in the civil liability treaties on oil pollution and nuclear damage, through its exclusive competence on certain aspects covered by those agreements, might have had a role in fostering the ratification of those treaties by the Member States, acting in the interest of the EU.

Having said that, a potential limitation of the present analysis is represented by its predominantly doctrinal perspective, which looked at the law and legal principles of EU external relations and examined, from that perspective, the extent to which they impact its role in international law-making. There are in fact other factors, dynamics and different forces, including at the political and institutional level, that contribute to shape the EU position in international negotiations and which may impact on the outcome of the interaction between EU and international law-making.[221] For example, it was observed that particularly in the context of international environmental negotiations, the Commission is often heavily influenced by non-official business actors or by Member States' interests, and this can in turn affect the substance of the international outcome of the negotiations and undermine the EU position as a unitary actor.[222]

Policy interests are also relevant in determining the attitude of the EU and of the Member States towards the adoption or ratification of international liability treaties. For example, the previous analysis discussed how the perceived appropriateness of pursuing action at the international level, as the most suited regulatory dimension to address damage caused by marine pollution caused by transport of oil and other hazardous substances, constituted an important rationale behind the EU's decision to authorise, and even encourage, Member States' ratification of the relevant international agreements. Whereas, in other cases (such as in the examples of the Lugano Liability Convention and the Kiev liability protocol), the interplay between EU law, through initiatives and developments related to the elaboration of an EU environmental liability regime, and international law has not succeeded in advancing the developments of international environmental liability regimes.

Notes

1 Previously, only the European Community had explicitly been granted legal personality under Article 281 EC Treaty, whereas the international legal personality of the EU remained disputed.

2 With the exception of commercial policy agreements which are negotiated and concluded according to the procedure laid down in Article 207 TFEU.

3 Article 218(8) specifies the cases where unanimity, instead of qualified majority, is required.

4 Article 218(9) TFEU.

5 Article 17(1) TEU; M. Buck, 'The EU's Representation in Multilateral Environmental Negotiations After Lisbon' in E Morgera (ed.), *The External Policy of the European Union: EU and International Law Perspectives* (CUP 2012) 81.

6 Ibid.

7 Buck (n 5); R Gosalbo Bono, ' The Organization of the External Relations of the European Union in the Treaty of Lisbon' in P Koutrakos (ed.), *The European Union's External Relations A Year After Lisbon* (2011) *CLEER Working Papers* 2011/3, 30. For examples in the field of environmental policy, see T Delreux, 'The Rotating Presidency and the EU's External Representation in Environmental Affairs: The Case of Climate Change and Biodiversity Negotiations' (2012) 8 Journal of Contemporary European Research 2, 210.

8 G De Baere, *Constitutional Principles of EU External Relations* (OUP 2008).

9 M Cremona, 'Who Can Make Treaties? The European Union' in DB Hollis (ed.), *The Oxford Guide to Treaties* (2nd ed., OUP 2020) 120.
10 M Cremona, 'External Relations of the European Union: The Constitutional Framework for International Action' in P Craig and G De Burca (eds.), *The Evolution of EU Law* (3rd ed., OUP 2021) 434.
11 Case C-22/70 *Commission v Council* (European Agreement on Road Transport, AETR/ERTA) EU:C:1971:32, [1977] ECR—263.
12 Ibid [16].
13 Ibid. [17].
14 Cremona (n 10); see in particular Opinion 1/03 EU:C:2006:8, [2006] ECR I-1145 on the existence of Community's competence to conclude the revised Lugano Convention.
15 Joined Cases 3/76, 4/76 and 6/76 *Cornelius Kramer and others* [1976] ECR 1279, ECLI:EU:C:1976:114.
16 Opinion 1/76 'Draft Agreement establishing a European laying-up fund for inland waterway vessels' EU:C:1977:63 [1977] ECR 741.
17 *Kramer* (n 15) [30].
18 Opinion 1/76 (n 16) [3]; Opinion 2/91, 'Convention No 170 of the International Labour Organization concerning safety in the use of chemicals at work' ECLI:EU:C:1993:106, [1993] ECR I-1061 [7].
19 (n 15) [115].
20 On this point concerning the distinction between the 'existence' and 'nature' of the EU external competence see C-600/14 *Federal Republic of Germany v Council of the European Union* EU:C:2017:935, [47–53].
21 Case C-600/14 (n 20). See P Van Elsuwege, 'The Duty of Sincere Cooperation and Its Implications for Autonomous Member State Action in the Field of External Relations' in M Varju (ed.), *Between Compliance and Particularism: Member State Interests and European Union law* (Springer 2019) 294.
22 Cremona 'External Relations of the European Union' (n 10) 433.
23 See especially Opinion 1/03 of 7 February 2006 on the Competence of the Community to conclude the new Lugano Convention, [2006] ECR I-1145 [114–119].
24 Opinion 2/91 of 19 March 1993 on the participation of the Community in the negotiation and conclusion of Convention No 170 of ILO [1993] ECR I-1061; Opinion 1/03 (n 23) [126]; reiterated in Opinion 1/13, 'Convention on the civil aspects of international child abduction' EU:C:2014:2303 [76].
25 Opinion 1/03 (n 23) [126].
26 Opinion 1/13 (n 24) [86].
27 Ibid [74].
28 Case C-45/07 *Commission v Greece* ECLI:EU:C:2009:81 [2009] ECR I-701.
29 Regulation 725/2004 on enhancing ship and port facility security [2004] OJ L 129/6.
30 See M Cremona, 'Extending the Reach of the AETR Principle: Comment on Commission v Greece (C-45/07)' (2009) 34 European Law Review 754, 756.
31 Ibid. 761.
32 *Commission v Greece* (n 28) [22–23].
33 N Lavranos, 'Protecting European Law from International Law' (2010) 15 European Foreign Affairs Review 265, 277.
34 M Cremona, 'Member States as Trustees of the Union Interest: Participating in International Agreements on Behalf of the European Union' in A Arnull and others (eds.), *A Constitutional Order of States: Essays in European Law in Honour of Alan Dashwood* (Hart Publishing 2011).
35 L Nengye and F Maes, 'The European Union and the International Maritime Organization: EU's External Influence on the Prevention of Vessel-Source Pollution' (2010) 41 Journal of Maritime Law and Commerce 581.
36 Opinion 2/00 on the Conclusion of the Cartagena Protocol ECLI:EU:C:2001:664, [2000] ECR 1–9713 [43–44].

37 For a possible reading of EU external environmental competence in this sense, see Buck (n 5) 87.
38 Opinion 2/00 (n 36) [43–44]; G De Baere, '"O, Where Is Faith? O, Where Is Loyalty" Some Thoughts on the Duty of Loyal Co-operation and the Union's External Environmental Competences in the light of the PFOS Case' (2011) 36 European Law Review 405, 412.
39 P Craig and G De Burca, *EU Law: Text, Cases and Materials* (7th ed., OUP 2020) 112–113.
40 Article 3(2) TFEU.
41 Craig and De Burca, *EU law* (n 39) 378; see also Case C-600/14 *Germany v Council* EU:C:2017:935 [46–51].
42 F Erlbacher, 'Recent Case Law on External Competences of the European Union: How Member States Can Embrace Their Own Treaty' (2017) CLEER Papers 2017/2, 11.
43 Opinion 2/00 (n 36) [5]; Case C-370/07 *Commission v Council* ('*CITES*') [2009] ECR I-8917, EU:C:2009:590 [47–49].
44 Cremona, 'Who Can Make Treaties?' (n 9) 125
45 Ibid. 126.
46 Case C-94/03 *Commission v Council* [2006] ECR I-001, ECLI:EU:C:2006:2 [55]; M Cremona, 'External Relations of the EU and the Member States: Competence, Mixed Agreements, International Responsibility and Effects of International Law', *EUI Working Paper LAW* No. 2006/22, 10.
47 CITES case (n 43) [44].
48 Opinion 2/00 (n 36) [22–23].
49 Ibid.
50 Case C-94/03 (n 46) on the annulment of Council Decision 2003/106/EC concerning the approval of the Rotterdam Convention [34–35].
51 Joined Cases C-164/97 and 165/97 *Parliament v Council*, ECLI:EU:C:1999:99 [14].
52 P Koutrakos, 'Legal Basis and Delimitation of Competence in EU External Relations' in M. Cremona and B. De Witte (eds.), *EU Foreign Relations Law: Constitutional Fundamentals* (Bloomsbury Publishing PLC 2008) 173.
53 A Rosas, 'EU External Relations: Exclusive Competence Revisited' (2015) 38 Fordham International Law Journal 1073, 1075.
54 On mixed agreements see further in section 3.1, text at nn 61–64.
55 Opinion 2/00 (n 36) and Case C-94/03 (n 46).
56 Opinion 2/00 (n 36) [41], referring in particular to the difficulties arising in the implementation of mixed agreements.
57 Ibid.
58 Opinion 2/15 of the Court on the Free Trade Agreement between the EU and the Republic of Singapore, 16 May 2017, ECLI:EU: C:2016:880.
59 Cremona 'Who Can Make Treaties?' (n 9) 125, also questioning on the appropriateness of the Court's strong bias towards a single legal basis.
60 See further in section 6.4 of this chapter, text at nn 151–153.
61 R Leal Arcas, 'The European Community and Mixed Agreements' (2001) 6 *European Foreign Affairs Review* 483.
62 P Eeckhout, *EU External Relations Law* (2nd ed., OUP 2011) 213–214.
63 Erlbacher (n 42) 17; Eeckhout (n 62) 214, who defines this type of shared competences as a 'potential' or 'virtual' external exclusive competences. In reality, the extent to which the EU alone can conclude agreements in areas of shared competence is often contested. Thus, in its Opinion 2/00 on the ratification of the Cartagena Protocol, the Court appeared to link the possibility of the EU concluding alone the treaty in an area of shared competence to the extent of harmonization achieved internally. It noted that since 'the harmonization achieved at Community level in the Protocol's field of application covers in any event only a very small part of such a field', the Community and its Member States share competence to conclude the Protocol, Opinion 2/00 (n 36) [46–47].

64 Court opinion 1/17 and 2/15; see also D Kleiman and G Kubek, 'The Signing, Provisional Application, and Conclusion of Trade and Investment Agreements in the EU—The Case of CETA and Opinion 2/15' *EUI Working Paper* RSCAS 2016/58.
65 Cremona, 'Member States as Trustees' (n 34).
66 A Rosas, 'The Status in EU law of International Agreements Concluded by EU Member States' (2011) 34 Fordham International Law Journal 1304.
67 Ibid. 1310.
68 Cremona, 'Member States as Trustees' (n 34).
69 Council Decision (EC) 2002/762 of 19 September 2002 authorising the Member States in the interest of the Community, to sign, ratify or accede to the International Convention on Civil Liability for Bunker Oil Pollution Damage, 2001 (the Bunkers Convention) OJ 2002 L 256/7.
70 Council Decision (EC) 2004/246 of 2 March 2004 authorising the Member States to sign, ratify or accede to, in the interest of the European Community, the Protocol of 2003 to the International Convention on the Convention on the Establishment of an International Fund for Compensation for Oil Pollution Damage, 1992, and authorising Austria and Luxemburg, in the interest of the European Community, to accede to the underlying instruments OJ 2004 L 78/22.
71 Case C-26/62, Van Gend & Loos [1963] ECR 1 [12]; Opinion 1/09 [2011] ECR I-1137 [65]; Opinion 2/13, EU:C:2014:2454 [157].
72 B de Witte, 'The Emergence of a European System of Public International Law: The EU and Its Member States as Strange Subjects' in J Wouters, A Nollkaemper and E de Wet (eds.), *The Europeanisation of International Law* (T.M.C. Asser Press 2008).
73 See Rosas 'Exclusive Competence Revisited' (n 53).
74 M Cremona, 'Defending the Community Interest: The Duties of Cooperation and Compliance' in M Cremona and B De Witte (eds.), *EU Foreign Relations Law: Constitutional Fundamentals* (Hart Publishing 2008).
75 On the link between the AERT exclusivity doctrine and the loyalty principle, see Eeckhout (n 62) 74 ff.
76 A Thies, 'The Search for Effectiveness and the Need for Loyalty in EU External Action' in M Cremona (ed.), *Structural Principles in EU External Relations Law* (Hart Publishing 2018).
77 There is an extensive literature on the implications of the duty of cooperation in the context of mixed agreements. See, among others, Cremona 'Defending the Community Interest' (n 74); J Heliskoski, *Mixed Agreements as a Technique for Organizing the International Relations of the Community and Its Member States* (Kluwer Law International 2001); M Klamert, *The Principle of Loyalty in EU Law* (OUP 2014) 183–206.
78 See, Opinion 1/94 WTO [1994] ECR-I-5267 [108].
79 In Opinion 2/91 (ILO) (n 24) [36–37] the CJEU held that 'cooperation between the Community and the Member States is all the more necessary in view of the fact that the former cannot, as international law stands at present, itself conclude an ILO Convention and must do so through the Member States'. Previously, in *Kramer and others* [42–45] (n 15) the CJEU emphasized the duty of Member States to proceed by common action and 'to use all the political and legal means . . . in order to ensure the participation of the Community in the convention and in other similar agreements'.
80 See *Commission v Greece* (n 28) [25]; Cremona 'Defending the Community Interest' (n 74), 157; F Casolari, 'The Principle of Loyal Co-operation: A 'Master Key' for EU External Representation?' in S. Blockmans and R. A. Wessel (eds.), *Principles and Practices of EU External Representation* (CLEER Working Papers 2012/5).
81 Case C-266/03 *Commission v Luxembourg (Inland Waterway)* [2005] ECR I-4805 [58] and Case C-433/03 *Commission v Germany (Inland Waterway)* [2005] ECR I-6985 [64].
82 Case C-246/07 *Commission v Sweden* (PFOS) ECLI:EU:C:2010:203 [2010] ECR I-3317.
83 Ibid. [39].
84 Ibid. [46].

85 *Commission v Greece* (n 28).
86 *Commission v Sweden* (n 82) [72].
87 See on this case Geert De Baere, 'O, Where Is Faith?' (n 38).
88 *Commission v Sweden* (PFOS) [102]. See on this Opinion of AG Maduro, C-246/07, Commission v Sweden, para 30, also discussed in G de Baere (n 38) 412–413.
89 For an excellent analysis and critique of this case-law, see R Pavoni, 'Controversial Aspects of the Interaction Between International and EU Law in Environmental Matters: Direct Effect and Member States' Unilateral Measures' in E Morgera (ed.), *The External Environmental Policy of the European Union* (CUP 2012), 369 ff.
90 Case C-459/03 *Commission v Ireland* [2006] ECR I-4635.
91 In this sense also Pavoni (n 89).
92 See as an example the reading of the Aarhus Convention in combination with the EU law principle of effective judicial protection, in the case C-240/09 *Lesoochranárske zoskupenie VLK v Ministerstvo životného prostredia Slovenskej republiky* (*Brown Bear* case). For more details, see discussion in Chapter 7, section 4, text at nn 58 ff.
93 M Mendez, 'The Enforcement of EU Agreements: Bolstering the Effectiveness of Treaty Law?' (2010) 47 Common Market Law Review 1719.
94 Case C-104/81 *Hauptzollamt Mainz v C A Kupferberg* [1982] ECR 3641 [11–13].
95 Ibid [2].
96 Klamert (n 77) 205–206. See Cases C-13/00 *Commission v Ireland* ECLI: EU:C:2002:184, [2002] ECR I-2943; and C-239/03 *Commission v France* ECLI:EU.C.2004:598, [2004] ECR I—9325.
97 Klamert (n 77) 202. G Van Der Loo and RA Wessel, 'The Non-Ratification of Mixed Agreements: Legal Consequences and Solutions' (2017) 3 *Common Market Law Review* 735.
98 Cremona 'Who Can Make Treaties?' (n 9) 128.
99 Klamert (n 77) 202.
100 Van Der Loo and Wessel (n 97) 745.
101 Cremona, 'Member States as Trustees' (n 34).
102 Opinion 2/91 (ILO) (n 24) [37–38].
103 See further in section 6.5, text at nn 154–155, with examples in the field of environmental liability.
104 Cremona, 'Member States as Trustees' (n 34) 6.
105 G De Baere, 'Mercury Rising; the European Union and the International Negotiations for a Globally Binding Instrument on Mercury' (2012) 37 European Law Review 5.
106 M Faure and K Kindji, 'Cross-Border Nuclear Safety, Liability and Cooperation in the European Union', Study for European Parliament, PETI Committee (February 2019); J Handrlica, 'Euratom Powers in the Field of Nuclear Liability Revisited' (2010) 3 International Journal of Nuclear Law 1.
107 Council Decision 2013/86/EU of 12 February 2013 on the conclusion on behalf of the European Union of the Nagoya-Kuala Lumpur Supplementary Protocol on Liability and Redress to the Cartagena Protocol on Biosafety, OJ L46/2, 19.2.2013. Recital 9 in Preamble to this Decision also explicitly refers to the fact that the 'Supplementary Protocol contributes to the achievement of the objective of the environmental policy of the Union'.
108 Ibid.
109 Ibid.
110 A Delgado Casteleiro, 'EU Declarations of Competence to Multilateral Agreements: A Useful Reference Base?' (2012) 17 European Foreign Affairs Review 491.
111 M Hedemann Robinson, 'EU Enforcement of International Environmental Agreements: The Role of the European Commission' (2012) European Energy and Environmental Law Review 2, 15. See also text at nn 92–98.
112 At the time of writing, 23 EU Member States are also Parties to the Nagoya-Kuala Lumpur Supplementary Protocol.

113 R Lefeber and J Nieto Carrasco, 'Negotiating the Supplementary Protocol: The Co-Chairs' Perspective' in A Shibata (ed.), *International Liability Regime for Biodiversity Damage: the Nagoya-Kuala Lumpur Supplementary Protocol* (Routledge 2014).
114 S Juncurt and N Schabus, 'Liability and Redress in the Context of the Cartagena Protocol on Biosafety' (2010) 19 Reciel 197.
115 Juncurt and Schabus (n 114) 201; G Singh Nijar, 'The Nagoya-Kuala Lumpur Supplementary Protocol on Liability and Redress to the Cartagena Protocol on Biosafety: An Analysis and Implementation Challenges' (2013) 13 International Environmental Agreements 271, 282.
116 Juncurt and Schabus (n 114).
117 European Commission, Proposal for a Council Decision on signing the Nagoya-Kuala Lumpur Supplementary Protocol on Liability and Redress to the Cartagena Protocol on Biosafety, COM (2011) 130 final.
118 A Lago Candeira, 'Administrative Approach to Liability: Its Origin, Negotiation and Outcome' in *International Liability Regime for Biodiversity Damage* (n 113).
119 Ibid.
120 AM Farmer (ed.), *Manual of European Environmental Policy—Institute of European Environmental Policy* (Routledge 2012).
121 See on this in particular, J Lefevere, 'Interactions of the EU Environmental Liability Regime' (FiELD 2003).
122 Expression borrowed from Lefevere (n 121).
123 Signed on 21 May 2003, text available at https://treaties.un.org/Pages/ViewDetails.aspx?src=IND&mtdsg_no=XXVII-16&chapter=27&clang=_en> accessed 21 January 2022.
124 COM (2003) 263 final.
125 Ibid.
126 See Article 7 of the Conventions on the Protection and Use of Transboundary Watercourses and International Lakes, according to which 'the Parties shall support appropriate international efforts to elaborate rules, criteria and procedures in the field of responsibility and liability'.
127 P Dascalopoulou-Livada and A Kolliopoulos, 'The Kiev Civil Liability Protocol and the Interaction between Civil and Administrative Liability Regimes' (2017) 19 International Community Review 518, 549.
128 European Commission, Staff Working Document—REFIT Evaluation of the Environmental Liability Directive, SWD (2016) 121 final, 59 [emphasis added].
129 For a comparison of the ELD and the Kiev Protocol see Dascalopoulou-Livada and Kolliopoulos (n 127). For a comparative analysis of the scope of application of the two instruments, see in particular M Pallemaerts, 'Study on National Legislation Needed to Implement the Protocol on Civil Liability and Compensation for Damage Caused by the Transboundary Effects of Industrial Accidents on Transboundary Waters', ECE/CP.TEIA/2012/7, 28 August 2012.
130 Pallemaerts (n 129) highlighted the complementarity between the ELD and the Protocol and the fact that the ELD only establishes minimum rules, which therefore do not prevent Member States from adopting or maintaining more stringent provisions, including where those provisions would result from the ratification and implementation of the Liability Protocol. On this basis, he argued that Member States' ratification of the Protocol would not be inconsistent with EU law. Yet, this point needs now to be read also in the light of more recent CJEU case-law, bearing in mind in particular the approach taken in the PFOS case.
131 In this sense, Pallemaerts (n 129) and Dascalopoulou-Livada and Kolliopoulos (n 127).
132 Pallemaerts (n 129).
133 Dascalopoulou-Livada and Kolliopoulos (n 127) arguing that, compared to the ELD, the Protocol 'is a more vigorous instrument which can constitute a satisfactory option for those States which are prepared to go further on a matter which is a very real concern'.

134 EU institutions nonetheless cooperate with IAEA in the framework of partnership agreements for specific projects or activities (see www.iaea.org/about/partnerships/european-union); moreover, the Supplementary Protocol No. 1 to the OECD Convention allows EU's representation and participation in the work of the organisations, although it does not envisage a fully-fledged membership.
135 H Ringbom, 'EU Regulation 44/2001 and Its Implications for the International Maritime Liability Conventions' (2004) 35 Journal of Maritime Law & Commerce 1.
136 Article 10(2) Bunker Liability Convention and Article 40(2) of the HNS Liability Convention.
137 International Convention on Civil Liability for Bunker Oil Pollution Damage (2001) ILM 1493, 40.
138 See the Explanatory Memorandum to the Proposal for a Council Decision authorising the Member States to sign and ratify in the interest of the European Community the International Convention on Civil Liability for Bunker Oil Pollution Damage, COM (2001) 675 final, OJ 051 E, 26.02.2002, 371. Importantly, these decisions concerning the accession by Member States to the Bunker and HNS Conventions in the interest of the Union with respect to the provisions governing jurisdiction and the recognition and enforcement of judgements are not applicable to Denmark, which opted out from Title V of Part Three TFEU; therefore, Denmark is exempted from the application of the EU Brussels Regulation regime.
139 Ringbom (n 135).
140 Cremona, 'Member States as Trustees' (n 34).
141 L Nengye and F Maes, 'Legal Constraints to the European Union's Accession to the International Maritime Organization' (2012) 43 Journal of Maritime Law and Commerce 2, 279.
142 Member States were already authorized to proceed with ratification of the 1996 HNS Convention by means of Council Decision 2002/971/EC. However, as the 2010 HNS Protocol led to the constitution of a new international agreement, a new Council Decision authorising Member States to its ratification was necessary.
143 Council Decision (EU) 2017/770 of 25 April 2017 on the ratification and access by Member States in the interest of the EU to the 2010 Protocol with regard to the aspects related to judicial cooperation in civil matters OJ L 115/18; and Council Decision (EU) 2017/769 of 25 April 2017 on the ratification and access by Member States in the interest of the EU to the 2010 Protocol with the exception of the aspects related to judicial cooperation in civil matters OJ L 115/15.
144 European Commission, 'Explanatory Memorandum to the Proposal for a Council Decision on the ratification and accession by Member States on behalf of the Union to the Protocol of 2010 to the International Convention on Liability and Compensation for Damage in connection with the Carriage of Hazardous and Noxious Substances by Sea with the exception of aspects related to judicial cooperation in civil matters', COM (2015) 304 final, 8.
145 Ibid.
146 Ibid. 6.
147 Ibid.
148 European Parliament, Committee on Legal Affairs, Interim Report on the draft Council Decision on the ratification and accession by Member States in the interest of the EU to the HNS 2010 Protocol with the exception of the aspects related to judicial cooperation in civil matters, 30.5.2016, A8–0191/2016.
149 Council Decision 2017/769 (n 143).
150 In this sense, recital 6 of the Preamble to the Commission's Proposal for a Council Decision on ratification and accession by Member States of the 2010 HNS Protocol, COM (2015) 304 final.
151 Council Decision on Member States ratification and accession to the 2010 HNS Protocol with the exception of the aspects related to judicial cooperation in civil matters (n 143).

152 It is worth mentioning that an interim report and a subsequent Recommendation by the European Parliament's legal committee emphasised the importance of safeguarding the integrity and effectiveness of EU legislation by ensuring that this is not undermined by discrepancies and normative conflicts between the two liability regimes. As to the legal basis, the Parliament, with an attempt at mediating between the two divergent positions of the Commission and the Council, proposed a triple legal basis for the Council Decision related to the ratification of the Convention with the exception of the judicial and civil cooperation aspects, which would include, besides Article 218 (6) TFEU, both Article 100(2) and 192(1) TFEU. See European Parliament, Interim Report, A8–0190/2016; and Recommendation, A8–0076/2017 of 27.3.2017.
153 A common practice in relation to mixed agreements is that the Council waits until all Member States have ratified the agreement before formally concluding the agreement on the part of the EU. In some cases, the Council may authorize the provisional application of the agreement, for the parts covered by EU competence, pending its ratification by all the Member States; Cremona, 'Who Can Make Treaties?' (n 9) 128.
154 For the Bunker Liability Convention, the date was 30 June 2006, whereas for the 2010 Protocol to the HNS liability convention was 6 May 2021.
155 Cremona, 'Member States as Trustees' (n 34) 7.
156 Rosas, 'The Status in EU Law of International Agreements' (n 66) 1334.
157 Klamert (n 77) 198; Van Der Loo and Wessel (n 97).
158 See, for example, G Spilker and V Koubi, 'The Effects of Treaty Legality and Domestic Institutional Hurdles on Environmental Treaty Ratification' (2016) International Environmental Agreements: Politics, Law and Economics 223.
159 Protocol of 12 February 2004 to amend the Paris Convention and Protocol of 12 February 2004 to amend the Brussels Supplementary Convention.
160 See, however, RJ Heffron, SF Ashley and WJ Nuttall, 'The Global Nuclear Liability Regime Post-Fukushima Daiichi' (2016) Progress in Nuclear Energy 90, 4, who argue that the requirement, pursuant to Council decision 2004/294/EC of 8 March 2004, of simultaneous ratification of the Protocol by the EU Member States had also impacted on and slowed down the pace of the ratification process.
161 HNS Convention, 'Positive progress reported during discussion on HNS matters at IOPC Funds' meetings', <www.hnsconvention.org/activity/france-prepares-for-ratification-of-hns-protocol/> accessed 1 March 2022.
162 J Klabbers, *Treaty Conflict and the European Union* (CUP 2008).
163 Case C-188/07 *Commune de Mesquer v Total France SA and Total International Ltd* [2008] ECR I-4501, Opinion of Advocate General Kokott, para 95.
164 Ibid.
165 CE Tuo and L Carpaneto, 'Connections and Disconnections between Brussels I Regulation and International Conventions on Transport Matters' (2016) Zbornik PFZ 66, 141.
166 Ibid. 146.
167 Eeckhout (n 62) 76.
168 Cremona, 'External Relations of the EU' (n 46) 4.
169 M Cremona, 'Disconnection Clauses in EU law and Practice' in C. Hillion and P. Koutrakos (eds.), *Mixed Agreements Revisited: the EU and its Member States in the World* (Hart 2010) 161, 168.
170 These decisions concerning the accession by Member States to the Bunker and HNS Conventions in the interest of the Union with respect to the provisions governing jurisdiction and the recognition and enforcement of judgements are not applicable to Denmark, on the basis of its opt-out from Title V of Part Three TFEU, which means Denmark is exempted from the application of the EU Brussels Regulation regime.
171 No such declaration/reservation is instead included in the Council decision concerning Member States' ratification, in the interest of the Union, of the 2004 Protocol to the Paris Convention on nuclear liability. See on this, European Commission, Explanatory Memorandum to the Council decision Proposal COM (2003) 409 final.

172 European Commission, Explanatory Memorandum to the Proposal for a Council Decision authorising the Member States to sign and ratify in the interest of the European Community the International Convention on Civil Liability for Bunker Oil Pollution Damage, COM (2001) 0675 final.
173 Ibid.
174 Ibid.
175 See the Explanatory Memorandum to the Proposal for a Council Decision authorising the Member States which are contracting parties to the 1960 Paris Convention to sign and ratify in the interest of the European Community the Protocol amending that Convention, COM (2003) 409 final, 5.
176 See European Parliament resolution of 8 June 2016 on the draft Council decision on the ratification and accession by the Member States, in the interest of the EU, to the Protocol of 2010 to the International HNS Convention, with regards to the aspects related to judicial cooperation in civil matters, OJ C 86/168 of 6.3.2018.
177 J. Handrlica, 'The Brussels I Regulation and Liability for Nuclear Damage' (2010) 2 Nuclear Law Bulletin 29, 33.
178 Ibid.
179 See further the discussion in Handrlica (n 177).
180 BIO Intelligence Service (2014), 'ELD Effectiveness: Scope and Exceptions' Final Report prepared for European Commission—DG Environment, 190.
181 Ibid.
182 On the compensation under the CLC and Fund Conventions and their relationship with the ELD, see W Oosterveen, 'Some Recent Developments Regarding Liability for Damage Resulting from Oil Pollution—from the Perspective of an EU Member State' (2004) 6 Environmental Law Review 223.
183 See more in detail in the discussion in Chapter 3.
184 BIO Intelligence Report (2014) (n 180) 184.
185 Annex II ELD (1.3.3).
186 BIO Intelligence Report (2014) (n 180) 183.
187 Article 2(1)(k) of the Vienna Convention as amended by the 1997 Protocol. BIO Intelligence Report (n 180) 231.
188 See Article 3(4) of the 1992 Civil Liability Convention which excludes compensation claims against the servants or agents of the owner, members of the crew, pilots, charterers and persons performing salvage operations, unless the damage resulted from their personal act or omission, committed with the intent to cause such damage, or recklessly and with knowledge that such damage would probably result.
189 European Commission, Communication from the Commission to the European Parliament and the Council on a Second Set of Community Measures on Maritime Safety Following the Sinking of the Oil Tanker Erika ('*Erika II Package*'), Brussels 6.12.2000, COM (2000) 802 final, 56.
190 J Liu and M Faure, 'Compensation for Nuclear Damage: A Comparison among the International Regime, Japan and China' (2016) 16 International Environmental Agreements 165, 184.
191 BIO Intelligence Report (n 180)179.
192 European Commission, REFIT Evaluation on the ELD (n 128).
193 Ibid. 56
194 Ibid.
195 European Commission REFIT Evaluation on the ELD (n 128) 55.
196 On the relationship between the TFEU and Euratom and the implications on the regulation of nuclear liability, Faure and Kindji, 'Cross-Border Nuclear Safety' (n 106) 76–77.
197 Commission REFIT Evaluation (n 128) 55.
198 See Council Decision (EU) 2017/769 on Member States ratification and accession to the 2010 HNS liability convention with the exception of aspects related to judicial

cooperation in civil matters, Recital 7 of the Preamble; Council Decision 2013/434/EU authorising certain Member States to ratify or accede to the Protocol amending the Vienna Convention; and Council Decision 2004/294/EC on authorising Member States which are contracting parties to the 1960 Paris Convention to ratify, in the interest of the European Community, the Protocol amending that Convention, Recital 5 of the Preamble.

199 Council Decision 2017/769 (n 198), Recital 10 of the Preamble. Also the Explanatory Memorandum to the Proposal for a Council Decision authorising the Member States to sign, ratify or accede, in the interest of the European Community, to the Protocol to the Paris Convention of 29 July 1960 on Third Party Liability in the Field of Nuclear Energy, COM (2003) 409 final, 6: 'The new Protocol . . . by improving protection for victims in the event of nuclear accidents, is particularly important for the European Community and its Member States'.

200 COM (2015) 304 final, 10.

201 European Commission *Erika II Package* (n 189) 59; BIO Intelligence Report (n 181) 190–91.

202 European Commission, Explanatory Memorandum to the ELD proposal, COM (2002) 17 final.

203 Ibid.

204 European Commission, 'Communication from the Commission to the European Parliament and the Council on the Safety of the Seaborne Oil Trade', Brussels 21.3.2000, COM (2000) 142 final ('*Erika I Package*').

205 European Commission, *Erika II Package* (n 189).

206 *Erika I Package* (n 204) 35.

207 *Erika II Package* (n 189) 50 ff.

208 *Erika I Package*, 34. *Erika II Package*, 59: 'The Commission recognises that an international liability and compensation regime provides important benefits in terms of uniformity and straightforwardness and in terms of sharing the cost for oil spills . . . among oil receivers world-wide'.

209 Yet, thus far, after two decades since these discussions took place, there has not been a formal revision of the CLC regime in the sense sought by the Commission.

210 Commission REFIT Evaluation of the ELD (n 128); BIO Intelligence Report (n 181) 265 ff.

211 REFIT Evaluation of the ELD (n 128) 54–55.

212 Ibid.

213 *Erika II Package*, 59

214 Proposal for a Regulation of the European Parliament and of the Council on the establishment of a fund for the compensation of oil pollution damage in European waters and related measures, COM (2000) 802 final—2000/0326 (COD), submitted by the Commission on 8 December 2000.

215 On the proposed COPE Fund, see G Gonsaeles, 'The Impact of EC Decision-Making on the International Regime for Oil Pollution Damage: The Supplementary Fund Example' in F Maes (ed.), *Marine Resource Damage Assessment, Liability and Compensation for Environmental Damage* (Springer 2005), 100–101. More generally, for an extensive analysis of developments at the EU level and their influence within IMO see S Poli, *La Responsabilità per Danni da Inquinamento Transfrontaliero nel Diritto Comunitario e Internazionale* (Giuffré 2006).

216 See also relevant discussion in Chapter 3.

217 See Explanatory Memorandum to the Commission Proposal for a Council Decision authorising the Member States to sign, ratify or accede to, in the interest of the Community, the Protocol of 2003 to the International Convention on the Establishment of an international Fund for Compensation for Oil Pollution Damage, COM (2003) 534 final, 4.

218 M Faure and H Wang, 'Smart Mixes of Civil Liability Regimes for Marine Oil Pollution' in J van Erp, M Faure, A Noellkamper and N Philipsen (eds.), *Smart Mixes for Transboundary Environmental Harm* (CUP 2019), 299.
219 Ibid. 299.
220 Thies (n 76) 265–66.
221 T Delreux, *The EU as an International Environmental Negotiator* (Routledge 2011).
222 S Cassotta, *Environmental Damage and Liability Problems in a Multilevel Context: The Case of the Environmental Liability Directive* (Kluwer Law International 2012) 119–120.

7 Substantive aspects of the interplay between EU law and international environmental agreements

1. Introduction

Environmental law in the European Union is increasingly characterised by the multilevel interaction of EU Member States' domestic law, EU regional law and international law. This chapter examines the interplay between different legal regimes in the context of the legal responses to environmental harm, by focusing on how international law provisions penetrate in the EU legal order and interact with EU law and domestic law. It seeks to ascertain whether and to what extent the coexistence and interplay of different legal frameworks in a multilevel context may strengthen opportunities to obtain redress for environmental damage and to achieve, more generally, effective responses to environmental harm. To this end, this chapter begins with an analysis of the legal principles and relevant CJEU case-law concerning the legal status and effects of international agreements in the EU legal order. It then applies those findings to the analysis of the interaction between EU law and international law in the field of liability and remedies for environmental damage, focusing in particular on the relationship between the ELD and relevant international law agreements. The analysis in this chapter will ultimately seek to understand whether the interplay between EU law and international law may be framed in a way to reinforce the effectiveness of the responses to environmental harm and ultimately facilitate the achievement of common environmental objectives.

2. The legal status and impact of international treaties to which the EU is a party in the EU legal order

International law is generally thought to be neutral regarding its legal effects in the national legal order, leaving those questions to be determined by national law. Within the EU legal order these questions are therefore a matter to be determined in accordance with EU law. Both the TEU and TFEU contain only general indications on the role of international law within the EU legal order. The most relevant provisions are Article 3(5) TEU, which sets out an open attitude of the EU legal order towards international law,[1] and Article 216 TFEU, which defines the impact in the EU legal order of the EU's participation in international

DOI: 10.4324/9781315676708-11

treaties. In addition, Article 351 TFEU deals with the impact of EU membership for those agreements to which Member States became party before the establishment of the EU or before their accession thereto. None of these treaty provisions, however, articulates in detail the legal implications arising from the relationship between international law and EU law or the place of international rules in the hierarchy of sources in the EU legal order. Consequently, most of the principles currently applicable to determine the role of international law within the EU legal order and its interaction with EU secondary legislation have been elaborated by the CJEU. It is therefore to the CJEU's jurisprudence that the analysis shall now turn.

2.1. The binding character of EU international agreements and the CJEU's jurisdiction over them

In examining the role and legal effects of international treaty provisions in the EU legal order, it is appropriate to recall the distinction—already outlined in the previous chapter—between treaties to which the EU is a party and those agreements that are instead concluded by the Member States in the interest of the EU. With respect to the former, Article 216(2) TFEU establishes that agreements concluded by the EU are binding upon EU institutions and its Member States. From this wording the CJEU, with an approach described by some as embodying a monist attitude to international law,[2] concluded that since their coming into force international agreements to which the EU is a party form an integral part of the EU legal order.[3] The provisions of these international treaties are therefore automatically incorporated and become directly applicable in the EU legal system.[4] A corollary of this assumption is the extension to these international provisions of the interpretative and adjudicative jurisdiction of the CJEU. Thus, through their incorporation in the EU legal order, the provisions of EU-concluded international agreements acquires the same (EU) legal status and displays the same effects across the EU Member States, while their uniform application is ensured by the exclusive interpretive jurisdiction of the CJEU. As the CJEU explained in *Kupferberg*, the rationale behind this approach is the need to ensure compliance by Member States and EU institutions with the relevant international commitments arising from the agreement for the due performance of which the EU had assumed responsibility.[5] Non-compliance with the agreements would in fact potentially give rise to the international responsibility of the EU vis-à-vis third contracting parties.[6]

Although Article 216(3) TFEU only refers to international treaties concluded by the EU, the CJEU has extended its relevance also to mixed agreements, equating their status to pure EU agreements for those parts falling within the scope of EU competence.[7] Moreover, the CJEU took an expansive approach to the question of EU competence over mixed agreements, and it was prepared to assert its exclusive jurisdiction for the interpretation of the mixed agreement where this relates to an area that is largely covered by EU law,[8] even if the specific issues at hand were not yet regulated by internal European legislation.[9] Thus, in a decision concerning

Article 9 of the Aarhus Convention—a mixed agreement to which the EU is a contracting party—it held,

> where a provision can apply both to situations falling within the scope of national law and to situations falling within the scope of EU law, it is clearly in the interest of the latter that, in order to forestall future differences of interpretation, that provision should be interpreted uniformly, whatever the circumstances in which it is to apply.[10]

Therefore, although the EU had not yet adopted relevant legislation to translate and implement the Aarhus Convention's access to justice requirements within the EU legal order, this aspect did not preclude the international provisions to display its impact in the EU legal order.

This conclusion is consistent with previous decisions on the EU's participation in mixed agreements, in which the Court clarified that whether a provision of a mixed agreement falls within EU's competence is a question 'which relates to the attribution and, thus, the very existence of that competence, and not to its exclusive or shared nature' (i.e. whether the EU has adopted secondary rules which are likely to be affected within the meaning of AETR).[11] Thus, in the *MOX Plant* case, the CJEU concluded that the existence of the EU's external competence in regard to the protection of the marine environment and thus its capacity to enter into relevant international agreements is not, in principle, contingent on the adoption of secondary legislation covering the area in question and potentially subject to the AETR effect.[12] Then, in assessing whether the MOX Plant dispute falls within its exclusive jurisdiction, the CJEU took into account whether the EU exercised that competence (namely, through the adoption of Community rules, which are then reflected in the Declaration of EU competences annexed to the decision to conclude the UNCLOS), considering to that effect that for a transfer to the EU of areas of shared competence to take place, it is not necessary that those Community rules be affected.[13]

2.2. Primacy of EU international agreements

The automatic incorporation in the EU legal order of international agreements concluded by the EU and their binding effects under Article 216(2) bear important implications for both the EU institutions and the Member States, which must properly implement and give effect to the agreement. From the point of view of the EU institutions, the adoption of secondary EU legislation incompatible with international law might result, at least in principle, in the annulment of the incompatible EU provisions. As the Court itself has clarified, agreements concluded by the EU rank in between primary treaty provisions and secondary legislation,[14] thereby retaining primacy over acts of EU institutions and secondary EU legislation. The provisions of these international treaties can therefore act as parameters to assess and review the validity of EU legislation when challenges against it are brought through direct action of annulment under Article 263 TFEU,[15] or through preliminary references procedures under Article 267 TFEU. The Court had been prepared in various occasions to judicially review EU measures in the light of international law[16] and has extended this effect not only to agreements to which the EU is a party, but also to fundamental rules of customary international law.[17] This approach has often been read as a sign of openness of the EU legal order to international law,[18] although, in reality the CJEU has almost always ended up upholding the validity of the relevant EU legislation. In fact, in a relatively more recent line of cases, the Court has significantly narrowed down the possibility to have the validity of EU legislation reviewed in the light of international law by restricting this effect only to those international agreements to which the EU is a party and which fulfil specific requirements of direct effect.[19]

The fact that international agreements concluded by the EU become an integral part of the EU legal order bears important consequences also for the Member States. First of all, the EU nature of these agreements means that under certain conditions they can be regarded to have direct effect. Direct effect is one of the most powerful tools, allowing individuals to enforce rights which are granted by EU law. In the environmental field, direct effect may work as an effective means to boost the implementation of EU and international environmental law.[20] The extension of this feature to provisions of international agreements has therefore the potential to further enhance the implementation of those agreements, strengthening their impact in the legal order of the EU and of its Member States.[21] The second implication arising from Article 216(2) TFEU is the duty, and therefore the responsibility, of the Member States to comply with international agreements to which the EU is a party. The CJEU clarified, 'in ensuring compliance with commitments arising from an agreement concluded by the Community institutions, the Member States fulfil, within the Community system, an obligation in relation to the Community, which has assumed responsibility for the due performance of the agreement'.[22] In other words, Member States' obligation to observe EU international law commitments qua EU law becomes a further guarantee of EU compliance on the international level.[23] This implies that a Member State's failure to perform in accordance with the terms of an agreement to which the EU is a party may entail their liability under EU law. In these cases, international agreements can in principle also benefit of the stronger enforcement system provided by the Commission's infringement procedure, an aspect that appears significant especially when compared to the lack of proper enforcement procedures under many MEAs.

In the field of environmental law, both direct effect and the possibility for EU enforcement against non-compliance are aptly illustrated by a set of proceedings arising in relation to the severe pollution of freshwater and damage to the aquatic environment of the Étang de Berre, a pond situated in southern France, in violation of the prescription of the Barcelona Convention for the protection of the Mediterranean Sea against pollution and its Protocol concerning pollution from land-based sources. The case gave rise to two parallel sets of proceedings. The first set of proceedings arose out of a preliminary ruling request by the French Court of Cassation and related to a domestic proceeding between the Syndicat professionnel coordination des pêcheurs de l'Étang de Berre and Electricité de France (EDF) and related to the interpretation of the Protocol to the Barcelona Convention.[24] In that case, the Court considered that Article 6(3) of the Protocol for the Protection of the Mediterranean Sea against Pollution from Land-Based Sources to the Barcelona Convention for the Protection of the Mediterranean 'contains a clear, precise and unconditional obligation to subject discharges of substances listed covered by Annex II to the Protocol to the prior issue of an authorization by the competent national authorities'.[25] The provision could therefore be regarded as having direct effect, meaning, 'any interested party is entitled to rely on those provisions before the national courts'. This would enable the claimants—an association of French fishermen concerned by the significant damage to the Étang de Berre's aquatic environment resulting from the discharge from a hydroelectric power station managed by the electricity company EDF—to invoke the international treaty provision before the national court in order to stop EDF's operations despite the failure of France to fully implement the Protocol. At the same time, the French government's failure to properly implement the Protocol's provisions was also the subject of an enforcement action by the European Commission leading to a Court's ruling condemning France for its non-compliance with the obligations under Articles 6(1) and 6(3) of the Protocol, due to its failure to take all appropriate measures to prevent, abate and combat heavy and prolonged pollution of the Mediterranean Sea area.[26] In that ruling, the Court stressed in particular,

> in ensuring respect for commitments arising from an agreement concluded by the Community institutions, the Member States fulfil an obligation not only in relation to the non-member country concerned but also and above all in relation to the Community which has assumed responsibility for the due performance of the agreement.[27]

The Étang de Berre proceedings offer an interesting example of how EU's participation in international environmental agreements and the consequent 'Europeanisation'[28] of the relevant international law provisions may contribute to boost compliance and the effective implementation of international environmental law. As the case related to an instance of significant marine pollution, it also shows how, in some cases, the combination and interplay of EU and international law may strengthen the range of remedies available and the effectiveness of the responses to environmental harms.

More generally, the fact that provisions of MEAs, through their incorporation in the EU legal order and their assimilation to EU law, may have direct effect offers a wider avenue for international law to penetrate in the legal order of the Member States. Direct effect can indeed be regarded 'as the most far reaching formal way for a legal order to be open to public international law',[29] almost reflecting a monist approach to international law.[30] Significantly, the uniform interpretation of the Court allows such effect to be granted across all the EU Member States, independently on their constitutional structure with respect to the incorporation of international law, thereby further opening up the EU system to a potential mutually reinforcing interaction with international law.

To this it must be added that the adoption by the EU of secondary legislation implementing an international environmental agreement to which the EU is a contracting party can also promote the proper implementation of the relevant international provisions, and their effectiveness, in the Member States' legal system. An example is represented by two CJEU rulings delivered prior to Brexit and concerning the UK's failure to properly transpose and implement certain access to justice provisions contained in EU secondary legislation,[31] which implemented in the EU legal order the public participation and access to justice requirements contained in the Aarhus Convention. The rulings, respectively delivered within the context of an infringement proceeding[32] and a request for preliminary ruling,[33] concerned in particular the failure of the UK to correctly implement the Aarhus/EU requirement concerning the costs of environmental litigation, and in particular that judicial proceedings on environmental matters should not be prohibitively expensive. These judicial developments at the EU level eventually led to the adoption of new provisions in the Civil Procedure Rules aimed at limiting the costs that could be awarded against parties in judicial review proceedings that fall within the scope of the Aarhus Convention. Therefore, this is a further example of how the combination and interplay between international law and EU law contributed to positive developments at the domestic level towards enhancing environmental standards of access to justice.

3. The CJEU's case-law and its approach to direct effect of international norms

The previous section has illustrated how the direct incorporation of international law provisions into the EU legal order and their equation to EU law offers an important avenue to boost the effectiveness of international norms contained in agreements to which the EU is a contracting party, strengthening both their proper implementation and the mechanisms available for their enforcement. These preliminary findings on the positive implications of the relationship between EU and the international legal order, and on the EU's openness towards international law, must however be assessed through a closer examination of certain developments in CJEU jurisprudence concerning the two main tools through which international law penetrates the EU legal order, namely direct effect and consistent interpretation. Yet, compared to an initially open attitude towards international law, in a relatively more recent line of cases, the CJEU seems to put forward a more restrictive approach to the direct applicability of international law provisions in the EU legal order and the possibility to rely upon them in judicial review challenges of the legality of EU secondary legislation, requiring to that end that the international norms in question satisfy a 'double test' of direct effect.[34] First, the CJEU applies the standard test for direct effect which is valid also for EU legal acts, whereby the provisions in question must 'appear to be as regards their content, unconditional and sufficiently precise'.[35] This means that the international norms need to contain 'a clear and precise obligation which is not subject, in its implementation or effects, to the adoption of any subsequent measures'. Second, with specific respect to the assessment of the direct effectiveness of international provisions, the CJEU has regard to the 'nature and broad logic of the agreement' in order to assess whether the international agreement in question is capable of conferring subjective rights on individuals.

This approach to the determination of the direct effect of international provisions has emerged in particular in the CJEU's case-law concerning challenges to the validity of EU legal acts and the possibility of using international law as a standard for the review of the lawfulness of secondary EU legislation. According to the CJEU, the possibility for international agreements to act as parameters for the validity of EU secondary legislation is subject not only to the requirement that the EU is a party to the agreement in question, but also to the condition that the international law provisions relied upon to challenge the validity of the allegedly incompatible EU legislation have direct effect. In the environmental field, this approach was put forward in *Intertanko*,[36] in which the Court ruled that the legality of Directive 2005/35 on ship-source pollution and on the introduction of penalties for infringements[37] could not be reviewed under the UNCLOS, since the nature and broad logic of the latter 'prevent the Court from being able to assess the validity of a Community measure in the light of that Convention'.[38] The CJEU noted in particular that UNCLOS 'does not establish rules intended to apply directly and immediately to individuals and to confer upon them rights or freedoms capable of being relied upon against States'.[39] This reasoning was then reiterated in the *ATAA* case,[40] where the Court excluded that the validity of Directive 2008/101[41] on the inclusion of aviation activities in the EU scheme for GHGs emission allowances could be assessed in the light of the Kyoto Protocol, since the latter confers on the parties a degree of flexibility in the implementation of the commitments set forth thereto,[42] and therefore the relevant provisions relied upon by the applicants cannot be regarded as being unconditional and sufficiently precise so as to confer on individuals the right to rely on them in legal proceedings to contest the validity of the EU directive. This trend continued in the environmental field with the cases involving the application of the Aarhus Convention, another MEA to which the EU is a party.[43] However, it was especially in the field of human rights, with the *Kadi* line of cases, that the CJEU's more restrictive approach to the penetration of international law had special resonance.[44]

This line of CJEU jurisprudence further narrows down the possibility for international law norms to display direct effects in the EU legal order and stands in apparent contrast with the seemingly open attitude to international law demonstrated in previous rulings.[45] Notably, in a previous ruling concerning the alleged incompatibility of the provisions of an EU directive on the legal protection of biotechnological inventions with the Convention on Biological Diversity (CBD), the CJEU had dismissed the Council's argument that the Directive's validity could not be challenged by reference to the CBD, noting in particular that the fact that

> the CBD contains provisions which do not have direct effect in the sense that they do not create rights which individuals can rely on directly before

> the courts . . . does not preclude review by the courts of compliance with the obligations incumbent on the Community as a party to that agreement.[46]

Similarly, in a ruling concerning the validity of certain provisions of an EU Regulation establishing common rules on the rights of passengers in the event of denied boarding, cancellation or long delay of flights,[47] the CJEU was prepared to review the legality of the EU provisions in the light of the Montreal Convention on the Unification of Certain Rules for International Carriage by Air.[48]

Compared to these rulings, the more restrictive approach brought by the Court has often been regarded as a yet further manifestation of the asserted autonomy, and almost disconnection, of the EU legal order from international law.[49] Scholars have also criticised the *de facto* blurring of the distinction between the concept of self-executing (direct applicability) and direct effect for the purpose of judicial review of EU measures,[50] arguing that while maintaining the direct effect requirement may be appropriate in those cases where individuals seek to rely and invoke rights deriving from an agreement, this same test may not be adequate to assess the questions of legality and validity, which are instead objective questions of law.[51] It was also noted that the requirement that the agreement in question is capable of conferring subjective rights might lead to an inconsistent reading of international agreements. As Cremona pointed out when confronting the CJEU's refusal in *Intertanko* to review the legality of the Directive in the light of UNCLOS with the more open attitude shown in the IATA case:

> in the identification of individual rights it is not easy to distinguish clearly between (for example) the collective interests of airline passengers at issue in the IATA case, where judicial review was accepted, and the 'interests and need of mankind as a whole' identified as an objective of the UNCLOS, where it was not.[52]

Looking at the practical impact of this approach, it can be noticed that while, admittedly, the CJEU's reluctance to use international law as a standard for reviewing the legality of EU acts has in several cases contributed to preserve EU legislation maintaining more stringent standards of environmental protection,[53] it may still preclude the successful use of international law to challenge lower EU standards.[54] That this may be the case is demonstrated in a more recent case involving the alleged incompatibility of Article 10 of Regulation 1367/2006 (so-called Aarhus Regulation, as it implements the requirements of the Aarhus Convention with respect to EU institutions) with Article 9(3) of the Aarhus Convention. The applicants, two environmental NGOs, challenged the restrictive approach taken by the Aarhus Regulation with respect to the type of EU acts that can be challenged by individuals and NGOs, and which according to the Regulation are limited only to 'administrative acts' having an 'individual scope'. While the General Court and the AG sided with the applicants, the CJEU concluded on this point, 'article 9(3) of the Aarhus Convention lacks the clarity and precision required for that provision to be properly relied on before the EU judicature for the purposes of assessing the legality of Article 10(1) of Regulation 1367/2006'.[55] Thus, in this ruling the Court lost the opportunity to use the interaction between international law and EU law as a means not only to contribute to enhance the effectiveness of international environmental law within the EU legal order, but also to further advance environmental standards. This is particularly striking with respect to an issue, such as access to justice, where the ethos of the Aarhus Convention is resonating globally in other regions of the world through the adoption of parallel agreements that uphold, if not even upgrade, the Aarhus standards.

4. Consistent interpretation

Direct effect is not the only avenue through which international law provisions can penetrate in the EU legal order. Consistent interpretation—that is, the requirement to interpret, insofar as it is possible, EU secondary legislation in accordance with the terms of the international agreements to which the EU is a party[56]—may equally lead to positive outcomes with respect to the application of international rules. In fact, in some cases consistent interpretation may prove to be even more helpful than direct effect. First, it may apply independently from the direct effect character of the relevant provisions and, as such, can make it easier for international environmental norms to 'penetrate' in the EU legal order. An example is represented by the CJEU decision concerning the possibility for an environmental NGO to rely on the provision of the Aarhus Convention, an agreement to which the EU is a contracting party, to challenge the validity of domestic law undermining their access to justice and participation rights under the Convention. The Court excluded that Article 9(3) of the Aarhus Convention could have direct effect since, despite the overall spirit of the Convention conformed with the requirement of conferring subjective rights to individuals, that provision 'does not contain clear and precise obligations capable of directly regulating the legal position of individuals' but 'is subject, in its implementation or effects, to the adoption of a subsequent measure'.[57] The lack of direct effect, however, did not prevent the Convention from having a far-reaching effect in the Member State's legal order via the avenue of interpretation. According to the CJEU, the domestic court shall 'interpret, to the fullest extent possible, the procedural rules relating to the conditions to be met in order to bring administrative or judicial proceedings in accordance with the objectives of Article 9(3) of that convention' as well as with 'the objective of effective judicial protection of the rights conferred by EU law, in order to enable an environmental protection organization . . . to challenge before a court a decision taken following administrative proceedings liable to be contrary to EU environmental law'.[58]

Second, by contrast with direct effect, which is reserved to EU-concluded international agreements on the basis of their equivalent status to EU secondary law, the Court extended the application of consistent interpretation also to general norms of international law and, albeit with some tweaks, also to international agreements to which only the Member States, but not the EU, are contracting parties, and which are therefore not directly binding on the EU institutions. Arguably, this is especially the case for international agreements in which all or most EU Member

States are contracting parties since, in these situations, the endeavour to interpret EU law in the light of the relevant international law provisions would stem not only from a general attitude of respect for international law, but also from more pragmatic considerations aimed at avoiding potentially disrupting conflicts between different legal regimes; for example because EU secondary legislation binding on the Member States diverge from their international commitments. Thus, in *Intertanko*, the Court found that, while the legality of Directive 2005/35 Directive could not be reviewed in the light of the MARPOL Convention,[59] the latter could have consequences for the interpretation of provisions of EU secondary law which fall within its field of application.[60] The Court paid particular attention to the fact that MARPOL was binding on all the Member States and considered that a duty take into account of MARPOL in the interpretation of relevant secondary EU legislation derived from 'the customary principle of good faith, which forms part of general international law' and of the duty of loyal cooperation.[61] Similarly, in the *Commune de Mesquer* case, nearly all Member States were contracting parties to the CLC, and the Fund Convention for oil pollution damage was regarded as reflecting the existence of 'a broad political consensus' for liability for oil pollution damage to be regulated by the relevant international framework.[62] Therefore, although the Convention could not be set to prevail over the EU Waste Framework Directive since the EU was not a party to it,[63] the duty of loyal cooperation binding the Union and the Member States would imply a requirement of consistent interpretation to ensure that normative conflicts between EU law and Member States' international commitments are avoided where possible.[64]

A similar reasoning can be found in a more recent decision concerning once again the relationship between Directive 2005/35 and certain international conventions applicable to the marine environment, namely UNCLOS, MARPOL and the 1969 Convention Relating to Intervention on the High Seas ('Intervention Convention').[65] This preliminary ruling was given in the context of domestic proceedings concerning a fine imposed on a shipping company (Bosphorus Queen Shipping Ltd) for an oil spill that allegedly caused significant damage in the Finnish EEZ. At stake in this case was therefore not a normative conflict but rather more generally the interpretation of certain provisions of Directive 2005/35 regarding the powers of Member States' authorities to impose penalties on vessels for polluting discharges arising from law infringements and causing major damage or threat of major damage to the coastline or related interest of the Member State concerned or to any natural resources in the relevant area. While the CJEU's reasoning focused mostly on the role and legal impact of the relevant provisions of UNCLOS (an agreement to which the EU is a contracting party) for the interpretation of legal concepts in Article 7 of the Directive, it also touched on the interpretative relevance of MARPOL and of the 1969 Intervention Convention. In that respect, the CJEU seemed to establish a subtle distinction between the legal significance of MARPOL and the Intervention Convention.[66] As to the former, which is binding on all the Member States, the Court stated that a duty of consistent interpretation finds its basis on the customary international law principle of good faith and on the EU principle of loyalty embodied in Article 4(3) TEU. Conversely, it noted that the Union has not acceded to the Intervention Convention, and not all the Member States are parties to it.[67] Accordingly, the CJEU found that it does not have jurisdiction to interpret that Convention, but the latter must nevertheless be taken into account since it is part of the relevant rules for the interpretation of UNCLOS.[68]

There are, of course, limitations to what can be achieved through the use of consistent interpretation. Unlike direct effect, consistent interpretation only allows an 'indirect' effect of the international legal rule in the EU legal order, meaning that international law cannot regulate directly the situation at stake. There are also limits posed by general principles of law[69] and by the impossibility for the court to reach a *contra legem* interpretation. Those limits came to play in the *Wolfgang Glatzel* case concerning the compatibility of a provision of Directive 2006/126/EC on driving licences with the articles of the Charter of Fundamental Rights.[70] The question was in particular whether the requirement of visual acuity laid down in the EU provision constitutes an interference with the rights of equality and non-discrimination under the EU Charter of Fundamental Rights. In that context, the CJEU considered necessary to examine the possible effects on that Directive's provision of the UN Convention on Disabilities, to which the EU is a party. On this point the CJEU, while reasserting the primacy of international agreements concluded by the EU on provisions of EU secondary legislation and the consequent duty to interpret that Directive in a manner that is consistent with the UN Convention on Disabilities, concluded that it was not possible to give that EU law provision an interpretation which would enable it to circumvent the clear rule laying down that minimum value requirement.

5. Towards a harmonious approach to the relationship between EU and international law

In the light of the above discussion, it can be argued that interpretative tools and approaches can open the way to a more nuanced and harmonious approach to the relationship between international law and EU law, particularly in those situations where international agreements and EU secondary legislation drive towards the achievement of the same objectives or aim at the protection of similar values. It has been suggested, for example, that the reluctance of the CJEU to apply international law to annul secondary acts of EU legislation needs to be read not so much in terms of a forced disconnection with international law, but rather and more positively as the attempt by the court to defend European values[71]—even if in some cases this may entail to make political choices as to what those values are.[72] The values at stake, which the court seeks to protect and uphold against interferences from international law,[73] are those associated with the European Rule of Law, including in particular those values that represent the 'very foundations of the Community legal order'.[74] It can be noted in that regard that in a number of areas such as environmental protection and human rights, the European values often converge with the values and objectives enshrined in international agreements. The question is therefore whether the relationship between the international and the European legal systems can be reimagined in a way that identifies and highlights the commonalities of the values and interests at stake and the convergence towards a similar aim. In other words, the question that needs to be explored is whether it is possible to envisage an interpretative approach to the relationship between EU and international law which rather than focusing on the form—on questions of hierarchy and primacy—centres instead on the substantive contents of the relevant norms and on the values that such norms aim to portray.

An approach that goes along these lines is arguably that proposed by the Advocate General's (AG) opinion in the *Intertanko* case. The AG did not only admit the possibility to review the legality of Directive 2005/35 in the light of UNCLOS, but also tried to reconcile the text of the EU directive, which put forward a more stringent standard of criminal liability compared to what was allowed under the MARPOL Convention for areas beyond the territorial jurisdiction, with the relevant international law standards.[75] In this interpretative endeavour, the AG stressed the appropriateness of going beyond the textual wording of the international law provisions, by taking account of the underlying objectives and functions of both MARPOL and UNCLOS, including in particular the aim of achieving 'the complete elimination of pollution and the minimization of accidental pollution' and 'to facilitate effective protection of the marine environment'.[76] It also noted that the achievement of those objectives in both MARPOL and UNCLOS would not require restricting liability to the master and the owner of the ship—thereby implicitly permitting the broadening of potentially liable subjects under the Directive.[77] Finally, drawing on the principle of consistent interpretation and asserting the need to prioritise an interpretation of EU law in conformity with international law,[78] the AG remarked that efforts to avoid conflicts between the relevant legal frameworks are not only dictated by the principle of cooperation between the EU institutions and the Member States (that are parties to international agreements and which can otherwise be subjected to competing requirements), but also by the need not to undermine the practical effectiveness of the relevant provisions of EU and international law.[79]

A similar interpretative reading was adopted at the domestic level by the French Court of Cassation when deciding on an analogous situation of incompatibility of French criminal law with MARPOL, in the context of criminal proceedings arising from the shipwreck of the *Erika* oil tanker and the consequent massive oil pollution of the French coast.[80] Among the submissions presented by the respondents, who also argued the lack of jurisdictional competence of the French court, was the discrepancy between French law on combating marine pollution and the requirements of MARPOL. In particular, French legislation established a wider range of potentially liable subjects and more stringent standard of criminal liability. According to Article 55 of the French Constitution, international treaties are hierarchically placed above domestic legislation. However, in upholding the validity of French legislation, the Court of cassation went beyond a purely textual reading of MARPOL Convention and adopted instead a theological approach to the interpretation of the relevant provisions, taking into account the spirit as well as the functions and objectives of MARPOL.[81]

6. Consistent interpretation and the mutual supportiveness of EU law and international law in the field of environment

In the multilevel legal order of the EU, consistent interpretation and other interpretative approaches not only may serve to connect and reconcile international provisions with EU law, but can also be employed to enhance the positive synergies arising from the interaction between EU law and international law. An interesting example of this dynamic is represented by the case-law on the application and interpretation of the Aarhus Convention. One of the first opportunities for the CJEU to pronounce on the legal nature of the Aarhus Convention's provisions was a reference for a preliminary ruling from the Supreme Court of the Slovak Republic in the *Lesoochranárske zoskupenie VLK* case (also known as the '*Brown Bear*' case) regarding the direct or self-executing effect of Article 9(3) of the Aarhus Convention.[82] The case stemmed from a challenge brought by an environmental protection association (i.e. Lesoochranárske zoskupenie VLK) against the refusal of the Slovakian administrative authority to confer to the association the status of 'party' to the administrative proceedings concerning the approval of derogations to the system of protection of species and protected areas under the Habitats Directive. This refusal had implications for the association's access to justice, since under Slovakian domestic law being a 'party to the proceedings' was a precondition to bringing a judicial review action against the decision taken or the procedure followed by the administrative authority.

In its decision, the CJEU dismissed the direct effect of Article 9(3) of the Aarhus Convention, but it observed that this provision despite being drafted in broad terms is intended to ensure effective environmental protection.[83] It then established a link between the Aarhus Convention's objective of ensuring effective protection of EU environmental law (namely, the protection offered by the Habitats Directive) and the EU law principle of effective judicial protection. According to the Court, 'if the effective protection of EU environmental law is not to be undermined, it is unconceivable that article 9(3) of the Aarhus Convention be interpreted in such a way as to make it in practice impossible or excessively difficult to exercise rights conferred by EU law'.[84] It added that since there were not yet EU rules implementing Article 9(3) in the EU legal order and governing questions concerning standing and access to justice of NGOs before domestic courts, it is left to the domestic legal system of each Member State to lay down the detailed procedural rules governing actions for safeguarding the rights that individuals derive from EU law, in this case the Habitats Directive.[85] Accordingly, national courts have to interpret,

> to the fullest extent possible, the procedural rules relating to the conditions to be met in order to bring administrative or judicial proceedings in accordance with the objectives of article 9(3) of the Aarhus Convention and the objective of effective judicial protection of the rights conferred by EU law.[86]

From the point of view of the relationship between EU and international law, this ruling features a shift in the CJEU reasoning from a main focus on the primacy arguments (i.e. the higher rank enjoyed by international agreements concluded by the EU within the EU legal order) to greater attention on the question of effectiveness of the relevant rules of international law and of EU law.[87] The duty of consistent interpretation is linked in this case to the need to ensure the effective judicial protection of EU environmental directives in domestic law.[88] By bringing together the objectives and principles of the Aarhus Convention with one of the basic principles of EU governance (the EU principle of effective judicial protection), the Court has led the way to a mutually reinforcing application of Article 9(3) of the Aarhus Convention with the EU law,[89] leading eventually to an extended protection of environmental rights in the domestic systems of the Member States. The CJEU ruling had impact at the domestic level. It was found that following the CJEU decision, the referring court in its follow-up judgment brought about 'a ground-breaking shift in case law at the national level from the point of view of statutory requirements of the environmental protection associations for bringing up administrative court proceedings in the field of environmental protection'.[90] Although, it was as well noted that the CJEU's legal opinion on the interpretation of Article 9(3) of the Aarhus Convention was not always respected in similar cases at the national level.

In a subsequent decision, delivered after the adoption of the Lisbon Treaty, which enhanced the legal status of the Charter of Fundamental Rights, the Aarhus Convention's right of access to justice had been further strengthened through the EU right to a fair trial, embodied in Article 47 of the Charter.[91] The proceeding in this case is related to the *Brown Bear* case as they concerned the same NGO's right to bring a legal action against the approval by the Slovakian authorities of a project to construct an enclosure on a protected site, while the parallel proceeding regarding its status as 'party to the procedure' was still pending. In this case, the CJEU ruled that the continuation of the administrative procedure relating to the application for a permit, even where the legal proceedings relating to a request to be granted the status of a party to the procedure is pending, would be contrary to the fulfilment of the right of judicial protection enshrined in Article 47 of the Charter read in conjunction with Articles 9(2) and 9(4) of the Aarhus Convention. The result of this combined reading of the Aarhus Convention with Article 47 of the Charter are significant both for the application of the EU Charter's right to remedy and for the enforcement of the Aarhus Convention itself. It was noted that 'Article 47 is notoriously difficult to apply through judicial review, especially regarding standing requirements'.[92] In this respect, the wording of Article 9 of the Aarhus Convention has enabled the Court to reveal the substantive contents and meaning of an Article 47's right to an effective remedy with respect to EU-derived environmental rights and enhanced its role in the enforcement of EU secondary legislation.[93]

7. Interim findings

By examining, in the light of the CJEU case-law, the relationship and interaction between norms of international agreements and EU law, the analysis so far illustrated how the interplay between EU and international law may contribute to strengthening the application and implementation of environmental standards. Particularly in those cases where the EU is a contracting party to international environmental agreements, the incorporation of the provisions of these agreements in the EU legal order, and their acquired EU law nature, may enhance their effectiveness. In this respect, the two proceedings related to the pollution of the Étang de Berre and the case-law concerning the national implementation of the Aarhus Convention show how the integration of international law provisions in the EU legal order opens significant possibilities to the European Commission to be able to use infringement proceedings to enforce the international norms against Member States' failure to properly implement the agreement. The discussion also revealed how, despite the more restrictive approach of the CJEU to grant direct effect to international law provisions, especially when those provisions are relied upon as parameter to review the legality of EU acts, interpretative principles and the doctrine of consistent interpretation can still enable a mutually supportive reading of EU and international law and may represent an important tool to build a harmonious relationship between the two legal orders. It has been submitted that such an approach, which rather than hinting at autonomy and disconnection reinforces the scope for mutual support and cooperation towards the pursuit of the same goals, is particularly appropriate in the field of environmental protection, where the European and international legal frameworks are often on a path of convergence in terms of interests and objectives, if not of standards, for the protection of a common good. In the light of these considerations, the following part of this chapter will explore more closely the potential for mutual supportive and constructive interaction between EU and international law in the specific context of environmental liability.

8. Between mutual supportiveness and complementarity in the CJEU's case-law on environmental liability

The previous analysis has attempted to show how synergic interactions between EU and international law may also arise through the combined and complementary reading of international law provisions in conjunction with EU secondary legislation. With specific respect to the question of liability and reparation for environmental damage, an example of a mutually supportive application of EU law and international law is the CJEU preliminary ruling in the proceeding brought by the French municipality of Mesquer against Total France SA and Total International companies—respectively the seller and the charterer of the ship—for the reimbursement of the costs undertaken for the operations of cleaning up and decontaminating its coastline as a result of the sinking of the *Erika* oil tanker in 1999.[94] This case therefore touches directly on the question of environmental liability and compensation for oil pollution damage. The devastating environmental consequences of the *Erika* incident on the French marine waters and coastline provoked a strong reaction among the French population and in Europe, and the accident prompted both criminal proceedings and civil compensation claims. As one of the most affected municipalities, the Commune de Mesquer decided to bring an action against Total, the oil charterer contracted to supply heavy fuel oil to Italy, for its responsibility for the severe pollution of the marine environment and the municipality's coastline. The claim was based on provisions of national law implementing the Waste Framework Directive, as interpreted in the light of the decision in the *Van der Walle* case, where the CJEU had previously held that soil contaminated as the result of an accidental spill of hydrocarbons could be considered waste. This classification as 'waste' had important implications in terms of the allocation of disposal cost under the Waste Framework Directive. According to Article 15 of that Directive, 'in accordance with the polluter pays principle', the costs of disposing waste must be borne by the holder of the waste and/or the previous holders or the producer of the product from which the waste came from. In the light of this, the preliminary ruling revolved around two main questions. First, whether in line with the previous Court's decision in the *Van der Walle* case, heavy oil accidentally spilled on the beaches could be considered waste within the meaning of that Directive. If the answer to that question was positive, the second question was whether the Total companies, in their quality as the producer, seller and/or charterer of that heavy fuel, could be regarded as 'holders' of the waste or 'producers of the product from which the waste came' under the Waste Framework Directive and, as such, be held responsible for the cost of the waste disposal—i.e. the costs related to cleaning up the oil spilled on the coastline. This aspect was particularly controversial as it touched directly on the relationship between EU secondary legislation and international law. In particular, a finding of liability of Total under the Waste Framework Directive would imply a potential conflict with the liability regime established by the 1992 oil pollution civil liability convention (CLC), which was the main liability framework applicable to the *Erika* oil pollution case. One of the main features of the CLC is the channelling of liability to the shipowner, to the exclusion of other potentially responsible parties, including the charterers and other actors listed in Article 4 of the Convention, unless the damage resulted from their personal act or omission, committed intentionally or recklessly and with the knowledge that such damage will probably result. The question for the CJEU was therefore how to reconcile the responsibility arising for Total under the EU directive on waste with domestic French law implementing the oil pollution liability convention. In other words, the issue was how to strike a balance between the respect of Member States' international commitments under the CLC and the need to preserve the effectiveness of the EU waste legislation.

On this point, both the Advocate General and the Court acknowledged the importance of a consistent interpretation, although they followed a slightly different reasoning. The Advocate General stressed the fact that the duty of loyal cooperation was also binding on EU institutions, thereby requiring an interpretation of the relevant provisions of EU law which, as far as possible, avoids conflicts with the Member States' international commitments. The CJEU, instead, focused mainly on the duty of national courts to interpret and apply national law, including domestic legislation based on international commitments entered into by the Member State, 'as far as possible in the light of the wording and the purpose of the Directive'.[95] In this case, the Court was clear in presenting the duty of consistent interpretation as aimed at ensuring that the objectives pursued by the Directive are attained, even if this would ultimately require interpreting and, if necessary, accommodating the application of international law in the light of EU law.

The different approaches of the CJEU and of the Advocate General led to different conclusions with respect to the question of liability and allocation of costs. In particular, while both the CJEU and the Advocate General based their reasoning on the polluter pays principle, which conceptually underpinned the responsibility of the producer and holder of waste under Article 15 of Directive, they adopted slightly different interpretations of this principle.[96] The Advocate General interpreted the polluter pays principle as permitting the general public, as the end consumer of the product and as such implicitly accepting the risk entailed by international oil transport, to bear part of the pollution costs arising from the oil spill. From this perspective, 'the exclusion from liability does not appear to be incompatible with Article 15 of the Waste Framework Directive, even if the person concerned contributed to causing the waste, but it is a permissible full utilization of the scope which the polluter pays principle allows the Member States in connection with implementation'.[97]

The CJEU took a rather different approach and concluded that the seller of the hydrocarbons and the charterer of the ship carrying them could be considered as the producer of the waste (i.e. the producers of the product from which the waste came from) under the Waste Framework Directive, and therefore held liable to pay the cost of disposal (i.e. clean-up), if the national court finds that they '*contributed* to the risk that the pollution caused by the shipwreck would occur, in particular if [they] failed to take measures to prevent such an incident, such as measures concerning the choice of ship'.[98] In reaching this conclusion the Court noted in particular that 'the application of the "polluter pays" principle within the meaning of . . . article 174(2) EC and article 15 of Directive 75/442 would be frustrated if such persons involved in causing waste escaped their financial obligations as provided by that directive'.[99] Applied to the case at hand, it meant that, insofar as the charter-seller contributed to the creation of the waste, they could be considered as producers or previous holder of waste, and therefore they could be held liable alongside the shipowner.

This slightly different interpretation of the polluter pays principle under the Waste Framework Directive reflects two different approaches to the relationship between this Directive and the international regime. In particular, while the Advocate General emphasises the respect for international law commitments and seeks to reconcile the Directive's requirements regarding the allocation of costs with the exclusion of certain actors from liability under the international regime, the reasoning of the CJEU is mainly centred on the need to ensure that the Directive's objectives, including those linked to the implementation of the polluter pays principle, are achieved. Indeed, in a relevant passage it held,

> if it happens that the cost of disposal of the waste produced by an accidental spillage of hydrocarbons at sea is not borne by that fund . . . and that . . . the national law of a Member State, including the law derived from international agreements, prevents that cost from being borne by the shipowner and/or the charterer, even though they are to be regarded as 'holders' within the meaning of . . . [the Waste Framework Directive], such a national law will then, in

order to ensure that article 15 of that directive is correctly transposed, have to make provision for that cost to be borne by the producer of the product from which the waste thus spread came.[100]

Like in the *Brown Bear* case, the reasoning behind the application of consistent interpretation in the relationship between international commitments and EU law is mostly concerned with the need to preserve the effectiveness (of EU law).[101] The difference being however that, unlike with the Aarhus Convention, the EU is not a party to the CLC, and therefore the relevant international provisions are not binding upon it. Nevertheless, faced with a potential conflict between EU secondary legislation and the Member States' international commitments, the Court did not hesitate to invoke the duty of consistent interpretation in a way not to undermine the effective application of the relevant norm of the Waste Directive. In that case, this meant that if the actual damage caused by an oil spill exceeds the maximum damage payment under the national law/international oil pollution regime, the national court must interpret that legislation as to make sure that the exceeding costs are borne by the producer of the product from which the waste came.

From an environmental law perspective, this interpretative approach, which essentially enables a complementary application of the provision of EU secondary legislation with the liability regime under the international convention, presents some important advantages. In the *Commune de Mesquer* case, the CJEU's interpretation of the polluter pays principle under Article 15 of the Waste Directive allowed to expand the scope of responsibility and liability for the oil pollution damage beyond the personal and financial limitations of the Convention. From the point of view of the potentially liable subjects, this is an important result that allows tackling one of the main criticisms raised to the CLC regime—namely the narrow channelling of liability onto a single subject, the shipowner, with the almost total exclusion of other actors involved in, and benefiting from, maritime transport of oil. It was also noted that this expansion of the potentially liable subjects might contribute to address the 'one ship, one company' phenomenon,[102] that is the creation of companies whose only asset lies in the ownership of a single ship. Once the ship disappears, these companies become insolvent and as such avoid compensation claims simply because of the factual lack of any assets.[103] That said, it is also important to note that, unlike the strict liability channelled onto the shipowner under the CLC, the liability of the seller-charterer is linked to their contribution to the creation of the waste and to the consequent risk that pollution would occur.[104] The CJEU does not specify in what does consist this 'contribution to the risk', although it clarifies that this is an assessment to be undertaken by the national court on the basis of the elements in its possession; however, a passage of the judgment hints at the fact that this is linked to the company being negligent. In sum, the decision seems to envisage the possibility for the charterers, and the other actors benefiting from the exclusion clause under the CLC, to be still held liable under certain circumstances, if their negligence contributed to cause the pollution. With respect to this, it is interesting to note that the negligent conduct of Total, as the charterer of the ship, was key in establishing its liability in the course of parallel criminal proceedings brought before the French courts against the shipmaster of the *Erika*, the representative of the registered owner of the vessel, the president of the vessel's managing company, the classification society (RINA) and against Total oil company. In a progressive, yet controversial, ruling the French Court of Cassation concluded that Total could not be exempted from liability under Article III (4) CLC, because of its negligent decision of chartering the *Erika* without having properly performed the vetting procedures in accordance with its internal regulations.[105]

9. Interactions and potential synergies between liability regimes in a multilevel context

The CJEU ruling in the *Commune de Mesquer* case is particularly relevant for the examination of the relationship between the ELD and the marine pollution regime. This question was touched on during the CJEU proceedings but eventually dismissed on the basis that the temporal scope of application of the ELD precluded its direct relevance to the *Erika* oil spill. However, this question is not merely theoretical, given that there is a potential overlap between the marine civil liability conventions and the ELD, at least for what concerns the question of compensation for damage to protected marine resources and habitats in the territorial sea and EEZ of the Member States. Of course, the application of the CJEU reasoning in *Commune de Mesquer* to the relationship between the ELD and the oil pollution conventions needs to take into account the important limitation represented by the exemption contained in Article 4(2) of the ELD, which excludes the application of the Directive

> to environmental damage or to any imminent threat of such damage arising from an incident in respect of which liability or compensation falls within the scope of any of the international Conventions listed in Annex IV, including any future amendments thereof, which is in force in the Member State concerned.

In highlighting that the Waste Framework Directive, even in its codified version resulting from Directive 2006/12, does not contain a similar provision, the CJEU in *Commune de Mesquer* seemed to implicitly infer that a different outcome could have been reached if the ELD were to apply.[106]

However, it has been noted that the wording of Article 4(2) ELD (and of Article 4(4) ELD with respect to the civil liability convention in the field of nuclear energy) leaves unclear the extent to which the international conventions listed in Annex IV and V of the ELD preclude its application in case of environmental damage.[107] In particular, it is unclear whether the EU legislator intended to completely bar the Directive's application in case of damage arising from incidents falling in the scope of the marine and nuclear conventions, or whether instead such exclusion is limited only to the extent to which there is an overlap in the scope of liability and compensation.[108] Opinions are divided on this question. From an environmental protection perspective, given the more limited approach to the reparation of environmental damage under the civil liability conventions for marine pollution, a complementary application of the ELD, which would include in the scope of reparation damage not covered under the international regime, would allow to fill an important gap and enhance the overall system of remedies available. However, some commentators have pointed to the risk that applying the ELD to incidents covered by the IMO conventions might be disruptive for the international regime and would create a normative conflict between the EU and the international provisions.[109] The risk would affect both the system of compensation available under the international conventions and the scope of potentially liable subjects. Compared to the almost exclusive shipowner liability under the IMO conventions, the definition of operator under the ELD is broader. However, the designation of the liable entity under the oil pollution liability regime reflects a carefully achieved compromise during the negotiation stages of these international treaties, in which the various commercial concerns were taken into account.

Given these considerations, the CJEU ruling in the *Commune de Mesquer* case and the way the court approaches the interaction of the EU and international law in the light of the polluter pays principle may provide some interesting insights on how to address the relationship between international and regional regimes of liability in a multilevel framework. Of particular relevance is the suggestion in the ruling that the channelling of liability and the related limitation and exclusion of actors from liability under the convention are not necessarily incompatible with the identification of a wider range of potentially liable parties under a regional legal framework (in this case the Water Framework Directive). With respect to the ELD, the question is therefore whether, in case of pollution damage within the meaning of the maritime liability conventions occurring to the coast and EEZ of an EU Member State, it is possible to follow the approach of the Court in the *Commune de Mesquer* case and read the ambiguous wording of the exemption clause in Article 4(2) as allowing the ELD to apply to 'environmental damage' for the part exceeding the liability amount provided by the relevant international conventions. The question concerns in particular how to overcome the divergences regarding the personal scope of application of the respective liability regimes and the different remediation standards. With respect to the liable persons, it must be noted that although the maritime conventions are based on the principle of channelling strict liability onto the owner of the ship to the exclusion of other players, this exclusion is not absolute. First of all, shipowners can lose their right to have liability limited to the amount provided in the CLC, if it can be proved that damage resulted from their personal act or omissions, committed with intentionality or recklessness.[110] This is indeed what happened in another case, involving the oil spill of the tanker *Prestige*, where the shipowner was found negligent in the course of domestic proceeding before the Spanish Supreme Court and as such lost its right to limit liability under the Convention.[111] Second, under the CLC, claimants can still bring civil liability or tort actions against other persons outside the framework of the Convention, but those claims must be based on the applicable national law. Finally, although the CLC and the HNS Convention prohibit compensation claims against the persons indicated in Articles III(4) and 7(5) respectively, the protection of those subjects from liability will cease if the damage results from their personal act or omission, committed with the intent to cause such damage, or recklessly and with the knowledge that such damage would probably result.[112] Indeed, in the criminal proceedings related to the damage resulting from the oil spill of the *Erika* tanker, the French Court of Cassation affirmed the criminal as well as the civil liability of four main players, including the registered shipowner, the executive and technical manager of the ship, as well as the charterer and the classification society for having deliberately sidestepped the need to perform structural repairs, in order to save costs at the expense of the safety of the ship. Although the oil spill and the consequent damage were unintentional, the Court considered that negligence of the oil company (Total) and the shipping operators in omitting the much needed restoration works and during the vetting and certification process contributed fundamentally to the disaster. Accordingly, it found that the exoneration of Article 4(III) of the CLC was not applicable.

The ruling of the French Court is also significant, for it confirms the Court of Appeal's decision recognising ecological damage as a distinct head of damage deserving compensation, finding that persons who are criminally liable because of their fault and lack of care should not be allowed to benefit from the Convention's immunity for damage caused to nature and to the environment as such. A passage of the decision mentions domestic legislation transposing the ELD, noting that although this directive is not applicable to the present case, its adoption represents a further important step towards the recognition of pure ecological damage in the French legal system.

In the light of the aforementioned, it is possible to argue that a progressive interpretative approach leading to a complementary application of the Directive and the civil liability convention is indeed possible, at least insofar as the blatant lack of care and negligence of liable parties would bring them outside the remit of the CLC's immunities and limitation of liability. Moreover, the notion of 'operator' under the Directive could in some cases be interpreted to include those persons who, while not formally qualifying as the ultimate owner of the ship, retained nevertheless control on important decisions regarding the ship's management and operation. This could be the case, for instance, of the registered owner of the two Liberian companies holding the capital of the Tevere Shipping company, which in turn owned the *Erika*. The French court considered that this person, while not strictly meeting the definition of shipowner under the CLC, was nevertheless the 'ultimate owner' of the *Erika*.[113] As in the *Erika* case, this complementary reading of the Directive and the Convention would in principle reinforce the persuasive impact of liability regimes towards promoting greater care in terms of ship safety.

The French court's decision also shows an interesting interrelation of civil and criminal liability and the way the careless conduct of the oil operators and shipping actors could lead to their criminal liability as well as to the duty to compensate environmental damage within and potentially also beyond the terms of the Civil Liability Convention. It also shows how the interplay between different legal systems—in that case, the international legal framework and domestic law and procedure—can in some cases open up to a broader scope of compensation and remedies. In the *Erika* case, a particularity of the French legal system is that criminal courts may also award civil remedies.

That said, expanding the scope of compensation beyond what is provided under the international civil liability conventions might not be always straightforward. Circumventing the personal exclusions provided in Article III(4) CLC may require the proof of specific evidence showing the recklessness conduct of the actors involved. Thus, in another significant oil spill damage to the marine environment involving the tanker *Prestige*, the Spanish government's liability and compensation claim, in US courts, against the US certification company (ABS) was rejected for insufficient evidence proving the recklessness conduct of the defendants. Subsequent attempts to file liability and compensation claims in the Spanish Court of First Instance against the captain of the ship, the chief engineer and the director of the merchant navy also proved unsuccessful for lack of sufficient evidence to render these persons criminally liable for environmental offences. The proceedings eventually ended up before the Spanish Supreme Court, which deemed the captain of the ship responsible for environmental crime and as such liable, under civil liability, for the damage caused. The Court also concluded that the shipowner had subsidiary liability and was not entitled to any liability limitation under the Convention for having negligently permitted the navigation of the vessel despite being aware of its deteriorated conditions. The Court's ruling also went beyond the limitations of the conventional text with respect to the scope of compensable damage. In contrast to the consolidated practice of the IOPC Fund, the Court decision suggested that the quantification of the damages (to be made at a later stage and in a separate legal proceeding on the basis of evidence submitted by the parties and of the experts' reports) will not necessarily be constrained by the criteria contained in the Fund's Claims Manual.[114] Applying criteria deriving from national law, the Court hinted at the fact that damage compensation may also include moral and purely environmental damage.[115]

This decision reveals once more how domestic court proceedings on the basis of national law may challenge the compensation and liability limits of the international regime, both in terms of the personal scope of application of the Convention and with respect to the type of compensable damage. Yet, while such an approach may be welcomed from an environmental law perspective, the extent to which domestic courts can apply standards and criteria derived from national law to expand the scope of liability and compensation beyond what established in international conventions, which are in force and are applicable in the domestic jurisdiction concerned, is not uncontroversial. Questions arise around the impact of such decisions both on the smooth functioning of the international regime and in terms of legal certainty.[116]

Notes

1 K Ziegler, 'Beyond Pluralism and Autonomy: Systemic Harmonization as a Paradigm for the Interaction of EU Law and International Law' (2016) 35 Yearbook of European Law 667, 670.

2 See A Rosas, 'The European Court of Justice and Public International Law' in J Wouters, A Nollkaemper and E De Wet (eds.), *The Europeanization of International Law: The Status of International Law in the EU and Its Member States* (TMC Asser Press 2008) 75.
3 C-181/73 *Haegeman v Belgian State*, judgment of the court 30 April 1974, ECLI:EU:C:1974:41, para 5.
4 Rosas (n 2).
5 C-104/81, *Hauptzollamt Mainz v C.A. Kupferberg & Cie KGa* ('*Kupferberg*'), ECLI:EU:C:1982:362, ECR [1982] 3641 [13–14].
6 M Mendez, 'The Enforcement of EU Agreements: Bolstering the Effectiveness of Treaty Law?' (2010) 47 Common Market Law Review 1719.
7 Case C-12/86 *Demirel* [1987] ECR 3719 [9]; Case C-13/00 *Commission v Ireland* [2002] [14].
8 Case C-13/00 (n 7) [16], [20].
9 Case C-239/03 *Commission v France* (Étang de Berre) ECLI:EU:C:2004:598, ECR [2004] I-9325 [29–30].
10 Case C-240/09 *Lesoochranárske zoskupenie VLK v Ministerstvo životného prostredia Slovenskej republiky* (*Brown Bear* case) ECLI:EU:C:2011:125 [42]. M Klamert, 'Dark Matter: Competence, Jurisdiction and 'The Area Largely Covered by EU law'—Comment on Lesoochranarske' (2012) 37 European Law Review 3.
11 Case C-459/03 *Commission v Ireland* (MOX Plant) [2006] ECR I-4635 [93].
12 Ibid. [94–95].
13 Ibid [106–111].
14 Case C-61/94 *Commission v Germany* [1996] ECR I-3989 [52].
15 CJEU, C-377/98 *Netherlands v Parliament and Council* [2001] ECR I-7079 (Biotech Directive case); C-344/04 IATA and ELFAA [2006] ECR I-0403.
16 Biotech Directive case (n 15) and IATA and ELFAA case (n 15).
17 Case C-162/96, *A Racke GmbH & Co and Hauptzollamt Mainz* [1998] ECR I-3655.
18 Rosas (n 2) 75; K Ziegler, 'International Law and EU Law: Between Asymmetric Constitutionalization and Fragmentation' in A Orakhelashvili (ed.), *Research Handbook on the Theory of International Law* (Edward Elgar 2011) 292–293.
19 See further discussion in section 3 of this chapter.
20 See S Marsden, 'Invoking Direct Application and Effect of International Treaties by the European Court of Justice: Implications for International Environmental Law in the European Union' (2011) 60 International & Comparative Law Quarterly 737.
21 Ibid.
22 *Kupferberg* case (n 5) [12].
23 F Martines, 'Direct Effect of International Agreements of the European Union' (2014) 25 European Journal of International Law 129, 133.
24 Case C-213/03 *Pêcheurs de l'étang de Berre v EDF*, ECLI:EU:C:2004:464, [2004] ECR I-7357.
25 Ibid. [36].
26 *Commission v France* (n 9).
27 Ibid. [26].
28 J Wouters, A Nollkaemper and E de Wet (eds.), *The Europeanisation of International Law: The Status of International Law in the EU and its Member States* (T.M.C. Asser Press 2008).
29 Ziegler 'Beyond Pluralism and Autonomy' (n 1) 672.
30 Ibid.
31 Directive 2003/35 of the European Parliament and of the Council of 26 May 2003 providing for public participation in respect of the drawing up of certain plans and programmes relating to the environment. This Directive implemented the Aarhus Convention and accordingly amended with regard to public participation and access to justice Council Directives 85/337/EEC on environmental impact assessment and 96/61/EC integrated pollution prevention and control.

32 Case C-530/11 *Commission v UK*, ECLI:EU:C:2014:67.
33 Case C-260/11 *Edward and Pallikaropoulos v Environment Agency* ECLI:EU:C:2013:221.
34 Martines (n 23) 141.
35 See C-366/10 *ATAA and Others v Secretary of State for Energy and Climate Change* ('*ATAA*') [2011] I-13755 [53–54].
36 Case C-308/06 *International Association of Independent Tanker Owners et al. v Secretary of State for Transport* ECLI:EU:C:2008:312 ('*Intertanko*').
37 OJ 2005 L 255.
38 *Intertanko* [65].
39 Ibid. [64].
40 *ATAA* case (n 35).
41 OJ 2009 L8.
42 *ATAA* case (n 35) [74–76].
43 See further at nn 53–55.
44 Joined Cases C-402/05 P and C-415/05 P *Yassin Abdullah Kadi and Al Barakaat International Foundation v Council of the European Union and Commission of the European Communities* ECR [2008] I-6351, ECLI:EU:C:2008:461.
45 R Pavoni, 'Controversial Aspects of the Interaction between International and EU Law in Environmental Matters: Direct Effect and Member States' Unilateral Measures' in E Morgera (ed.), *The External Environmental Policy of the European Union* (CUP 2012) 350.
46 Case C-377/98 *Kingdom of the Netherlands v European Parliament and Council* (Biotech case).
47 Regulation (EC) No 261/2001, OJ 2004 L46.
48 Case C-344/04 *IATA and ELFTA v Department of Transport* ECLI:EU:C:2004:598 [39].
49 Ziegler 'Beyond Pluralism and Autonomy' (n 1) 681 ff; Pavoni (n 45).
50 Pavoni (n 45) 348–349.
51 Martines (n 23). For a slightly different opinion on the appropriateness of the requirement of direct effect also in relation to legality challenges, see P Eeckhout, 'Case C-308/06, The Queen on the Application of Intertanko and Others v Secretary of State for Transport' (2009) 46 Common Market Law Review 2041, 2054.
52 M Cremona, 'External Relations and External Competence of the European Union: The Emergence of an Integrated Policy' in P. Craig and G. De Burca (eds.), *The Evolution of EU Law* (2nd ed., OUP 2011) 242.
53 See in particular the cases of *Intertanko* and *ATAA*.
54 In this sense, see Pavoni 356.
55 Joined Cases C-401/12 P and C-403/12 P, 13 January 2015, *Vereniging Milieudefensie and Stichting Stop Luchtverontreiniging Utrecht v Council of the European Union, European Parliament and European Commission* ECLI:EU:C:2015:4.
56 Case C-61/94 *Commission v Germany*, ECLI:EU:C:1996:313.
57 *Brown Bear* case (n 10) [45].
58 Ibid. [50].
59 International Convention for the Prevention of Pollution from Ships (London 2 November 1973, entered into force 2 October 1983), supplemented by the Protocol of 17 February 1978 (MARPOL 73/78), 2 ILM 1319 (1973).
60 *Intertanko* [52].
61 Ibid.
62 Opinion of Advocate General (AG) Kokott in Case C-188/07 *Commune de Mesquer v Total France SA and Total International Ltd* ECLI:EU:C:2008:174 [99].
63 The AG's opinion was quite elaborated on this point, considering different hypotheses whereby the convention could be held to set aside the Directive's conflicting provisions.
64 Ibid. [101].
65 Case C-15/17 *Bosphorus Queen Shipping Ltd Corp v Rajavartiolaitos* ECLI:EU:C:2018:557.

66 Ibid. [45].
67 Ibid. [46].
68 Ibid.
69 G Betlem, 'The Doctrine of Consistent Interpretation: Managing Legal Uncertainty' (2002) 22 Oxford Journal of Legal Studies 397.
70 Case C-356/12 *Wolfgang Glatzel v Freistaat Bayern*, ECLI:EU:C:2014:350 [71].
71 J Klabbers, 'The Validity of EU Norms Conflicting with International Obligations' in E Cannizzaro, P Palchetti and RA Wessel (eds.), *International Law as Law of the European Union* (Brill 2011).
72 Ibid. 131.
73 N Lavranos, 'Protecting European Law from International Law' (2010) 15 European Foreign Affairs Review 265.
74 Klabbers (n 71). Cfr however K. Ziegler 'Beyond Pluralism and Autonomy' (n 1) 683, who noted that in Opinion 2/13 concerning the EU accession to the European Convention on Human Rights, the CJEU 'seemed to have abandoned what might have been considered a still defensible rationale of restricting the openness of EU law towards international law: to uphold important values of the EU legal order' and seems instead 'motivated by more parochial concerns, as it demonstrates the extent of the CJEU's reluctance to subject EU law and itself to the jurisdiction of the European Court of Human Rights'.
75 See AG Opinion in *Intertanko*, especially para 90.
76 Ibid. [87] (referring to the objectives of Marpol) and [90] (referring to the objectives of UNCLOS).
77 Ibid. [89–90].
78 Ibid. [108].
79 Ibid. [78].
80 Cour de Cassation, Chambre Criminelle, 25 September 2012, Arret No 34349.
81 See MP Camproux-Duffrene and D Guihal, Cour de cassation, Chambre criminelle, 25 Septembre 2012, SA Total et a., n° 3439, Case-note (2013) 3 *Revue Juridique de l'Environnement* 457.
82 (n 10).
83 Ibid. [46].
84 [49].
85 [47].
86 Ibid [51].
87 F Casolari, 'Giving Indirect Effect to International Law within the EU legal Order: The Doctrine of Consistent Interpretation' in E Cannizzaro, P Palchetti and RA Wessel (eds.), *International Law as Law of the European Union* (Brill 2012) 407.
88 For an analysis on how the court had already established a link between consistent interpretation and effective judicial protection in its case-law concerning the relationship between EU secondary legislation and domestic law, see M Klamert, *The Principle of Loyalty in EU Law* (Oxford University Press 2014) 133–134.
89 See in this sense also K Lenaerts and JA Gutierrez-Fons, 'To Say What the Law of the EU Is: Methods of Interpretation and the European Court of Justice', *EUI Working Papers*, AEL 2013/9, 35.
90 L Squintani and S Kalisvaart, 'Report on Judicial Cooperation in Follow-Up Judgements in Environmental Matters' – EU Forum of Judges for the Environment < https://www.eufje.org/images/docConf/visio2021/Report_based_on_EUFJE_questionnaires_on_follow-up_judgments_-_Definitive_06-11-2021.pdf>; see also ACA-Europe, 'Follow-Up of Preliminary Rulings' – Overview from mid-September to December 2018 < https://www.aca-europe.eu/flash/suivi/en/Flash-suivi-1-2019_En.pdf> accessed March 2023.
91 Case C-243/15 *Lesoochranárske zoskupenie VLK v Obvodný úrad Trenčín* ECLI:EU:C:2016:838.

92 M van Wolferen, 'Case C-243/15 Lesoochranárske zoskupenie VLK v Obvodný úrad Trenčín' (2017) 14 Journal for European Environmental & Planning Law 136.
93 Ibid.
94 Case 188/07 *Commune de Mesquer v Total France SA and Total International Ltd* [2008] ERC I-4501 ('*Commune de Mesquer*').
95 Ibid. [84].
96 J Adshed, 'The Application and Development of the Polluter-Pays Principle across Jurisdictions in Liability for Marine Oil Pollution: The Tales of the "Erika" and the "Prestige"' (2018) 30 Journal of Environmental Law 425.
97 Opinion of AG Kokott in Case C-188/07, 13 March 2008, ECLI:EU:C:2008:174 [135].
98 *Commune de Mesquer* case (n 94) [78] [emphasis added].
99 Ibid. [72].
100 Ibid. [82].
101 Casolari (n 87) 412.
102 N de Sadeleer, 'Liability for Oil Pollution Damage Versus Liability for Waste Management: The Polluter Pays Principles at the Rescue of the Victims' (2009) 21 Journal of Environmental Law 2.
103 V Rebeyrol, 'The Erika Case: An Incitement to Rewrite the CLC' (2013) European Energy and Environmental Law Review 33, 37.
104 *Commune de Mesquer* case [77] and [82].
105 Rebeyrol (n 103).
106 *Commune de Mesquer* case [87–88].
107 BIO Intelligence Service (2014), 'ELD Effectiveness: Scope and Exceptions, Final Report Prepared for European Commission—DG Environment', 169.
108 Ibid.
109 M Jacobbson, 'Perspective of the Global Compensation Regimes; the Relationship between EU Legislation and Maritime Liability Conventions' (2012) 4 European Journal of Commercial Contract Law 63, 70.
110 Article V(2) CLC.
111 Spanish Supreme Court, Criminal section, 14 January 2016 no. 865/2015.
112 Interestingly, the Bunker Liability Convention does not provide for similar exclusion.
113 See CA Paris, March 30, 2010, case no 08–02278, 422. See also Rebeyrol (n 103) 35.
114 See IOPC Fund, IOPC/APR16/3/2, 30 March 2016.
115 G Caballero and D Soto-Onate, 'Environmental Crime and Judicial Rectification of the Prestige Oil Spill: The Polluter Pays' (2017) 84 Marine Policy 213.
116 With respect to the Spanish Supreme Court decision in the Prestige case, see A Betancor Rodríguez, *Responsabilidad y Aseguramiento por Danos Ambientales. El Caso Prestige* (Agencia Estatal Boletín Oficial del Estado 2018).

Conclusions

1. An evolving scenario

The need to find concrete and effective responses to the problem of environmental damage caused during the operation of hazardous, yet lawful, economic and industrial activities led to the development of a plethora of legal instruments to provide redress to victims of environmental harm and prompted the emergence of different approaches to the question of environmental liability. The analysis carried out in this work demonstrated how the legal landscape in the field of liability and remedies for environmental harm has been gradually evolving. The growing importance of environmental protection has led to the integration of environmental concerns into liability systems, prompting both a re-elaboration and revision in an environmental perspective of the functions and objectives traditionally attributed to liability, and an adjustment of the classic structures of liability to the new realities. Whilst the earliest applications of liability rules to address the harmful consequences of environmental pollution have focused on their reparative and corrective function, there is now a better understanding of the regulatory function that liability can perform, both as a complement to regulation and as an integral part of environmental protection strategies. This has in turn led to a better appreciation of the relationship of continuity between prevention and risk management, one the one hand, and between liability and reparation, on the other.

At the same time, a discernible feature that characterises recent developments in this field is the emergence of new approaches to the question of liability and reparation for environmental harm, which are better tailored to the specificities of environmental damage. Accordingly, the classic private law remedies (such as tort law and civil liability), which for a long time represented the main instruments to implement environmental liability, now tend to coexist with and be complemented by administrative law schemes of liability and by other mechanisms of redress, such as the creation of funds and the promotion of voluntary frameworks of environmental responsibility and accountability.

Nevertheless, despite the enhanced and growing interest in the topic both at an academic level and in the policy-making context, the establishment of appropriate and effective mechanisms of redress for environmental harm still remains a largely unresolved item on the international law-making agenda. This question has

DOI: 10.4324/9781315676708-12

however begun to find some more concrete responses in certain domestic legal systems and within the EU, both through the elaboration of specific remedies for damage to natural resources and, more recently, through the development of legislative proposals aimed at improving access to justice for the victims of corporate environmentally harmful activities.

Against this backdrop of legal developments and academic discussions, this book has sought to develop a response to the allegedly underdeveloped status of international law in the field of environmental liability by exploring whether a more fruitful approach to strengthening the remedies for environmental damage, particularly when such damage assumes a transboundary or transnational dimension, can be found by examining the interactions of different regulatory frameworks in a multilevel context and by identifying ways to maximise potential synergies arising from such interactions. This broad aim inspired the research underlying this book and informed its contents and structure.

This concluding chapter summarises and presents the findings of this research. Following the scope and objectives of the book, as set out in the introduction, this chapter articulates the findings according to the two dimensions of interaction which have been explored in this volume. First, it will draw some conclusions from the comparative analysis of the EU law and international law in the field of environmental liability carried out in Parts I and II of the book and provide some reflections on the extent to which there are patterns of convergence between developments in the two legal systems that may potentially contribute to forge a consensus on a set of common principles in the field of environmental liability at the global level. Second, this chapter will draw conclusions from the analysis of the relationship and interplay between the EU and international law, providing some reflections on the extent to which EU action and interaction with international law developments may contribute to further strengthen the range of remedies available for victims of environmental damage.

2. General trends and emerging principles

Parts I and II of this book have each aimed to offer an extensive examination of the existing legal frameworks and relevant developments in the field of environmental liability within, respectively, international law and the European Union. While the relevant chapters had in part an informative purpose, they also offered a comparative examination of the relevant legal developments taking place in the EU and at the international law level. In so doing, the analysis applied the comparative method to the multilevel context of the relationship between EU and international law with a view to ascertain whether it is possible to discern some emerging common trends among the various legal responses to the problem of liability and reparation for environmental harm. While traditionally legal comparative analysis has been conducted horizontally (i.e. among legal systems at the national level), there is a growing interest in cross-echelon comparisons occurring vertically among legal systems not belonging to the same level or echelon.[1] Within the latter methods of comparison, scholars have further distinguished between top-down vertical comparison, which occurs typically in the context of the 'internalization of international norms' by domestic legal orders, and bottom-up vertical comparison, which 'refers to the transposition of legal concepts, or the ideas behind them, from national to the international level'.[2] This type of comparison has become particularly interesting in the environmental field, stimulating further enquiry into 'how, why and when these trans-echelon transplantations occur'.[3]

Scholars have also increasingly advocated the need to rethink the application of the comparative legal method to take into account laws and legal developments which sit beyond the traditional realm of the 'municipal law of nation states', which was classically the remit and main scope of comparative legal analysis, to include new transnational law developments beyond the State,[4] including forms of regulation and normative developments put forward by non-state actors (private or public) and forms of soft law. Challenges to traditional approaches to comparative analysis also come from the transformative impact exerted on law and legal processes (and on society and the economy more generally) by globalisation.[5] By fostering increasing interconnections between actors, jurisdictions, and legal systems, globalisation has led to a 'relativization of jurisdictional boundaries as markers of rule-generating and rule-administering spaces',[6] bringing scholars to suggest that comparative law may need to 'abandon its state-oriented view of law' to 'embrace a pluralist and socio-legal view'.[7] Indeed, comparative law and methods can arguably usefully complement and enhance the transnational and global law research agenda by enabling an investigation into whether and to what extent the interconnections favoured by globalisation are promoting mechanisms of convergence or of divergences among legal systems and among legal responses to societal problems,[8] which (especially in the case of converging trend) may lead to identify the emergence of common principles or approaches to legal issues. As noted in the introduction, scholars tend to identify the distinctive features of global law in its forward-looking and aspirational qualities or, to express it in the words of Neil Walker, in its 'practical endorsement of, or commitment to the universal or otherwise global in general warrant of some laws or dimensions of law'.[9] It is suggested that those features would make a global (environmental) law approach, in combination with a comparative method and a transnational approach to legal analysis, particularly apt to capture the scope and aim of this book's research, particularly insofar as it seeks to explore the normative implications of the interconnections and substantive interactions between different legal frameworks across different levels of regulation and governance.

With specific respect to the analysis of legal developments in the field of environmental liability, the application of the comparative method in combination with the conceptual approaches offered by transnational and global environmental law has enabled identifying some important trends of convergence across the various relevant legal frameworks in the EU and in international law. These trends reflect the normative trajectory of the law of environmental liability over the past decades, suggesting an emerging consensus around a few general principles.

First of all, one of the distinctive features of more recent developments in the law of environmental liability in EU law and in international law is the widened notion of environmental damage to encompass, alongside traditional forms of damage to persons and property, the ecological dimension of environmental harm. Recent environmental liability instruments tend to use terms like 'ecological damage', 'natural resources damage' or in some cases 'environmental damage' to indicate the inclusion of harm to the environment *per se* in the scope of reparation, although the type of remedies and the extent of compensation vary across the different regimes. The examination of several international environmental liability agreements in Chapter 3 of this book demonstrated the existence of a clear consensus at the international level on the inclusion of 'damage to the environment' within the scope of compensable damage, while the analysis of recent developments in the field of the international law of State responsibility, in Chapter 1, illustrated how the recognition of natural resources damage has now penetrated the realm of the customary rules on State responsibility.

The analysis of the various environmental liability regimes also revealed how this 're-conceptualisation' of environmental damage goes hand in hand with the progressive recognition of the environment and of natural resources as deserving legal protection in themselves and as a self-standing value, independently from their utility to humans. This idea emerges clearly from the ELD, as well as in some of the more recent international environmental liability instruments addressing biodiversity damage and damage to the Antarctic environment. A particularly interesting application of this approach can be found in the idea of 'natural resources services'. For instance, under the ELD the existence of an 'environmental damage' relevant to trigger the application of the liability regime is ascertained also on the basis of the adverse effects impacting 'both the State of a natural resource and the beneficial *functions performed by the natural resource for both other natural resources* and the public'.[10] In that context, the term 'natural resources services' indicates the functions that natural resources provide not only to the public, but also to each other, thereby acknowledging that human economic activities can have adverse effects also on the 'interdependencies and dynamic relationships within and between natural resources' and on the services that they perform.[11] The inclusion of natural resources services in the ELD is significant as it signals a step towards adopting a more eco-centric approach to environmental harm, that is, an approach that does not only value the utility that the environment and natural resources provide to humans but also to other species and ecosystems.[12] In fact, while other liability instruments contain references to the idea of services and goods provided by the environment and by natural resources,[13] they often leave unclear whether they include in the definition also services provided to other natural resources.

Besides specific question regarding the scope of compensable damage and the definition of environmental damage, the legal recognition of ecological damage and its inclusion in the scope of application of environmental liability regimes has also prompted discussions in Europe and at the international level regarding the development of specific remedies for this type of damage and specific approaches to its valuation and assessment. On this point, the analysis of the remedial measures available under the ELD and the similarities with methods for damage assessment and valuation under US statutes revealed interesting instances of normative borrowing and diffusion in a multilevel context. Similarly, the recognition of natural resources damage in the work of the UNCC and more recently in the case-law of the ICJ[14] pointed out the potential of borrowing and mutual learning across domestic, regional and international law with respect to the methodology for natural resource damage evaluation.

Furthermore, there are new perspectives to the question of liability and reparation for environmental harm which are emerging in connection with the growing environmental awareness and the acknowledgment of natural resources' intrinsic value. The analysis in Parts I and II of this book evidenced how, alongside their classic function as an almost ad hoc and *ex post* legal tool to provide compensation to private victims of environmental pollution, liability rules are increasingly integrated into environmental protection strategies both as a mechanism to ensure the restoration of impaired natural resources and as a complementary tool in the efforts to promote compliance with and enforce environmental standards. In this perspective, the regulation of liability becomes closely linked conceptually with the idea of prevention. The adoption of the EU ELD is a plain example of this conceptual and regulatory trend. The ELD envisages a new model of environmental liability, which seeks to capture the collective and public nature of the environment as a common good. Whilst it borrows some of the primary features from more traditional regimes of civil liability for environmental damage—such as the causation requirements and the endeavour to harmonise strict liability for harm caused by hazardous activities—the ELD also places greater emphasis on the preventive dimension of liability, and overall it aims at setting up a more sophisticated regime that combines in a single framework the twin goals of prevention and restoration. It was noted (Chapter 4) that a similar trend towards the integration of liability rules as a central component of environmental protection regimes is also discernible at the international law level, particularly through the adoption of liability protocols and annexes to MEAs.

The comparative analysis further shows how there is a two-fold dimension of the relationship between environmental liability and prevention, which concerns not only the aims and objectives assigned to liability rules, but also its impact on the structure of liability regimes through the inclusion of specific duties of '*ex post* prevention' and response action, which are due to operate after the potentially harmful event and aimed at mitigating and containing further damage or even avoiding irreversible damage. While the scope and legal nature of those preventive duties vary across the various regimes, they overall point to a line of functional and conceptual continuity between liability and prevention. This trend is particularly interesting at the international law level. Both international conventions and customary international law developments signal the emergence of a series of duties of prompt response action, cooperation and emergency assistance that apply in the immediate aftermath of environmental damage or in the imminent threat of damage, and which therefore sits in-between prevention and reparation. It is suggested here that, at least from the point of view of State responsibility, these duties of *ex post* prevention challenge somehow the classic distinction between primary and secondary rules, by blurring the line of demarcation between primary duties of harm prevention and secondary obligations of liability and reparation.

Overall, the interface between international law and EU law with respect to the legal tools available to obtain reparation for environmental damage, rather than revealing contradictions and incoherencies, reveals a path of convergence and a common effort at finding effective solutions to the problem of environmental damage. Seen in this perspective, certain features, such as the progressive broadening of liability to encompass specific duties of prevention and minimisation of environmental damage; the coexistence of different approaches and regimes of liability, touching upon the private law and the public law aspects of the damage; and the reconceptualisation of liability in a regulatory perspective as a tool to promote prevention and compliance with environmental standards, can all be regarded as different manifestations of this common effort.

Finally, when examined from a global and integrated perspective, which brings together under a unitary lens the different rules and legal mechanisms on environmental liability and reparation available at the international level and in the EU, it also becomes apparent how there is an intrinsically and distinctive 'layered' structure that characterises the law of environmental liability globally. The various layers reflect the different dimensions of this field of law. Environmental liability operates through different levels of regulation and governance (i.e. domestic, EU, international) at which environmental liability regimes and/or mechanisms for reparation of environmental harm have been adopted and implemented. It potentially involves different liable actors, be these the State, private economic operators, or a combination of both. Finally, there are layers of liability which correspond to the different approaches or systems of attributing responsibility, namely whether through classic rules of tort liability under private law, administrative regimes, or even criminal law (although developments concerning criminal liability for environmental harm were not covered in this book). One of the main features emerging from the analysis carried out in this book is indeed the coexistence and potential complementarity between the classic rules of civil liability and the new administrative type of approaches to environmental liability in providing responses to environmental damage.

With these findings and considerations in mind, the next question that this book sought to address concerns the relationship between the different layers and legal frameworks of environmental liability and, namely, the extent to which the coexistence and interaction of different liability regimes may be harnessed effectively to provide more effective responses to environmental harm. The book addressed this question by examining the multilevel interaction between EU and international law. It is to the findings of this enquiry that we now turn.

3. Environmental harms and the relationship between EU and international law: towards mutual supportiveness?

One of the main objectives underlying the research leading to this book has been to try and ascertain whether and to what extent the scarce progress towards the definition of a harmonised set of legally binding rules on liability and reparation for environmental harm can be somehow compensated by a better understanding of the interaction between different liability regimes and legal frameworks in a multilevel context. With this perspective in mind, the book has embarked on a multilevel analysis of the relationship between EU law and international law. In summarising here the main findings of this enquiry, it is useful to refer to the concept or idea of 'mutual supportiveness' as a conceptual frame to examine and interpret the relationship between EU and international law in this context. The concept, or principle, of mutual supportiveness has been used in international law scholarship mainly in two respects. It has been used notably in the ILC Report on the fragmentation of international law[15] which mentions briefly mutual supportiveness as a 'technique' to curb potential normative conflicts between different regimes by reading the relevant provisions in the light of 'their contribution to some generally shared—"systemic"—objective'.[16] In this context, mutual supportiveness becomes an interpretative principle or technique to be used by those vested to interpret or apply the law when dealing with potential conflicts between different norms and legal obligations, and as a means to overcome the challenges, or even to appease the anxieties, raised by the phenomenon of the fragmentation of international law. In the relationship between different international legal regimes, mutual supportiveness has therefore often been invoked in the context of efforts to reconcile different potentially competing policy objectives coexisting across distinct legal regimes (i.e. trade and environment coming across the WTO and CBD for example) or within a single regime.[17]

It was further noted that the legal principle of mutual supportiveness also has a law-making dimension in that it operates not only at the level of interpretation, implementation and application of the legal rules, by demanding an approach that enhances the complementarity and synergies between the different regimes and legal framework, but it is also relevant *ex ante*, during the formation of legal regimes by guiding law-making.[18] Pavoni sees this law-making dimension of mutual supportiveness in a quite progressive fashion in that it would require 'a proactive attitude on the part of the States according to which they are bound to promote and support negotiations aimed at amending agreements which cannot otherwise be reconciled with other regimes, protecting essential values of the international community'. Thus, here mutual supportiveness would represent an expression of the general international law principle of good faith and would apply both during the negotiation and formation of new international regimes and as a guiding principle for negotiating amendments and adjustments thereof when there is a potential conflict of rules with other treaty frameworks in order to address and 'resolve conflicts *before* they arise'.[19] In any event, both when it operates as an interpretative technique and when it applies at the law-making level during the formation of new regimes or the amendment of an existing one, the principle of mutual supportiveness requires an approach that seeks to achieve coordination and complementarity among different regimes and to promote a synergic, non-hierarchical application of the normative framework with a view to protect the fundamental values and interests of the international community.

While the ILC Report deals specifically with horizontal instances of fragmentation (i.e. between different international law regimes), and although legal references and scholarly discussions on mutual supportiveness have normally been limited to the level of international law (typically, by examining the normative relevance of this principle in promoting reconciliation and complementarity between competing and potentially conflicting treaty regimes), the idea of mutual supportiveness may also be relevant in a multilevel context, given the increasing interconnections and interactions of international law with domestic and supranational/EU law. Therefore, as an interpretative principle, mutual supportiveness may also be relevant and useful in the analysis of the multilevel relationship between EU and international law.[20] From an EU law perspective, the idea of a harmonious application of EU and international law finds one of its expressions in the well-established principle of consistent interpretation. However, it is submitted that an interpretative technique inspired by mutual supportiveness goes beyond the endeavour of consistent interpretation, in that it is not limited to reading the EU secondary rule in the light of the allegedly superior norm of international law, but it rather purports a reading which seeks to identify and enhance the synergies between the two legal frameworks with a view to advance a common shared objective in relation to the protection of the environment.

In this perspective, mutual supportiveness can provide an interesting analytical lens by acting as an ideal or an aspirational standard against which to examine and assess the relationship between the EU and international law in the field of environmental liability. By adopting this approach in reviewing the findings of the analysis of the interplay between EU and international law carried out in Chapters 6 and 7 of this book, the following conclusions can be drawn. First, with respect to the contribution of the EU to the development of international law in the field of environmental liability, Chapter 6 identified some interesting and positive synergies. It was noted that the EU involvement as a contracting party in international environmental agreements might have in many instances a positive effect in promoting Member States' ratification of the relevant treaty, with positive implications on the treaty's prospects of entering into force. The analysis has further shown how the EU involvement of international liability treaties could in some cases have the positive impact of proposing novel solutions which allow to resolve deadlocks and facilitate achieving consensus. Yet, it was also noted that the scope for synergies and mutual support is maximised when there is an alignment of the EU interest with that pursued by the international regime. Moreover, it was suggested that from an EU perspective, concerns for protection and preservation of the EU interest in the integrity, effectiveness and uniformity of EU law are often treated as paramount in the relationship of the EU with the international legal order, even when they lead to outcomes which are not fully in line with the needs of environmental protection as a common and fundamental value of the international community as a whole. On the other hand, the soft normative power of the EU in advancing developments at the international law level was discussed in the second and third part of the book, with respect to both the ELD and how it represented a model for the definition of international environmental liability regimes focused on damage to natural resources and to the environment, and in relation to current proposals on corporate due diligence and environmental liability.

A similar set of remarks stems from the analysis of the relationship between EU and international law in Chapter 7. Having examined the role and status of international law within the EU legal order, the analysis demonstrated how the ratification by the EU of an international agreement and the consequent incorporation of the international provisions in the EU legal order and their assimilation to EU law may play an important role in enhancing the effectiveness of the relevant international norms. In that respect, the analysis of relevant case-law of the CJEU illustrated the scope for positive and synergic interactions between EU law and international norms and the potential for interpretative approaches that go beyond consistent interpretation to achieve coordination and complementarity between the different norms and legal frameworks to enhance the achievement of environmental protection standards and objectives.

4. Closing remarks

Environmental degradation is one of the major challenges that the international community is facing nowadays. An effective response to the problem requires concerted and coordinated solutions at the national, regional (EU) and international levels. It also requires the use in a coherent and coordinated fashion of legal and policy instruments, so as to maximise the achievement of the common objective of environmental protection and the effectiveness of the responses to environmental harm.

This book has sought to apply this understanding to the analysis of the relationship between EU and international law in the field of environmental liability, with a view to explore synergies and elements of complementarity emerging from the coexistence and interaction of the different legal frameworks and liability regimes. Moreover, given the difficulties to develop harmonised and legally binding frameworks in the field of liability and reparation for environmental harm at the international level, this book also sought, in part, to offer a response to the underdeveloped status of international law in this context by ascertaining whether and to what extent progress in the definition of legal responses to environmental harm may be achieved at the global level through the multilevel interaction of different legal systems and regulatory frameworks. In both respects, the analysis carried out in this book reveals two levels on which these synergic relationships can take place. First, at the normative and conceptual level, it (especially Chapters 2 to 5) reveals, through the comparative analysis of relevant developments in international and in EU law, a two-way trajectory of convergence and of reciprocal influence on the definition of certain structural and conceptual elements of an environmental liability law framework, thereby contributing to shape an emerging consensus around main concepts. It also illustrates how this process involves the interaction between both formal (i.e. positive law) and informal types of law-making and the participation of a different type of actors, including States but also non-state actors, learned societies as well as judges when applying and interpreting the law.[21]

Second, it (especially Chapters 6 and 7, but in part also Chapter 5) has revealed the existence of synergic interactions at the more practical level of law-making and application of the law.

Yet, the analysis has also revealed elements of inconsistency and of lack of coordination in the interplay between EU and international law, or simply instances where the potential for a fully synergic relationship maximising the responses to environmental harm was not properly captured. These findings then call for a future research agenda, which would further investigate from an integrated perspective the relationship between different legal frameworks in the field of liability and responsibility for environmental harms with a view to devising and proposing appropriate approaches to achieve better coordination and to maximise the effectiveness of the legal responses to environmental damage.

Such an 'integrated' approach[22] to the analysis of environmental liability is further warranted in the light of the multifaceted and cross-cutting nature of environmental issues, which means that questions concerning liability and reparation for environmental harm can be addressed through different regimes and in different normative contexts. The growing human rights jurisprudence addressing claims for environmental pollution and the environmental dimension of some recent investment arbitral awards are but remarkable examples of the increasing penetration of environmental concerns into other branches of international law. There is therefore also scope to expand the framework of the analysis beyond the examination of the multilevel relationship between EU and international environmental law liability regime to encompass other instances and venues in which questions of environmental harm are negotiated and addressed.

Notes

1 A Momirov and A Naudé Fourie, 'Vertical Comparative Law Methods: Tools for Conceptualising the International Rule of Law' (2009) 3 Erasmus Law Review 291, 295.
2 Ibid. 296.
3 JB Wiener, 'Something Borrowed for Something Blue: Legal Transplants and the Evolution of Global Environmental Law' (2001) 27 Ecology Law Quarterly 1295, 1297.
4 In this sense, R Scarciglia, 'Diritto Globale e Metodologia Comparativa: Verso un Approccio Verticale?' (2015) 17 Diritto Pubblico Comparato ed Europeo 1011; M Siems, *Comparative Law* (3rd ed., OUP 2022) 350 ff.
5 Siems (n 4) 349.
6 P Zumbansen, 'Transnational Comparison: Theory and Practice of Comparative Law as a Critique of Global Governance' (2012) Comparative Research in Law & Political Economy. Research Paper No 1/2012 <https://digitalcommons.osgoode.yorku.ca/cgi/viewcontent.cgi?article=1003&context=clpe> accessed 22 December 2023, 4.
7 Siems (n 4) 349, citing J Husa, *A New Introduction to Comparative Law* (Hart 2015) 55; R Michaels, 'Transnationalising Comparative Law' (2016) 23 Maastricht Journal of European and Comparative law 352.
8 Scarciglia (n 4).
9 N Walker, *Intimations of Global Law* (CUP 2014) 11–14.
10 European Commission, 'Guidelines providing a common understanding of the term "environmental damage" as defined in Article 2 of Directive 2004/35/EC on environmental liability with regard to the prevention and remedying of environmental damage', C(2021) 1860 final, 14.

11 Ibid.
12 H Washington and others, 'Why Ecocentrism Is the Key Pathway to Sustainability' (2017) 1 The Ecological Citizen 35.
13 Cfr ELD with the Nagoya-Kuala Lumpur Liability Protocol, Article 2(3)(c).
14 See Chapter 1.
15 Report of the Study Group of the International Law Commission finalized by M. Koskenniemi (2006) 'Fragmentation of International Law: Difficulties Arising from the Diversification and Expansion of International Law', UN Doc A/CN.4/L 682, 207, para 412.
16 L Boisson de Chazournes and MM Mbengue, 'A Footnote as a Principle. Mutual Supportiveness and Its Relevance in an Era of Fragmentation' in HP Hestermeyer et al. (eds.), *Coexistence, Cooperation and Solidarity—Liber Amicorum Rudiger Wolfrulm*, Vol II (Springer 2011) 1615.
17 See E. Lydgate, 'Sustainable Development in the WTO: From Mutual Supportiveness to Balancing' (2012) 11 World Trade Review 621, 622, who however seems to use the idea of mutual supportiveness with a more limited or at least neutral connotation as somehow a concept which does not necessarily allow giving priority to environmental concerns: 'MS suggests a non-intrusive role for the concept with regard to the WTO mandate of trade liberalization'.
18 R Pavoni, 'Mutual Supportiveness as a Principle of Interpretation and Law-Making: A Watershed for the 'WTO-and-Competing-Regimes' Debate? (2010) 21 European Journal of International Law 649.
19 Ibid. 668.
20 E Morgera, 'Ambition, Complexity, and Legitimacy of Pursuing Mutual Supportiveness Through the EU's External Environmental Action' in B Van Vooren, S Blockmans and J Wouters (eds.), *The EU's Role in Global Governance: The Legal Dimension* (CUP 2013).
21 This last point is discussed especially in Chapter 6 when examining the role of courts when dealing with concepts of duty of care and corporate liability in transnational tort litigation.
22 Expression borrowed from M Faure and S Ying (eds.), *China and International Liability: Legal Remedies for Transboundary Pollution* (Edward Elgar 2008) 1–2.

Bibliography

Abraham KS, 'The Relation between Civil Liability and Environmental Regulation: An Analytical Overview' (2002) 41 Washburn Law Journal 379.

Adshead J, 'The Application and Development of the Polluter-Pays Principle across Jurisdictions in Liability for Marine Oil Pollution: The Tales of the "Erika" and the "Prestige"' (2018) 30 Journal of Environmental Law 425.

Akehurst MB, 'International Liability for Injurious Consequences Arising Out of Acts Not Prohibited by International Law' (1985) Netherlands Yearbook of International Law 3.

Alpa G, 'Interessi Diffusi: Una Categoria Rivisitata' (2014) 2 Economia e Diritto del Terziario 167.

Aragão A, 'Les intérêts diffus, instruments pour la justice et la démocratie environnementale' (2015) Vertig0—La revue électronique en sciences de l'environnement—Hors-série 22 <www.journals.openedition.org/vertigo>.

Aragão A and Carvalho AC, 'Taking Access to Justice Seriously: Diffuse Interests and Actio Popularis. Why Not?' (2017) ELNI Review 2.

Azoulai L, 'The Acquis of the European Union and International Organisations' (2005) European Law Journal 196.

Barboza J, *The Environment, Risk and Liability in International Law* (Martinus Nijhoff Publishers 2011).

Baughen S, 'Environmental Damage and UK Offshore Operations: Uncertain Liabilities in Deep Waters' (2016) 28 Journal of Environmental Law 497.

Baxi U, 'Human Rights Responsibility of Multinational Corporations, Political Ecology of Injustice: Learning from Bhopal Thirty Plus?' (2016) 1 Business Human Rights Journal 21.

Bellamy J, 'Civil Liability for Nuclear Damage in Countries Developing Nuclear New Build Programmes', (2019) 12 Journal of World Energy Law and Business 108.

Bergkamp L, 'The Environmental Liability Directive and Liability of Parent Companies for Damage Caused by their Subsidiaries (Enterprise Liability)' (2016) 13 European Company Law 183.

Berkes A, 'Extraterritorial Responsibility of the Home States for MNCs Violations of Human Rights' in Y Radi (ed.), *Research Handbook on Human Rights and Investment* (Edward Elgar 2018).

Betancor Rodríguez A, *Responsabilidad y Aseguramiento por Danos Ambientales. El Caso Prestige* (Agencia Estatal Boletín Oficial del Estado, 2018).

Betlem G, 'Standing for Ecosystems—Going Dutch' (1995) 54 Cambridge Law Journal 153.

Betlem G, 'The Doctrine of Consistent Interpretation: Managing Legal Uncertainty' (2002) 22 Oxford Journal of Legal Studies 397.

Betlem G, 'Scope and Defences of the 2004 Environmental Liability Directive: Who Is Liable for What? (2005) 6 ERA Forum 376.

Betlem G and Faure M, 'Environmental Toxic Torts in Europe—Some Trends in Recovery of Soil Clean-Up Costs and Damages for Personal Injury in Belgium, England, Germany and the Netherlands' (1998) 10 Georgetown International Environmental Law Review 855.

Beyerlin U, 'Different Types of Norms in International Environmental Law: Policies, Principles and Rules' in D Bodansky, J Brunnée and E Hey (eds.), *The Oxford Handbook of International Environmental Law* (OUP 2012).

Bianchi A, 'The Harmonization of Laws on Liability for Environmental Damage in Europe: An Italian Perspective' (1994) 6 Journal of Environmental law 21.

Bianchi A, 'Harm to the Environment in Italian Practice: The Interaction of International Law and Domestic Law' in P Wetterstein (ed.), *Harm to the Environment: The Right to Compensation and the Assessment of Damages* (Clarendon Press 1997).

BIO Intelligence Service, 'Implementation Challenges and Obstacles of the Environmental Liability Directive' (2013), Final Report Prepared for European Commission—DG Environment.

BIO Intelligence Service, 'ELD Effectiveness: Scope and Exceptions' (2014), Final Report prepared for European Commission—DG Environment.

Bocken H, 'Developments with Respect to Compensation for Damage Caused by Pollution' in BS Markesinis (ed.), *The Gradual Convergence; Foreign Ideas, Foreign Influences, and English Law on the Eve of the 21st Century* (Clarendon Press 1994).

Boisson de Chazournes L and Mbengue MM, 'A Footnote as a Principle. Mutual Supportiveness and Its Relevance in an Era of Fragmentation' in HP Hestermeyer et al. (eds.), *Coexistence, Cooperation and Solidarity—Liber Amicorum Rudiger Wolfrulm, Vol II* (Springer 2011).

Boutonnet M, 'l'environnement' (2010) 5 Hokkaido Journal of New Global Law and Policy 67.

Bowman M, 'Biodiversity, Intrinsic Value, and the Definition and Valuation of Environmental Harm' in M Bowman and A Boyle (eds.), *Environmental Damage in International and Comparative Law: Problems of Definition and Valuation* (OUP 2002).

Boyle A, 'Nuclear Energy and International Law: And Environmental Perspective' (1989) 60 British Yearbook of International Law 257.

Boyle A, 'State Responsibility and International Liability for Injurious Consequences of Acts Not Prohibited by International Law: A Necessary Distinction?' (1990) 39 International and Comparative Law Quarterly 11.

Boyle A, 'Reparation for Environmental Damage in International Law: Some Preliminary Problems' in M Bowman and A Boyle (eds.), *Environmental Damage in International and Comparative Law: Problems of Definition and Valuation* (OUP 2002).

Boyle A, 'Globalising Environmental Liability: The Interplay of National and International Law' (2005) 17 Journal of Environmental Law 3.

Boyle A, 'Liability for Injurious Consequences of Acts Not Prohibited by International Law' in J Crawford, A Pellet and S Olleson (eds.), *The Law of International Responsibility* (OUP 2010).

Boyle A, 'Human Rights and the Environment: Where Next?' (2012) 23 European Journal of International Law 613.

Boyle A, 'Soft Law in International Law Making' in MD Evans (ed.), *International Law* (5th ed., OUP 2018).

Boyle A and Harrison J, 'Judicial Settlement of International Environmental Disputes' (2013) 4 Journal of International Dispute Settlement 245.

Boyle A and Redgwell C, *Birnie, Boyle and Redgwell's International Law and the Environment* (4th ed., OUP 2021).

Brans EHP, *Liability for Damage to Public Natural Resources—Standing, Damage and Damage Assessment* (Kluwer Law International 2001).

Brans EHP, 'Liability for Damage to Public Natural Resources under the 2004 EC Environmental Liability Directive—Standing and Assessment of Damages' (2005) 7 Environmental Law Review 90.

Brans EHP, 'The Environmental Liability Directive: Legal Background and Requirements' in L Bergkamp and B Goldstein (eds.), *The EU Environmental Liability Directive. A Commentary* (OUP 2013).

Braswell J, 'Quando Chi Inquina non Paga: la Fuoriuscita di Acqua Contaminata da Cianuro a Baia Mare e l'Irrisolto Problema della Responsabilità Internazionale per Danni Ambientali Trasfrontalieri' (2001) Rivista Giuridica dell'Ambiente 909.

Bratspies RM and Miller RA (eds.), *Transboundary Harm in International Law* (CUP 2009).

Brown-Weiss E, 'The Changing Structure of International Law' in C Lambrechts and M Prieur (eds.), *Les Hommes et L'Environnement—Quel Droits pour le Vingt-et-Uniemen siècle?* (Frison-Roche 1998).

Brown-Weiss E, 'Invoking State Responsibility in the Twenty-First Century' (2002) 96 American Journal of International Law 798.

Brownlie I, *System of the Law of Nations—State Responsibility—Part I* (Clarendon Press 1983) 50.

Brüggemeier G, 'Enterprise Liability for Environmental Damage in German Law and EC Law' in G Teubner, L Farmer and D Murphy (eds.), *Environmental Law and Ecological Responsibility* (Wiley & Sons 1994).

Brüggemeier G, 'European Civil Liability Outside Europe. The Example of the Big Three: China, Brazil, Russia' (2011) 2 Journal of European Tort Law 1.

Brunnée J, 'The Responsibility of States for Environmental Harm in a Multinational Context—Problems and Trends' (1993) 34 Les Cahiers de Droit 827.

Brunnée J, 'Of Sense and Sensibility: Reflections on International Liability Regimes as Tools for Environmental Protection' (2004) 53 International and Comparative Law Quarterly 351.

Brunnée J, 'International Legal Accountability through the Lens of the Law of State Responsibility' (2005) 36 Netherlands Yearbook of International Law 3.

Buck M, 'The EU's Representation in Multilateral Environmental Negotiations After Lisbon' in E Morgera (ed.), *The External Policy of the European Union: EU and International Law Perspectives* (CUP 2012).

Buesseler K, Dai M, Aoyama M, Benitez-Nelson C, Charmasson S, Higley K, Maderich V, Masqué P, Morris PJ, Oughton D and Smith JN, 'Fukushima Daiichi-Derived Radionuclides in the Ocean: Transport, Fate, and Impacts' (2017) 9 Annual Review Marine Science 173.

Burlington L, 'Valuing Natural Resources Damages: A Transatlantic Lesson' in G Betlem and EHP Brans (eds.), *Environmental Liability in the EU—The 2004 Directive Compared with US and Member States Law* (Cameron May 2006).

Bush RB, 'Between Two Worlds: The Shift from Individual to Group Responsibility in the Law of Causation of Injury' (1986) 33 UCLA Law Review 1473.

Caballero G and Soto-Onate D, 'Environmental Crime and Judicial Rectification of the Prestige Oil Spill: The Polluter Pays' (2017) 84 Marine Policy 213.

Calabresi G, 'Some Thoughts on Risk Distribution and the Law of Torts' (1961) Yale Law Journal 499.

Camproux-Duffrène MP and Guihal D, 'Pollution Maritime. Naufrage de l'Erika. Responsabilité Pénale. Loi du 5 juillet 1973. Convention MARPOL. ZEE. Responsabilié civile pour Dommages Causés à l'Environnement par des Hydrocarbures en Mer. Réparation du prejudice écologique pur' (2013) 3 Revue Juridique de l'Environnement 457.

Cane P, *The Anatomy of Tort Law* (Hart 1997).

Cane P, 'Are Environmental Harms Special' (2001a) 13 Journal of Environmental Law 3.

Cane P, 'Distributive Justice and Tort Law' (2001b) New Zealand Law Review 401.

Cane P, 'Using Tort Law to Enforce Environmental Regulations?' (2002) 41 Washburn Law Journal 428.

Cappelletti M and Garth B, 'Access to Justice: The Newest Wave in the Worldwide Movement to Make Rights Effective' (1978) 27 Buffalo Law Review 181.

Cappelletti M, Garth B, and Trocker N, 'Access to Justice. Variations and Continuity of a World-Wide Movement' (1982) 46 Rabels Zeitshrift fur auslandisches und internationals Privatrecht 664.

Cardesa-Salzmann A and Morgera E, 'The EU's External Action after Lisbon: Competences, Policy Consistency and Participation in International Environmental Negotiations' in M Peeters and M Eliantonio (eds.), *Research Handbook on EU Environmental Law* (Edward Elgar 2020).

Casolari F, 'Giving Indirect Effect to International Law within the EU legal Order: The Doctrine of Consistent Interpretation' in E Cannizzaro, P Palchetti and RA Wessel (eds.), *International Law as Law of the European Union* (Brill 2012a).

Casolari F, 'The Principle of Loyal Co-operation: A 'Master Key' for EU External Representation?' in S Blockmans and RA Wessel (eds.), *Principles and Practices of EU External Representation* (CLEER Working Papers 2012b) 5.

Cassotta S, *Environmental Damage and Liability Problems in a Multilevel Context: The Case of the Environmental Liability Directive* (Kluwer Law International 2012).

Clarke C, 'Updated Comparative Legal Study on Environmental Liability' (Study Contract No 201919/MAR/B3, 2001). <https://ec.europa.eu/environment/legal/liability/pdf/legal-study_full.pdf> (last accessed 16 December 2021).

Cook K, 'No Liability, No Protocol' in C Bali, R Falkner and H Marquand (eds.), *The Cartagena Protocol on Biosafety: Reconciling Trade in Biotechnology with Environment and Development?* (Royal Institute of International Affairs 2002).

Cotterel R, 'What is Transnational Law?' (2012) 37 Law & Social Inquiry 500.

Craig P and de Burca G, *EU Law: Text, Cases and Materials* (7th ed., OUP 2020).

Crawford J, 'Responsibility for Breaches of Communitarian Norms: An Appraisal of Article 48 of the ILC Articles on Responsibility of States for Internationally Wrongful Acts' in U Fastenrath, R Geiger, D-E Kahn, A Paulus, S von Shorlemer and C Vedder (eds.), *From Bilateralism to Community Interest: Essays in Honour of Bruno Simma* (OUP 2011).

Crawford J, *Brownlie's Principles of Public International Law* (8th ed., OUP 2012).

Cremona M, 'The Union as a Global Actor: Roles, Models and Identity' (2004) 41 Common Market Law Review 553.

Cremona M, 'External Relations of the EU and the Member States: Competence, Mixed Agreements, International Responsibility and Effects of International Law' (2006) EUI Working Paper LAW No. 2006/22.

Cremona M, 'Defending the Community Interest: The Duties of Cooperation and Compliance' in M Cremona and B De Witte (eds.), *EU Foreign Relations Law: Constitutional Fundamentals* (Hart Publishing 2008).

Cremona M, 'Extending the Reach of the AETR Principle: Comment on Commission v Greece (C-45/07)' (2009) 34 *European Law Review* 754.

Cremona M, 'Disconnection Clauses in EU Law and Practice' in C Hillion and P Koutrakos (eds.), *Mixed Agreements Revisited: The EU and Its Member States in the World* (Hart 2010) 161.

Cremona M, 'External Relations and External Competence of the European Union: The Emergence of an Integrated Policy' in P Craig and G De Burca (eds.), *The Evolution of EU Law* (2nd ed., OUP 2011a).

Cremona M, 'Member States as Trustees of the Union Interest: Participating in International Agreements on Behalf of the European Union' in A Arnull and others (eds.), *A Constitutional Order of States: Essays in European Law in Honour of Alan Dashwood* (Hart Publishing 2011b).

Cremona M, 'Who Can Makes Treaties? The European Union' in DB Hollis (ed.), *The Oxford Guide to Treaties* (2nd ed., OUP 2020).

Cremona M, 'External Relations of the European Union: The Constitutional Framework for International Action' in P Craig and G De Burca (eds.), *The Evolution of EU Law* (3rd ed., OUP 2021).

Cusato C, Jones E, Ohdedar B and Bueno de Mesquita J, 'Symposium Introduction: Critical Perspectives on Global Law and the Environment' (2022) 12 Asian Journal of International Law 1.

Daniel A, 'Civil Liability Regimes as a Complement to Multilateral Environmental Agreements: Sound International Policy or False Comfort?' (2003) 12 Review of European Community and International Environmental Law 225.

Darpö J, 'Principle 10 and Access to Justice' in L Kramer and E Orlando (eds.), *Principles of Environmental Law—Elgar Encyclopaedia series* (Edward Elgar 2018).

Dascalopoulou-Livada P and Kolliopoulos A, 'The Kiev Civil Liability Protocol and the Interaction between Civil and Administrative Liability Regimes' (2017) 19 International Community Review 518.

Deakin S, 'The Evolution of Tort' (1999) 19 Oxford Journal of Legal Studies 537.

De Baere G, *Constitutional Principles of EU External relations* (OUP 2008).

De Baere G, '"O, Where Is Faith? O, Where Is Loyalty" Some Thoughts on the Duty of Loyal Co-operation and the Union's External Environmental Competences in the Light of the PFOS Case' (2011) 36 European Law Review 405.

De Baere G, 'Mercury Rising; the European Union and the International Negotiations for a Globally Binding Instrument on Mercury' (2012) 37 European Law Review 5.

De Burca G, 'Legal Principles as an Instrument for Differentiation' in B De Witte, D Hanf and E Vos (eds.), *The Many Faces of Differentiation in EU Law* (Intersentia 2001).

de Graaf K and Jans J, 'Liability of Public Authorities in Cases of Non-Enforcement of Environmental Standards' (2007) 24 Pace Environmental Law Review 377.

De La Fayette L, 'Nuclear Liability Revisited' (1992a) 1 Review of European Community and International Environmental Law 443.

De La Fayette L, 'Towards a New Regime of State Responsibility for Nuclear Activities' (1992b) 50 Nuclear Law Bulletin 7.

De La Fayette L, 'The Concept of Environmental Damage in International Liability Regimes' in M Bowman and A Boyle (eds.), *Environmental Damage in International and Comparative Law: Problems of Definition and Valuation* (OUP 2002).

de la Rue C, 'TOVALOP and CRISTAL—A Purpose Fulfilled' <www.colindelarue.com/publications/> (last accessed 16 December 2021).

Delgado Casteleiro A, 'EU Declarations of Competence to Multilateral Agreements: A Useful Reference Base?' (2012) 17 European Foreign Affairs Review 491.

Delmas-Marty M, Supiot A and Frieyro M, 'L'Internationalisation du droit: Degradation ou recomposition?' (2012) 389 Esprit 35.

Delmas-Marty M, 'Governing Globalisation Through Law' (2020) European Journal of Risk Regulation 195.

Delreux T, 'The Rotating Presidency and the EU's External Representation in Environmental Affairs: The Case of Climate Change and Biodiversity Negotiations' (2012) 8 Journal of Contemporary European Research 2.

Delreux T, 'The EU as an Actor in Global Environmental Politics' in A. Jordan and C. Adelle (eds.), Environmental Policy in the EU. Actors, Institutions and Processes (Routledge 2012).

Delreux T, *The EU as an International Environmental Negotiator* (Routledge 2011).

De Sadeleer N, 'Liability for Oil Pollution Damage Versus Liability for Waste Management: The Polluter Pays Principle at the Rescue of the Victims' (2009) 21 Journal of Environmental Law 299.

De Witte B, 'The Emergence of a European System of Public International Law: The EU and Its Member States as Strange Subjects' in J Wouters, A Nollkaemper and E de Wet (eds.), *The Europeanisation of International Law* (TMC Asser Press 2008).

Doeker G and Ghering T, 'Private or International Liability for Transnational Environmental Damage—The Precedents of Conventional Liability Regimes' (1990) 2 Journal of Environmental Law 3.

Doherty B, 'Very Hard Life Now: 12 Years after the Montara Oil Spill, Indonesians are Still Fighting to Be Heard' *The Guardian* (15 January 2022).

Dolidze A, 'Bridging Comparative and International Law: Amicus Curiae Participation as a Vertical Legal Transplant' (2015) 26 European Journal of International Law 851.

Dupuy PM, *La Résponsabilité Internationale des Etats Pour les Dommages D'Origine Technologique et Industrielle* (Pédone 1976).

Dupuy PM, 'The International Law of State Responsibility: Revolution or Evolution?' (1989) 11 Michigan Journal of International Law 105.

Dupuy PM, 'Soft Law and the International Law of the Environment' (1991) 12 Michigan Journal of International Law 420.

Dupuy PM, 'A Propos des Mésaventures de la Responsabilité International de l'État Dans Ses Rapports Avec la Protection International de l'Environnement' in M Prieur and C Lambrechts (eds.), *Les Hommes et l'Environnement: Quels Droits pour le Vingt-et-unième Siècle? Études en Hommage à Alexander Kiss* (Frison-Roche 1998).

Dupuy PM and Viñuales J, *International Environmental Law* (CUP 2018).

Dupuy PM, Le Moli G and Viñuales J, 'Customary International Law and the Environment' (2018) C-EENRG Working Papers 2018-2 <www.ceenrg.landecon.cam.ac.uk/system/files/documents/CEENRG_WP_19_CustomaryInternationalLawandtheEnvironment.pdf> (last accessed 12 July 2022).

Duvic-Paoli LA, *The Prevention Principle in International Environmental Law* (CUP 2018).

Ebbeson J, *Access to Justice in Environmental Matters in the EU* (Kluwer Law International 2002).

Eeckhout P, 'Case C-308/06, The Queen on the Application of *Intertanko* and Others v Secretary of State for Transport' (2009) 46 Common Market Law Review 2041.

Eeckhout P, *EU External Relations Law* (2nd ed., OUP 2011).

Eisenhammer S, 'Brazil Mine Disaster Could Devastate Ecosystem for Many Years' *Insurance Journal* (November 2015). <www.insurancejournal.com/news/international/2015/11/16/389012.htm> (last accessed 15 September 2022).

Eliantonio M, 'Soft Law in Environmental Matters and the Role of the European Courts: Too Much or Too Little of It?' (2018) 37 Yearbook of European Law 496.

Enneking L, 'Judicial Remedies: The Issue of Applicable Law' in JJ Alvarez Rubio and K Yiannibas (eds.), *Human Rights in Business—Removal of Barriers to Access to Justice in the European Union* (Routledge 2017).

Erlbacher F, 'Recent Case Law on External Competences of the European Union: How Member States Can Embrace Their Own Treaty' (2017) CLEER Papers 2.

European Commission, 'Guidelines for the Establishment of the Natural 2000 Network in the Marine Environment. Application of the Habitats and Birds Directive' (May 2007) < https://ec.europa.eu/environment/nature/natura2000/marine/index_en.htm> (last accessed March 2023).

European Commission, DG Environment, 'Answers Given by DG Environment on the Implementation of the Industrial Emissions Directive—Chapter 1', 'Definition of "Operator"' <ec.europa.eu/environment/industry/stationary/ied/implementation.htm> (last accessed July 2022).

European Commission, *Fifth Environmental Action Programme (EAP)* 'Towards Sustainability: A European Community Programme of Policy and Action in Relation to the Environment and Sustainable Development', COM (92) 23 final, OJ C 138/5, 17.5.93.

European Commission, *Green Paper on Remedying Environmental Damage*, COM (93) 47, OJ C 149/12, 29.5.93.

European Commission, *White Paper on Environmental Liability*, COM (2000) 66 final, Brussels 9.2.2000.

European Commission, Staff Working Document—REFIT Evaluation of the Environmental Liability Directive, Accompanying the document 'Report from the Commission to the European Parliament and to the Council pursuant to Article 18(2) of Directive 2004/35/EC on environmental liability with regard to the prevention and remedying of environmental damage', SWD (2016) 121 final.

European Commission, Notice, Guidelines Providing a Common Understanding of the Term 'Environmental Damage' as defined in Article 2 of Directive 2004/35/EC on environmental liability with regard to the prevention and remedying of environmental damage, C/2021/1860, OJ C 118, 7 April 2021.

Farmer AM (ed.), *Manual of European Environmental Policy—Institute of European Environmental Policy* (Routledge 2012).

Fasoli E, 'The Possibilities for Nongovernmental Organizations Promoting Environmental Protection to Claim Damages in Relation to the Environment in France, Italy, the Netherlands and Portugal' (2017) 26 Review of European Comparative and International Environmental Law 30.

Faure M, 'Economic Aspects of Environmental Liability: An Introduction' (1996) 4 European Review of Private Law 85.

Faure M, 'Regulatory Strategies in Environmental Liability' in F Cafaggi and H Muir Watt (eds.), *The Regulatory Function of European Private Law* (Edward Elgar 2009).

Faure M and Fiore K, 'An Economic Analysis of the Nuclear Liability Subsidy' (2009) 2 Pace Environmental Law Review 419.

Faure M and Jing L, 'Compensation for Environmental Damage in China: Theory and Practice' (2014) 31 Pace Environmental Law Review 226.

Faure M and Kindji K, *Cross-border Nuclear Safety, Liability and Cooperation in the European Union* (Study for European Parliament, PETI Committee 2019).

Faure M and Nollkaemper A, 'International Liability as an Instrument to Prevent and Compensate for Climate Change' (2007) 26 Stanford Environmental Law Journal 123.

Faure M and Van den Borre T, 'Compensating Nuclear Damage: A Comparative Law and Economic Analysis of the US and International Liability Schemes' (2008) 37 William and Mary Environmental Law and Policy Review 219.

Faure M and Wang H, 'The International Regimes for Compensation of Oil Pollution Damage: Are They Effective?' (2003) 12 Review of European Community and International Environmental Law 242.

Faure M and Wang H, 'Smart Mixes of Civil Liability Regimes for Marine Oil Pollution' in J Van Erp and others (eds.), *Smart Mixes for Transboundary Environmental Harm* (CUP 2019).

Faure M and Ying S (eds.), *China and International Liability: Legal Remedies for Transboundary Pollution* (Edward Elgar 2008).

Fitzmaurice M, 'International Responsibility and Liability' in D Bodansky, J Brunnée and E Hey (eds.), *The Oxford Handbook of International Environmental Law* (OUP 2007).

Fogleman V, 'Enforcing the Environmental Liability Directive: Duties, Powers and Self-executing Provisions' (2006) 4 Environmental Liability 127.

Fogleman V, 'The Threshold for Liability for Ecological Damage in the EU: Mixing Environmental and Conservation Law' in H Schoukens et al. (eds.), *The Habitats Directive in its EU Environmental Law Context* (Routledge 2015).

Fogleman V, 'The Duty to Prevent Environmental Damage in the Environmental Liability Directive; A Catalyst for Halting the Deterioration of Water and Wildlife' (2020) 20 ERA Forum 707.

Fogleman V, 'Improving financial security in the context of the Environmental Liability Directive' (May 2020) <https://ec.europa.eu/environment/legal/liability/pdf/Final_report.pdf> (last accessed 10 January 2022).

Foster C, 'The ILC Draft Principles on the Allocation of Loss in the Case of Transboundary Harm Arising Out of Hazardous Activities: Privatizing Risk' (2005) 14 Review of European Community and International Environmental Law 3.

Foster C, 'Diminished Ambitions? Public International Legal Authority in the Transnational Economic Era' (2014) 17 Journal of International Economic Law 355.

Francioni F, 'Exporting Environmental Hazards through Multinational Enterprises: Can the State of Origin be Held Responsible?' in F Francioni and T Scovazzi (eds.), *International Responsibility for Environmental Harm* (Graham & Trotman 1991).

Francioni F, 'Liability for Damage to the Common Environment: The Case of Antarctica' (1994) 3 Review of European Community and International Environmental Law 223.

Francioni F, 'Dispute Avoidance in International Environmental Law' in A Kiss, D Shelton and K Ishibashi (eds.), *Economic Globalization and Compliance with International Environmental Agreements* (Kluwer Law 2003).

Francioni F, 'Alternative Perspective on International Responsibility for Human Rights Violations by Multinational Corporations' in W Benedek, K De Feyter and F Marrella (eds.), *Economic Globalization and Human Rights* (CUP 2007a).

Francioni F, 'The Rights of Access to Justice under Customary International Law' in F Francioni (ed.), *Access to Justice as a Human Right* (OUP 2007b).

Francioni F, 'Realism, Utopia, and the Future of International Environmental Law' in (The Late) A Cassese (ed.), *Realizing Utopia: The Future of International Law* (OUP 2012).

Francioni F and Bakker C, 'The Evolution of the Global Environmental System: Trends and Prospects in the EU and the US' in F Francioni and C Bakker (eds.), *The EU, the US and Global Climate Governance* (Ashgate 2014).

Galizzi P and Sands P, 'The 1968 Brussels Convention and Liability for Damage' (1999) 64 Nuclear Law Bulletin 7.

Ghering T and Jachtenfuchs M, 'Liability for Transboundary Environmental Damage: Towards a General Liability Regime?' (1993) 4 European Journal of International Law 92.

Glinsky C, 'Corporate Social Responsibility and Corporate Liability for Environmental Damage' in B Pozzo and V Jacometti (eds.), *Environmental Loss and Damage in a Comparative Law Perspective* (CUP 2021).

Gobbato S, 'Legal Standing of Environmental Associations: The New 'Democratic Approach' of the Italian Supreme Administrative Court' (2007) 19 Journal of Environmental Law 259.

Godt C, 'Enforcement of Environmental Law by Individuals and Interest Groups: Reconceptualizing Standing' (2000) 23 Journal of Consumer Policy 79.

Goldie LFE, 'Concepts of Strict and Absolute Liability and the Ranking of Liability in Terms of Relative Exposure to Risk' (1985) 16 Netherlands Yearbook of International Law 175.

Golub J, 'New Instruments for Environmental Policy in the EU: An Overview' (1998) EUI Working Paper RSC No 98/12.

Gonsaeles G, 'The Impact of EC Decision-Making on the International Regime for Oil Pollution Damage: The Supplementary Fund Example' in F Maes (ed.), *Marine Resource Damage Assessment, Liability and Compensation for Environmental Damage* (Springer 2005).

Goransson M, 'Liability for Damage to the Marine Environment' in A Boyle and D Freestone (eds.), *International Law and Sustainable Development: Past Achievements and Future Challenges* (OUP 1999).

Gosalbo Bono R, 'The Organization of the External Relations of the European Union in the Treaty of Lisbon' in P Koutrakos (ed.), *The European Union's External Relations a Year After Lisbon* (CLEER Working Papers 1/3 2011).

Grieve MS, 'The Private Enforcement of Environmental Law' (1990) 65 Tulane Law Review 339.

Guttinger P, 'Allocation of Responsibility for Harmful Consequences of Acts Not Prohibited by International Law' in J Crawford, A Pellet and S Olleson (eds.), *The Law of International Responsibility* (OUP 2010).

Hadjiyanni I, 'The European Union as a Global Regulatory Power' (2020) 41 Oxford Journal of Legal Studies 243.

Handl G, 'State Liability for Accidental Transnational Environmental Damage by Private Persons' (1980) 74 American Journal of International Law 525.

Handl G, 'National Uses of Transboundary Air Resources: The International Entitlement Issue Reconsidered' (1986) 26 Natural Resources Journal 405.

Handl G, 'Environmental Security and Global Change: The Challenge to International Law' in W Lang, H Neuhold and K Zemanek (eds.), *Environmental Protection and International Law* (Graham & Trotman 1991).

Handl G, 'International Accountability for Transboundary Environmental Harm Revisited: What Role for "State Liability"?' (2007a) 37 Environmental Policy and Law 116.

Handl G, 'Transboundary Impacts' in D Bodansky, J Brunnée and E Hey (eds.), *The Oxford Handbook of International Environmental Law* (OUP 2007b).

Handl G and Lutz RE (eds.), *Transferring Hazardous Technologies and Substances: The International Legal Challenge* (Graham and Trotman 1989).

Handl G and Svendsen K (eds.), *Managing the Risk of Offshore Oil and Gas Accidents: The International Legal Dimension* (Edward Elgar 2019).

Handrlica J, 'Euratom Powers in the Field of Nuclear Liability Revisited' (2010) 3 International Journal of Nuclear Law 1.

Hanley N, 'The Economic Value of Environmental Damage' in M Bowman and A Boyle (eds.), *Environmental Damage in International and Comparative Law: Problems of Definition and Valuation* (OUP 2002).

Hanqin X, *Transboundary Damage in International Law* (CUP 2003).

Harrison J, 'Conflicting Interpretations—The Slops Incident and the Application of the International Oil Pollution Liability and Compensation Regime to Offshore Storage and Transfer Operations' (2008) 20 Journal of Environmental Law 455.

Harrison J, 'Regime Pluralism and the Global Regulation of Oil Pollution Liability and Compensation' (2009) 5 International Journal of Law in Context 379.

Harrison J, 'Reflection on the Role of International Courts and Tribunals in the Settlement of Environmental Disputes and the Development of International Environmental Law' (2013) 24 Journal of Environmental Law 501.

Hedemann Robinson M, 'EU Enforcement of International Environmental Agreements: The Role of the European Commission' (2012) European Energy and Environmental Law Review 2.

Heffron RJ, Ashley SF and Nuttal WJ, 'The Global Liability Regime Post-Fukushima Daiichi' (2016) 90 Progress in Nuclear Energy 4.

Heliskoski J, *Mixed Agreements as a Technique for Organizing the International Relations of the Community and Its Member States* (Kluwer Law International 2001).

Hemming AD, 'Liability Postponed: The Failure to Bring Annex VI of the Madrid Protocol into Force' (2018) 8 The Polar Journal 315.

Hervé-Fournerau N, *National Report FRANCE* (Avosetta Meeting, Helsinki 2013).

Hey E, *Advanced Introduction to International Environmental Law* (Edward Elgar 2016).

Heyvaert V, 'Transnationalization of Law: Rethinking Law through Transnational Environmental Regulation' (2017) Transnational Environmental Law 205.

Hinteregger M (ed.), *Environmental Liability and Ecological Damage in European Law* (CUP 2008).

Hoffmeister F, 'The Contribution of EU Practice to International Law' in M. Cremona (ed.), *Developments in EU External Relations Law* (OUP 2008).

Holtby KL, Kerr WA, Hobbs JE, *International Environmental Liability and Barriers to Trade—Market Access and Biodiversity in the Biosafety Protocol* (Edward Elgar 2007).

Husa J, *Law and Globalization* (Edward Elgar 2018).

ILC, Survey of Liability Regimes Relevant to the Topic of International liability for Injurious Consequences Arising Out of Acts Not Prohibited by International Law', ILC 47th Session (1995), UN General Assembly, A/CN.4/471.

ILC, 'Draft Articles on Responsibility of States for Internationally Wrongful Acts, with commentaries' in (2001) Report of the International Law Commission on the Work of its Fifty-third Session, Official Record of the UN General Assembly 56th Session, Supplement No. 10, UN Doc A/56/10.

ILC, 'Draft Articles on the Prevention of Transboundary Harm from Hazardous Activities' in (2001) *Yearbook of the International Law Commission*, vol. II, Part II, Report of the Commission to the General Assembly on the Work of its Fifty-third Session, UN Doc. A/56/10.

ILC, 'Principles on Allocation of Loss in the Case of Transboundary Harm Arising Out of Hazardous Activities, with Commentaries' (2006) *Yearbook of the International Law Commission*, vol 2, Part II, Report of the Commission to the General Assembly on the Wok of its Fifty-eight Session, UN Doc A/61/10.

Jacobsson M, 'Oil Pollution Liability and Compensation: An International Regime' (1996) 2 Uniform Law Review 260.

Jacobsson M, 'Perspective of the Global Compensation Regimes; The Relationship between EU Legislation and Maritime Liability Conventions' (2012) 4 European Journal of Commercial Contract Law 63.

Jacobsson M and N Trotz, 'The Definition of Pollution Damage in the 1984 Protocols to the 1969 Civil Liability Convention and the 1971 Fund Convention' (1986) 17 Journal of Maritime Law and Commerce 467.

Jessurun d'Oliveira HU, 'The Sandoz Blaze: The Damage and the Public and Private Liabilities' in F Francioni and T Scovazzi (eds.), *International Responsibility for Environmental Harm* (Graham & Trotman 1991).

Johnson M, 'Liability for Environmental Damage in Antarctica: The Adoption of Annex IV to the Antarctic Environmental Protocol', (2006–2007) 19 Georgetown International Environmental Law Review 33.

Josefsson H, 'The Environmental Liability Directive, the Water Framework Directive and the Definition of "Water Damage"' (2018) 20 Environmental Law Review 151.

Jungcurt S and Schabus N, 'Liability and Redress in the Context of the Cartagena Protocol on Biosafety' (2010) 19 Review of European Comparative and International Environmental Law 2.

Kamminga MT and Zia-Zarifi S (eds.), *Liability of Multinational Corporations under International Law* (Kluwer Law International 2000).

Keating GC, 'Distributive and Corrective Justice in the Tort Law of Accidents' (2000) 74 Southern California Law Review 193.

Kerbrat Y, 'Le droit international face au défi de la réparation des dommages à l'environnement. Rapport général sur le thème de la deuxième demi-journée' in Société Française pour le Droit International (SFDI) (ed.), *Le Droit International Face au Défi de la Protection de l'Environnement* (Pedone 2010).

Kingston S, 'Mind the Gap: Difficulties in Enforcement and The Continuing Unfulfilled Promise of EU Environmental Law' in S Kingston (ed.), *European Perspectives on Environmental Law and Governance* (Routledge 2012).

Kiss A, 'Present Limits to the Enforcement of State Responsibility for Environmental Damage' in F Francioni and T Scovazzi (eds.), *International Responsibility for Environmental Harm* (Graham & Trotman 1991).

Kiss A, 'The Common Concern of Mankind' (1997) 27 Environmental Policy and Law 244.

Klabbers J, *Treaty Conflict and the European Union* (CUP 2008).

Klabbers J, 'The Validity of EU Norms Conflicting with International Obligations' in E Cannizzaro, P Palchetti and RA Wessel (eds.), *International Law as Law of the European Union* (Brill 2011).

Klamert M, 'Dark Matter: Competence, Jurisdiction and 'The Area Largely Covered by EU law'—Comment on Lesoochranarske' (2012) 37 European Law Review 3.

Klamert M, *The Principle of Loyalty in EU Law* (OUP 2014).

Klamert M, 'What We Talk About When We Talk about Harmonisation' (2015) 17 Cambridge Yearbook of European Legal Studies 360.

Klaphake A, 'The Assessment and Restoration of Biodiversity Damages—Some Remarks on Environmental Damages under the Directive 2004/35' (2005) 4 Journal of European Environmental & Planning Law 268.

Kleiman D and Kubek G, 'The Signing, Provisional Application, and Conclusion of Trade and Investment Agreements in the EU—The Case of CETA and Opinion 2/15' (2016) *EUI* Working Paper RSCAS 2016/58.

Koskenniemi M, 'Report of the Study Group of the International Law Commission, Fragmentation of International Law: Difficulties Arising from the Diversification and Expansion of International Law' (2006) UN Doc A/CN.4/L 682, 207.

Koutrakos P, 'Legal Basis and Delimitation of Competence in EU External Relations' in M Cremona and B De Witte (eds.), *EU Foreign Relations Law: Constitutional Fundamentals* (Bloomsbury Publishing PLC 2008).

Kramer L, 'Differentiation in EU Environmental Policy' in B De Witte, D Hanf and E Vos (eds.), *The Many Faces of Differentiation in EU Law* (Intersentia 2001).

Kramer L, 'Directive 2004/35 on Environmental Liability' in G Betlem and E Brans (eds.), *Environmental Liability in the EU* (Cameron May 2005).

Kramer L, 'Regional Economic International Organizations: The European Union as an Example' in D Bodansky, J Brunnée and E Hey (eds.), *The Oxford Handbook of International Environmental Law* (OUP 2007).

Kramer L, 'The Environment and the Ten Commandments' (2008) 21 *Journal of Environmental Law* (Forewords) 5.

Kulovesi K, Mehling M and Morgera E, 'Global Environmental Law: Context and Theory, Challenge and Promise' (2019) 8 Transnational Environmental Law 405.

Lago Candeira A, 'Administrative Approach to Liability: Its Origin, Negotiation and Outcome' in A Shibata (ed.), *International Liability Regime for Biodiversity Damage. The Nagoya-Kuala Lumpur Supplementary Protocol* (Routledge 2014).

Lavranos N, 'Protecting European Law from International Law' (2010) 15 *European Foreign Affairs Review* 265.

Leal Arcas R, 'The European Community and Mixed Agreements' (2001) 6 European Foreign Affairs Review 483.

Lee M, 'From Private to Public: The Multiple Faces of Environmental Liability' (2001) 7 European Public Law 375.

Lee M, 'Regulatory Solutions to GMOs in Europe: The Problem of Liability' (2003) Journal of Environmental Law and Practice 311.

Lee M, 'Safety, Regulation and Tort: Fault in Context' (2011) 74 Modern Law Review 555.

Lee M, 'The Intersection Between Environmental Law and Tort Law' in L Paddock, RL Glicksman and NS Bryner (eds.), *Decision Making in Environmental Law* (Edward Elgar 2016).

Lefeber R, *Transboundary Environmental Interference and the Origin of State Liability* (Kluwer Law International 1996).

Lefeber R, 'The Prospects for an Antarctic Environmental Liability Regime' in D Vidas (ed.), *Implementing the Environmental Protection Regime for the Antarctic* (Springer 2000).

Lefeber R and Nieto Carrasco J, 'Negotiating the Supplementary Protocol: The Co-Chairs' Perspective' in A Shibata (ed.), *International Liability Regime for Biodiversity Damage: The Nagoya-Kuala Lumpur Supplementary Protocol* (Routledge 2014).

Lefevere J, *Interactions of the EU Environmental Liability Regime* (Field 2003).

Lenaerts K and Gutierrez-Fons JA, 'To Say What the Law of the EU Is: Methods of Interpretation and the European Court of Justice' (2013) EUI Working Papers, AEL 2013/9.

Lin J, 'Climate Change and the Courts' (2012) 31 Legal Studies 35.

Liu J and Faure M, 'Compensation for Nuclear Damage: A Comparison Among the International Regime, Japan and China' (2016) 16 International Environmental Agreements: Politics, Law and Economics 165.

Lopez C, 'Legal Liability for Business Human Rights Abuses Under the Revised Draft of a Treaty on Business and Human Rights' *Cambridge Core Blog* (11 September 2019). <www.cambridge.org/core/blog/2019/09/11/legal-liability-for-business-human-rights-abuses-under-the-revised-draft-of-a-treaty-on-business-and-human-rights> (last accessed 27 December 2022).

Lydgate E, 'Sustainable Development in the WTO: From Mutual Supportiveness to Balancing' (2012) 11 World Trade Review 621.

MacKay D, 'The Proposed Antarctic Treaty on Environmental Damage', (1999–2000) ILSA Journal of International and Comparative Law 473.

Magraw DB, 'Transboundary Harm: The International Law Commission's Study of "International Liability"' (1986) 80 American Journal of International Law 305.

Maljean-Dubois S, 'International Litigation and State Liability for Environmental Damages: Recent Evolutions and Perspectives' in JR Yeh (ed.), *Climate Change Liability and Beyond* (National Taiwan University Press 2017).

Manners I, 'Normative Power Europe: A Contradiction in Terms?' (2002) 40 Journal of Common Market Studies 235.

Marsden S, 'Invoking Direct Application and Effect of International Treaties by the European Court of Justice: Implications for International Environmental Law in the European Union' (2011) 60 International & Comparative Law Quarterly 737.

Martines F, 'Direct Effect of International Agreements of the European Union' (2014) 25 European Journal of International Law 129.

Marx A et al, 'Access to Legal Remedies for Victims of Corporate Human Rights Abuses in Third Countries' *EU Study* (February 2019) www.europarl.europa.eu/RegData/etudes/STUD/2019/603475/EXPO_STU(2019)603475_EN.pdf (last accessed 15 July 2022).

Mason M, 'Transnational Compensation for Oil Pollution Damage: Examining Changing Spatialities of Environmental Liability' (2002) LSE Research Papers in Environmental and Spatial Analysis (No. 69) <http://eprints.lse.ac.uk/570/>.

Mason M, 'Civil Liability for Oil Pollution Damage: Examining the Evolving Scope for Environmental Compensation in the International Regime' (2003) 27 Marine Policy 1.

Mayer B, 'State Responsibility and Climate Change Governance: A Light Through the Storm' (2014) 13 Chinese Journal of International Law 539.

McCorquodale R and Simons P, 'Responsibility Beyond Borders: State Responsibility for Extraterritorial Violations by Corporations of International Human Rights Law' (2007) 70 Modern Law Review 598.

McGillivray D and Wightman J, 'Private Rights, Public Interests and the Environment' in Hayward and O' Neill (eds.), *Justice, Property and the Environment—Social and Legal Perspectives* (Ashgate 1997).

McRae B, 'The Compensation Convention: Path to a Global Regime for Dealing with Legal Liability and Compensation for Nuclear Damage' (1998) 61 Nuclear Law Bulletin 25.

McRae B, 'The Convention on Supplementary Compensation for Nuclear Damage: Catalyst for a Global Nuclear Liability Regime' (2007) 79 Nuclear Law Bulletin 17.

Mendez M, 'The Enforcement of EU Agreements: Bolstering the Effectiveness of Treaty Law?' (2010) 47 Common Market Law Review 1719.

Mensah TA, 'Civil Liability and Compensation for Vessel-Source Pollution of the Marine Environment and the United Nations Convention on the Law of the Sea' in N Ando et al. (eds.), *Liber Amicorum Judge Shigeru Oda*, Vol. II (Kluwer Law International 2002).

Merialdi A, 'The *Patmos* and *Haven* Cases: Recent Developments' (1994) 9 International Journal of Marine and Coastal Law 389.

Michaels R, 'Transnationalising Comparative Law' (2016) 23 Maastricht Journal of European and Comparative Law 352.

Milieu Ltd, 'Towards a Common Understanding of ELD Key Terms and Concept—Support in the Implementation of REFIT actions for the ELD—phase I' (2017) DOC5–05/10/2017.

Milieu Ltd/IUCN, 'Experience Gained in the Application of ELD Biodiversity Damage' in *Final Report,* European Commission—DG Environment (Brussels 2014).

Momirov A and Naudé Fourie A, 'Vertical Comparative Law Methods: Tools for Conceptualising the International Rule of Law' (2009) 3 Erasmus Law Review 291.

Montjoie M, 'The Concept of Liability in the Absence of an Internationally Wrongful Act' in J Crawford, A Pellet and S Olleson (eds.), *The Law of International Responsibility* (OUP 2010).

Morgera E, 'Ambition, Complexity, and Legitimacy of Pursuing Mutual Supportiveness Through the EU's External Environmental Action' in B Van Vooren, S Blockmans and J Wouters (eds.), *The EU's Role in Global Governance: The Legal Dimension* (CUP 2013).

Morgera E, 'Global Environmental Law and Comparative Legal Methods' (2015) Review of European Comparative and International Environmental Law 254.

Mullerat B, 'European Environmental Liability: One Step Forward' (2005) 16 International Company and Commercial Law Review 26.

Nengye L and Maes F, 'The European Union and the International Maritime Organization: EU's External Influence on the Prevention of Vessel-Source Pollution' (2010) 41 Journal of Maritime Law and Commerce 581.

Nengye L and Maes F, 'Legal Constraints to the European Union's Accession to the International Maritime Organization' (2012) 43 Journal of Maritime Law and Commerce 2.

Nichols J, 'Admissibility of Claims: Development of the IOPC Funds' Policy' in *The IOPC Funds' 25 Years of Compensating Victims of Pollution Accidents* (The IOPC Funds 2003).

Nijar GS, 'Civil Liability in the Supplementary Protocol' in A Shibata (ed.), *International Liability Regime for Biodiversity Damage: The Nagoya-Kuala Lumpur Supplementary Protocol* (Routledge 2014).

Nocera F, *The Legal Regime of Nuclear Energy* (Intersentia 2005).

Nollkaemper A, 'Cluster-Litigation in Cases of Transboundary Environmental Harm' in Faure and Ying (eds.), *China and International Liability: Legal Remedies for Transboundary Pollution* (Edward Elgar 2008).

Nollkaemper A and Jacobs D (eds.), *Distribution of Responsibilities in International Law* (CUP 2015).

OECD, 'Recommendation of the Council for the Implementation of a Regime of Equal Right of Access and Non-Discrimination in Relation to Transfrontier Pollution' (1977) OECD/LEGAL/0152 < https://legalinstruments.oecd.org/public/doc/17/17.en.pdf> (last accessed March 2023).

Okowa P, 'Responsibility for Environmental Damage' in M. Fitzmaurice, DM Ong and P Merkouris (eds.), *Research Handbook on International Environmental Law* (Edward Elgar 2010).

Ong D, 'The Relationship between Environmental Damage and Pollution: Marine Oil Pollution Laws in Malaysia and Singapore' in M Bowmann and A Boyle (eds.), *Environmental Harm in International and Comparative Law* (OUP 2002).

Oosterveen W, 'Some Recent Developments Regarding Liability for Damage Resulting from Oil Pollution—from the Perspective of an EU Member State' (2004) 6 Environmental Law Review 223.

Orlando E, 'Public and Private in the Law of Environmental Liability' in F Lenzerini and AF Vrdoljak (eds.), *International Law for Common Goods: Normative Perspectives on Human Rights, Culture and Nature* (Hart 2014).

Orlando E, 'From Domestic to Global? Recent Trends in Environmental Liability from a Multi-Level and Comparative Law Perspective' (2015) 24 Review of European Comparative and International Environmental Law 289.

Orlando E, 'Principles, Standards and Voluntary Commitments in International Environmental Law' in E Techera and others (eds.), *Routledge Handbook of International Environmental Law* (2nd ed., Routledge 2020).

Orrego Vicuna F, 'Responsibility and Liability for Environmental Damage under International Law—Final Report Prepared for the Eight Committee of the Institut de Droit International' (1998) 10 Georgetown Environmental Law Review 279.

Orrego Vicuna F, 'Current Trends in Responsibility and Liability for Environmental Harm under International Law' in K Koufa (ed.), *Protection of the Environment for the New Millennium—2000 International Law Session* (Sakkoulas Publications 2002).

Osofosky HM and Peel J, 'The Role of Litigation in Multilevel Climate Change Governance: Possibilities for a Lower Carbon Future?' (2013) 30 EPLJ 303.

Pallemaerts M, 'Study on National Legislation Needed to Implement the Protocol on Civil Liability and Compensation for Damage Caused by the Transboundary Effects of Industrial Accidents on Transboundary Waters', ECE/CP.TEIA/2012/7, < https://unece.org/fileadmin/DAM/env/documents/2012/wat/WG/Joint_meeting_july/background_docs/IEEP_UNECE_final_report.pdf> (last accessed 28 August 2012).

Papadopoulou D, 'The Role of French Environmental Associations in Civil Liability for Environmental Harm: Courtesy of "Erika" ' (2009) 21 Journal of Environmental Law 87.

Pauwelyn J, Wessel RA and Wouters J, 'When Structures Become Shackles: Stagnation and Dynamics in International Lawmaking' (2014) 25 European Journal of International Law 733.

Pavoni R, 'Mutual Supportiveness as a Principle of Interpretation and Law-Making: A Watershed for the 'WTO-and-Competing-Regimes' Debate? (2010) 21 European Journal of International Law 649.

Pavoni R, 'Controversial Aspects of the Interaction Between International and EU Law in Environmental Matters: Direct Effect and Member States' Unilateral Measures' in E Morgera (ed.), *The External Environmental Policy of the European Union* (CUP 2012).

Payne CR, 'Pulp Mills on the River Uruguay' (2011) 105 American Journal of International Law 94.

Payne CR, 'Legal Liability for Environmental Damage: The United Nations Compensation Commission and the 1990–1991 Gulf War' in C Bruch, C Muffett and S Nichols (eds.), *Governance, Natural Resources and Post-Conflict Peacebuilding* (Earthscan/Routledge 2016).

Pellet A, 'Les Fondements Juridiques Internationaux du Droit Communautaire' (1994) V-2 Collected Courses of the Academy of European Law 193.

Pelzer N, 'Concept of Nuclear Liability Revisited: A Post-Chernobyl Assessment of the Paris and Vienna Conventions' in P Cameron et al. (eds.), *Nuclear Energy Law After Chernobyl* (Graham & Trotman 1988).

Percival RV, 'Liability for Environmental Harm and Emerging Global Environmental Law' (2010) 25 Maryland Journal of International Law 37.

Percival RV, Cooper KH and Gravens MM, 'CERCLA in a Global Context' (2012) Southern Western Law Review 727.

Petersen M, 'The Environmental Liability Directive—Extending Nature Protection in Europe' (2009) 11 Environmental Law Review 5.

Phillips D, 'Samarco Dam Collapse: One Year on from Brazil's Worst Environmental Disaster' *The Guardian* (5 October 2016). <www.theguardian.com/sustainable-business/2016/oct/15/samarco-dam-collapse-brazil-worst-environmental-disaster-bhp-billiton-vale-mining> (last accessed 20 July 2022).

Plakokefalos I, 'Prevention Obligations in International Environmental Law' (2012) 23 Yearbook of International Environmental Law 1.

Poli S, 'Shaping the EC Regime on Liability for Environmental Damage: Progress or Disillusionment?' (1999) 8 European Environmental Law Review 299.

Poli S, *La Responsabilitá per Danni da Inquinamento Transfrontaliero nel Diritto Comunitario e Internazionale* (Giuffré 2006).

Politi M, 'The Impact of the Chernobyl Accident on the State's Perception of International Responsibility for Nuclear Damage' in F Francioni and T Scovazzi (eds.), *International Responsibility for Environmental Harm* (Graham & Trotman 1991).

Pontin B, *Nuisance Law and Environmental Protection: A Study of Nuisance Injunctions in Practice* (Lawtext 2013).

Prieur M, 'La Responsabilité Environnementale en Droit Communautaire' (2004) 2 Revue Juridique de l'Environnement 5.

Rabin RL, 'Environmental Liability and the Tort System' (1987) 24 Houston Law Review 28.

Rabin RL, 'Some Thoughts on the Ideology of Enterprise Liability' (1996) 55 Modern Law Review 1190.

Rao PS, 'First Report on the Legal Regime for Allocation of Loss in Case of Transboundary Harm Arising Out of Hazardous Activities' (2003) United Nations General Assembly, Doc. A/CN.4/531 <https://digitallibrary.un.org/record/494252?ln=en> (last accessed April 2023).

Rebeyrol V, 'The Erika Case: An Incitement to Rewrite the CLC' (2013) European Energy and Environmental Law Review 33.

Rehbinder E, 'Extraterritoriality of Pollution Control Laws from a European Perspective' in G Handl, J Zekoll and P Zumbansen (eds.), *Beyond Territoriality: Transnational Legal Authority in an Age of Globalisation* (Brill 2012).

Ridley K and Shabalala Z, 'BHP Labels $ Billion UK Case Over Brazilian Dam Failure Pointless' (July 2020) <www.reuters.com/article/us-bhp-britain-court-dam-idUKKCN24N187> (last accessed 15 September 2022).

Ringbom H, 'EU Regulation 44/2001 and Its Implications for the International Maritime Liability Conventions' (2004) 35 Journal of Maritime Law & Commerce 1.

Rosas A, 'Issues of State Liability for Transboundary Environmental Damage' (1991) 60 Nordic Journal of International Law 29.

Rosas A, 'The European Court of Justice and Public International Law' in J Wouters, A Nollkaemper and E De Wet (eds.), *The Europeanization of International Law: The Status of International Law in the EU and its Member States* (TMC Asser Press 2008).

Rosas A, 'The Status in EU Law of International Agreements Concluded by EU Member States' (2011) 34 Fordham International Law Journal 1304.

Rosas A, 'EU External Relations: Exclusive Competence Revisited' (2015) 38 Fordham International Law Journal 1073.

Rosenthal L and Raper C, 'Amoco Cadiz and Limitation of Liability for Oil Spill Pollution: Domestic and International Solutions' (1985) 5 Virginia Journal of Natural Resources Law 259.

Rudall J, 'Certain Activities Carried Out by Nicaragua in the Border Area (Costa Rica v Nicaragua)' (2018) 112 American Journal of International Law 288.

Sachs N, 'Beyond the Liability Wall: Strengthening Tort Remedies in International Environmental Law' (2008) 55 UCLA Law Review 837.

Sand PH, 'Compensation for Environmental Damage from the 1991 Gulf War' (2005) 36 Environmental Policy and Law 244.

Sands PH and Peel J, *Principles of International Environmental Law* (4th ed., CUP 2018).

Sandvik B and Suikkari S, 'Harm and Reparation in International Treaty Regimes: An Overview' in P Wetterstein (ed.), *Harm to the Environment: The Right to Compensation and the Assessment of Damages* (Clarendon Press 1997).

Scarciglia R, 'Diritto Globale e Metodologia Comparativa: Verso un Approccio Verticale?' (2015) 17 Diritto Pubblico Comparato ed Europeo 1011.

Schwabach A, 'The Sandoz Spill: The Failure of International Law to Protect the Rhine from Pollution' (1989) 16 Ecology Law Quarterly 443.

Scott J, 'Extraterritoriality and Territorial Extension in EU Law' (2014) 62 American Journal of Comparative Law 87.

Scott J, 'The Global Reach of EU Law' in M Cremona and J Scott (ed.), *EU Law Beyond EU Borders: The Extraterritorial Reach of EU Law* (OUP 2019).

Scovazzi T, 'State Responsibility for Environmental Harm' (2002) 12 Yearbook of International Environmental Law 43.

Scovazzi T, 'The Mediterranean Guidelines for the Determination of Environmental Liability and Compensation: The Negotiations for the Instrument and the Question of Damage That Can Be Compensated' in A Von Bogandy and R Wolfrum (eds.), *Max Planck Yearbook of United Nations Law*, Vol 13 (Martinus Nijhoff Publishers 2009)

Shaffer GC, 'Transnational Legal Ordering and State Change' in GC Shaffer (ed.), *Transnational Legal Ordering and State Change* (CUP 2012).

Shavell S, *The Economic Analysis of Accident Law* (Harvard University Press 1987).

Shelton DL and Kiss A, 'Strict Liability in International Environmental Law' in TM Ndiaye and R Wolfrum (eds.), *Law of the Sea, Environmental Law and Settlement of Disputes: Liber Amicorum Judge Thomas A Mensah* (Brill Academic Publishers 2007).

Shibata A, 'How to Design an International Liability Regime for Public Spaces: The Case of the Antarctic Environment' in T Komori and K Wellens (eds.), *Public Interest Rules of International Law* (Routledge 2009).

Shibata A, 'The Nagoya-Kuala Lumpur Supplementary Protocol on Liability and Redress' in A Shibata (ed.), *International Liability Regime for Biodiversity Damage: The Nagoya-Kuala Lumpur Supplementary Protocol* (Routledge 2014).

Siems M, *Comparative Law* (3rd ed., CUP 2022).

Simma B, 'From Bilateralism to Community Interest in International Law' (1994) 250 Recueil des Cours de l'Académie de Droit International 233.

Soyer B, 'Emergence of EU and Maritime Law' in D Patterson and A Sodersten (eds.), *A Companion to European Union and International Law* (Wiley and Blackwell 2016).

Spilker G and Koubi V, 'The Effects of Treaty Legality and Domestic Institutional Hurdles on Environmental Treaty Ratification' (2016) International Environmental Agreements: Politics, Law and Economics 223.

Squintani L and Kalisvaart S, 'Report on Judicial Cooperation in Follow-Up Judgements in Environmental Matters' – EU Forum of Judges for the Environment < https://www.eufje.org/images/docConf/visio2021/Report_based_on_EUFJE_questionnaires_on_follow-up_judgments_-_Definitive_06-11-2021.pdf>

Stephan PB, 'Privatizing International Law' (2011) 97 Virginia Law Review 1537.

Stevens & Bolton LLP (2013), 'The Study on Analysis of Integrating the ELD into 11 National Legal Frameworks', Final Report Prepared for the European Commission—DG Environment.

Taylor P, 'Common Heritage of Mankind and Common Concern of Humankind' in L Kramer and E Orlando (eds.), *Principles of Environmental Law, Elgar Encyclopaedia of Environmental Law* (Edward Elgar 2018).

Teubner G, 'The Invisible Cupola: From Causal to Collective Attribution in Ecological Liability' in G Teubner, L Farmer and D Murphy (eds.), *Environmental Law and Ecological Responsibility: The Concept and Practice of Ecological Self-Organization* (Wiley & Sons 1994).

Thieffry P, 'Environmental Liability in Europe: The European Union's Project and the Convention of the Council of Europe' (1994) 29 International Lawyer 1083.

Thies A, 'The Search for Effectiveness and the Need for Loyalty in EU External Action' in M Cremona (ed.), *Structural Principles in EU External Relations Law* (Hart Publishing 2018).

Tladi D, 'Civil Liability in the Context of the Cartagena Protocol: To Be or Not to Be (Binding)?' (2009) 10 International Environmental Agreements 15.

Tuo CE and Carpaneto L, 'Connections and Disconnections between Brussels I Regulation and International Conventions on Transport Matters' (2016) 66 Zbornik PFZ 141.

UNECE, Task Force on Access to Justice, 'Study on the Possibilities for Non-Governmental Organisations Promoting Environmental Protection to Claim Damages in Relation to the Environment in Four Selected Countries: France, Italy, the Netherlands and Portugal' (2015) <www.unece.org/fileadmin/DAM/env/pp/a.to.j/AnalyticalStudies/TFAJ_Study_env_damage_final.pdf>.

UNEP/OCHA, Assessment Mission, 'Cyanide Spill at Baia Mare Romania' (Report, March 2000) <https://reliefweb.int/report/romania/cyanide-spill-baia-mare-romania-unepocha-assessment-mission-advance-copy> (last accessed April 2023).

Van Der Loo G and Wessel RA, 'The Non-Ratification of Mixed Agreements: Legal Consequences and Solutions' (2017) 3 Common Market Law Review 735.

Van Elsuwege P, 'The Duty of Sincere Cooperation and Its Implications for Autonomous Member State Action in the field of External Relations' in M Varju (ed.), *Between Compliance and Particularism: Member State Interests and European Union law* (Springer 2019).

Van Wolferen M, 'Case C-243/15 Lesoochranárske zoskupenie VLK v Obvodný úrad Trenčín' (2017) 14 Journal for European Environmental & Planning Law 136.

Vigni P, 'A Liability Regime for Antarctica' (2006) The Italian Yearbook of International Law 214.

Vogler J, 'The European Union as an Actor in International Environmental Politics' (1999) 8 Environmental Politics 24.

Voigt C, 'State Responsibility for Climate Change Damages' (2008) 77 Nordic Journal of International Law 1.

Voneky S, 'The Liability Annex to the Protocol on Environmental Protection to the Antarctic Treaty' in D Doing, P Tobias Stoll and R Volker (eds.), *International Law Today: New Challenges and the Need for Reform?* (Springer 2008).

Walker N, *Intimations of Global Law* (CUP 2014).

Washington H, Taylor B, Kopnina H, Cryer P and Piccolo JJ, 'Why Ecocentrism Is the Key Pathway to Sustainability' (2017) 1 The Ecological Citizen 35.

Wenneraas P, 'Permit Defences in Environmental Liability Regimes—Subsidizing Environmental Damage in the EC' (2005) 4 Yearbook of European Environmental Law 149.

Weston P, 'Victims of Brazil's Worst Environmental Disaster to Get Day in UK Courts' *The Guardian* (22 July 2022) <www.theguardian.com/environment/2022/jul/08/uk-court-of-appeal-case-victims-brazil-mariana-dam-collapse-aoe> (last accessed 15 September 2022).

Wiener JB, 'Something Borrowed for Something Blue: Legal Transplants and the Evolution of Global Environmental Law' (2001) 27 Ecological Law Quarterly 1295, 1297.

Wilde M, 'Locus Standi in Environmental Torts and the Potential Influence of Human Rights Jurisprudence' (2003) 12 Review of European Community and International Environmental Law 3.

Wilde M, *Civil Liability for Environmental Damage—Comparative Analysis of Law and Policy in Europe and the US* (2nd ed., Kluwer Law International 2013).

Wilkinson D, 'Moving the Boundaries of Compensable Environmental Damage Caused by Marine Oil Spills: The Effect of Two New International Protocols' (1993a) 5 Journal of Environmental Law 71.

Wilkinson D, 'The Council of Europe Convention on Civil Liability for Damage Resulting from Activities Dangerous to the Environment: A Comparative Overview' (1993b) European Law Review 130.

Winter G, Jans HJ, Macrory R and Kramer L, 'Weighing Up the EC Environmental Liability Directive' (2008) 20 Journal of Environmental Law 163.

Wouters J, Nollkaemper A and de Wet E (eds.), *The Europeanisation of International Law: The Status of International Law in the EU and Its Member States* (TMC Asser Press 2008).

Wurzel RKW and Connelly J (eds.), *The European Union as a Leader in International Climate Change Politics* (Routledge 2010).

Yang T, 'Environmental Regulation, Tort Law and Environmental Justice: What Could Have Been' (2002) Washburn Law Journal 607.

Yang T and Percival RV, 'The Emergence of Global Environmental Law' (2009) 36 Ecology Law Quarterly 615.

Yang Y, 'Liability and Compensation for Oil Spill Accidents: International Regime and Its Implementation in China' (2017) 57 Natural Resources Journal 465.

Zahar A, 'Mediated Versus Cumulative Environmental Damage and the International Law Association's Legal Principles on Climate Change' (2014) 4 Climate Law 217.

Ziegler K, 'International Law and EU Law: Between Asymmetric Constitutionalisation and Fragmentation' in A Orakhelashvili (ed.), *Research Handbook on the Theory of International Law* (Edward Elgar 2011).

Ziegler K, 'Beyond Pluralism and Autonomy: Systemic Harmonization as a Paradigm for the Interaction of EU Law and International Law' (2016) 35 Yearbook of European Law 667.

Zumbansen P, 'Transnational Comparison: Theory and Practice of Comparative Law as a Critique of Global Governance' (2012) Comparative Research in Law & Political Economy. Research Paper No 1/2012 < https://digitalcommons.osgoode.yorku.ca/cgi/viewcontent.cgi?article=1003&context=clpe> (last accessed March 2023).

Index